OFFICIAL HISTORY
OF
WHITFIELD COUNTY, GEORGIA

BY

WHITFIELD COUNTY HISTORY COMMISSION
APPOINTED

by

The Grand Jury
In accordance with Legislative action
July, 1930

HISTORY COMMISSION:

MRS. R. M. HERRON, SR., CHAIRMAN

MISS WILLIE WHITE
MRS. CLARENCE FRAKER
W. C. MARTIN

MRS. W. C. MARTIN
MRS. B. A. TYLER*
W. M. SAPP

Southern Historical Press, Inc.
Greenville, South Carolina

This volume was reproduced
from a personal copy located in
the Publishers private library

All rights reserved. No part of this publication may be reproduced,
stored in a retrieval system, transmitted in any form, posted
on the web in any form or by any means without the
prior written permission of the publisher.

Please direct all correspondence and book orders to:
SOUTHERN HISTORICAL PRESS, Inc.
1071 Park West Blvd.
Greenville, SC 29611

Published 1936:
   Dalton, GA.
ISBN #978-1-63914-673-4
Printed in the United States of America

Contents

CHAPTER I

NORTH GEORGIA INDIANS 1
        Miss Willie S. White

CHAPTER II

WHITFIELD'S BEGINNING 39
        Mrs. R. M. Herron

CHAPTER III

WAR BETWEEN THE STATES 55
        Mrs. W. C. Martin

CHAPTER IV

RECONSTRUCTION ERA 71
        Mrs. R. M. Herron

CHAPTER V

CHURCHES AND SCHOOLS 84
        Mrs. C. H. Fraker

CHAPTER VI

ORGANIZATION OF CLUBS AND SOCIETIES 130
        W. M. Sapp

CHAPTER VII

MODERN WHITFIELD 154
        Mrs. B. A. Tyler*

CHAPTER VIII

GREATER WHITFIELD COUNTY 171
        Mrs. R. M. Herron

APPENDIX 175
        W. M. Sapp, Mrs. B. A. Tyler*

---

*Deceased.

DEDICATION

TO THE PEOPLE OF WHITFIELD COUNTY:

To those pioneers whose sacrifice and service laid well the foundations, and whose careers illustrated an exalted conception of citizenship;

To those who followed them, and after the clouds of war had lifted, gathered together the fragments of their fallen fortunes and built again a greater community;

To those, who mindful of the heritage of the past, are participants in the progress and development of the county today, this volume is respectfully dedicated.

Introduction

*T*HE General Assembly of Georgia on August 23, 1929, passed a resolution with an earnest appeal to the judges of the Superior courts of the state, to give in charge to the grand jury of each county in their several circuits the urgent request that they secure the consent of some competent person, or persons, to write a complete history of the formation, development and progress of said county.

These histories were to be ready in 1933, and a copy of each to be deposited in the state Department of Archives and History in Atlanta, Georgia.

Pursuant to this appeal Judge C. C. Pittman instructed the grand jury in July, 1930, to appoint a committee to comply with this request of the General Assembly.

The grand jury, of which T. D. Ridley was foreman, appointed the following committee: Mrs. R. M. Herron, Chairman; Miss Willie S. White, Mrs. B. A. Tyler, Mrs. W. C. Martin, Mrs. Clarence H. Fraker, W. C. Martin and W. M. Sapp.

The committee thus appointed began the work and vigorous efforts were made to gather all available material pertinent to the subject.

This request of the General Assembly was complied with and a typed copy of the Whitfield County history was presented at the specified time.

Copies were made of records in the Bureau of the Census, War Department, Congressional Library, Washington, D. C.; Confederate Roster Commission and State Department of Archives and History and the Carnegie Library, Atlanta, Georgia. The records of Murray and Whitfield counties have been consulted.

This has been augmented from many other sources, notably the files of the Dalton Citizen and a bound copy of the Dalton Argus from 1882 to 1892, presented by the late H. A. Wrench.

Material and records preserved over a number of years by the late Mrs. Warren R. Davis have been of great value. A number of articles published some years ago by the late J. C. Head, of Tunnel Hill, have yielded valuable material on the early history of the county.

Our thanks are due Miss Ruth Blair, State Historian, the Bryan M. Thomas Chapter United Daughters of the Confederacy, the Governor John Milledge Chapter, Daughters of the American Revolution, the Service Star Legion, the Ordinary, Judge O. M. Stacy, the Ex-county Commissioners: Messrs. J. A. Thomason, Troy G. Kirk, S. H. Wilson, and G. C. Stafford, who made a suitable appropriation for typing the history, and to the present Commissioner, Judge Harlan J. Wood, who has co-operated in every way with this commission.

Appreciation is likewise expressed for aid contributed by John S. Thomas, Miss Eloise Bryant, Mrs. Penelope J. Allen, of Chattanooga, Tennessee; Ivan Allen, Atlanta, Georgia; Dr. W. K. Morehead, Andover, Massachusetts; and to the Yale University Press, New Haven, Connecticut.

Some histories are written for fame, some for the hope of material gain, and some for personal advancement. This history was written for none of these motives. It has been a labor of love by this committee, love for the noble men and women who laid a foundation for much of the happiness and prosperity we now enjoy.

Mrs. R. M. Herron, Sr., Chairman

Miss Willie S. White	Mrs. Clarence Fraker
Mrs. B. A. Tyler*	W. C. Martin
Mrs. W. C. Martin	W. M. Sapp
	History Commission.

---

*Deceased.

Foreword

*I*T is as well for a county, a state or a nation, as it is for an individual, to pause for a while now and then and cast a long look down the backward trail. It is well to bring to mind again the scenes of the past and to read therein the story of the development of the life of that community.

It might seem to the casual observer that Whitfield county is but a counterpart of many others in Georgia, but such is not the case for there is a wealth of history and romance that center around this county.

There are stories written large across these far blue hills, stories of years of battle, years of victory won in peace, years that have sculptured these hills, years that have painted them in colors strangely wonderful. There is legend and story here, there is history written in storm and sunshine, in war and peace.

These scenes of history that we are seeking to preserve concern those who, in the main, played well their parts, whose patriotism, courage, determination and hardy resolution were not excelled by the people of any time. Is it not well for us to tenderly gather each thread and lovingly record each memory of these, our own people? These bits of facts and incidents recorded in these pages are typical of our knowledge of those stirring periods of our county's history. A little here and a little there has been recorded and remembered, but many of the thrilling details are lost beyond recall.

There are epochs in the history of every place that are characterized by a nobler type of citizenry than that which falls to the ordinary lot of mankind, and which leaves its impress on those who come after. We can but feel that the generation whose memory has not yet grown dim in our minds, was of that type— that past which "being dead—yet speaketh" with tender and heroic grace.

These men and women of Whitfield county speak to us of a great past, yet they speak to us more eloquently of the present and the future, bidding us to face a new age with courage and to go forward with new duties which our country's larger mission in the world now lays upon us.

WILLIE DAVIS HERRON.
(Mrs. Robert M. Herron).

PREFACE

to

The Cherokee Indians of North Georgia

*I*N presenting this historical sketch of the Indian occupancy of Whitfield county the writer finds it necessary to state that the Cherokee lands were created December 26, 1831, by legislative act into one vast county—Cherokee.

From this original county Murray county was formed December 3, 1832. It included within its boundaries that area which December 30, 1851, was cut off and became by legislative act Whitfield county.

The city of Dalton, first called Cross Plains, came into existence about 1836 and remained for fifteen years in Murray county.

Thus we trace our lineage and claim by rightful heritage the Cherokee Indian history of our mother county—Murray.

CHAPTER I

The Cherokee Indians of North Georgia

by
Willie Stewart White

A WEALTH of Indian history exists in Whitfield county and surrounding counties and affords a wide field to those who are searching for historic landmarks and legends which will help to a clearer understanding of the aboriginal inhabitants—the Cherokees.

This brave and stalwart race offers some of the most striking and picturesque types yet produced by any race of people. It is important that the legends, traditions, and historical events, in which they had a leading part, be preserved.

Before entering on a discussion of the Indians of north Georgia, who, less than a century ago, roamed the mountains and made their homes in the fertile river valleys, we will turn our faces backward for a brief glance at the early history of this tribe.

In the southern Appalachian region human drama had doubtless been unfolding for hundreds, perhaps thousands of years—long before the first European ship sailed along the shores of the new world.

EARLY CHEROKEE HISTORY

Recorded history begins when the Cherokees first made acquaintance with Europeans in 1540. Then it was that DeSoto and his companions, in their search for gold, marched through Georgia on their way to the Mississippi. These early Spaniards described the Cherokees as "lean, naked, unwarlike, and given to hospitality to strangers."

At that time the Cherokees were in possession of the southern Allegheny region extending from the headstreams of the Kanawha and the Tennessee southward almost to the site of the present Atlanta, and from the Blue ridge on the east to the Cumberland range on the west. This area is now included in the states of Virginia, Tennessee, North Carolina, South Carolina, Alabama and Georgia.*

They were the mountaineers of the south holding the great mountain barrier between the English settlements on the Atlantic seacoast and the Spanish and French garrisons on the Gulf region and along the Mississippi.

They called themselves Yun-wi-yah, meaning real or principal people. The name Cherokee has been given several interpretations. One authority says it came from A-che-la, meaning "He takes fire," the belief being that the Great Spirit gave the Cherokees a sacred fire, which must be kept perpetually burning.** Their northern kinsmen, the Iroquois, called them Oyata'-ge-ronon—"inhabitants of the cave country"—which is unlike any other mountainous area in North America. Pickett tells us "their whole country was the most beautiful and romantic in the known world. Their springs of delicious water gushed out of every hill and mountain side. Their lovely rivers meandered through fertile valleys and rushed over cataracts and through mountain gaps. The forests were full of game, the rivers abounded with fish, and the mountains with fruit."***

Adair, the historian and trader, who lived for forty years among the American Indians, says, "the natives make two divisions of their country, Ayrate (low); Ottare (mountainous)."**** Later writers make three divisions—lower, middle and upper Cherokee. Tdheir principal towns lay upon the head-

---

*Mooney, James, Myths of the Cherokee, in Nineteenth Annual, Rep. Bureau of Ethnology, p. 14.

Note: James Mooney is an acknowledged authority on Cherokee Indian history. His book, "Myths of the Cherokee", is an invaluable contribution to American Ethnology. He wrote from material gathered from association with the Cherokees living in western North Carolina (1887). He supplemented this with information obtained in the Indian Territory, chiefly from old Cherokees who had emigrated west from Georgia and Tennessee.

**Starr, Emmet, Early History of Cherokees, p. 7.
***Pickett, Albert, J., History of Alabama, p. 14.
****Adair, J., History of the American Indians (1735-1755), p. 237.

waters of the Savannah, the Hiwassee, and the Tuckasegee rivers, and along the entire length of the Little Tennessee.* In 1735 there were sixty-four villages, the number of people being not less than sixteen thousand. Their ancient capital Itsa'-ti, on the Little Tennessee, by early historians was written Chote, Chota, and Echota. It was the "sacred peacetown" as well as the meeting place of the General Council before 1800.

In physical appearance the Cherokees were a fine race, tall and athletic, with an olive complexion. An English traveler describes the women as slender with delicate frames. The men were erect, having an air of superiority and independence. They were "honest, just and liberal and always ready to sacrifice every pleasure and gratification, even their blood and life itself, to defend their territory and maintain their rights."**

We may add that they were a religious people, with a fixed belief that a Great Spirit made the world and was in unceasing warfare with a Spirit of Evil, the Good Spirit finally triumphant. They believed in rewards and in punishments, as is shown by their reply to Mr. Martin, a preacher, "who having preached scripture till his audience and he were heartily tired, was told at last that they knew very well that if they were good, they should go up; if bad, down; that he could tell no more."***

In 1721 a momentous transaction took place—the first formal treaty between the Cherokees and the English was signed in Charleston, South Carolina, and a small cession of land made, the first land grant in the history of the tribe. In a little more than a century thereafter they had signed away their whole original territory. The Cherokees resisted every treaty and finally signed only under pressure. A treaty to the white man proved to be merely a scrap of paper. Before the signatures were dry, overtures were under way for more of the red man's land.

The advancing tide of white pioneers pressed into the

---

*An aboriginal map setting out the "Location of the Overhill Towns made by Lieutenant Timberlake 1762" is included in his Memoirs, 1756-1765. Reprint by Hon. Samuel Cole Williams, LL.D. (1927).

**Bartram—Travels through North and South Carolina and Georgia, etc., p. 366 (1792).

***Timberlake, Lieut. Henry, Memoirs (1756-1765), p. 87.

Indian country from the east and northeast, destroying the exposed upper towns and forcing the Cherokees further south, where they made new settlements. Their ancient capital was abandoned, and Ustanali, near the present Calhoun, Georgia, became their capital and central gathering place.

The Federal government before 1800 began a new civilizing policy in their dealings with the Cherokees. An agent, with headquarters on the Hiwassee river, was appointed to settle disputes between the whites and the red men and to distribute free, hoes, plows, spinning wheels, cards and looms, teaching their use to the Cherokees, who seemed "better fitted to follow the white man's road" than other Indians.

At the close of the eighteenth century the Cherokee hunting grounds had nearly vanished, but the Indians still retained their ancestral home and were at peace with mankind. By the terms of their treaty of October 2, 1798, the United States government had declared in all sacredness they would continue the guaranty of the remainder of their country forever.

A progressive spirit animated the tribe. Rich in courage and faith they faced the future.

1800

At the beginning of the nineteenth century the Cherokees were the most enlightened and the most powerful of all North American Indians. Their lands, though greatly diminished, still covered a large territory. A small part lay in western North Carolina, about the same extent in Tennessee, a small section in northeastern Alabama, and a large area in upper Georgia.

FIRST MISSION ESTABLISHED IN 1801

At this auspicious time in the history of the Cherokees the Society of the United Brethren, known as Moravians, authorized, in 1799, Reverend Abraham Steiner of Bethlehem, Pennsylvania, to establish a mission in the Cherokee nation.

Christian Frederick de Schweinitz volunteered to assist

NOTE: Moravian Missions Among Southern Tribes has been of valuable assistance and grateful acknowledgment is made to the author, Rev. Edmund Schwarze, Ph.D.

Steiner and went with him to Knoxville, Tennessee, where they secured passes permitting them to travel in the Cherokee country.*

When they reached Tellico, they found the chiefs away on a hunting expedition.

They went again to Tellico in September, 1800. Among the first chiefs to arrive at the council were Little Turkey, Glass, Doublehead, and Bloody Fellow. The meeting was held one mile below Tellico across the Tennessee river, with about thirty chiefs present sitting on rail fences under the open sky. They presented their appeal and much discussion followed, the chiefs making many objections and excuses. Finally Charles Hicks, the interpreter, became interested and offered his help. Encouragement came from James Vann, who, learning the missionaries would teach religion, said: "Come to me in my section among the upper Cherokees. You can accomplish more among them than in the lower towns."**

It was at last decided on October 6, 1800, to let the missionaries come into the Cherokee nation and make a trial. Steiner and de Schweinitz went with James Vann to his upper Georgia home; they explored the country and looked over other territory for a suitable place for the mission. Their report to the conference at Salem, North Carolina, suggested four situations. It was decided to locate in the vicinity of James Vann.***

Abraham Steiner and Gottlieb Byhan were selected to begin the work; they arrived at James Vann's home April 30, 1801, which was two and one-half miles north of the place intended for the mission. In a short time Vann bought the plantation—Springplace,**** owned by a Mr. Brown. It became the property of the Moravians and the site of the first mission to the Cherokee Indians. They built a little cabin and on the

---
*David Henley, Superintendent of Indian affairs, gave the passes.
**Schwarze, Edmund, Moravian Missions Among Southern Indian Tribes, p. 55.

***Salem was the seat of Moravian church Government in the Southern Section—Cherokee Missions were under their control.
****The present town of Springplace, Murray county, Georgia, is built on this site. Rev. Edmund Schwarze in Moravian Missions Among Southern Indians, writes Springplace as one word during the years of the Moravion Mission (1801-1832).

evening of July 13th they dedicated the place and themselves to the service of God. Forty acres were cleared lands largely rich bottom soil; a field near the mission was called the missionaries' field and has been cultivated many years.

The Springplace Mission was about eighty miles from Tellico on a trail between Georgia and South Carolina and with Ustanali belonged to the upper towns, the Conasauga river being the boundary between the lower and upper Cherokees. Here the British had maintained an agency during the Revolutionary war.

Because of ill health Steiner gave up his post. Byhan and his wife carried on alone until joined by Mr. and Mrs. J. J. Wohlfahrt, December, 1802. They began the mission school March 26, 1802, with two pupils—Sally, Vann's youngest daughter, and a cousin, Polly. One hour a day was given to teaching. Sally married in 1803 and went to Coosawattee Old Town to live.

Many obstacles were in the way of progress. The need of an interpreter was keenly felt. The missionaries were greatly handicapped in not knowing the Cherokee language and soon found that it would take years to learn.

Indians made frequent visits to Springplace, for it was in the midst of an old and populous community. Fifteen miles south was Rabbit Trap; about seventeen miles south was Coosawattee Old Town, near the Coosawattee river; just above the junction of the Conasauga and Coosawattee was the capital Ustanali. Seven miles north of Springplace was Sumach; to the northwest Red Clay; Dogwood, Crayfish Town, and Chestnut Town to the west. Indian trails led to these places through an almost unbroken forest, as the Cherokees had not yet permitted roads in their north Georgia country.

As a result of a great council held June 5, 1803, at Ustanali a letter, signed by Chiefs Chuleoa and Sour Mush, was sent to the mission which, in substance said that the missionaries must open a school in six months or leave the nation.

James Vann and Colonel Return J. Meigs, Indian Agent, rallied to the support of the distressed missionaries. In due time the school was built. The first boy to arrive was Gentleman Tom's eight-year-old son; next came the nephew of Chief Bark; then George Hicks was brought by his uncle, Big Half-breed.*

However, before the school was opened, Byhan and Wohlfahrt built two houses, each 20 x 24 feet, a story and a half high with wooden chimneys lined with clay. Roofs of clapboards were held in place by heavy poles. The houses were built of logs felled by Wohlfahrt and Byhan assisted by Vann's negroes. W. J. Cotter, who saw the mission first in 1832, wrote of "the beautiful site," saying "the comfortable, roomy buildings were of good timber well prepared and well put up."**

The year 1805 saw John Gambold and his wife installed at the mission. Mrs. Gambold's amiability, sense of responsibility, and genius for imparting knowledge made her the guiding spirit of the mission.***

A routine day at the mission was not for the sluggard. All arose at daybreak. First came family prayers, breakfast next, followed by school lasting until dinner. Then an intermission until three o'clock; during this time outdoor work in field and garden by boys, while other boys, with blow-guns and arrows, were sent to shoot squirrels and birds. The girls learned to weave, sew, knit and spin. Early to bed was the rule following evening song and prayer.

James Vann was murdered in 1809 at the age of forty-one. Though a dissipated man, he had been a constant friend to the mission which could not have been established or maintained without his generous aid.

The first convert to Christianity, in 1810, was his widow, Margaret Vann.**** The second was Charles Hicks, assistant principal chief.

Colonel Return J. Meigs, Indian Agent, was always a welcome guest at the mission. Mr. and Mrs. Gambold were the re-

---

*Schwarze E., Moravian Missions, p. 80.

**Cotter, Rev. W. J., My Autobiography, p. 70.
***Mrs. Gambold, before her marriage in 1805, as Anna Rosina Kleist, had been a teacher at the Moravian Seminary, Bethlehem, Pa.

****Mrs. Margaret Scott Vann, born August 20, 1783, was the daughter of Walter Scott who had been British agent to the Cherokees.

cipients of his unvarying kindness and were free to seek his advice in all matters as the following letter* testifies.

"Springplace 18th May, 1814.

"Dear Sir:

"The bearer of this, Young Deer, affords me an opportunity to address a few lines to you. He goes to see you with an Intention to beg you for some Iron to get him a Plough made, or rather if it were possible, to get a ready made one from you, as he wishes to exert himself in providing for his family; as he is at present in very low circumstances, he likewise begs you to assist him with Corn and Meal.

"About 10 or 12 Days since Mrs. Gambold addressed some lines to you of similar Import in Behalf of one named Woodpecker, which we suppose has been presented ere now. These poor People, who in general had very poor Crops last Year, have been by their serving against the Creeks, prevented from making provision for their families by Hunting, of course their little stock is consumed, and now they wish to cultivate the ground, which prevents them from procuring Sustenance by Hunting.

"Having a Letter to the Revd. Jacob van Vleck in Salem, lying here ever since Easter Day, we venture to send it along with this to your kind care, hoping it will come to your Hands.

"Our family is still favored with the Enjoyment of good Health, and as the Contest with our neighbors the Creeks is happily ended, we have reason to hope that we shall remain unmolested in our Undertaking.

"May good Health and every other Blessing be showered on you abundantly is the Wish and prayer
of

Dear Sir,

Your Sincere Friends

JOHN & AN. GAMBOLD."

"Colo. Return J. Meigs
Highwassee Garrison."

1815—1820

In 1815 the council provided for a standing committee to look after financial matters. This committee developed into

---

*The original letter is in the possession of Mrs. Penelope J. Allen, Chattanooga, Tenn. This letter has not yet been published, and is now used with Mrs. Allen's consent.

the upper house of the legislature, while the general council became the lower house. In 1817 it was reorganized and a standing body of legislators created which assembled in October of each year at New Echota,* the new capital near the present Calhoun, Georgia.

The council in 1820 divided the nation into eight civil and judicial districts; in each was located a council house where twice each year court was held.

The eight districts were:**

    1—Chickamaugee***   5—Hickory Log
    2—Challoogee   6—Etowah
    3—Coosawattee   7—Tahquohee
    4—Amoah   8—Aquohee

John Ross, in 1819, became president of the national council, holding the office for eight years. To prevent further land cessions a law was enacted which made it a death penalty to sign a treaty ceding Cherokee land. A cession of land could be made only by the national committee and the national council in joint action.

In the early part of 1817 Reverend Cyrus Kingsbury, acting under the instructions of the American Board of Commissioners for Foreign Missions, Boston, Massachusetts, opened a mission on Chickamauga creek, named it Chickamauga and a year later changed the name to Brainerd. The site of this mission is about six miles from Chattanooga, near the present town of Brainerd.

Mission stations established in Georgia, Alabama and Tennessee were:****

	Opened	Closed
Brainerd, Tennessee	1817	1838
Taloney (later Carmel), Georgia	1819	1839
Creek Path (now Guntersville), Alabama	1820	1837
Will's Town, Alabama	1823	1839

    *First mentioned as the capital October 26, 1819.
    **Battey, G. M., Jr., History of Rome and Floyd County, pp. 386-388.
    ***The territory now known as Whitfield was included in the Chickamaugee district. See appendix.
    ****Walker, Robert Sparks, Torchlights to the Cherokees, pp. 69, 70.

Turnip Mountain (later Haweis), Georgia	1823	1834
Etowa (Hightower), Georgia	1823	1831
Candy's Creek, Tennessee	1824	1839
Amohee, Tennessee	1831	1833
Red Clay, Tennessee	1835	1839
Running Water, Tennessee	1835	1836

Mr. Ainsworth E. Blunt of Amherst, New Hampshire, joined the missionaries at the Brainerd mission in March 1822. The following November he married Miss Harriet Ellsworth, also a Brainerd missionary. The Morse family of Dalton are descendants of this union. After the removal of the Cherokee Indians to the west he had charge of the mission property and, in order to protect the graves of the missionaries, he bought the little mission cemetery with money furnished by the American Board.

His wife died in 1847 and is buried in the Brainerd mission cemetery.

Mr. Blunt came to Dalton in 1843. His second marriage was to Miss Elizabeth C. Ramsey in February, 1848. The Kirby family of Dalton are their descendants. Mrs. Lillie Blunt Kirby, his daughter, has preserved the pewter communion service used at Brainerd mission.

Mr. Blunt was admired and respected by the Cherokee chiefs and his advice was often sought. Mrs. Kirby recalls a visit paid her father by Chief John Ross and a friend who came to talk over early Indian affairs—years before they had been associated with him at the Brainerd mission.

Mr. Blunt died December 21, 1865, and is buried in Dalton.

In 1819 a religious wave swept the country. Among the converts were Clement Vann, a white man, and his Indian wife, Wa-wli—the parents of James Vann.

The Federal government had at various times donated one hundred dollars to the Springplace school. They now announced an allowance of two hundred and fifty dollars annually. Welcome news to the missionaries, as they provided shelter, food and clothes in addition to teaching, preaching and entertaining visitors. The missionaries were developing a lasting love for the Cherokees, thus proving the truth of Colonel

Sevier's words, "it is want of acquaintance we have disliked you."

In 1818 Leonard Hicks and Buck Watie were sent from the Springplace school to the Foreign Mission school at Cornwall, Connecticut.* The next year John Ridge, David Steiner Tauchee-chee, and John Vann followed. At Cornwall, Buck (Galagi-na) met the philanthropist, Dr. Elias Boudinot, who was much pleased with him, promising him support and bestowing on him—as was the custom of the time—his own name.

On November 10, 1819, John Gambold was appointed the first postmaster at Springplace. This was the second post-office in the nation. The first was established at Rossville in 1817 with John Ross as postmaster.

INFLUENCES FOR CIVILIZATION

It was now no longer a question whether the Cherokee Indian could be civilized, for it was apparent that the tribe, under the influence of education and religion, was making remarkable progress.

Historians are convinced that this advance was in part due to intermarriage with white men. At first traders and soldiers married into the nation. Later men of the back settlements, of excellent English, Irish and Scotch stock, took Indian wives. The Vann, Rogers, Hicks, Taylor, Adair, McDonald, Martin and Ross families had a large part in the political life and history of the Cherokee nation.

The opening of roads was another great influence for civilization. The white people of Tennessee, South Carolina and Georgia complained that the trails were so narrow that communication was difficult. Chief Doublehead replying said, "the narrow trails were wide enough for the white people to find the red man's land."

By 1816 treaties had been made permitting the opening of roads between Georgia and Tennessee and the territory directly west. One of the most beautiful and historic highways built at this period is now known as

---

*Buck (Galagi-na) was the son of David Watie. John Ridge the son of Major Ridge. David Watie and Major Ridge were brothers. Among the Cherokees, in early days, brothers rarely had the same family name.

Anderson, Mrs. Mabel W., Life of Gen. Stand Watie, p. 7.

THE OLD FEDERAL ROAD

This road comes into Georgia from Tennessee at the present Tennga and runs southward for many miles, then turns east over the mountains to the older settlements of Georgia. It lies on the west side of a lofty and majestic range, the Blue Ridge, a part of the southern Appalachians locally known as the Cohutta mountains.

It follows an old, old trail etched by the padding feet of Indian braves of long ago. General Andrew Jackson passed over this road in 1818 on his way to "Fort Scott via Fort Hawkins."* A marker erected by the Governor John Milledge Chapter Daughters of the American Revolution, Dalton, Georgia, marks the federal road and records this historic incident.

Located on this road were the homes of several prominent Indians of mixed blood. The names of those who kept "public stops" were David McNair, Ellis Harlan, James Monroe, George Harlan, Judge John Martin and John Bell**.

ROCK SPRING

The most noted of these homes stands at Rock Spring where George Harlan, a rich and prominent man with some Cherokee blood, lived. His wife, Anna, was a daughter of William May, a member of a well known white family. Mr. Cotter says that Mrs. Anna May Harlan was "a superior woman in every respect." Their home, a two-story building with exterior of wide clapboards, was the best house in that section.*** It was painted white with green shutters, and long hinges extended almost the width of the shutters. The doors have the same type of hinge. The windows have small panes of glass, and over them scroll work. Just inside the front door ascends the unique stairway, and opposite is the high mantel with a wide fireplace. At the foot of the elevation on which the house stands, is a spring gushing forth from under a limestone rock; from this spring the place derives its name.

When the Indians went west, Mr. Farish Carter, a large slave and land owner of Scottsboro, Georgia, became the possessor of

---

*Extract from letter written to Secretary of War.
**Cotter, W. J., "My Autobiography", p. 74.
***Ibid pp. 23, 75, 76.

this beautiful place of fifteen thousand acres, which continues in the hands of his descendants. A grandson, Mr. Sam Carter, occupies the old Indian house built more than a century ago. It is unchanged, as its narrow stairway, tiny windows and high hand-carved mantels bear mute witness.

ANCIENT MOUNDS

A few miles south of Rock Spring are three ancient mounds near the site of Coosawattee Old Town. We are aware that there lived in Georgia a race of people antecedent to the Cherokees and that the artificial mounds were their burial grounds, containing the bones, and often the ornaments and implements which they used in daily life.

In March, 1928, Dr. W. K. Moorehead* began exploration of the largest mound by permission of the owner, Mr. Sam Carter. About two weeks were spent in examination of this mound where many Indian skeletons were found buried. It was here that a most significant find was made. Dr. Moorehead says, "It is not surprising, in view of the public interest concerning DeSoto, that our discovery of swords, heavily oxidized, caused considerable comment in the press. The longest of these objects is six and one-half inches while the lengths of the others are, one sword fragment three and three-quarter inches, the other four and one-half inches. The slender pointed objects are four and three-quarter and five and three-quarter inches. These fragments of swords and pike points, or whatever they are, were found with skeleton 'H', fairly well preserved; and buried some six feet below the surface. The ground was disturbed and we considered 'H' as an intrusive interment. We concluded the Indians had constructed a crude pen over 'H'.

"Our little collection of iron implements were sent to the Metropolitan Museum of Art, New York, where each specimen was examined by an official familiar with arms and armor. In his opinion as to whether they were Spanish swords, he was cautious, but stated they were old, and not of American Colonial

---

*By written permission of Dr. W. K. Moorehead, Director of the Dept. of Archaeology, Phillips Academy, Andover, Mass. Also by permission of the Yale University Press Publisher, New Haven, Conn.

period. There were no hilts, or maker's marks, and the dates could not be distinguished."*

Beautiful pottery vessels, engraved shells portraying plumed serpents, pipes, beads, pennate or winged stones, ornaments, unfinished birds and polished hatchets were found with various burials. "On the chest of one skeleton lay the largest shell gorget found . . . being about seven inches in diameter and beautifully carved."

PREHISTORIC INDIAN ARTICLES

The Indian relics shown above are from the collections of W. M. Sapp and Willie Stewart White. Many were found in Whitfield County. Celts, discoidals, axes, tomahawks, pipes, skinning knives, arrows and spearheads are of stone. The ax in the center, and the four spearheads near it are unusually fine specimens. The pottery Effigy bowl represents a frog.

FORT MOUNTAIN

About four miles east of Spring Place is an outstanding peak of the Cohutta mountains, near the crest of which is an old fort

---

*Moorehead, Dr. W. K., Exploration of Etowah Site in Georgia, pp. 151-154.

whose origin is shrouded in the mists of tradition. This historic landmark is known as Fort Mountain. Some of the legends which still persist connect the building of this ancient fort with the passing of DeSoto through Georgia in 1540, but we cannot readily believe the accounts which credit it to the Spaniards.

At the request of Mr. Ivan Allen, of Atlanta and Dalton, the distinguished archaeologist, Dr. W. K. Moorehead, explored the fort in 1928. He states that "the total length of all stone walls, including bastions and curves, is something less than one thousand feet. Originally the height must have been approximately five feet, yet in numerous places the wall has tumbled down. Numerous outcrops of stone upon the crest and a great many fragments, varying from ten to forty pounds, are available. The Indians constructed their breastwork from this material. . . . That the stones were laid to form a defensive position no one can deny, since there are crude bastions or projections from the main wall. Inside each is a depression, called locally, sentry pits. . . . We came to the conclusion that although a large body of Indians came up the mountain and constructed this work, they did not tarry more than two or three days and were not attacked. They would have left definite traces had they remained here for some time. . . . It is inconceivable that DeSoto would have taken his large body of men and horses up the mountain-side to so inaccessible a position. It was easier for him to oust natives from their villages and occupy the best houses—which he did."*

If we accept Dr. Moorehead's views we can but agree that this fort—one of the most impressive and ancient ruins of North America—was built by Indians doubtless long before DeSoto passed through North Georgia.

Following Dr. Moorehead's exploration Mr. Allen generously deeded this prehistoric fort and several acres of land to the state of Georgia for a state park. Mrs. M. E. Judd, of Dalton, Georgia. holds the office of State Park Authority and has worked untiringly in the accomplishment of all state park projects. From her the writer learns that a beautiful stone look-out tower has been built and is in use. A picnic shelter is nearing completion and a road is under construction from highway No. 2 to the very fort

---

*Moorehead, Dr., Exploration of the Etowah Site in Georgia, p. 55.

itself. The number of visitors constantly increases. They come not only to see the old fort but to view the magnificent panorama which unrolls nearly three thousand feet below.

HISTORIC INDIAN PLACES IN DALTON AND VICINITY

The present town of Dalton, Whitfield county, was included in the Chickamaugee district and a number of Cherokees lived here and in the vicinity. Chief Red Bird made his home at a beautiful place now known as Hamilton Spring. He lived in a double log house with stone chimneys, to the northwest of the spring. The outline where the house was built was visible a few years ago. Red Bird devoted much of his time to racing, his race-track extending southward from his home the length of the street now known as Thornton avenue. While engaged in racing he was thrown from his horse and died of his injuries and was buried not far west of his home. His grave is now covered by a railroad embankment.* His name appears in the list of Indians who attended the council at Running Water—near the present Rome, Georgia, July 19, 1835.**

Drowning Bear, a sub-chief, also was present at Running Water council in 1835, and we find his name with others of the Chickamaugee district.

An interesting story was told the writer by Mrs. C. W. McFarland in connection with Drowning Bear and his home.

"About 1838 my grandparents, Mr. and Mrs. G. W. Keith, came to Cross Plains, now Dalton, and purchased the Drowning Bear place about two miles south of the town. The land was on the east side of the road from the old Bowie, now Speck place, and extended from the brow of the hill south to Drowning Bear creek. Some of the land was already cultivated, and one field had been so long under cultivation that it was free from stumps and wild growth. The home of Drowning Bear was made of hewn logs, and my grandmother said that the flat, smooth logs on the inside of the rooms greatly interested her, for they were covered with drawings. One wall showed a trail down which Indians

---

*The writer is indebted to the late Mr. G. W. Hamilton, Sr., for the information about Red Bird. Col. John Hamilton (father of G. W. Hamilton) bought the Red Bird place about 1838

**Battey, G. M., Jr., A History of Rome, p. 390.

were driving turkeys; on another was an Indian riding a pony with a woman and children walking, while still another drawing portrayed an Indian with a deer on his shoulder.

"The Cherokee Indians were at this time being removed west, and at night the sound of marching feet on the nearby road often kept my grandmother awake. Years afterward she said that she regretted that she had not preserved some of the logs with their Indian drawings."*

One of the popular pastimes of the Cherokee Indian was the ball game, so interesting and strenuous that it attracted many spectators. It is said, on reliable authority, that the present Dalton was a favorite place and that the memorial park, where now stands the monument to Confederate heroes of 1861-1865, together with the Presbyterian church yard, were once parts of an Indian ball ground. Here the Indian braves, with brightly painted faces, played, always using a racquet somewhat similar but much smaller than is used in tennis, for the ball must not be touched by hand. The players made a special prayer to the "flying squirrel and the bat for help, these being symbols of quick and dexterous movement." Players were oftentimes crippled, sometimes killed, in this national sport, but the game went on until one side was victorious.**

About nine miles north of Dalton at Kenan Spring*** was the home of Rattling Gourd; the house has disappeared but a field to this day is called "Old Rattling Gourd Field." He made claim to the United States for spoliation on October 2, 1838, before C. H. McDonald, agent collecting claims east for:

"One rifle gun worth $32.00
One brass kettle 5.00
Shot bag 1.00

"The claimant says that about twelve years ago he and some others went to the Chickasaw nation on a hunting expedition and on their way home they got to drinking—and that white men Citizens of the United States took the property."

his
RATTLING X GOURD.
mark

---
*The Civitan club, Dalton, Ga., in 1932 marked the site of the Drowning Bear home and creek. John S. Thomas, chairman.
**Also marked by Civitans.
***Owned by the late Mrs. Pearce Horne and sold to Mr. Bart Wilson.

CHARLES R. HICKS

Charles R. Hicks was a member of the Moravian church at Springplace and a loyal friend to all missionaries. His home was in Dogwood valley, about nine miles northwest of the present Dalton, in that part of Chickamaugee district which is now Whitfield county. He is admitted to have been one of the most remarkable and influential men in the Cherokee nation. He was born December 23, 1767, at Tomotley, on the Hiawassee river. His father, Nathan Hicks, was a white trader and his mother a Cherokee.

Emmet Starr, Indian historian, quotes from the memoirs of Elias Cornelius in this wise—"Charles Hicks speaks the English language with utmost facility and reads better than one-half of the white people and writes an easy hand. For thirty years he has been an interpretor for the United States government. A man of integrity, temperance and intelligence."* He died in 1827, less than two weeks after he became principal chief.

A description of his home in 1817 by the same writer shows the style of log house used by the chiefs: "The house is of hewn logs, is 26 x 18, two stories high, with a double piazza the whole length of the house, ornamented with handrails and banisters and covered with a good roof of shingles."

Mr. C. L. Easley, of Dalton, who for years owned this place, says that this description fits the house as he remembers it when he first saw it, that the house was torn down about 1929.**

RED CLAY COUNCIL GROUND

Red Clay (Elawa'-diyi) is situated a few miles north of Dalton and is described by Mooney as "a former council ground known in history as Red Clay, at the site of the present village of that name in Whitfield county, Georgia, adjoining the Tennessee line."***

Here some of the most stirring events of Cherokee history were enacted. Today it is a deserted village whose glory lies wholly in its historic past for almost every foot of this section is replete with history and tradition.

---
*Starr, Emmet, Early History of the Cherokees, pp. 45 and 46.
**The writer is reliably informed that when this house was demolished there was found inscribed, on one of the smooth logs, the name "Ch. R. Hicks."
***Mooney, Myths of the Cherokee, p. 517.

Many Indians made their homes in this community. Living in Georgia and over the line in Tennessee, were Deer-in-the-water on Chatata creek, Sleeping Rabbit at Red Clay, Rattling Gourd near Kenan Spring; and not far distant were the homes of Otter-lifter (also written Auter-lifter), Seven Nose and Black Fox.

Between 1831 and 1838 many Cherokee councils were held at Red Clay, where the question of removal west was debated in what is officially described as tumultuous and excited meetings. The last council met here on August 7, 1837, for the purpose of protesting the New Echota treaty of December 1835; it was largely attended by the Indians, but their pleas were unheeded by the United States government.

Following the removal of the Cherokee Indians Mr. James H. Huff came into possession of the council ground—making it his home.* Mrs. W. C. Huff, his daughter-in-law, lived here between 1880 and 1890 and tells the writer that the log house, known to all in that section as the council house, was standing in 1886 quite near the old Huff residence and on Georgia soil.

Many traditions still cling to this beautiful and historic spot. Here Mrs. Margaret McGhaughy Huff (wife of James H. Huff) made her home for many years, garnered the Indian legends and told them to her children and long years afterward repeated them to her grand-children. Miss Mattie Lee Huff recalls the following ancient and enduring legend which her grandmother delighted in telling:

"When the dusky warriors and maidens were gathered together for removal westward, the assembled chiefs and counselors met at the council ground under the spreading oaks and murmuring pines, and after smoking the pipe of peace, in imploring attitudes turned their dark eyes to heaven, pulled the swinging limbs to them and, in their wild devotion, bedewed the sprigs and branches with their tears. When the final departure drew near, all arms were taken from the Indians and they were marched between files of soldiers. Tradition says that a chief known as Big Bear had but a short time before buried his wife and only

---

*Letter to writer from Rev. A. R. T. Hambright which gives a list of early settlers who came into possession of the Indian land and homes. The writer in 1913 had the privilege of a visit to Red Clay with Mr. Hambright as guide—he was then 84 years old. His memory was clear and accurate and the writer is indebted to him for a wealth of Indian information.

child, and that in his deep grief he implored that he be spared the life of an exile. His prayers were unheeded and he was forced to take up the march. He secured a bayonet, hiding it under his blanket, and as he passed by the graves of his loved-ones, broke from his companions and threw himself across the mound, and, falling upon the sharp bayonet was pierced to the heart, thus dying by those he loved dearer than life."

In November, 1935, the Georgia Society Daughters of the American Revolution and the Georgia Society Sons of the American Revolution erected jointly a memorial to mark the site of the former council ground of the Cherokee Indians at Red Clay. The memorial erected is a large granite boulder with bronze tablet. It was placed just east of the site of the old Cherokee council house.

The marker bears the following inscription:

Red Clay
"Elawadiyi—Red-earth place"
A former council ground of the Cherokee Indians
"Heaven hath angels watching 'round
The Indians forest-mound,
And they have made it holy ground."

—John Greenleaf Whittier.

Erected by
The Georgia Society D. A. R.
The Georgia Society S. A. R.
1935

The tablet carries an Indian head at the top and at the bottom the insignia of each organization.

The dedication and unveiling exercises were held Sunday, November 10, 1935.* Much credit is due Mrs. J. L. Beeson, state historian Georgia D. A. R., for her untiring efforts in securing and placing the marker at this historic place.

LAST YEARS OF THE SPRINGPLACE MISSION

On October 13, 1820, John R. Schmidt and wife came to the mission to relieve Mr. and Mrs. Gambold, who were to establish a mission at Oochgelogy.* Mrs. Gambold, who had been ill for several months, succumbed to a heart attack February 19, 1821, while still at Springplace. Always modest and unassuming in the work of the mission, yet she had a large part in extending its influence throughout the nation. She was buried close by the grave of Margaret Vann Crutchfield, who died October 18, 1820.** The little graveyard was in the midst of a fenced orchard. Today this spot is a part of a cultivated field. The writer has often visited this place but the graves have long since disappeared. Mr. C. N. King, of the present town of Spring Place, has a vivid memory of the little cemetery which he says lay east of the mission buildings. He also distinctly recalls the log mission buildings which were demolished about 1865. Mrs. R. J. McCamy and Mrs. J. Q. Steed, Sr., once residents of Spring Place, now living in Dalton, give interesting descriptions of the old mission.

Mr. Gambold, on April 11, 1821, left the Springplace mission to establish the second Moravian Mission in the Cherokee nation at Oochgelogy.

The location selected was about four miles south of the present town of Calhoun, Georgia. He remained there until his death November 7, 1827. He was buried on the hill east of the mission, and a small headstone marks his grave. In 1831 the mission closed. The building still stands on the west side of the old Dixie highway.

November 8, 1827, the Byhans returned to Springplace. They were followed by Henry C. Clauder, April 18, 1832, who remained as missionary and postmaster until January, 1833. The Cherokee lands had, prior to this time, been distributed by lottery and a Mr. Nix drew the Springplace lots. The place passed into other hands, and Mr. Clauder was forced to give up the mission premises and leave for Tennessee.

In 1931 the Governor John Milledge Chapter, D. A. R., Dalton, Georgia, marked the site of the Moravian Mission, thus preserving for future generations the spot where heroic men and women labored to christianize and civilize the Cherokee Indians.

---
*Now called Oothcaloga.
**Margaret Vann married July 9, 1812, Joseph Crutchfield at one time overseer on Vann's estate.—Schwarze, Moravian Missions, p. 118.

JOSEPH VANN

To the northwest of the Springplace mission Joseph Vann, a son of James Vann, built his home on an elevation overlooking the surrounding valley—it stands today a reminder of the tragic history of the Cherokees.

We learn from Rev. W. J. Cotter, who lived on the federal road, north of the Carter plantation from 1832 to 1840, that Chief Joseph Vann was six feet six inches in height and of

THE VANN HOUSE
Brick residence built by Chief Joseph Vann early in the nineteenth century at Springplace, Georgia.

fine appearance. He owned many slaves and had his negro quarters about 4 miles out at Mill Creek. He built his home from brick made about four hundred yards away.* The house faces south, and, including basement and attic, is four stories high. The entrance has large double doors with a transom of fan-shaped glass. The wide hall extends the length of the house and at the right is a hand-carved stairway which is so constructed that it ascends without visible support. The two rooms on the main floor are large with high ceilings of wood and the floors are of wide boards. The room to the right has secret

---
*Cotter, Rev. W. J., My Autobiography, p. 70.

drawers placed beneath the windows, and when built, were, no doubt, skillfully concealed, but now can be clearly seen. The room on the left, at the west side of the hall, has a hand-carved mantel which extends to the ceiling. The third floor has a large open space where the stairway ends; to the east is a small room which, from its shape, is known as the coffin room.

In 1833 Joseph Vann owned about eight hundred acres of cultivated land, not to speak of his extensive improvements. In the fall of the year he was called away from home on business and before leaving "employed a Mr. Howell, a white man, to oversee for him in the year 1834—to commence on the first day of January, 1834. He returned about the 28th or 29th of December, 1833, and learning that Georgia had prohibited any Cherokee from hiring a white man, told Mr. Howell he did not want his services. Yet Mr. Bishop, the State's agent, represented to the authorities of Georgia that Mr. Vann had violated the laws of that state by hiring a white man, had forfeited his right of occupancy and that a grant ought to issue for his lands."*

Conflicting claims arose. Mr. Bishop and a Mr. Riley each took possession and a pitched battle ensued. Riley kept his position and Bishop set fire to the house and succeeded in dislodging Riley who surrendered. The fire was extinguished. Vann and his frightened family were then driven out, unprepared, in the dead of winter and forced to make their way into the state of Tennessee.

"Indian Office.   Washington, D. C.

"Cherokee Valuations by Young & McMillan 1835.

"A list of the appraisements of Cherokee Indians. Improvements in that part of the nation included in Murray county, Georgia, made under the 9th article of the Treaty concluded at New Echota, on 29th of December 1835,

by Jno. S. Young and Jo W. McMillan, Appraisers.

"No. 158   Joseph Vann (⅛ Cherokee), Spring Place, Murray County, Georgia.

"Nov. 11, 1836.

"1 Brick house 47x30—2½ stories high loft passage—5 rooms 24'.
12 ten light windows—5 four light windows, 11 panel doors—back and front

---

*Cong. Doc's. 1835-36, Doc. 286, p. 6. Courtesy of Miss Mary Louise Horan.

porticos, the whole finished in a workman like manner	$ 6,000
Hew'd log kitchen	100
&c &c	445

"List of his cabins covers 2 pages
Grist and saw mill, dam 8' high, 9' wide.
Garden, apple and peach trees

total	$18,902.25
"Cabins traced from descriptions destroyed after he was dispossessed	625

NOTE: The foregoing claimant was dispossessed under the laws of Georgia, of his mills and 448 acres of land in the spring of 1834.

"It is submitted to the commission to allow him $400. annual rent for his mills and $3.00 per acre for his land up to the end of the year 1836—total	$5,232

"Of his brick house and other tenements together with the remaining 357 acres of land he was dispossessed in the spring of 1835.
"Allowed $3.00 per acre and $400. annual rent for his house.

Total	2,942
	$8,174

"March 8, 1837.
  "The suggestions and returns of the valuing agents were considered.

Cut to	$7,374.00"*

SEQUOYAH

In 1821 an event occurred which exerted a far-reaching influence on the future history of the Cherokees. A mixed-blood Cherokee, known to the whites as George Gist (or Guess) and among his own tribe as Sikwayi, invented the Cherokee alphabet. His mother is said to have been a Cherokee of the Paint clan.** As to his father—by some authorities it is said he was a wandering German peddler; others have stated he was the son of Captain Nathaniel Gist, a friend of Washington. Hon-

---

*Courtesy of Mrs. P. J. Allen, Chattanooga, Tenn.

**Starr, Emmet, Early History of the Cherokees, p. 9. Names of the seven clans were Wolf, Deer, Bird, Long Hair, Paint, Blind Savannah and Holly. The clan was always inherited from the mother.

orable S. C. Williams, of Johnson City, is of the opinion that Captain Nathaniel Gist "was the father of the greatest of red Tennesseeans."

Sequoyah's early youth was probably spent in Tuskegee town, in Tennessee. He could neither read nor write and never learned to speak the English language. When and how he became a cripple authorities differ, but all agree as to his dexterity as a craftsman in silver work.

Sequoyah's attention was called to the white man's ability to communicate thought by writing. He told his friends that he would make the "leaf" talk to the Indian as well as to the white man. For paper he used bark and for a pencil a piece of charcoal and set himself to the task of recording the separate sounds found in the Cherokee language. After repeated failures he evolved his syllabary—eighty-five* character representations for eighty-five distinct sounds. At this time he was living in Willstown, Alabama. In 1821 Sequoyah presented the new syllabary and "within a few months, without school or other expense of time or money, the Cherokees were able to read and write in their own language." In 1823 the Cherokee council awarded Sequoyah a silver medal carrying a commemorative inscription in both languages.

Following an active correspondence with the Cherokees who had moved west, he made his permanent home in Arkansas in 1823.

The state of Oklahoma presented a statue of Sequoyah to Statuary Hall, in the United States Capitol, which was unveiled with appropriate ceremonies June 6, 1917.

THE CHEROKEE PHOENIX

In 1827 the Cherokee council resolved to establish a national newspaper in the Cherokee language. The type was cast in Boston, a printing press bought and early in 1828 shipped by water to Augusta, then carried by wagon to New Echota. On February 21, 1828, the first number of the Cherokee Phoenix appeared with Elias Boudinot as editor. It was printed in both English and Cherokee, and was the first newspaper ever pub-

---

*Some authorities give the number at eighty-six.

lished in an Indian language. The first printers were two white men, Isaac N. Harris and John F. Wheeler. The Reverend S. A. Worcester was the leading spirit.

ELIAS BOUDINOT

When Elias Boudinot (Galagi'-na) attended the missionary school at Cornwall, he met and loved Harriet Gold, daughter of Colonel Benjamin Gold. Bitter opposition developed in the Gold family and great excitement prevailed in the town, for a short time before, John Ridge, a cousin of Elias Boudinot, had married Sarah Northrup, of Cornwall, Connecticut. It was said that this marriage had a bad effect on the mission school. It was now felt that a second marriage of an Indian to a white girl would "annihilate the institution." However, Harriet's family became reconciled and the marriage took place May 1, 1826. Elias Boudinot brought his wife to Oothcaloga, Cherokee nation to live and she was soon engaged in assisting her husband in his work. Many interesting letters were written by Mrs. Boudinot to her parents and it is a matter of regret that they are too long to be included in this sketch of the Cherokee Indians.

Colonel Benjamin Gold and his wife drove with their own horse and carriage the long distance to New Echota, where the Boudinots were living in 1829. Colonel Gold wrote his brother that "Mr. Boudinot has much good company and is as much respected as any man of his age. His paper (the Cherokee Phoenix) is respected all over the United States and is known in Europe."

Harriet Boudinot died at New Echota, August 15, 1836, aged thirty-one. She is buried in the tribal cemetery and her grave is marked by a simple headstone. A house known as the Boudinot's home still stands in New Echota but opinions to the contrary exist.

General Brinsmade in 1830 visited the Boudinots and spent some of his time traveling in the Cherokee nation. He kept a record of the people and places, which is included at this time as originally written:

"JOURNAL OF OUR JOURNEY TO CREEK PATH

"We started on the first Monday in May, to-day we went to Major Ridge's farm and his house presents a fine appearance. The house is an elegant painted mansion with porches upon each side as the fashion of the country is; we saw in the house likeness of John Ridge, Esq., accurately painted, hanging in a large frame in the position of writing which was his principal business.

"Tuesday: We visited John Ross, the principal chief, his house is a long two story building, inside has the appearance of neatness and elegance, here we crossed the Coosa, and passed the tomb of the Cherokee, who was so barbarously murdered by the Georgians. We went along Van's valley, to David Van's; his house is elegantly painted outside, and in, and is beautifully located and furnished with the nicest of furniture, his wife amused us in the evening by playing most charmingly on her piano. They are both descendants of Cherokees.

"Wednesday: Went 33 miles to Lasleys, of Turkey Town, we had butter, cheese and every desirable on the Cherokee tables, and were treated extraordinarily hospitably, on account of our connection with Mr. Boudinot.

"Thursday: We rode to Mr. Jack Ross', a native of New Jersey, brother-in-law to the principal Chief.

"Friday: We traveled over the Raccoon Mountain, which is about 20 miles from the brow of the Mountain on one side to the brow on the other side; we arrived at Creek Path in the evening, here is a flourishing school, superintended by Mr. and Mrs. Potter, from our native state. There is some seriousness in the school at this time.

"Saturday: One of the scholars and myself mounted our horses, and rode between two Mountains, in the beautiful valley of Creek Path, to David Carter's, found his wife weaving, the slaves we saw about the plantation. Mr. Carter's wife is a descendant of the Cherokees, and is as white as the Northern ladies, dresses well; left an invitation for herself and husband to visit at Mr. Potter's, in the evening, as he was not at home. Went to Col. Gilbreath's, who married a sister of David and Catharine Brown, Mrs. Gilbreath favors her brother David very much in looks, disposition, and actions, she invited me to take dinner, which was fritters, butter, honey and thick milk, I am very fond of it.

"Sabbath: 10th of May, attended meeting at the Creek Path School House, sermon by Mr. Potter (interpreted by Samuel Gunter), alternately in Cherokee and English. David Carter, and his wife presented their child to be baptized by Mr. Potter.

"Monday: Took a ride with Dr. Carter Dempsey Fields, to Gunter's Landing, fields of corn and cotton in this part of Creek Path Valley looked fine. We called at Mr. Edward Gunter's, a member of the Cherokee Committee. He is an excellent man, a member of the Methodist Episcopal Church.

"Tuesday: We parted with our Cherokee friend at Creek Path, traveled over the Mountain to Wills' Valley, 35 miles to Col. Mulkey's, who is a native of Georgia, and brother-in-law to the principal chief, Mrs. Mulkey is the youngest daughter of Mr. Daniel Ross. There as in other places we were treated cordially and hospitably.

"Wednesday: We rode to Willstown, called by the way on many Cherokees, among whom was Judge Huss, Judge of the Supreme Court of the Cherokee nation. None of the family could talk English, but my imperfect Cherokee made them understand that my father and mother were the parents of Mrs. Boudinot. They expressed much satisfaction on seeing us. We gave Judge Huss' daughter the Cherokee Phoenix, which she fluently read in the Cherokee language.

"Thursday: We visited the families of the Lowerys, and Rosses, of Willstown. There we saw some of the families of the Guess', and went under the very shade trees where Guess studied upon his syllabolic alphabet.

"Friday: We rode to Mr. Benges in company with Mr. Chamberlin, Minister of Willstown, some of the Benge family belong to Mr. Chamberlin's church. Friday we rode the whole day under the lofty Lookout Mountain, passed the residence of an ancient chief near the end of the Lookout. We saw some mounds about the place in the form of pyramids about 10 feet high and about 15 thick where the bones of ancient chiefs lie deposited. As we passed over the Lookout Mountain, the Tennessee was to be seen winding its course below the high mountain. This I think is the highest mountain I ever crossed in a wagon. At the end of this mountain is the plantation of Mr. Joseph Coody, Father of William S. Coody, Clerk of Cherokee Delegation at Washington. There we talked and had a short visit with Mr. Coody's family. Mrs. Coody is a native, sister of John Ross, the principal chief. Traveling 8 miles farther on we came in sight of the bare chimneys of the Brainerd Station. The meeting house and some other houses at a distance escaped the conflagration. There we saw Cherokees flocking to the meeting house to attend a preparatory lecture.

"We spent Sabbath at Brainerd, there three of the missionaries of the American Board, providentially met on Monday, viz. the Rev. Mr. Worcester, Rev. Mr. Thompson, and Rev. Mr. Chamberlin, at 4 o'clock in the evening, and Monday following rode as far as the house of Hon. Richard Taylor.

"Tuesday: We arrived at the beloved City of the Cherokees, New Echota. I should like to give you many more particulars, but fail for want of time.

"(Gen) D. D. Brinsmade, May 22, 1830. (H. S. Gold)

"P. S. Our Cherokee friends at Creek Path say they shall all love the people of the North for the part they have taken for them, and for their sending such missionaries.

"All the places where we stayed would not have a cent, but said they were glad to have us call on them."*

EVENTS LEADING TO REMOVAL

We turn to note the march of events which culminated in the forced removal of the Cherokees from their beloved ancestral home to a western wilderness. As the population of Georgia increased there was a growing demand for the removal of the Indians, who, it was said, were an obstacle in the path of progress. The Federal government in 1802 had entered into a compact to extinguish for the benefit of Georgia the Indian title to land lying within the state "as early as same can be peaceably obtained on reasonable terms." Georgia in 1822 complained to congress that the United States was not keeping

*Courtesy of Miss Fanny P. Brown, Washington, Conn.

her part of the agreement and soon afterward an appropriation was made and a commission appointed to negotiate with the Cherokees for a cession of their land lying in Georgia.

The Cherokees at once declared, without a dissenting voice, they would make no more treaties for the purpose of land cessions. Persistent, but unsuccessful efforts, continued to be made for the Cherokee land; secret methods were employed to bring about either a cession or emigration but to no avail.* The Cherokee council in July, 1827, resolved to establish a republican form of government based on a written constitution. In this remarkable document, modeled after the Federal constitution, the Indians claimed independence as one of the distinct and sovereign nations of the earth. Governor Forsyth, of Georgia, made a vigorous protest to the president against the setting up of a separate government within the limits of the state. It is asserted that this act more than anything else was the reason for Georgia's attitude towards the Cherokees.

The Governor and the people of the state were determined to prevent the formation of an independent Cherokee nation within our borders. The legislature then passed an act, December 26, 1828, annexing the Cherokee lands and giving the courts of Georgia authority over them. Other laws were passed that deprived the Cherokees of legal protection and made life intolerable for them. The Cherokee country was mapped into counties, surveyed into land lots and distributed among the white Georgia citizens by public lottery. Each Cherokee head of a family was permitted a reservation of one hundred sixty acres, but no deed was given.

Meanwhile the venerable Path-Killer, leader of the nation, died January 8, 1827, and tradition asserts that he was buried at New Echota.

Path-Killer was followed in office by second chief, Charles R. Hicks, who outlived him only thirteen days. By his own wish Charles R. Hicks was buried in the mission graveyard at Springplace.

To fill the unexpired term of Path-Killer and Charles R. Hicks the council in 1827 appointed William Hicks as principal,

---

*Mooney, Myths of the Cherokee, pp. 114-115.

and John Ross as second chief. When the next election came, John Ross defeated Hicks and became principal chief.

JOHN ROSS

In October, 1828, Ross entered on his duties as principal chief of the young republic.* By education and experience in Cherokee public life, he was well fitted to be the leader of his people. One-eighth Cherokee and seven-eighths Scotch, he knew Cherokee nature as no white man could possibly understand it. His influence was supreme in the councils and until his death on August 1, 1866, he remained their leader.

After his marriage to Mrs. Quatie Brown Henley, he moved from Ross' Landing to the head of the Coosa (now Rome, Georgia). He also lived at Rossville, Georgia, in the house owned by his grandfather, John McDonald, which is said to have been built around 1770. This house was in his possession until disposed of by the Georgia land lottery.

MAJOR RIDGE

Major Ridge was one of the most outstanding men of the tribe. He was born at Hiwassee about 1770. He could neither read nor write and his advancement in public life was due to native ability. For nearly thirty years his influence in the policy of the government was paramount.

His home was about two miles north of the Ross home on the Oostanaula and there, in a comfortable house, he lived for forty-three years. John Ridge, his son, lived on Two Run a few miles away.

JOHN MARTIN

Judge John Martin was the first chief justice and also the first treasurer of the Cherokee nation. His home, Coosawattee, was on the federal road about three miles south of Rock Spring. He was a man of wealth, had an extensive farm with large wheat fields. Not far from his home he built his quarters for about one hundred slaves.

In 1835 Judge John Martin received the following letter:

---

*Ross was born Oct. 3, 1790, at Turkeytown (Tahnoovayah), Ala.

"Murray county, Georgia
January 20, 1835.
"Mr. John Martin:
Sir: The legal representative of lots of land:

No.	95	25 district	2d section
	86	25 "	"
	93	25 "	"
	89	25 "	"
	57	25 "	"

has called on me as States agent, to give him possession of the above described lots of land, and informs me that you are the occupant upon them. Under the laws of the State of Georgia, passed in the years 1833 and 1834, it is my duty to comply with his request, you will therefore prepare yourself to give entire possession of said premises, on or before the 20th day of February next, fail not under penalty of the law"

WM. N. BISHOP, States Agent"*

In February, 1835, Judge Martin was compelled to seek a new residence in Tennessee.**

W. J. Cotter in "My Autobiography" says, "When the family left the Coosawattee home he was present and saw the daughter Susanna sweep the house for the last time, burn the broom for good luck and leave in the family carriage."

APPEALS TO THE SUPREME COURT
1830—1831

In January, 1831, the Cherokee nation, through John Ross, appealed to the Supreme Court of the United States for an injunction against the application of Georgia laws. This bill claimed that they were "a foreign nation not owing allegiance to the United States, nor to any state in the Union." They further said that they were an independent, sovereign state; also that former treaties had recognized their claim by guaranteeing the inviolable right of the Cherokees to their lands. This suit was dismissed on the ground that the Cherokees were not a foreign nation within the meaning of the constitution.

---

*Cherokee Indian Cong. Doc. No. 286, pp. 4, 5, 6, 1835.

**Judge Martin was a member of a distinguished English family which intermarried with the Cherokee tribe. The romantic history of his forbears is related by Emmet Starr, History of the Cherokees, pp. 612, 641.

Soon after this decision four missionaries and a white printer —Wheeler—were arrested as they declined to take the oath of allegiance to Georgia. Three reconsidered, took the oath and were released. Worcester and Butler refused and were sentenced to four years in the penitentiary. This case was carried, as a test case, to the Supreme Court. A decision in favor of Worcester was given which declared unconstitutional the extension of Georgia laws over the Indian country. It is said that President Jackson, on hearing the decision of the supreme court remarked, "John Marshall has made his decision; now let him enforce it."

DISSENSIONS

In 1832 a council was called to meet at Red Clay council ground. This was the year for the national election of all officials, but, owing to conditions, it was decided to continue in office all present officials. This action did not meet the approval of the Ridges and their friends, who, it was rumored, were inclining toward removal west. This disaffection was the beginning of a new party favoring removal and numbered among its members the Ridges, Boudinot, Vann and Andrew Ross. Heretofore the Ridges had bitterly opposed emigration, but now, seeing that voluntary or forced removal was confronting the nation, came out openly for emigration on the best terms obtainable.

In August and again in October, 1834, the council met at Red Clay. The two factions were now in controversy over the course the Cherokee people should take. In the winter of 1835 the two leaders went to Washington—Ross to fight for home and national existence and Ridge to negotiate for removal. Proposals and counter proposals were made and no decision reached. Finally President Jackson appointed Reverend J. F. Schermerhorn to arrange a treaty with Ridge, which he (Ridge) signed. It stipulated that it was not binding until approved by the Cherokee people assembled in regular council.

RED CLAY COUNCIL OF 1835

Many important councils were held at Red Clay, but the council that convened on October 12, 1835, was the most important ever held in the Cherokee nation. Leading men of the Cherokees together with about eight hundred Indians, were present. Several prominent white men were there. John Howard Payne attended as the guest of John Ross. The question of ceding Cherokee territory was of vital importance and was to be decided at this time. Mr. Curry and Mr. Schermerhorn were on hand to urge the signing of the treaty which had been drawn in Washington in the spring. To their astonishment the two factions became reconciled and "agreed to bury in oblivion all unfriendly feelings and act unitedly in treaty with the United States for the relief of their nation." As a result the Schermerhorn treaty was unanimously rejected, both the Ridges and Boudinot working against it.* Almost at once trouble arose among the newly reconciled parties, personal grievances crept in, and bitter accusations were made. A committee of twenty members had been selected from both parties to arrange a new treaty. John Ridge and Boudinot resigned from this committee.

JOHN HOWARD PAYNE

John Ross and his guest, John Howard Payne, were arrested by the Georgia Guard about midnight November 7th at the home of Ross at Flint Spring.** All of Ross' correspondence and Payne's papers were seized. Following this they were carried to Springplace, where they were confined in a small log hut with two sentinels on guard.*** Ross was detained nine days; then his papers were returned, and, without explanation, he was released.

Payne was ordered to depart four days later. His papers were given him and he was roughly commanded to leave the country. Payne had been collecting historical and ethnological information in the Cherokee country. An interesting feature of his arrest came when he heard one of the guards, on the way to Spring Place, humming "Home Sweet Home". He revealed himself as the author, but an incredulous look was the response.

NEW ECHOTA TREATY

Mr. Schermerhorn, before leaving the Red Clay council in October, posted a notice of a meeting to be held at New Echota

---

*Eaton, Rachel C., John Ross and the Cherokee Indians, p. 95.
**John Ross and his family sought refuge within the limits of Tennessee in 1835 when ejected from their home at the head of the Coosa. They lived in a small log house near Flint Spring.
***Battey, G. M., Jr., History of Rome, pp. 56, 59.

in December for the purpose of negotiating a treaty. Threats and inducements were made to secure a large attendance, but the report made by Schermerhorn only shows from three hundred to five hundred men, women, and children present. The smallness of the attendance and the absence of the principal officer of the nation—Ross was then in Washington—did not deter Schermerhorn. A committee was appointed to arrange the details of a treaty. The main articles, briefly stated, were as follows:

> The Cherokee nation east to be ceded for $5,000,000. A common joint interest in the territory already occupied by the western Cherokees.
>
> All improvements made by the Cherokees to be paid for by the United States Government. Removal to take place within two years from ratification of treaty.
>
> Provision was made for debts due the Indians and for pensions, etc.*

On December 29, 1835, the treaty was signed by Governor William Carroll, of Tennessee, and Reverend J. S. Schermerhorn as United States commissioners. It is said that the solemn ceremony of signing the treaty, by the committee of twenty took place at midnight at Boudinot's home March 29, 1835. The names signed are:

Major Ridge,	his X mark
James Foster,	his X mark
Test-ta-esky,	his X mark
Charles Moore,	his X mark
George Chambers,	his X mark
Tah-yeske,	
Achilla Smith,	his X mark
Andrew Ross,	
William Lassley,	
Cae-te-hee,	his X mark
Tah-gaheske,	his X mark
Robert Rogers,	
John Gunter,	
John A. Bell,	
Charles F. Foreman,	
William Rogers,	
George W. Adair,	
Elias Boudinot,	
James Starr,	his X mark
Jesse, Halfbreed,	his X mark

---

*Mooney, Myths of the Cherokee, pp. 122, 123.

In compliance with instructions of the council at New Echota, we sign this treaty.

STAND WATIE,
JOHN RIDGE.

March 1, 1836.

The treaty, in spite of strenuous opposition against the ratification, passed the United States senate by a majority of one vote and was signed and proclaimed by the president May 23. 1836.

NEW ECHOTA MEMORIAL

Today a granite memorial of lasting beauty marks the site of New Echota, last capital of the Cherokee Indians east. Through the efforts of Congressman M. C. Tarver, this shaft was erected and an appropriation of twenty-five hundred dollars secured from the United States Government.

The formal dedication of this memorial took place September 16, 1931.

COMPULSORY REMOVAL

We will not dwell on the heart-breaking days that ensued. The Cherokees "like all other mountaineers, adored their country, held to it and defended it with a heroic devotion, a pathetic constance and an unyielding tenacity." Their trust was placed in Ross who refused to believe that the removal would be consummated.

On January 20, 1838, the following notice was issued by the Superintendent of Cherokee Removal:

"NOTICE

"The Cherokees are informed that the Superintendent of their removal west, will have Suitable Steam Boats ready for their transportation at the Agency on the 5th day of Feby. capable of taking one thousand persons at a time, with comfort and safety to their new homes in fifteen days. The removal by land with unavoidable exposure and fatigue will require at least Seventy days; the choice of way is however given to the emigrant. The places of Rendezvous will be at the Agency, Ross' Landing and a point opposite Bellefonte, at each of which places the Boats will stop to take in Emigrants.

---

*Starr, Emmet, History of the Cherokee Indians, p. 95.

"The Superintendent takes the occasion to repeat that he has been instructed by their great father the President to treat the Cherokees with kindness and Friendship, and to assure them that to linger in the midst of a white population suffering oppression and encroachment, ruin and extermination must inevitably fall on them. In tenderness then to their persons and interests, he would urge them in the most friendly manner, assuring them at the same time that the treaty will not be altered, to make speedy preparations, settle their business with the Commissioners, and remove before the 23rd of May, when the time arrives for the application of Military Force.
Cherokee Agency, East)
January 20, 1838   )

NAT SMITH,
Supt. Ch. Removal."

In the spring of 1838 General Winfield Scott appeared at the capital, New Echota. He issued, on May 10th, a proclamation to the Cherokees warning them "that before another moon had passed every Cherokee man, woman and child must be in motion to join his brethren in the west."

Then began the last act of the Cherokee tragedy, which, in grief and pathos, exceeds any other chapter of American history. Stockade forts were built for assembling and holding the Indians. Five of these were in Georgia; one was placed in Murray county near the federal road and called Fort Coosawattee.*

The work of removal began in June at three points—at Calhoun, Tennessee, Ross' landing (now Chattanooga), and Gunter's landing (now Guntersville, Alabama), where the Indians were put on steamers and carried to the Mississippi. From there their journey was continued by land. Many deaths resulted from the heat and the long wearisome journey.

Ross and other chiefs then proposed to General Scott that they take over the business of emigration and the request was granted on condition that all should be on the march not later than October 20th.

The detachments were placed under the following conductors:**

Conductor: Hair Conrad, started August 28, 1838, arrived January 17, 1839, 143 days on road.
Conductor: Elijah Hicks, started September 1, 1838,

---
*The site of the old fort is near the McIntyre cemetery.
**Starr, Emmet, History of the Cherokee Indians, p. 103.

arrived January 4, 1839, 126 days on road.

Conductor: Rev. Jesse Bushyhead, started September 3, 1838, arrived February 27, 1839, 178 days on road.

Conductor: John Benge, started September 28, arrived January 11, 1839, 106 days on road.

Conductor: Situwakee, started September 7, 1838, arrived February 2, 1839, 149 days on road.

Conductor: Captain Old Field, started September 24, 1838, arrived February 23, 1839, 153 days on road.

Conductor: Moses Damel, started September 20, 1838, arrived March 2, 1839, 164 days on road.

Conductor: Choowalooka, started September 14, 1838, arrived March 1, 1839, 162 days on road.

Conductor: James Brown, started September 10, 1838, arrived March 5, 1839, 177 days on road.

Conductor: George Hicks, started September 7, 1838, arrived March 7, 1839, 189 days on road.

Conductor: Richard Taylor, started September 20, arrived March 24, 1839, 186 days on road.

Conductor: Peter Hilderbrand, started October 23, 1838, arrived March 25, 1839, 154 days on road.

Conductor: John Drew, started December 5, 1838, arrived March 18, 1839, 104 days on road.

When the steamer Victoria arrived at Little Rock in March, 1839, bearing Chief John Ross, the last of the Cherokees were nearing their destination, more than four thousand having perished on the way. The fateful road the exiles trod is known to this day as "The Trail of Tears."

CHAPTER II

Whitfield's Beginning

THE land known as the Cherokee purchase embraced all the territory north of the Chattahoochee river to the Tennessee line, and from Alabama eastward to North Carolina—an empire in extent.

In 1828, Georgia had extended her criminal jurisdiction over all this territory which was claimed by the Cherokees, and had passed many laws intended to operate upon that people.

In 1831, a survey of lands, with a view to occupancy by citizens of Georgia, was ordered by the Georgia legislature, and this was done in April of that year. The United States government had resolved sometime previously to remove the Cherokees to lands west of the Mississippi, and in preparation for the settlement of the lands by the white people, the whole territory was divided into sections, and these into districts nine miles square. The land was divided by lottery which commenced the twenty-second of October, 1832. The land lots were drawn in parcels of one hundred sixty acres and forty acres, the latter being called gold lots. In this division of the Cherokee lands into lots for distribution, the influence of the gold-fever then prevailing was in evidence in the lottery. The land districts which were thought to contain gold were laid off into lots of forty acres apiece while the others were laid off in one hundred and sixty acres apiece. These lots were drawn, and settlement was rapidly accomplished.

Even before the removal of the Indians two-thirds of their land was organized into Cherokee county; and soon after, Murray county was made from Cherokee with the county site at Spring Place, which was already a thriving settlement.

There were, of course, no railroads at that time, but when the Western and Atlantic railroad was built in 1847, it was laid out in the western part of the county, and new towns and settlements came into existence there, which made it necessary to establish a new county.

Whitfield was formed in 1851, and the county site of the new county was placed at Dalton.

WHITFIELD COUNTY*

This county was named after the celebrated GEORGE WHITEFIELD. He was the son of Thomas Whitefield, and was born in 1714, at the Bell Inn, in Gloucestershire, England, which was then kept by his mother. At twelve years of age he was sent to a grammar school in Gloucester. There he made considerable progress in the Latin classics, and in oratory. From this school he was transferred to Pembroke College, at Oxford, where he became acquainted with the Wesleys, and attached himself to a religious club, of which they were leaders.

On the 30th of June, 1736, he was ordained by Bishop Benson, and on the next Sunday preached his first sermon in the church in which he was baptized. A week after this he went to Oxford, where he took his Bachelor's degree and then complied with an invitation to visit London, where he continued two months, preaching with great effect to large and admiring audiences. About this time he received a letter from the Wesleys, who were then in Georgia, which induced him to determine to offer himself as a missionary to the Trustees. His offer was accepted, and he arrived at Savannah on the 7th of May, 1738.

Having resolved to establish an orphan house, he left Georgia for the purpose of collecting money to enable him to accomplish his object. Arriving in Charleston, he preached on several occasions to immense crowds, and then embarked for London, and after a voyage of nine weeks, he arrived at Limerick. Remaining there a short time, he sailed for England, and arrived September 30, 1738.

Having collected about one thousand pounds he set sail from England and landed at Philadelphia. After preaching at various places in New York, New Jersey and Pennsylvania where great crowds attended his ministry. He arrived in Savannah on the 11th of June, 1740.

---

*From "Historical Collections of Georgia by Rev. George White, M. A. 1854. Material and Picture presented to the county history by Ivan Allen of Atlanta, Ga.

WHITFIELD'S BEGINNING 41

REV. GEO. WHITEFIELD

The trustees of Georgia received him cordially and presented him with the living of Savannah and granted him five hundred acres upon which to erect an orphans' home.

He died on the 30th September, 1770, fifty-six years old.

The new county embraced two hundred eighty-one square

From the Historical Collections of Georgia, by the Rev. George White, M.A., 1854. Picture and material presented to the County of Whitfield by Ivan Allen, Atlanta, Ga., 1935.

miles, or about one hundred seventy-nine thousand eight hundred forty acres.

The land embraced in the county is unusually well watered and traversed by many streams. Cooahulla, the largest creek, traverses the county for thirty-four miles, emptying into the Connasauga river. Mill creek rises in John's mountain, races along its base for six miles, through a picturesque valley, and then courses around for eighteen miles till swallowed up by the Cooahulla. Within its boundaries there are ten miles of Swamp creek, eight miles of Bear creek, seven miles of West Chickamauga, six miles of Meadow creek and six miles of Deep Spring creek, besides over two hundred fifty miles of smaller creeks flowing into these streams. Mill creek, especially, affords unlimited water power for manufacturing purposes. Wherever these streams wind they form rich bottom lands. There is scarcely a quarter section in the county without a spring of never-failing water.

Whitfield is bounded on the north by Tennessee, on the east by Murray county, on the south by Gordon county, on the west by Catoosa and Walker counties, the latter forming a portion of the southern line also.

The Connasauga river divides it from Murray county on the east.

Two railway systems traverse the county, crossing one another diagonally at Dalton; these are the Southern and the Louisville and Nashville, through the latter's control by lease of the Western and Atlantic, the state road.

Before the removal of the Indians many white settlers had come into the territory and they perfected their titles to the land they had taken up as soon as Georgia had established sovereignty over the territory. One of these early settlers was Captain J. C. Head who came with his father, James A. Head, to what is now Tunnel Hill before 1836. Many years later he wrote a description of the country as he saw it in that early day, which is so vivid and interesting that the following is taken from it:

"It was then a forest, perhaps as beautiful and rich as the eye of man ever looked upon. The trees, in great variety on the plains and valleys, were large, tall and straight. On the highlands and ridges they were beautiful, but not so tall, nor so great in variety, being mostly pine and oak of the different varieties, and hickory.

"The lands everywhere were covered with luxuriant grass, and vines, forming a very fine range for cattle and horses.

"In this territory are numerous hills and small mountains which contribute largely to the beauty of the country, notably Dug Gap, Mount Rachel, Rocky Face and Dick's Ridge and Tunnel Hill Ridge. The best lands lie in the valleys and plains between these hills and mountains, but the lands on most of the hills are fertile and productive, and well adapted to orchards and vineyards.

"The whole country is well watered by numerous springs, branches, creeks and the Connasauga river. West of the Connasauga, is Cooahulla creek running out of Tennessee in a southerly direction and emptying into the river at a point about seven miles east of Dalton. Deep Springs, one of the largest and most beautiful springs anywhere, forms the Norton Mill creek and flows into the Connasauga. In the northern part of Whitfield county are several creeks formed mainly from beautiful springs and running in a southeasterly direction through good bodies of land and emptying into Cooahulla creek.

"In or about the year 1834, while the Indians occupied the country and were waiting for the government to settle the matter of their removal to the Indian Territory, where, according to the treaty made with them a short while before that time, they were to receive lands in exchange for their homes here, a few hardy and adventurous persons, anxious to secure homes in the beautiful Cherokee Purchase, as it was then called, moved in and began to make settlements.

"Two years later (in the year 1836) when this scribe, then a boy, came to this country with his father and family, it had come to be generally understood that the Indians were soon to be removed, and a large number of white families, assured of protection by the government, moved in that year from Georgia, North Carolina, South Carolina and Tennessee. After searching out and finding the section of land, each one claimed title to as drawer or purchaser, he settled down and began to make improvements as he had opportunity and ability, being careful not to infringe on the improvement of any Indian who might be living on the same lot of land; his right of occupancy having been guaranteed to him until he was legally removed according to the existing treaty.

"The first business of the newcomer was to build himself a cabin for the protection of his family, and stalls for his stock, and then clear land to cultivate in corn the ensuing summer to make bread for his family. Also to clear and enclose a rich plat to cultivate in potatoes, beans and other vegetables. In the meantime he had to look out for provisions for his family and stock. There was nothing at that time in the country to sell. The Indians sometimes had a venison ham, but no corn, bacon or provender to sell.

"Ross' landing (now Chattanooga) on the Tennessee river, was the nearest point where provisions could be obtained. There was then but one wagon road in this section, and that was a government road, leading from the Coosawattee river in a northerly direction to Ross' landing; but soon other ways were opened along the trails through the valleys and over the ridges from settlement to settlement, and from the settlements leading into the principal road to the landing, and to the county towns, Spring Place in Murray county, and LaFayette in Walker county. The writer helped to cut out that section of the Spring Place and LaFayette road passing through Dogwood valley from the point where Mount Vernon church now stands to the top of Taylor's ridge in the spring of 1836. All the white men, liable to road duty, living in the 27th land district, which is nine miles square, were called together to help do this work. The number, according to the recollection of this scribe, was about thirty, and it required three days to open the road. From this statement it may be inferred, that neighbors were not crowded together very closely, but they neighbored together, and were neighbors indeed. They were drawn together in the strongest ties of friendship, and assisted each other as a band of brothers. When one had a cabin to raise, or logs to roll, all in the same neighborhood, extending four or five miles around, cheerfully met at his place and helped him do his work. At such gatherings it was not uncommon for persons to meet who lived seven or eight miles apart.

"The every day occupation of the settlers was for the most

part farming, although milling, store keeping, and building were a part of the pioneers' work.

"The social and religious events such as corn shucking, log-raisings, and quilting were considered as social events, while church meetings and old-fashioned singing parties and camp meetings were important events in their lives.

"When supplies were needed, two or three teams and wagons were banded together and sent to the Landing for such things as were needed by anyone in the same community. This was a sort of necessity, as the roads were new and rough, and the streams which had fords were unbridged and difficult to cross.

"This was a time when men felt their dependence, one upon another, and they were ready to combine together to assist and protect each other. Friendships were formed then which continued for life, and may be traced to-day through the second and third generations of those early settlers.

"During the fall and winter of 1836, a good many more whites moved in and settled upon the lands to which they usually had some show of title, either as drawer or purchaser, and thus by the summer of 1837, a pretty good force of pale faces could be paraded in case of emergency, and they were ready to respond whenever danger was threatened, or an actual trespass had been committed upon the person or property of any individual."

Candler's History of Georgia states that the county is rich in minerals, iron, bauxite, manganese, silica, marble, sandstone and other building stone being found within its borders. The clay in certain portions of the county makes excellent brick. The farming land in the county embraces almost every character of soil from the rich chocolate loam of the river and creek bottoms to white gravelly and rotten shale of the uplands, but none so poor as to fail to respond to intelligent and energetic culture. It is a splendid stock country with many springs and spring branches.

The county was laid off into militia districts by the justices of the inferior court, practically as the districts now are, February 19, 1852, by virtue of the following order: "Whereas, by an act of the legislature of this state, creating a new county out of the county of Murray, and for other purposes, it is made the duty of the justices of the inferior court of the county of Whitfield to lay off said county into militia districts. It is therefore ordered that the said county of Whitfield be divided into districts with the following justices: F. W. McCurdy, John Hamilton, Hugh Burke, Joseph Robertson, Winston Gordon." (Extract from minutes of court, February 28, 1852).

DALTON THE COUNTY SEAT

The city of Dalton, long a thriving settlement known as Cross Plains, was incorporated in 1847 under the following charter:

"Sec. 1. Be it enacted by the Senate and the House of Representatives of the State of Georgia in General Assembly met and it is hereby enacted by authority of the same, That from and after the passage of this act, the village of Cross Plains, in Murray county, shall be incorporated under the style and name of the City of Dalton, in Murray county.

"Sec. 2. And be it further enacted by the authority aforesaid, That the corporate limits of said city shall extend one mile in every direction from the Railroad Depot in said city, and the municipal authorities shall be the Mayor and six members of Council with such other officers as they may appoint, or as may be hereinafter authorized, to be styled and designated the Mayor and Council of the City of Dalton.

"Sec. 3. And be it further enacted, that on the first Saturday in January in Eighteen Hundred and Forty-eight, and on the first Saturday in January in each and every year hereafter, the inhabitants of the city of Dalton, who are entitled to vote for members of the General Assembly of this State, who have resided for six months immediately preceding the election within the corporate limits of said city, unless absent therefrom on lawful business, and who have paid all taxes imposed by the city authorities and which they have had opportunity of paying, shall elect by ballot a Mayor and Council, of individuals likewise inhabitants, who upon accepting the office shall take and subscribe the following oath: 'I, A. B., do solemnly swear, or affirm, that I will well and truly perform the duties of Mayor and member of Council for the City of Dalton, by the adoption and enforcement of such measures as to me appear conducive to the general welfare and permanent good of the City of Dalton.'

"They shall convene the first Tuesday after their election and the said members of council and Mayor shall serve twelve months from the date of their election, and until their successors are elected and qualified.

"Sec. 4. And it is further enacted that John Thomas, Samuel R. McCary and Alexander M. Wallace be and they are hereby appointed superintendents of the election for members of Council and Mayor of said city on the first Saturday in January next, and in the absence of one of those individuals, the remaining two shall have power to appoint some other individual, a citizen of Dalton.

CHARLES J. JENKINS, Speaker
House of Representatives.

ANDREW J. MILLER, President
State Senate of Georgia.

APPROVED: December 29, 1847.

GEORGE W. TOWNS,
Governor."

*"Much of the land thus incorporated was owned by a syndicate headed by Captain Edward White, a native of Massachusetts, and in laying out the city he set aside tracts for parks, schools, churches and other public buildings on a scale suited to the real city he confidently expected Dalton would some day become. There was then no town of any size between Knoxville, Tennessee, and Augusta, Georgia. At that time Ross' Landing, now Chattanooga, and Marthasville, later Atlanta, were mere clusters of cabins, and Captain White believed his new city would become a metropolis.

"The principal streets were laid out a mile in length, and a hundred feet wide, and all the streets were named for prominent citizens. The main business street was named Hamilton in honor of Colonel John Hamilton; the principal residence street, Thornton Avenue for Colonel Mark Thornton; Pentz street for Frederick Pentz, and Morris street for James and Franklin B. Morris.

"The city was named in honor of Captain White's mother, whose maiden name was Mary Dalton,** a daughter of General Tristam Dalton, at one time speaker of the house of represen-

---

*NOTE: The above information was collected by the late Mrs. Warren R. Davis and published in "Georgia Memorials and Landmarks."—Knight.

**From an article in the Atlanta Constitution Nov. 2, 1913, entitled: Origin of names of towns traced by the United States Geographical Survey with the assistance of the Georgia Historical Society "Dalton was so called in honor of General Tristam Dalton, Speaker of the House of Representatives of Massachusetts."

tatives of Massachusetts. A member of Captain Edward White's family is authority for this statement.

"If there ever was a Dalton citizen who deserved a loving memorial in the midst of Dalton's activities, Edward White is that one. He was capitalist, but with a vision, the manager of a New England company, who foresaw the economic relations of the new Southwest to the eastern Atlantic slope.

"With the building of the East Tennessee, Virginia and Georgia railroad from Bristol, he used his influence that it might be brought to Dalton. It formed the first direct line of rail

WHITFIELD COUNTY COURT HOUSE

from eastern points to this section, and for several years the main artery of travel and traffic between eastern points and New Orleans. When this was accomplished, he conceived the necessity of the Selma, Rome and Dalton railroad and largely with Dalton capital procured charter, made survey and began the grading, which later attracted greater help. This brought larger traffic through Dalton, maintained large transfer forces, and made Dalton hotels—four of them—famous."

HOTELS

Even at an early date arrangements were made for entertaining the public and a number of Dalton's hotels have been noted for their hospitality and the excellence of their cuisine. One of the oldest was the Cross Plains Tavern which was located on the present site of the McCutchen home on Thornton Avenue.

Another of the oldest was the "Chester House", built by Judge W. P. Chester, who came to Dalton in 1844 and erected a large three story hotel with double deck galleries on the lot now occupied by Mitchell and Ingram Drug Company. An old photograph of this building is in the possession of his granddaughter, Mrs. Ernest Allen. This building was used as a hospital during the War Between the States and left a wreck by the armies.

Another hotel built by Judge Chester was destroyed as well as his commodious home at the intersection of Hamilton street and Chattanooga Avenue.

The Henderson Hotel owned by Mr. Ed Henderson, the Brown Hotel owned by Mr. Bean Brown, afterward by Major W. A. Camp, who was blind from a gunshot wound received in the war, were well-known hostelries.

The National Hotel was owned by Col. W. H. Tibbs, who had been a member of the Confederate Congress.

The Duff Green House was a well known hotel owned and managed by Col. Ben E. Green. It was situated on the vacant lot east of the Citizen office. This hotel was bought by J. Q. A. Lewis who operated it for many years. This hotel gained quite a reputation for Dalton and the trains arranged their schedules so that stops could be made at Dalton for meals. This was before the advent of diners on many trains.

The Hotel Dalton, built in 1890, was a credit to any city. It was owned by a company and leased to different managers. For a number of years it was under the management of Mrs. Dollie Lewis Dettor. Under her capable direction this hotel prospered and became well known as a resort for summer and winter visitors. Its hospitality was proverbial and it was a social center for the city.

This hotel was burned in the great fire of 1911, and for a number of years Dalton had no large hotel but a number of smaller hotels served the public most acceptably, notably the Hotel Horan and the Shell House and others.

Hotel Dalton was rebuilt in 1923 and is an up-to-date and modern hotel. (For further description see Chapter Six).

In the first ten years of Dalton's growth there were four hotels, two wagon and buggy factories, the Cherokee Furniture

HOTEL DALTON

factory, the Dalton Machine and Foundry Company, a large cabinet shop, a large saw and grist mill, a tin shop, a jug factory, other small interests and several retail stores.

From the birth of Dalton full train loads of hogs and cattle driven over the highways from East Tennessee were loaded and shipped from Dalton. Train loads of wheat from the fields of Whitfield and Murray were shipped from Dalton by the grocery and grain firm of Blount & King. At times grain was piled to the ceiling of the old depot, and all the platforms were filled, clogging the railroad to capacity. Dalton was the shipping point of the Ducktown copper mines, and the wagon trains came in half-mile lengths. With the beginning of settlement around Dalton, wagon train after wagon train came over the mountains and, as they said, were coming to the new Egypt.

In 1844, a German colony under the leadership of Count Frederick Charles settled in the northern part of what is now Dalton, and many of these have descendants still living in this vicinity. Among the settlers were: Peter and Adam Kreischer, Herman and Augustus Yeager, A. Lippman, Charles Knorr, A. Bolander, Henry Rauschenberg, Augustus Guntz, Adam Pfancokuche and John Setzefand.

In 1845, there were only ten families within the boundary of Cross Plains: Silas Mote, Colonel Mark Thornton, B. C. Morse, A. E. Blount, Judge William I. Underwood, William P. Hackney, Frederick Cook, Finley Riley, Dr. I. S. Waugh, and Colonel John Hamilton. At this time there were only two small stores, a post office, a blacksmith shop and a saloon in Cross Plains. Colonel Malone kept the Cross Plains Tavern situated where the late F. K. McCutchen formerly lived.

The first mayor of Dalton was A. E. Blount and the wartime mayor Judge Elbert Sevier Bird. The first ordinary of the county was William Gordon; the first sheriff, Captain Fred Cox; the first clerk of the court, John Anderson, and the first will probated was made by Thomas Wylie.

Until the beginning of the War Between the States, Captain White's dream of Dalton's greatness seemed on the way to realization as it was a busy and prosperous little city, with handsome churches, a good business section and many beautiful homes with a refined and cultured people of whom their descendants have a right to be proud.

An interview with Ed E. Chapman, published in the July, 1911, issue of the Dalton Argus, states that he came to Dalton fifteen years before Whitfield was made a county, this was in 1836. He also stated that at the time the county was separated from Murray, there were only five houses, and double log houses at that, here.

"Mark Thornton, for whom Thornton avenue was named, lived in a double log house on the lot now occupied by the home of Chas. Deakins.

"John Parks lived at the southern end of Thornton avenue on the corner lot on the east side. This was afterward known as the Fischer place. Otto Fischer was the father of Messrs. Will, Lou, and Otto Fischer, jewelers of Chattanooga.

"Judge Underwood built on a lot in northeast Dalton, now known as the Doctor Sams home.

"Colonel John Hamilton lived at what is known as Hamilton Spring.

"Dick Hill lived at the J. P. Daves place.

"These were the only families living here then."

Some of the early settlements in the county were, Varnells, Cohutta, Tunnel Hill, Red Clay, Rocky Face, Tilton and Dawnville.

TUNNEL HILL

Tunnel Hill was named for the Western and Atlantic railroad tunnel which penetrates the mountain there. The tunnel at the time it was built was considered a marvelous feat of engineering.

"Excavation for the tunnel began July 15th, 1848, and the first opening effected October 31, 1849, the first train of cars passed through May 9, 1850. The length of excavation, west end 575 feet, tunnel 1477 feet.

"George Towns, Governor, William Mitchell, chief engineer, Benj. C. Morse, chief assistant engineer, B. E. Wells, assistant engineer, John D. Gray & Co., Contractor. Railroad runs directly east and west through the tunnel."

The above data appears on the west end of the tunnel.

The opening of the tunnel was marked by a great celebration. The Hon. W. L. Mitchell decided to celebrate by the firing of a national salute. He gave the order for a cannon to be made for the occasion and when it came it was placed over the tunnel. Amid a large concourse of people who had gathered to listen to the speeches, the cannon was fired and the salute ended. After that they determined that the cannon should not be used for any other purpose and it was loaded with such a heavy charge that it was blown to pieces.

Tunnel Hill was the scene of several sharp engagements in

the war between the states, notably on November 28, 1863; February 23rd and May 6th and 7th, 1864.

Some of the early settlers were Jas. A. Head, Joseph M. Cain, Geo. W. Harlan, Benjamin Clark, Absolem Foster.

It is said to have been the first town in the country to have had a commission form of government.

OTHER EARLY TOWNS

Varnells, Red Clay and Cohutta, in the northern part of the county, are old settlements. All are thriving communities and were the homes of many splendid citizens of the county, and have interesting histories. Rev. W. G. Cotter, a noted Methodist minister and writer of his day, mentions the following families who were there in 1840: The Pitners, Nortons, McGuagheys, Stantons, Johnsons, McCombs and others. Colonel Jones had a home near Cohutta and Reverend Jos. Johnson had a large farm in the vicinity. Judge Kenan settled on the Chief Rattling Gourd place, the house was built in 1837. A. R. T. Hambright was another early settler, as was Jesse Wade. The Reverend Peyton Wade had a summer home near Varnells. He is said to have had over three hundred slaves.

J. H. Huff owned the house that was the scene of the councils of the Indians at Red Clay, which was one of the council grounds of the Cherokee Indians. Benjamin F. Prater settled near Varnells in 1852, coming as did most of the other families mentioned, from East Tennessee.

Rocky Face, in Mill Creek Gap, is located in one of the most picturesque parts of North Georgia. The towering mountains, with palisades along the crest, stretching for miles, all heavily wooded, with smiling valleys below through which winds Mill Creek, make it a place of beauty, and added to this is the historical interest of Rocky Face.

Mill Creek Gap has been called the Thermopylae of the Southern Confederacy because at the battles of Rocky Face, in the gap, February 25, May 8, 10, 12, 1864, the Confederates successfully held the pass against Sherman's forces. There are still in existence today (1936) traces of old breastworks and cannon emplacements on the mountains nearby.

Mill Creek Gap was the early home of many fine citizens of

the county. Isham Wood, father of the present county commissioner, Judge Harlan J. Wood, was an early settler. Adam Calhoun was another who came there at an early date. He came with his family in 1850.

Dawnville is another early settlement, although it was not named until after the war. Most of these early settlers came from East Tennessee; they were: Isaac Hair, George P. Fraker, Andrew Fraker, Ethelred Tarver (J. P.), grandfather of the present congressman, Hon. Malcolm C. Tarver, John Broadrick, Wilson Norton, D. L. Cline, Lewis Quillian and Milligan Quillian.

The settlement now known as Pleasant Grove had some pioneer settlers, notably Andrew Watt*, the first white man to settle in that vicinity, who came from South Carolina in 1836. Charles A. Cook came in 1838, and the Hammonds, Jewells and Stevensons came a few years later.

Mineral Springs, another small settlement, was named for the springs that flow out of the mountain which are said to be very beneficial to health.

Tilton is on the line of the Western & Atlantic railroad, also on the Conasauga river. Some of the first settlers were the Browns, Treadwells, Maynards and others.

Carbondale is another settlement in the southern part of the county. Honorable N. A. Bradford for many years representative of Whitfield county in the legislature, lived there.

Hill City is another small community center.

Beaverdale and Waring are well known communities.

Freeman Springs, now in Whitfield county, was originally in Walker county. Benjamin F. Freeman came there in 1836. Two of his sons, Judge Jesse P. Freeman and W. H. C. Freeman, held official positions in Whitfield county.

All these early settlements still thrive and, in their citizenry are still found the descendants of the early pioneers, bearing out not only the names but also carrying on their spirit of enterprise and service, which has won for Whitfield county rank among the most progressive counties of Georgia.

---

*Authority, Mr. Will Watt, his son.

CHAPTER III

War Between the States

When it became apparent that the North and South were hopelessly divided, the legislature of Georgia called a state convention of delegates to be elected by the people, to decide whether or not Georgia should secede from the union.

When the convention met at Milledgeville on the sixteenth of January, 1861, many eloquent speeches were made for and against secession. On the final test vote it was found that one hundred and sixty-four delegates favored secession, while one hundred and thirty-three favored co-operation with fifteen other southern states in securing constitutional guarantees for the protection of their rights and property. Following the result of the vote Georgia was declared a free and independent republic. In February, 1861, the Southern Confederacy was formed, and Georgia entered, thus becoming one of the Confederate states.

Whitfield county was represented in this convention by duly elected delegates. Avery's History of Georgia states that Whitfield county was represented by J. M. Jackson, F. A. Thomas and Dickson Taliaferro. Jackson and Taliaferro voted "No" on the ordinance of Secession and Thomas voted "Yes". It is interesting to note that only one delegate from Whitfield county to the convention voted for secession.

MILITARY HISTORY*

"At the outbreak of hostilities between the North and South, Dalton had one organized military company: The Dalton

---
*This article was prepared by John S. Thomas for the Anniversary Edition of The Citizen and is published with his permission. Authorities consulted: Gen. Joseph Johnston's "Narrative of the campaign from Dalton to Atlanta;" "Campaigns of Wheeler's Cavalry;" "A Staff Officers Diary;" "Mountain Campaigns" in Georgia by Joseph M. Brown.

Guards, commanded by Captain Tom Cook, who lost his life at Fredericksburg, Virginia, and was brought back to Dalton and buried in the old Presbyterian cemetery.

The Dalton Guards were ordered to Big Shanty and formed a part of the famous Phillips Legion of General T. R. R. Cobb's brigade, and fought through the long four years under General Lee, taking part in all the great battles that the Army of Virginia engaged in. A number of Whitfield county and Murray county men joined the 36th Georgia, commanded by Colonel Glenn, and the 34th Georgia, commanded by McConnell, who was killed at Missionary Ridge while leading his regiment in a charge; others joined Colonel Avery's Fourth Georgia Cavalry and served with General Joe Wheeler.

The Confederate government had a pork packing establishment erected on Mill Creek near what we know as Willow Dale. This was in charge of W. J. M. Thomas, J. G. S. Weatherford and W. M. Nichols.

Soon after the war started the government commenced the manufacture of cartridge boxes and belts in a portion of the unfinished hotel that stood on the lot where our post office building now stands.

Dalton saw its first Confederate troops when, in the summer of 1862, most of General Bragg's army came from North Alabama and Mississippi via Atlanta and Rome on the way to concentrate at Chattanooga in preparation for the Kentucky campaign. Not long before this the town was set in a frenzy by the wild race of the engine General chased by the Texas as they raced through Dalton. The race ended near Catoosa station and most of the raiders were captured and hung. In September, 1863, General Longstreet's veteran corps passed through Dalton on their way to take part in the great battle of Chickamauga. They were met by the people of Dalton with baskets of food, and greeted with cheers and wild enthusiasm. In only a few days the roar of cannon and rattle of musketry were plainly heard in Dalton, for the great battle that lasted nearly three days was being desperately fought; the Confederate army finally driving the Union army from the field.

The wounded were sent to Dalton by the hundreds. Soon every house or church that could care for or handle the wounded was full. The ladies of Dalton gave up for bandages every linen table cloth, and every sheet they possessed. And thousands of wounded were hauled in all kinds of box and flat cars, to cities and towns farther south.

On a dark, cold, rainy day in December, 1863, news of the defeat of the Southern army at Missionary Ridge reached Dalton, and the whole town was hushed in gloom and despair. Some gathered together what household goods they could pack and ship, closed up their homes, and refugeed to South Georgia and Alabama.

The next day the advance guard of the Army of Tennessee reached Dalton. Cleburne's gallant division of less than 5,000 muskets had fought Hooker's corps to a standstill at Ringgold Gap, and stopped the pursuit of Bragg's army. Bragg's wagon train extended from Ringgold almost to Dalton. It reached Dalton, thanks to Cleburne's fight and repulse of Hooker's corps at Ringgold Gap. Unmolested, on arrival at Dalton, General Bragg telegraphed President Davis at Richmond and asked to be relieved of the command of the Army of Tennessee. General W. J. Hardee assumed temporary command and made his headquarters at a home on South Depot street that burned many years ago, now replaced and owned by the Horne family. On one of the walls of the old house was a complete map of Dalton and Whitfield county drawn by army engineers.

On December 26, 1863, General Joseph E. Johnston was assigned to the command of the army and reached Dalton on that date and assumed command the next day. General Johnston first occupied a house on Selvidge street, then owned by the Cook family, and now owned by Mrs. William C. Huff. When the Spring campaign opened, General Johnston moved his headquarters to a house known as the Tibbs' house on North Hamilton street. This statement was verified by Major Frank Jackson of the 34th Georgia infantry, who was appointed provost marshal of Dalton by General Johnston.

During December and January the different divisions of the army were camped all around Dalton. The winter of '63 and '64 was an exceedingly cold one and the Confederate army, poorly supplied with clothing and shoes, suffered greatly; oftentimes food was scarce and the soldiers foraged for miles around.

In late January, or early February, a heavy snow fell and blanketed the country with two feet of fleecy whiteness. All drills and inspections were for the time abolished, and from a small tossing and throwing of a few snowballs the whole army engaged in a great snow battle that lasted nearly all day.

When the weather permitted, the soldiers were put to building corduroy roads. Every main road out of Dalton was made passable for artillery. In General Johnston's account of the Dalton to Atlanta campaign he says that Dalton was not strong strategically, as it could be flanked on the east via the Cleveland wagon road, and a flanking movement west of Rocky Face was screened by mountains.

DEFENSE OF DALTON

When the Union army advanced via Ringgold Gap, Johnston made ready to defend Dalton. His army was posted in Mill Creek Gap in line of battle extending along Rocky Face northeast so as to cover the Tennessee Railroad and the Cleveland highway. On the 5th of May, the Confederate army was in line of battle as follows: Stewart's and Bates' division in Mill Creek gap, in which they had constructed slight defensive works, the former on the right of the stream; Cheatham on Stewart's right occupied about a mile of the crest of the mountain; Walker's division in reserve; Stevenson's across Crow Valley, its left joining Cheatham's right on the crest of the mountain; Hindman's on the right of Stevenson's; and Cleburne's immediately in front of Dalton and behind Mill Creek across the Cleveland road.

In General Joseph Hooker's account of Sherman's campaign from Dalton to Atlanta, he says that under Sherman's orders, he inspected, from a high hill with field glasses, General Johnston's line of battle, and reported to Sherman that it was one of the strongest positions ever occupied and defended by an army, and advised that the position be flanked as a direct assault would cost thousands of lives.

On the 9th of May, Newton's division of the Fourth Union army corps assaulted the positions on the ridge in Crow Valley held by Brown's and Pettus' Confederate brigades. The Union forces were driven back with considerable loss.

On the 8th of May, two small regiments of Confederate cavalry were driven from Dug Gap three miles west of Dalton. General Johnston ordered Granberry's Texas brigade to retake the Gap, which they did in a gallant charge up the steep, rough mountain side.

On that same day Wheeler's cavalry encountered a large body of Union cavalry near Varnells Station. Wheeler attacked and routed the Union Cavalry, capturing over one hundred prisoners. Among them three captains, five lieutenants and Colonel LaGrange who commanded a brigade. Continual picket firing and skirmishing was constantly going on at and in front of Mill Creek Gap. The Confederate artillery which occupied the two high ridges west and northwest of the Springfield farm, checked the Union advance by rapid and well directed fire.

During the winter a man who turned out to be a Union spy, who posed as a peddler selling small notions, was closely watched and when arrested had almost a complete record of the number and positions held around Dalton by the Confederate forces. He was found guilty by court-martial and hanged near our court house square.

On the 13th of May, General Johnston was informed of Sherman's flanking movement, screened by Rocky Face and Taylor's ridge and through Snake Creek Gap. To meet this movement of the Union army, General Johnston, on the date, ordered his troops to give up the Mill Creek Gap and Crow Valley lines so successfully held by them, and to march to Resaca.

When the news spread over Dalton that our army was giving up Dalton to the enemy, panic took possession of the few remaining families and they left on foot, in wagons and carriages or any vehicle they could secure. Homes and most of their household goods were abandoned. Those attempting to leave by wagons found the roads blocked by Confederate troops.

On the 14th and 15th of May, the two armies struggled for advantage at Resaca. The roar of cannon, and rattle of small arms, were plainly heard at Dalton.

Then the first Union troops entered Dalton. They were part of Sherman's fourth corps, his other corps marched west of Dalton and passed through Snake Creek gap. The first Union flag to be put up in Dalton was raised on Thornton Avenue on the lot now occupied by the home of L. J. Allyn. Later in the summer of 1864, Wheeler's cavalry came into Dalton. A Union regiment was camped on North Thornton Avenue and on the ground where we now have our City Park. The Union troops were taken by surprise, as most of them were preparing their noonday meal. They offered little resistance, most of them taking refuge on Fort Hill. Wheeler's men took possession of the nearly prepared dinner and all abandoned camp material. At that time a Union sutler had his headquarters in the basement of the hotel owned by Judge W. P. Chester, who had refugeed with his family. Wheeler's men found the sutler's establishment and filled their knapsacks with eatables, and completely eptied the place.

In the meantime, the Union forces had erected fortifications on school hill and mounted artillery. Wheeler, in another raid, charged and captured this fort, taking several hundred prisoners. He attacked from the east side from Morris street.

In October, General Hood's army reached Dalton. Cheatham's division placed cannon on cemetery hill and demanded the surrender of the fort on school hill. Knowing it was useless to refuse, the Union forces surrendered and marched away as prisoners with Hood's troops. Dalton was again garrisoned by Union troops who remained undisturbed until Lee's surrender ended the war.

Nearly every building on Hamilton street was destroyed. The most wanton outrage was the destruction of the Presbyterian church. Not a brick was left standing. Mrs. Andy Calhoun, formerly a Miss Loner, was a small girl when Mill Creek gap was the Confederate line of battle. Her family occupied a house belonging to the Glaze family. She said the Union artillery elevated their guns to shoot at the Confederate troops on the top of Rocky Face, and some of the shells passed over the top of the mountain and fell in the orchard near the house. The women and children went under the house until the firing ceased.

While our army was camped in and around Dalton, a great protracted meeting was held. Some of the South's most famous preachers came to Dalton to help in the services; and hundreds of soldiers professed religion. General Hood was baptized by General Leonidas Polk who before the war had been an Episcopal bishop of Louisiana, and who was killed at Kennesaw mountain.

General Johnston reviewed his entire army while at Dalton, a reviewing stand being erected on Ridge street on the eastern side of our cemetery. Artillery, cavalry and infantry all marched by, over forty thousand strong.

The army of Tennessee remained longer at Dalton than at any other place, with the exception of the time spent at Tullahoma, Tennessee, during the period of the war. A sham battle was fought on the property now owned by the American Thread mill. As stated in the beginning of this article, the winter was cold and hard, and to make matters worse smallpox broke out among the troops. A smallpox hospital was established on the Antioch road, and many of our soldiers died there and were buried nearby on what was then known as the Worthy farm. The bodies were never removed.

No road out of Dalton but that felt the tramp of marching feet, and at night the surrounding hills were covered by thousands of camp fires.

A lady now living in Dalton, who was a small girl, tells of the retreat of our army after the disaster at Missionary Ridge. She said that on that cold December afternoon the advance brigade of the army came down Chattanooga avenue marching in columns of four. They were ragged, some were without hats or caps, some marched without shoes, but their heads were up and their bright bayonets shone in the evening sun. They had had no food that day, and had marched over seventeen miles of muddy roads. That night the entire Confederate army, with the exception of Cleburne's division that remained at Tunnel Hill, and camped there for several weeks, camped in and around Dalton. Very few of the Confederate soldiers had overcoats, and they had few tents. On bitter cold nights they came in from nearby camps and asked to sleep under houses or on the porches. Every Dalton home soon parted with every spare blanket and comfort they possessed.

Soon after General Johnson assumed command at Dalton, he telegraphed the War Department at Richmond, that 13,400 of his men were without shoes. That meant that one-fourth of his army was without shoes and snow on the ground. Hardships were cheerfully endured, and the officers and soldiers divided their slim rations with the few women and children left in the town.

In Wheeler's raids he met and charged the Union line of pickets near the intersection of Walnut avenue. Several of the Union dead were buried near our Confederate dead on the eastern slope of the cemetery, and in 1866 or '67 when our soldiers were moved to where they now rest, the Union soldiers were moved too, and their graves have always been decorated just as our own on Confederate memorial day.

On the crest of the western portion of Rocky Face for sixty years a Kentucky soldier has slept. A stone placed by the boy scouts of Dalton reads: "George W. Disney, Co. K. Kentucky Volunteers—May 9th, 1864."

Johnston's retreat from Dalton to Atlanta was a masterly retreat. Sherman with his far superior forces, could flank Johnston out of his well chosen positions, but always he found a Confederate battle line in his front, and every foot of ground bitterly contested. With a little handful of men, comparatively speaking, he menaced and harrassed General Sherman, who had a vast army, until it must have seemed to him impossible to make the distance from Dalton to Atlanta, taking him something like a hundred days to go a hundred miles."

WAR MEMOIRS

The following interesting bits are taken from the memoirs of Mrs. Emma Love Thompson, a Dalton woman who, as a girl, participated in many of the stirring events during the early days of the war:

"The first regiment that I saw was one that came through Dalton in May, 1861. It was the fourth Alabama regiment, which stopped over in Dalton for several days.

"The Dalton Guards left some weeks later. They were commanded by Captain Tom Cook. He was killed in battle and was brought back to Dalton and buried Christmas day. He was to have been married on that day to Miss Jemima Black, daughter of Dr. Black.

"The next company enlisted for six months. This company was commanded by Captain John Walker. They were sent to Savannah. My brother, R. R. Love, was a member of this com-

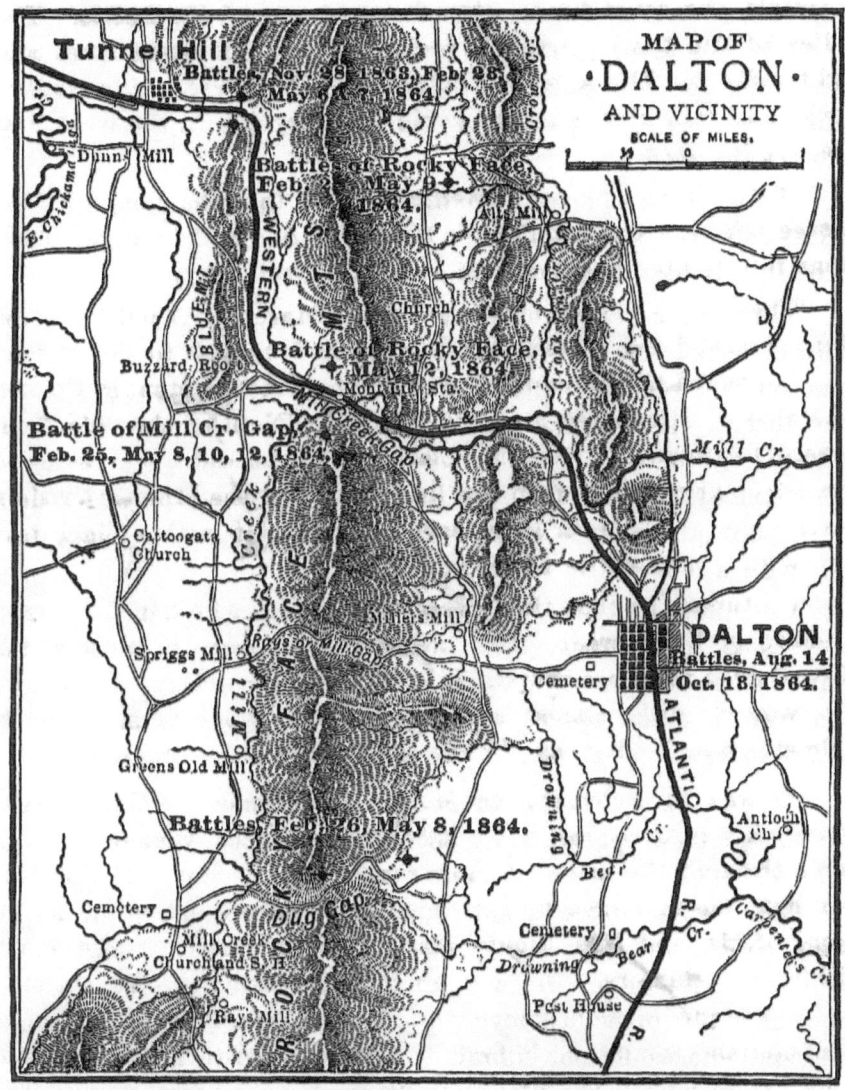

MAP OF BATTLEFIELDS OF WHITFIELD COUNTY

pany. A large number of the young men looked upon the war as a picnic for they supposed they would return in six or twelve months with laurels on their brows, but they were doomed to disappointment. Their chivalry and ardor were considerably dampened before the close for they suffered often from lack of food and clothing.

"I think it was in 1862 they turned all the public houses into hospitals, the court house, churches and one of the hotels. The ladies of the town formed a cooking society to make soup and light rolls for the sick and wounded. They secured a vacant house and four or five ladies would go every day in the week and prepare the food.

"It was in October or November of '63 that the army of Tennessee fell back to Dalton after the battle of Chickamauga. They went into winter quarters and remained until May.

"They had a review of the troops in March or April. Colonel Gordon asked me to escort him, which I agreed to do, but he was compelled to command his regiment as the Lieutenant Colonel was absent. He asked a friend, Colonel O'Neill of the 29th Tennessee Regiment, to take his place, which he did. He reviewed the whole army, riding up one line and down the other. I rode a black pony and wore a long black riding habit with a black turban with a long white feather in it.

"Costumes, at that time, were very scarce whether for street, evening or home wear. Our house dresses were homespun, the thread dyed and then woven on looms in the country. The southern women made almost every thing they wore from shoes to palmetto hats. That was in the last two years of the war.

"It was in February or March that General Hill, Provost Marshal, sent a request for a lady to search two women who had come through the lines. I can't remember the name of the first, nor how she managed to get through. She was stopping at the home of Mr. and Mrs. Blount just across the street from General Hill's headquarters. He sent an orderly with us. We went in and made our mission known to her. She became very indignant and said she would not submit to it. I turned to the orderly and told him to watch her while I went across the street to see General Hill. He told me to tell the orderly to see that his orders were carried out. When I got back she was putting some papers in the stove. She reluctantly consented to having her baggage searched. She had a large Saratoga trunk. It was packed but we went to the bottom of it, piling the things on the bed. When we got through she thought we should pack it again. I told her we had no orders to do that. We found no papers to convict her of being a spy; if she had any she had destroyed them.

"We went from there to my father's, J. P. Love, where Dr. Mary Walker was under guard. She was taken prisoner at Tunnel Hill. She had gone to the picket lines to send some mail. It was supposed that her principal object was to get a view, or learn something about our army, or she may have expected to be taken and exchanged, and by going through the southern states she would gain some knowledge of the situation of the army and other conditions. She was kept prisoner in Dalton about two weeks; she was then sent to Richmond where she was exchanged after being kept there some time. She was a surgeon in the army with a rank of Major. She wore a blue cloth bloomer suit with a red sash across her shoulder, a cocked felt hat and boots. When we went in and told her of General Hill's order, she agreed at once and was very agreeable. We had her disrobe as she had no baggage. I had her take her boots off, but I failed to find anything. After Sherman came to Atlanta she came back through Dalton."

Joseph M. Brown, ex-governor of Georgia, in his book, "The Mountain Campaigns in Georgia," says:

"In none of the campaigns of the gigantic 'War between the States' was there a more notable display of adroit, wary, far-reaching, strategic genius and prudent, patient, watchful care on the part of the great commanders, of skillful leadership by their officers, or of more heroic bravery and cheerful endurance by the men than in that memorable retreat which began in Whitfield county.

"The south had sent her brainiest and bravest leaders to endeavor, with fifty thousand men, to stem the tide of invasion which was rolling through Georgia.

"To the essayist, wishing to immortalize with his pen the deeds of great men, here is opened one of history's favorite chapters; to the artist eager to depict the romantic and picturesque, here, too, is displayed the scenery which thrills the emotions; while to the patriot who delights to tell of achievements of men who dared face death for their country, their cause and their flag, here is shown the theatre of their toils and their glory."

OTHER BATTLES

In Whitfield county there were thirteen fierce struggles at arms between Federal and Confederate armies, but so impregnable was she from her natural barriers that the exhausted army of General Bragg really went into winter quarters, while a few thousand men held the Federal army at bay, from November 28, 1863, till the 13th of the following May.

The more important engagements were the Battle of Ringgold, Pat Cleburne's ambuscade, only fourteen miles from Dalton on the Western & Atlantic railroad, November 27, 1863. This is near the famous Catoosa springs. Battles of Tunnel Hill, eight miles from Dalton by rail, November 28, 1863, and February 23rd, May 6th and 7th, 1864. Battles of Mill Creek gap, near Dalton, February 25th, May 9th and 10th, 1864. Battles of Rocky Face, seen from Dalton, February 25th, May 12th, 1864. Battles of Dug Gap, near Dalton, February 26th, May 8th, 1864. Recapture of Dalton and Federal garrison, October 13, 1864, by General Hood.

General Wheeler's race with a Federal locomotive, for stone bridge, on East Tennessee, Virginia & Georgia railroad, near Dalton, October 13, 1864.

Resaca, where four days' hard fighting occurred in May, 1864, is twelve miles south of Dalton. The "Atlanta Campaign" was opened May 1, 1864, at Dalton by Sherman with 98,797 men and 254 cannon, and Johnston with 42,856 men and 120 cannon. On August 15, 1864, Dalton was captured by Wheeler's cavalry, who were raiding Sherman's communications. The Confederates secured two hundred prisoners and destroyed considerable army stores, etc., and then went northward. Dalton was also captured by Hood's army, on its grand retrograde movement, after the fall of Atlanta. There was a sharp fight south of the town. The Confederates here captured the garrison, a regiment of negro troops. This was on October 13, 1864.

On April 9, 1865, General Robert E. Lee, Commander-in-Chief of the Confederate army, surrendered to the Federal army and was followed a few days later by General Joseph E. Johnston. By June 1st, all the Confederates had surrendered, and thus the great war came to a close, leaving the whole south destitute and exhausted. Dalton and Whitfield county suffered greatly because they were in the line of the invading army, and endured all the horrors incident to the situation.

RESTORATION

With a courage unequaled in any time they began the restoration of their beloved land.

All honor to the veterans of that struggle, the pioneers of the new south, who kept heart when all about them was ruin, and kept faith when all before them seemed darkest peril. They carried forward the torch of their civilization and had they failed there would be no such south as exists to-day. The war with its blighting desolation is gone. We are one people, and with Grady we can say, "there is no north, south, east or west," but it is fitting that those who made history and fought for what they thought was right, be remembered.

A beautiful spirit of patriotism was ever present among both the men and women of Whitfield county, and they did not fail to respond to a single demand for war relief. While the men were away many brave loyal women organized a Soldiers' Aid Society, and met daily to make uniforms, knit socks, make bandages, scrape lint, and send boxes to the boys at the front. When there were wounded and sick men, special food was prepared regularly in the homes of those devoted women. During the last part of the war, they nursed the sick and wounded, and in some instances, buried the dead.

The aid society grew into the Ladies' Memorial Association which had never failed to observe Memorial Day until it was merged into the Bryan M. Thomas Chapter United Daughters of the Confederacy. This organization has continued the observance each year since it was merged with the older organization. The Memorial association erected the monument at Memorial Park on Thornton avenue.

This monument is of Italian marble and is surmounted by a figure of a Confederate soldier with arms at rest. This statue was made in Italy. It stands in a beautiful park in the center of the city.

It took many years of patient effort and undaunted courage on the part of this organization to raise the funds in those lean years after the war and erect this beautiful monument. The inscription is as follows:

Confederate Memorial
Erected by the Ladies
Memorial Association
of
Whitfield County
To the Memory of
Our Confederate Dead
1892

Around the base are the names of four battlefields, Resaca, Dalton, Rocky Face, Chickamauga.

Some of the most distinguished orators of the south have delivered addresses on Memorial Day in Dalton.

Whitfield county lost many splendid men in the war. Their ashes rest in many soldiers' cemeteries in the southland. There are three hundred Confederate soldiers and four Union soldiers buried in the Confederate cemetery west of Dalton. The memory of their heroic deeds and loyal, patriotic service will ever be remembered by the citizens of Whitfield county.

JOSEPH E. JOHNSTON MONUMENT

In 1912 a monument in Dalton, Georgia, was erected in honor of General Joseph E. Johnston, the only one ever erected to his memory. This has a base of Georgia granite in the form of a semi-circle, rising in three tiers which diminish in size until the block of granite on which the statue stands is reached. On each side large wings extend handsomely carved in laurel leaves. At the front of the stone on which the statue rests is inscribed the following, directly under a laurel wreath:

The Inscription.
JOSEPH E. JOHNSTON.
1807—1891
Brigadier General, U. S. A.
General C. S. A.

Given command of the confederate forces at Dalton in 1863, he directed the 79 days' campaign to Atlanta, one of the most memorable in the annals of war.

Erected by the Bryan M. Thomas Chapter United Daughters of the Confederacy, Dalton, Ga., 1912.

Standing fifteen feet high, is the bronze statue of General Johnston, with his hat in one hand and his sheathed sword, pointing down, in the other, wearing full confederate uniform. This was erected at a cost of six thousand dollars.

There is a fund of history and romance in and about Dalton symbolized by its numerous ante-bellum homes. Many of the

JOSEPH E. JOHNSTON MONUMENT

homes served as headquarters for famous officers, prominent in both northern and southern ranks; homes that were used as hospitals; rooms where slain officers of both armies lay; and buildings and landmarks that have defied the ravages of time.

Two of these old homes were at different times the headquarters of General Joseph E. Johnston. The headquarters of General Hill were on Thornton avenue. Upon the authority of the late Mrs. M. E. Bitting the headquarters of General Pat Cleburne were at her country home several miles from Dalton.

It is a city with a history not yet grown dim, for it is fresh in the memory of the passing generation, and continually brought to mind by substantial relics in whose walls are entombed the memories of a fertile past.

The experiences that have made these old buildings sacred,

and that characterize their past, cover a wide field varying from the thrilling war-time tragedies, to the pretty fetes and courtships of ante-bellum days.

In addition to the headquarters of famous generals, there are buildings that have housed many brilliant social functions of the old south, and the courtships, marriages and births of men and women who have achieved both state and national recognition, have imbued the place and its surroundings with a charm of antiquity that pervades few cities now grown modern with the progress of the age.

CHAPTER IV

The Reconstruction Era

And so the War was over.

Whitfield county was in the path of the conflict; both armies were encamped within its borders for various lengths of time toward the end of the period and both city and county paid the price. Within the limits of Dalton very few buildings were left standing, mainly those used as headquarters, hospitals or commissaries by one army or both. The wonderful old oaks that had made the quiet village streets green lanes of beauty were, for the most part, gone. The soldiers, coming back, found their homes in ruins, their stock gone, the slaves freed, and nothing left but the firm spirit of determination to take up life again and carry on. Four years of army discipline had caused many to lose touch with civilian duties but their splendid reaction was what one might expect and the little city of their dreams, despite discouragement and poverty and unaccustomed toil, began to rise again from the ashes and take shape before their eyes.

Of the buildings remaining must be mentioned the old National Hotel. It was headquarters, commissary and hospital for both armies at different times. After the Federal troops occupied the city, they also used it as headquarters, as a hospital and as a prison, and the basement became a stable. It was estimated that ten thousand sick and wounded soldiers of both armies were sheltered under its roof at various times.

Fortunately Whitfield had never been a district of large slave owners, but rather a county of small farms, largely tended by the owners and their stalwart sons, so that there was not the wholesale change of habit necessary in some other sections. And within a few years new buildings and new stock had restored agriculture in the county to some semblance of the years before the war. Those halcyon days had departed, never to return, but they had built into the citizenry of the county here, as elsewhere, a deep conviction that no part of the world was as desirable as the home county and state. And where that spirit is prevalent and encouraged to bloom, the section must grow steadily toward the ideal held of it.

So it is not surprising that Whitfield county shortly covered the scars of war with a new growth of prosperity. One of the most important forward steps was taken in 1868 when the first county fair was held. Unfortunately there is no data concerning this, and the first succeeding fairs, in existence, so far as known prior to 1874. But a printed copy of the prize list of that year is now in the possession of Mrs. H. L. Jarvis, whose father, John H. Bitting, was secretary in that year and it is from this prize list that the following information is taken.

The name of the organization was The North Georgia Agricultural and Mechanical Association, and was officered by the following public-spirited citizens: T. J. Eason, president; G. W. Sapp, vice-president for Whitfield; John Bryant, vice-president for Murray; John H. Bitting, secretary; W. J. Underwood, treasurer; Ben E. Green, W. W. Cooksey, Dr. Moses Quinn, Dr. Folsom, L. W. Barrett, W. H. Tibbs, L. D. Palmer, Stephen Phillips, T. H. Pitner, J. D. Bivings, B. F. Prater, John Brooker, James L. McIntire, R. E. Kingsley, R. W. Jones, and Hon. C. D. McCutchen, directors.

At the fair of 1874 there were five departments: Domestic, Ornamental and Art, Agriculture, Mechanical and Live Stock. There was a speed ring and races were enthusiastically supported. Each day an address was given by a prominent speaker; in an old copy of The Dalton Argus it is stated that Belva Lockwood delivered an address.

The fair lasted four days and the admission charge was fifty cents.

Under the Domestic Department the prizes were for such items as the best six yards of jeans, best six yards of linsey, flannel, linen and rag carpet, best pair of woolen blankets, best bedspread, best pound of linen sewing thread and best pound of cotton sewing thread. This department was in charge of Frank Stanford and Silas Clemons.

The dairy and household division of this department had prizes offered for best ten pounds of dried beef, corned beef, cured sides, hard soap, soft soap, candles and starch, all to be home-made. J. W. Bivings and W. W. Gidden had this department in charge.

There were the usual prizes for preserves and pickles, grape and blackberry wine. This department was in charge of B. Moyers and John W. Stocks.

The second department offered prizes for plain and ornamental hand needlework, embroidery, patchwork quilts, braided work, darned work, knitting—socks and stockings; wax, hair, shell, bead and rustic work, millinery, and artificial flowers. This department being in charge of D. Bukofzer, J. W. Williamson, B. Z. Herndon, B. T. Luttrell, W. W. Higgins, B. F. C. Loughridge, Martin Berry and Professor King.

The livestock department was much the same as the usual county fairs of a later period. It included horses, mules, cattle, sheep, swine and pairs of graded cashmere goats. One division of this department included poultry, pigeons, rabbits, singing birds and bees. The superintendents were A. P. Roberts, D. E. Allen, Dr. M. M. Quinn, Henry Davis, J. F. Prather and B. B. Brown.

The committee to arrange for speakers consisted of George W. Sapp, D. E. Allen and R. J. Keith.

The third department—Agriculture—had three divisions: field crops; garden products; orchard, vineyard and nursery. The prizes were in the main for the usual farm products including red and white wheat, oats, buckwheat, rye, barley, etc. The superintendents of this department were: D. W. Mitchell, G. P. Fraker, J. A. Maddox, E. J. Tarver and J. M. Maddox.

The fourth department was the mechanical. It is interesting to note the number of articles that were then manufactured in the county as evidenced by the prizes offered for the best family carriage by maker; best buggy, wheelbarrow, horse collar, harness, saddle, plow-gear, and bridle by maker; best pair of boots, men's brogans, ladies' shoes; best bedstead and bureau; best side of sole leather and harness leather. This division was in charge of E. D. Wood and W. H. Kenner.

It is also interesting to note the advertisers on this old premium list as giving some names of families still represented here, as well as others long passed on to other fields of endeavor. Doctors Weaver and Fann, dentists, have a business card; R. P. O'Neill advertises provisions, fancy groceries, imported liquors and wines, as well as imported porter on draught and Cincinnati lager beer for family use; the City Drug Store, owned by L. P. Gudger & Company, has a list of the things offered for sale in drug stores, then as now; Mr. Hirschburg advertises books, fancy goods and toys. The only full page space advertises general merchandise to be sold by McCutcheon and Luttrell.

These fairs were continued for a number of years and were a great benefit to the county.

OLD HOMES

When we come across the statement in White's historical Collections published in 1847 that Dalton was the largest town between Knoxville, Tennessee, and Augusta, Georgia, we gain a better perspective of her past history. There was no little wealth centered in this point in pioneer days. The people reared substantial homes, employed the best teachers in the schools and gave to the virgin wilderness an atmosphere of culture while the tracks of the Indians were still fresh in the forest.

The homes of a number of her citizens were built with that stateliness of proportion and simple elegance of design so typical of southern homes of that time. There are few towns in the state around whose old homes there clusters more of architectural beauty and social charm or of historic renown. Some of them stand to-day as fine old landmarks such as the old Hamilton house which was built by Colonel John Hamilton on the site of an Indian village. It was used as a hospital during the War between the States.

The Frank Manly home on Thornton Avenue is reminiscent of the South's palmiest days. The home was rebuilt a number of years ago by Mr. Manly.

The Harben house on Selvidge street, now owned by Mr. and Mrs. Ogburn Alley, is another ante-bellum home. It was here that Will N. Harben, the noted author, spent his young manhood.

THE RECONSTRUCTION ERA 75

The Kirby home on Thornton Avenue was built by a pioneer citizen of Dalton, Ainsworth Emery Blunt, who came to Dalton in 1843 and served the town as its first mayor and postmaster. It is one of the few homes that is occupied by the descendants of the man who built it, being the home of Mrs. Lillie Blunt Kirby, a daughter of Ainsworth E. Blunt.

The old Davis home on Selvidge street built by Henry Davis, is another ante-bellum house, now the property of Mr. and Mrs. L. A. Brown. The foundations of this home were laid in the virgin forest before the street was laid out.

The Huff home on Selvidge street is another fine old landmark. Its history is given elsewhere; also that of the Tibbs house on North Hamilton street.

There are many other old homes that are still standing that have been almost entirely rebuilt but have retained the general style of architecture as the older building, such as the handsome colonial home of Mr. and Mrs. Will Moore on Thornton Avenue.

These homes are still standing, but there were many others that yielded to the torch of the invader.

The summit of Fort Hill, which was then terraced, was crowned with three beautiful homes. In the center, the home of Colonel J. A. R. Hanks, a brick building of pure colonial design; at the southern end of the hill was the Norris home, a splendid house half hidden in a grove of trees; on the northern end of the hill stood the Johnston house built by Colonel J. A. W. Johnston, one of the leading lawyers of the state. In the rear of these three homes were the negro quarters, which made almost a village in itself.

There were many others that have been burned or destroyed by the march of progress. The Fitzgerald house, built by Reverend Archibald Fitzgerald, once the home of the country club, the old Chester house, built by William P. Chester, the Glenn house in North Dalton, built by Jesse P. Glenn, the McCohen house, the W. J. Manly house, which stood on the elevation now occupied by the home of Mr. and Mrs. George Horan.

Another old home with a historic past is the brick, colonial house some miles south of Dalton known as the John Brown homeplace. It was built by the late Amos Sutherland, by slave labor, many years before the war between the states, as Mr. Sutherland was a large slave-holder.

SOCIAL LIFE

Dalton has from the beginning been the center of a delightful social life for the surrounding counties. One of the first social affairs was the "New County Ball" to celebrate the separation from Murray County.

There are several printed copies of invitations to social affairs, some of them on beautifully embossed paper, that are in the possession of Mrs. D. E. Allen. One of them dated August 2, 1855, is to a "Military Soiree" in honor of the Cadets of the Georgia Military Institute. This was at the Academy.

The managers of this event bring to mind many names prominent in the business as well as social life of Dalton. They were: Gen'l S. Dunn, Col. L. W. Earnest, Col. W. J. Underwood, Col. J. A. W. Johnson, Col. G. W. Roberts, Col. Wm. Gordon, Col. John Thomas, Major W. P. Chester, Capt. James Morris, Capt. J. W. Anderson, Dr. W. Gordon, Col. J. F. B. Jackson, Col. J. R. Brown, Col. Wm. K. Moore, Col. D. P. Wright, A. B. Holt, Wm. C. Mangum, Wm. A. Waugh, J. H. Hamilton, R. A. Holt, Jr., J. A. Nelson, R. G. Whitman.

Another event was a Washington Anniversary party given by the Dalton Guards at the Court House February 22, 1861. This paper is embossed and has a picture of Washington. Another invitation was a "Grand Social Hop" at Trevitt Hall in 1871. It too contains names familiar to many old Daltonians. Such as: S. Percy Greene, Dr. T. L. Kelly, Thos. R. Jones, W. H. Brooker, M. H. Bogle, Dr. R. Warren, Henry C. Hamilton, R. A. Rushton, Henry Lansdell, B. F. C. Loughridge, John Miller, Chas. Chester, D. E. Allen, W. H. Davis, D. Bukofzer, John Towns, R. P. O'Neill, T. M. Kirby.

From there and many other sources we gain faint glimpses of those happy days "before the war." We know that in after years the memories of those times, whatever fate may have done, were bright dreams of the past that could not be destroyed.

POST OFFICE

The post office was housed for many years in various rented

buildings and it was not till 1910 that the present handsome building was erected. The Hon. Gordon Lee was the representative in Congress and he secured the appropriation for the building.

It stands on the corner of Hamilton and Crawford streets and is a credit to the city. It is said to be a replica of Independence Hall in Philadelphia, Pa.

THE DALTON POST OFFICE

Due to the increase in the amount of business handled by the office an addition was made in 1931.

It is built of brick and stone and is well adapted and equipped for taking care of the postal business of the city.

The men and women who have served the office have always been representative citizens.

UNITED STATES POST OFFICE
Dalton, Whitfield County, Georgia

This office was established as Cross Plains, Murray County, Georgia, August 30, 1837.

Postmasters	Date Appointed
Ambrose McGhee	August 30, 1837
Frederick Cox	December 4, 1838
William I. Underwood	July 9, 1839
Robert Baker	September 4, 1841
Frederick Cox	June 9, 1842
Benjamin C. Morse	November 14, 1843
Ainsworth E. Blunt	June 26, 1845

The name of this office was changed to Dalton, March 27, 1847.

Postmasters	Date Appointed
Edward H. Edwards	April 14, 1853

This office was changed to Whitfield County.

Postmasters	Date Appointed
William P. Chester	January 12, 1858
Tolliver M. McHan	September 15, 1865
Lorenzo P. Gudger	March 16, 1869
John C. Ballew	January 8, 1874
Jesse A. Glenn	January 26, 1877
James G. Riley	March 31, 1880
Thomas H. Triplett	April 30, 1884
Jefferson T. Whitman	June 14, 1888
Columbus Browning	September 28, 1889
Mrs. Elizabeth Taylor	October 22, 1890
William M. Denton	January 10, 1895
John A. Crawford	January 10, 1899
Buford L. Heartsell	January 27, 1916
John A. Crawford (Acting)	November 12, 1920
John A. Crawford	March 13, 1922
Mrs. Josie M. Crawford (Acting)	July 18, 1923
Mrs. Josie M. Crawford	February 10, 1925
Thomas A. Hopper (Acting)	May 16, 1933
William M. Denton	May 22, 1934

This is an authentic list of the Postmasters furnished from the records of the Post Office Department by Hon. W. W. Howe, First Assistant Postmaster General, at the request of the committee through William M. Denton, Postmaster.

GROWTH OF DALTON

The population of Dalton in 1870 was listed as eighteen hundred; by 1880 this number was increased to two thousand five hundred sixteen and the citizenry began to become city minded. The Dalton Argus, of which a file from 1880 to 1890 furnishes much of the material for this chapter, is full of agitation for water-works, macadam streets, a public school system and various other city necessities. The grand jury in 1884 recommended the establishment of a county farm to care for the county poor. And also took occasion to offer congratulations on the fact that the county had voted "to abolish the retail liquor traffic in their midst." It is not perhaps generally known that this was the first county in any state to vote bone-dry.

The county tax digest for 1882 gives some interesting figures: White tax-payers, one thousand five hundred thirty-four, colored, three hundred seven; lawyers, fourteen; doctors, fifteen; dentists, two; number of acres listed, one hundred seventy-five thousand three hundred thirty-four, valued at $805,503; town and city property, value $470,653. This shows an increase of taxpayers of ninety-one over the preceding year, and a considerable increase in values.

Whitfield's school population in that year is given as: Males, white, fourteen hundred eighty-six; females, white, thirteen hundred ninety-three; colored, total, six hundred twenty-six; an increase of nearly four hundred from the preceding year. This does not mean that these children were in school as the public school system was not established until February, 1883. It was bitterly opposed in some quarters, and the Inferior Court at first refused to make appropriation for its support. But the school board was made up of men who saw clearly that the county could never go forward to take its proper place unless the coming citizens had a chance for an education, and finally an appropriation was made. This school board numbered among its members, W. K. Moore, chairman; J. P. Freeman, T. H. Pitner, W. C. Richardson and John H. Bitting. The City of Dalton had no public schools at this time, nor till some years later, but several excellent private schools were supplemented by a free school for children not otherwise provided for, supported by the Ladies Dorcas Society and held in the late Dr. Gudger's home on Thornton Avenue, beginning in October, 1884.

The Crown Cotton Mill was opened January 24, 1885. This was the first large manufacturing plant in the county though there had been several smaller plants of various kinds as early as 1882, and perhaps earlier, including a flour mill, an axe handle plant, a hub and spoke factory, a planing mill and small furniture factory, a cotton press, two gins, a number of saw mills and a small tannery. One of the first meat packing plants in the state was started in 1882, shipping sausage and cured meats in some quantity. The Argus speaks in this year of "Happy Dalton on a boom." But so much of Dalton's early prosperity and so much of its present wealth came from the Crown Cotton Mills that the date of its opening deserves special mention.

The Opera House was opened in August, 1885, It was owned and operated by Messrs. F. T. Hardwick, R. M. Herron, D. K. McKamy and Ben Gudger. Many plays with actors and actresses of national reputation were brought to Dalton as well as many distinguished lecturers and entertainers. It was used as a ball room and many notable social affairs took place there. It was burned in the great fire and was never rebuilt.

Street lighting was first seriously discussed in 1885 though it was several years before it became a fact.

During 1887, charters of organization were granted to the Dalton Building and Loan Association, the Dalton Electric and Gas Light Company and the Dalton Land and Improvement Company, as well as to several small manufacturing companies. The tax receiver's report showed a gratifying increase in the number of tax payers, and in the value of taxable property.

A most thrilling experience, calculated to make all Dalton city-conscious, was the turning on of water from the new plant which occurred on Saturday, August 4, 1888, though the plant was not actually completed till some weeks later. An impromptu banquet at the Lewis House celebrated the occasion.

In July, 1901, Dalton entertained the Fifth Regiment of State troops. They camped on the hill west of Dalton and the camp was called Camp Warren Davis, in memory of a prominent citizen of Dalton and a Confederate veteran. Governor Candler reviewed the troops camped here which consisted of ten companies.

It is axiomatic that a good newspaper makes a good town, and while all the credit for Dalton's advance does not belong to the newspapers of the county, it is certain that they have been more than helpful. The first of these, published while the ink on Whitfield's incorporation charter was still wet, was called The Mountain Eagle which began life in 1847 with J. A. Ware and a Mr. Wyatt as editors; later J. A. R. Hanks edited the paper for some time, and in 1862, we find it in the hands of J. T. Whitman as editor, under the name of the Daily North Georgia Times.* It is unfortunate that the old files of both these papers were destroyed by fire so that the date of this change of name, and the later change to the North Georgia Citizen, is not certainly known. But it is certain that the Daily Times shortly became a weekly paper again, and that J. T. Whitman was still the editor in 1866 by which time the paper had almost its present name. During the War Between the States J. T. Whitman was the editor and proprietor of the Daily North Georgia Times, now the Dalton Citizen. He was one of the most cultured of the several editors who have guided the destinies of this newspaper. He was a true Southerner of the old school and came to Dalton from Athens. Later editors of this newspaper were J. Troup Taylor, later secretary of the Georgia State Senate; Frank T. Reynolds, from whose voluminous scrap book much of this material is taken; and the present editor, T. S. Shope, under whose able direction the North Georgia Citizen, and under its later name the Dalton Citizen has won golden honors.

In October, 1865, J. A. R. Hanks, a former editor of the present Citizen, established the Cherokee Georgian but it lasted only a year or so.

Colonel H. A. Wrench, once an associate of Colonel Henry Watterson, of honored memory, moved back to Dalton about 1870, and established The Dalton Headlight which he edited for a time, sold to Walter Jefferson, Ben F. Carter, Gordon Russell and Frank T. Reynolds, and after a short time took it back, and edited it for some years, finally changing its name to the Dalton Argus, which was still being edited in 1890, standing always for the up-building of the county and a power in this part of the state.

There have been other ventures in the newspaper field, but none that made any permanent impression on the county prior to 1890, except these mentioned.

---

*From an editorial in the Anniversary Edition of the Dalton Citizen August 25, 1932.

The Dalton News was organized in 1927 with William M. Harris editor, and Gordon Kettles business manager.

The next year it was incorporated with Mr. Van Kettles as publisher and Mr. R. E. Hamilton as editor.

Mr. J. A. McFarland is the present president of the company. Mr. R. E. Hamilton is editor and manager.

In 1929 The News edited a fifty-two page special industrial and agricultural edition.

It has won the Hal M. Stanley trophy for typographical excellence and several smaller trophies.

In another particular the county has been unusually fortunate, and that is in its banks. It is a matter of pride that Whitfield has never had a bank failure from the organization of the county till this day. The first of its several banks was organized before this county was cut off from Murray, and was known as the Bank of Murray. In 1855 the Planters and Mechanics Bank, of which James Morris was president and T. B. Thompson, cashier, was a going concern but in November, 1862, Mr. L. Fullilove, who owned most of this bank, sold his entire interest in Planters and Mechanics to the Bank of Whitfield, of which M. Burns was president and John B. White, cashier.

Another early bank of which there seems to be no definite record, was the Cherokee Insurance & Banking Company, of which W. J. M. Thomas was cashier, and James D. Bard, president. A dollar bill issued in 1862, by this bank is still in existence. As the name appears in none of the records of the county, it was probably short lived and merged with one of the other banks of the time.

Mr. Frank T. Hardwick opened his bank in 1873 in partnership with his father and his brother, John Hardwick, under the name of C. L. Hardwick and Company. This was located in the old National Hotel, before mentioned, which stood on the corner now occupied by Hotel Dalton.

In 1888, the First National Bank was organized with R. I. Peak, of Lexington, Kentucky, J. D. Williamson, John Bryant, T. R. Jones, J. H. Kenner, T. M. Felker, R. J. McCamy, Sam B. Scott and T. Starr, as directors; R. J. McCamy was president; R. I. Peak, cashier; and S. B. Scott, teller. Later on Paul B.

Trammell reorganized this bank whose later history is given further on.

With many thriving industries, two unusually well managed newspapers, a good hotel and two sound banks, as well as many handsome homes, Dalton had reason to consider herself thriving. It is true there was not a foot of paving in the city; not a sidewalk, except the rough brick on Hamilton street, and not a public school of any kind within the city limits in 1890. But when one looks back twenty-five years beyond that date to what there was to work with at the close of the war, the progress already made was remarkable. The foundation for further growth had been well and firmly laid. And if it is true—which no one will deny—that the first step in any successful building is to make a foundation that will support any superstructure that is to follow, then we must gratefully admit that these city fathers of ours built well.

CHAPTER V

Churches and Schools

THE following extracts are from a discourse delivered before the Georgia Historical Society on the 12th day of February, 1845, by Dr. Church, President of the University of Georgia:

"Though our state laboured under peculiar difficulties during her colonial existence and for a considerable period after our independence, its history shows that our fathers were not less attentive to the great subject of general education than those who first settled our sister states.

"The first constitution of Georgia was adopted the 5th of February, 1777, only a few months after the Declaration of Independence. The 54th section of this constitution declares, 'Schools shall be erected in each county and supported at the general expense of the State.' This is an important record in the history of our education. On the 31st of July, 1783, the Legislature appropriated one thousand acres of land to each county for the support of free schools. In 1784 the Legislature passed an act appropriating four thousand acres of land for the endowment of a college or university. This act commences with the remarkable preamble: 'Whereas, the encouragement of religion and learning is an object of great importance to any community, and must tend to the prosperity and advantage of the same.'"

The oldest available printed records of churches and schools of Whitfield county are contained in White's Statistics of Georgia published in 1847 by W. Thorne Williams of Savannah. Whitfield was then a part of Murray county, Whitfield county not being laid out until 1851.

Under the headings "Religious Sects, Education, Character of the People and Amusements," Mr. White says: "The religious sects are missionary and anti-missionary Baptists, Cumberland Presbyterian, Methodists, Presbyterian, Roman Catholic and Universalists. The inhabitants are beginning to interest themselves in the subject of education. Number of poor children, 322; educational fund, $279.26.

"Murray county is settled by persons from different parts of Tennessee, North Carolina and Georgia, and it is, therefore, difficult to say precisely what are the peculiar traits in their character. Upon the whole, we think we may venture to state that religion and morality are on the advance. Practices which were formerly countenanced, have now but few advocates. The amusements are dancing, racing, cock-fighting, gander-pulling and bear fights."

History, a student once said, deals largely with omissions. Records of untold value were destroyed during the War between the States and for this reason credit due many individuals is necessarily omitted. Tradition is all that remains of their early struggles and accomplishments.

The missionaries of the Cherokee nation were the founders of the first churches in this section. Buildings erected of logs, hand-hewn by the pioneers were furnished with punch-board seats without backs. Some of these old benches are retained as memorials in the Macedonia Baptist church at Dawnville. These buildings were centers of all community activities. It was here that the old field schools were held and here the members of all denominations met for worship. The annual camp meeting formed an important part of the life of the pioneer settler. Meredith camp ground was one of the historic spots for Whitfield's religious assemblages. Another camp ground was at Pleasant Grove. Services were held three or four times daily under huge brush arbors. Cabins built expressly for the purpose, housed families who came for the duration of the meeting which was usually from ten days to two weeks. These meetings were held after crops were laid by. Many of the churches whose history is recorded in this chapter are the direct result of camp meetings.

DALTON METHODIST EPISCOPAL CHURCH, SOUTH*

"In the year 1835, Reverend D. F. Fulton and Reverend Ring were sent as missionaries of the Methodist church to the Indians then occupying this part of the country, as well as the few scat-

---
*From "History of Dalton Methodist Church," by Rev. Levi Brotherton.

tering whites then settled in the Indian nation. The first presiding elder was Reverend David Cummings whose district, covering the whole territory occupied by the Indians, extended from the Hiawassee River on the north to the Chattahoochee on the south, and from the line of South Carolina on the east to the Tennessee River on the west. He remained on the district until the year 1838, when the Indians were removed to the West. His immediate successor was Joseph B. Dawtery, followed by Thomas

FIRST METHODIST CHRURCH

Stringfield, the first editor of the Nashville Christian Advocate. The next was Reverend Timothy Sullins.

"This brings us down to 1845, the first year after the lines of the conference were changed. Russell Rineau, who was in charge of the circuit at the time of the change, was the first presiding elder thereafter. His district covered what is now the Dalton district, part of the Rome district, part of the Marietta district, and all of the Dahlonega district. He was succeeded in turn by Alfred T. Mann, J. B. Payne, J. C. Simmons, J. W. Yarborough, J. W. Glenn, B. A. Arbogast, A. G. Haygood, W. P. Harrison, H. J. Adams, W. J. Scott, R. W. Bigham, D. J. Myrick, A. M. Thigpin, W. A. Parks, J. F. Mixon, W. F. Quillian, W. T. Irvine, S. B.

Ledbetter, J. F. Yarbrough, S. A. Harris, Frank Quillian, J. R. Turner and A. M. Pierce.

"In 1836 Madison C. Hawk was sent to this territory to preach. He was followed in 1838 by Daniel B. Payne, and he, in turn, by Elijah Still. The next year two preachers were sent to this circuit, Wm. Rush and J. C. Tartar, and later Chas. K. Lewis. The following years Wm. Hickey with John Corn as his assistant. Russell Reneau was the next on this work and during 1844 the general conference changed the lines and took in all the Holston conference lying in Georgia, except Dade county, and added the Cherokee territory to the Georgia conference. Very near, if not quite all, the preachers working in this territory cast their lots with the Georgia conference.

"At the time of the change of the lines of the conference, the Spring Place circuit comprised all of what is now Murray, Whitfield and parts of Catoosa, Gordon and Bartow counties.

"In the year 1844, Reverend David Crenshaw was assigned to the Spring Place circuit as assistant preacher. The next year Jackson Reynolds served this work. In 1846 the circuit was left to be supplied, and the presiding elder put the Reverend Levi Brotherton in charge of the work. During this year the town of Dalton was located and named by Edward White, it having formerly been known as Cross Plains.

"The Methodists had a small membership and worshipped at a place then known as Clear Springs academy, just out of the limits of Dalton on the north. Here were perhaps twenty-five or thirty members, composed principally of the families of Captain Wm. Hammond, Reverend Levi Brotherton, George Chappell and B. E. Wells. During the fall of the year, on consultation, the place of worship was moved to the log school house in Dalton. The next year Mr. Edward White built a neat frame church on the lot where the Presbyterian church now stands, and bought and put up the bell which is still used by the Presbyterians He paid $250.00 for it. Reverend Levi Brotherton was asked by Mr. White to take charge of the church as town preacher and to preach or find a substitute every Sunday so that the people might be sure of hearing the gospel. The Methodist removed to this house in 1847.

"At the session of the annual conference held at Madison that year, Dalton was made a station, and attached to it were three country appointments, viz: the Cove, Union and Sugar Valley. Reverend Levi Brotherton was placed in charge.

"In 1849 the station at Dalton, not being able of itself to support a preacher, was thrown back into a circuit and Mr. Simmons was returned to the work. It should have been before stated that the Reverend James Quillian was the presiding elder in charge of Spring Place circuit in the year 1847.

In 1850 Mr. White offered to donate a lot to the Methodists for a church, and the site was selected where the present church now stands. Mr. White conveyed the lot selected to Captain Wm. Hammond, George Chappell, John Odell, J. E. Wells and Levi Brotherton, in trust for the church.

During the year 1851 five hundred dollars was subscribed for the building of a church. In this house the congregation worshiped until after the war, when it was removed to make room for a more commodious building. During the year 1851 there was a union protracted service held in the church erected by Mr. White. This meeting lasted forty days and was conducted principally by Reverends Archibald Johnson, of the Presbyterian church, Geo. W. Selvidge, of the Baptist, and Levi Brotherton, of the Methodist church, and Reverend John Strickland, presiding elder of the circuit. During this revival there were nearly one hundred conversions. The churches, very weak up to this time, were all greatly strengthened by additions to their number. In the fall of 1851 the new Methodist church was finished, and Reverend Levi Brotherton preached the first sermon in it. Dalton was left in the circuit from 1849 till 1851. The preachers who served this work from this time up to the war were Clayton Quillian, Louis B. Payne, W. F. Conly, R. H. Waters, M. C. Smith, Robert F. Jones, J. D. Anthony, John Murphy, C. A. Moore and M. A. Clontz. In 1857 Dalton was again made a station. The pastors in order were: M. A. Clontz, J. M. Dickey, J. W. McGhee; and then Wesley D. Pledger, who was here in 1861, and in 1862, John W. Turner. The war having come on, there was no regular preacher when the Reverend John M. Richardson, a local preacher living near, took charge."

The preachers in charge of the Dalton station after the war

were: first, W. C. Mallory, then John P. Duncan, D. D. Moore, Francis A. Kimball, George W. Yarbrough, George C. Smith, Wm. P. Kramer, G. W. Hardaway, Daniel J. Myrick, Thos. A. Searle, P. B. Ryburn, J. H. Baxter, J. T. Lowe, J. W. Lee, Simon P. Richardson, J. B. Robbins, A. B. Quillian, B. F. Fraser, L. G. Johnson, W. F. Quillian, H. J. Ellis, T. C. Betterton, R. A. Edmondson, J. A. Timmerman, W. R. Foote, S. B. Ledbetter, J. D. Hammond, R. M. Dixon, H. C. Emory, C. M. Lipham, G. F. Venable, C. P. Harris, W. G. Crawley and L. M. Twiggs.

In 1883, the church built a parsonage at a cost of $3,000.00 and in 1886-87 the church was remodeled and beautified. Again in 1907 the church was greatly enlarged by the addition of a Sunday school annex; and a new parsonage built in 1924-25 valued at $20,000.00.

The present membership of the church is approximately six hundred and seventy-five.

Presiding Elders of the Dalton District from 1870 to 1935 (list provided by J. R. Turner):

H. J. Adams, G. J. Pierce, R. G. Bigham, J. D. Myrick, A. M. Thigpin, W. A. Parks, J. F. Mixon, W. F. Quillian, J. M. Lowery, A. G. Worley, J. B. Robins, W. C. Dunlap, H. J. Adams, A. W. Williams, B. P. Allen, Ford McRee, W. P. Lovejoy, J. T. Christian, W. T. Ervine, S. B. Ledbetter, J. F. Yarbrough, A. S. Harris, Frank Quillian, J. R. Turner and A. M. Pierce.

THE FIRST PRESBYTERIAN CHURCH, DALTON

The minute book of the church tells simply this story of organization:

"The Presbyterian Church of Dalton, Georgia, was organized October 31, 1847. Ministers present: Reverend John Jones and Reverend J. M. Waddell. Members of the church, John Anderson, Jane Anderson, James McSpadden, Susan McSpadden, D. S. Waugh, W. M. Murray, A. E. Blunt, Ann S. Newell, Emily Tilliotson, Mary Rosenbaugh, Martha E. Morse and Andrew (colored boy of J. I. Hamilton). Elders elected: A. E. Blunt and James McSpadden. First baptism. John Emery, son of B. C. and Martha E. Morse.

"In 1847 the little frame building which Edward White had built for a town hall, was bought by a small band of Presby-

FIRST PRESBYTERIAN CHURCH

terians, and a church was organized with twelve members, the first organized church in the town.

"This little church had a high boxed-in pulpit from which the good pastor expounded good old fashioned Presbyterian doctrine, his congregation being divided by a high center-board down through the center of the church, the jackets and trousers on one side, the bonnets and petticoats on the other.

"A church bell was bought and hung with much pride, as it was then the only bell within a radius of one hundred miles.

"The building was destroyed by Sherman's army, but the bell, the melodian, the communion service and the pulpit Bible were hidden and kept by the women of the church and they became the nucleus for the new church which stood on the same site and was completed in 1868. A fine pipe-organ was soon installed and is still in use in this church. A steeple was added and the bell hung in it, the bell having been previously hung in a scaffold on the church grounds.

"In 1900 the manse was completed and in 1913 the whole church was rebuilt of cream brick.

"Reverend John Jones was the first pastor, and then followed Reverend A. G. Johnson, Reverend H. C. Carter, Reverend J. A. Wallace, Reverend H. C. Carter, Dr. A. W. Gaston, Reverend G. F. Robertson, Dr. Mark A. Matthews, Dr. John Mecklin, Dr. Walter L. Lingle, Reverend E. W. Way, Dr. F. K. Sims, and Dr. Wilkes Dendy.

In the ministry from this church, Rev. E. M. Green, Rev. O. E. Buchholz.

Elders who have served this church:

A. E. Blount, Jas. McSpadden, R. W. Jones, W. K. Moore, Sr., L. E. Wilson, W. R. Berner, V. Thompson, W. J. Manly, B. Moyers, J. T. Whitman, J. M. Lowry, J. F. Groves, G. L. O'Barr, E. W. Green, A. J. Showalter, A. W. Lynn, T. R. Jones, Sr., W. G. Liddell, R. A. Rushton, R. A. Patterson, J. F. Denton, H. L. Smith, G. W. Hamilton, Sr., T. M. Kirby, W. M. Denton, R. M. Herron, Sr., W. K. Moore, Jr., W. N. Morse, R. P. Gregory, G. W. Hamilton, Jr.

FIRST BAPTIST CHURCH*

The Baptists here first worshipped in a community chapel, or town hall, which was used by all denominations, and for other meetings as well. This building was about where the Presbyterian church now stands.

The First Baptist Church was organized in November, 1847, with seven charter members. At that time Dalton was in Murray county; the history of the First Baptist Church antedates by a little the history of Whitfield county. The first pastor of the church was Reverend G. W. Selvidge. His name is perpetuated in the name of the street which extends from the Baptist church northward to Chattanooga avenue.

In 1851-52, a two-story wooden building was erected on the site now occupied by the present building. The upper story was for the church services, the lower story was used as a school and displaced the old school house that stood in the park nearby. The deed to the Baptist property recites a consideration of twenty-five dollars. White street, the short street between the park and the church, was named for Mr. Edward White, a very public spirited citizen and a Baptist.

It was in this old First church that Judge Edward Harden made his famous speech to the first contingent of the Dalton Guards on the eve of their departure to give their services in the cause of the Confederacy. This was in July, 1861. Before the conclusion of the great conflict, this church had contributed thirty soldiers to the armies of the South. The church building was used as a hospital during the days following the battle of Chickamauga.

The present building was erected in 1873-4. This was accomplished mainly by the zeal and enterprise and devotion of the late Mr. J. A. Blanton. W. B. Farrar and W. T. McCarty were other helpful leaders. The bell was presented by Archibald Fitzgerald and is said to be made of unusually fine material. After the war was over, the bell was returned to its place, and is still used to call the Baptists of Dalton to worship.

The old communion service of the church was presented to the church by General Duff Green, who was a staunch Baptist. When Sherman's army came through Dalton it was taken to

---
*Dr. Crudup, History of the Dalton Baptist Church.

Union Springs, Alabama, for safe keeping by Mr. and Mrs. Henry Davis who had refugeed to that place. They were charter members of the church.

The parsonage was built in 1891.

The South Dalton church was a mission of the First Baptist

FIRST BAPTIST CHURCH

church for a number of years, and at its organization into a church it received about forty members from the First church.

Pastors who have served the First Baptist Church of Dalton include the following: G. W. Selvidge, A. E. Vandiver, George F. Cooper, A. S. Morrell, J. M. Stansberry, J. M. Grambell, J. A. R. Hanks, G. A. Loftin, N. A. Bailey, W. C. Wilkes, F. M. Daniel, H. T. Hanks, W. C. Luther, W. C. McCall, W. N. Jones, Waylan

Johnson, A. H. Mitchell, T. M. Calloway, B. F. Hunt, W. H. Cooper, E. M. Dyer, S. A. Goodwin, H. P. Fitch, O. C. Peyton, M. N. McCall, O. L. Martin, P. A. Gatlin, George P. White, J. S. McLemore, O. D. Fleming, Josiah Crudup, A. B. Couch, Gower Latimer, and J. L. Clegg.

SAINT MARK'S EPISCOPAL, DALTON

In 1864 there was only one Episcopalian in Dalton, Miss Cornelia Holiday. Two years later Colonel and Mrs. Ben E. Green moved from Washington, D. C., and soon formed a Sunday school held in Colonel Green's law office, then in the court house.

A church was built in 1871 on Depot street on lots donated by Colonel and Mrs. Green for church and rectory. That year Bishop Beckwith held the first services in the new church. In his report he says: "The congregation in Dalton, after many trials, are in possession of a handsome Gothic church with seating capacity for three hundred."

In 1896 a new church was built on Pentz street, fifty-six communicants being enrolled. The new church was much smaller than the original, and for some time had only occasional services.

Bishop Beckwith died in 1890 and Bishop C. K. Nelson succeeded him. As a tribute to his last official act being performed in Saint Mark's, Dalton, Bishop Nelson presented a handsome brass cross and vases for the communion table.

The church has many other memorials. The altar from the first Saint Mark's has been restored, and placed upon it are the above mentioned cross and vases in memory of Bishop Beckwith; on either side are brass candlesticks to match, memorials for Colonel and Mrs. Green from their daughter, Miss Carrie Green. The alms basin was presented by Mr. and Mrs. C. M. Hollingsworth in memory of their son, Latimer, a soldier of the World War. The book rest for the altar is a gift from the rector, Reverend Thomas Duck, and the processional cross is in memory of Joseph M. Self from his brothers. The old pipe organ given in early days to the parish, is now one of the treasured antiques of Saint Philip's Cathedral, Atlanta, being the one used by John Wesley in his first Sunday school held in Christ Church in Savannah. In its place is a double manual Estey combination pipe and reed organ.

General Bryan M. Thomas, Mr. and Mrs. John Black and family, Captain and Mrs. Pierce Horne and family, Col. and Mrs. B. E. Green and family, Charles Flowers and family, Mr. and Mrs. Gibson, Mr. and Mrs. Self and family, Major and Mrs. Lucas, Capt. T. C. Thompson and others were all active members and their names will always be held dear in the church.

The present vestry are John Black, senior warden; John Ratcliffe, junior warden; E. Burton Shaw, Frank Hawkins, H. W. Nevin, L. B. Lawton, Miss Annie Horne, Miss Carrie Green, Mrs. Swift Maddox, and Mrs. C. L. Bradley. (Rev. John H. Soper is the present rector, 1936.)

HAMILTON STREET METHODIST, DALTON

Hamilton Street Methodist church was founded in 1888 by Reverend E. M. Stanton and erected by W. F. Bender.

The following pastors have served the Hamilton street charge: E. M. Stanton, W. F. Hamby, J. R. Speck, M. D. Smith, J. T. Turner, Myers M. Church, M. M. Walraven, J. M. V. Morris, G. L. Chastain, J. M. Hawkins, J. L. Bryan, R. P. Tatum, A. B. Pendleton, M. L. Harris, E. G. Thomason, C. L. Martin, N. A. Parsons, J. E. Russell, J. W. Veatch, W. H. Spear, D. A. McBrayer, S. A. Bales, John M. Legg, C. H. Williams, J. T. Pendley, W. L. Jolley, F. H. Ray, H. A. King, J. E. Ward, C. A. Reece, B. M. McHan and J. L. Varner.

Some of the charter members were: W. A. Renfro, John Hill, Sr., R. H. Durham, Ross Pope, John Huckabee and S. B. McCamy.

SOUTH DALTON BAPTIST

The South Dalton Baptist church was founded in 1915. This church was formerly a small mission school organized by E. F. Hamilton and H. L. McEntyre and called Elk City Mission School. The first meetings were held in a store house. After securing a charter, the Reverend J. A. Boyd was appointed pastor. After a revival conducted by Reverend W. E. Roberts and Reverend J. O. Dantzler in 1930, one hundred and forty new members were added to the church. Mr. C. A. Payne was the chief instigator of a plan for a new church building. This building contains a main auditorium and three Sunday school rooms with a seating capacity of six hundred and twenty-five.

The following men have served as pastors since its organization: Reverend J. A. Boyd, Reverend Morris, Reverend Charles Maples, Reverend Hogan, Reverend Mealor, Reverend Thornton, Reverend J. H. Cargal, Reverend S. P. Chitwood and Reverend W. E. Roberts.

EAST SIDE BAPTIST CHURCH, DALTON

The East Side Baptist church was organized April 24, 1927. The building has a large basement which serves as Sunday school rooms. The auditorium has a seating capacity of five hundred. The entire cost of the building and equipment was approximately $5,000.00.

The pastors of this church have been Reverend C. S. Shugart, Reverend E. T. Tiffany, Reverend J. H. Cargal, Reverend E. O. Davis and Reverend W. E. Roberts.

MOUNT RACHEL BAPTIST CHURCH, DALTON

Mount Rachel Baptist church was organized January 19, 1892, with Elders J. E. Hudson, H. S. Gilbert and Joseph T. Nichols present to organize the church. It began with twenty-six members and has grown to a membership of around four hundred.

The following pastors have served the church: Reverend Hudson, Reverend B. F. Hunt, Reverend W. B. Bridges, Reverend W. E. Dawn, Reverend Taylor, Reverend J. H. Cargal, Reverend J. M. Hudlow, Reverend B. F. Farrar, Reverend Joe Maples, Reverend Charles Maples and Reverend W. M. Kelley.

GREEN STREET BAPTIST, DALTON

Green Street Baptist Church was first known as Smith's Chapel. The church was built with funds raised by W. F. Smith. After a revival conducted by Rev. J. O. Dantzler in 1926, the church was dedicated. There were twenty-six charter members. The membership now numbers about sixty-five.

The pastors have been W. F. Smith, J. O. Dantzler, and George Fletcher.

CROWN VIEW BAPTIST CHURCH

The church records list the following as members in 1912-13: J. N. Reynolds, Newton Sims, Mrs. Rachel Westmoreland, Mr. and Mrs. Augustus Conklin and Mrs. Mattie Elder. In 1914 a building committee composed of J. A. Maples, John Reynolds, W. H. Cronic, and J. H. Wells, was appointed and the building now in use was erected.

Pastors who have served this church are J. A. Maples, B. E. Bolden, E. O. Davis, and M. H. Welch and J. A. Thacker.

The church has a membership of more than four hundred.

MORRIS STREET METHODIST EPISCOPAL CHURCH

The movement for this new church was begun in a notable prayer-meeting in February of 1927. Among those present were Mr. and Mrs. I. G. Duckett, Mr. and Mrs. D. M. Millsap, J. F. Smith, Mr. and Mrs. Roscoe Long, Mr. and Mrs. J. T. Tatum, the Rev. T. Frank Cook of Fuller's Chapel M. E. Church who was assisted by Samuel H. Millsap in tent and other services, and Mrs. S. H. Millsap.

The Rev. W. L. Hampton was appointed their first pastor in November of 1928. The congregation endeavored to build a new church upon the property acquired at the corner of East Morris and Green streets but did not do so until after a parsonage had been built, six years later.

The Rev. E. B. Carlock became pastor in November of 1933. The new church was begun with the added charter members of Mr. and Mrs. Charlie Millsap, Miss Estelle Millsap, Mrs. Nora Long, Mr. and Mrs. Ernest Black, Mrs. Glen Patterson, Mrs. Elizabeth Smith, Misses Ina and Bertha Smith, Mrs. R. B. Stancill, Mr. and Mrs. Wheeler Headrick, Misses Edith and Frankie Lankford and other associated peoples in February of 1934. The new brick veneered church building was dedicated in October, 1935.

CHURCH OF THE NAZARENE

This church was organized in November, 1930, with seven charter members. The Church of the Nazarene is located on North Hamilton street. Rev. H. H. Hendershot was the organizing pastor. The members were: Mr. and Mrs. H. O. Miller, Mr. and Mrs. H. H. Hendershot, Mr. and Mrs. H. C. Clark and Mrs. Mattie L. Reed.

CATHOLIC

There are a number of Catholic communicants in Dalton who formerly had a church at the corner of West Morris and Pentz streets, the last priest in charge being the late Father Clifford. The church was given up about thirty-five years ago.

THE CHURCH OF CHRIST

This church was organized in 1915 by A. M. Richardson. The members held services in the court house auditorium for several months, later moving to a store building on North Hamilton street. The Cumberland Presbyterian church was rented for two years and then was purchased by the members.

The charter members were: W. A. Weaver, Mr. and Mrs. Cass Hall, Miss Flora Faulkner, Mr. and Mrs. Jason Stanley, Mrs. Della Reaves and Mrs. Clarice Hicks.

THE HOLINESS

The Church of God was organized in March of 1920. The pastor was W. M. Goings. The first members were A. W. Williams, Lillie Williams, and Sallie Poge.

The Church of God of the Union Assembly was organized in 1921 with C. T. Pratt as pastor. Members who have been active in support of the church since its organization are L. C. Whitener, Joe Vaughan, Alec Ledford, T. R. Bell and Claud Jones.

The Church of God over which A. J. Thomaston is general overseer was organized in 1923. Charter members were Mr. and Mrs. Albert Williams, Mr. and Mrs. J. R. Tudor and Mr. and Mrs. Dennis Keys.

ANTIOCH CHURCH

Organized in 1850, Antioch Baptist church has grown to a membership of three hundred and fifty.

Among the members during the early years of the church were: Elijah and Carolina Kirby and son, Walter, Mrs. Molly Connally, Mr. and Mrs. James Holland, Mr. and Mrs. William

West, Mr. and Mrs. H. L. Nichols, Mr. and Mrs. William Whitener, Mr. and Mrs. Washington Cavender, Mr. and Mrs. Felix Bradley and Mrs. Henry Bartenfield.

Pastors of the church were: Joseph Terry, John Compton, John J. Gilbert, H. D. Gilbert, B. F. Foster, Joe T. Nichols, Charlie Maples, James Austin, John Head —. —. Acree, J. O. Dantzler and W. E. Roberts.

BETHEL

The information which follows was furnished by Misses Ella and Nan Richardson and J. L. Randolph.

Bethel Methodist church was built before the War between the States on land given by Buford Randolph. Among the pioneers composing its membership were William Richardson and wife, Nancy, William C. Richardson and wife, Eliza, John M. Richardson and wife, Martha, Lee Richardson and wife, Ann, the widow and children of Alfred H. Richardson, Buford Randolph and wife, Elizabeth, John Wesley Fincher and wife, Rhoda, Mrs. Eliza Harris Tillman, Charlie Cochran, Mary Jane and Ann McCurdy, Churchwell Morris and family, William O'Dell and Luther Rodgers and family.

The colored members of the congregation occupied pews in the rear of the church. Among the most devout of these were Uncle Lewis Richardson and his wife, Aunt Jane.

The pastors of Bethel have been Thomas Pledger, ——— Hamilton, J. R. Speck, A. J. Hughes, ——— McFarland, J. L. Bryan, ——— Gober, G. L. Chastain, W. R. Kennedy, E. M. Stanton, W. T. Hamby, R. P. Tatum, H. D. Pace, J. V. M. Morris, J. M. Hawkins, A. B. Pendleton, M. L. Harris, E. G. Thomason, C. L. Martin, N. A. Parsons, J. E. Russell, J. W. Veatch, W. H. Spear, D. A. McBrayer, S. A. Bales, John M. Legg, C. H. Williams, J. T. Pendley, W. L. Jolley, F. H. Ray, H. A. King, J. E. Ward, C. A. Reece, B. M. McHan and J. L. Varner.

CARBONDALE CHURCHES

The Baptist church at Carbondale, known as the Swamp Creek church, was organized before the War between the States. The building now in use was erected shortly after the war ended.

The Carbondale Methodist church was organized in a log building occupied by the present building soon after the war ended. The building now in use was erected more than fifty years ago.

The Baptist church of the Carbondale section organized more than thirty years ago as Bethlehem is now known as the Union Baptist church.

CONCORD BAPTIST CHURCH

A church whose influence has played an important part in Whitfield county is Concord. It is one of the oldest churches in the county and while complete records are not available, a list of pastors since its organization establishes its history as having begun long before the War between the States.

The following named pastors have served: Giles Dunn, Levi Dunn, Henry Head, Joshua W. Patty, W. C. Haddock, Jesse T. Huffaker, Dan Lewis, W. M. Lowry, Wm. Davenport, ―――― Ensley, ―――― Elliott, H. A. Winstead, W. J. Darnell, A. R. Breeden, ―――― Franklin, ―――― Chastain, J. S. Williams and Fred Harper.

(Information given by T. J. Cooper.)

COHUTTA PRESBYTERIAN

This history of this church is given in the church record, now in the possession of Mrs. H. F. Shugart, of Cleveland, Tennessee:

"Red Clay, Ga.,
August, 3rd Sabbath, 1858.

"The following persons living in this vicinity were organized into a Presbyterian church to be known by the name of Pisgah and to be under the care of Kingston Presbytery.

"Sam'l Minnis, Mary Minnis, Thos. J. Minnis, Susan Minnis, Elizabeth J. Minnis, John A. Haskins, Rachel K. Haskins, Andrew J. McCallie, H. J. A. McCallie, Robt. Lindsay, Mary Mitchell. In August, 1858, the following members were received into the church: Sarah Pitner, Margaret Norton, J. D. Haskins, Mary J. Haskins, Martha J. Haskins and Florence J. Lindsay.

"John A. Haskins and Andrew J. McCallie were unanimously elected and regularly ordained to the office of Ruling Elder. In this organization Rev. Wm. B. Brown, the state minister to this people, was assisted by Rev. Thomas Brown and Rev. Wm. E. Caldwell.

"The Red Clay Presbyterian church building was situated about one mile east of the village of Red Clay. For years the little band of members struggled to have regular services in their beloved church, but as time passed, the senior elder passed over the river to his eternal home, his family moved away, and the ranks were further thinned by deaths and removals till they reached that crisis when it became evident it was a change or extinction. Many hearts clung to the dear old house with its sacred memories and the little city of the dead that lay near it, but they chose removal.

"The place chosen for rebuilding was at Cohutta, a small town on the Southern railroad. A beautiful lot was donated by Major T. H. Pitner for a building site. The deed was made to J. F. Groves, H. F. Shugart and L. W. Roy.

"Dr. J. F. Groves, the only living elder in the church, being instrumental in getting the removal made, together with Mr. H. F. Shugart, began the taking down of the old house in December, 1887.

"Kind friends of every denomination lent a helping hand to the good cause. Free from debt, it was rededicated to the worship of God on the fourth Sabbath of May, 1888.

"Reverend James S. Hillhouse, assisted by Reverend R. F. Taylor, conducted the services.

"After the change of location Presbytery was petitioned for a change of name which was granted before the Presbytery in session at Calhoun in April, 1891. It was given the name of Cohutta."

Among pastors serving this church have been R. F. Taylor, James Lane, J. L. King, A. G. Johnston, J. B. Hillhouse, W. W. Brinson, D. L. Buttolph, M. D. Smith, B. R. Anderson, K. T. Simmons, and J. T. Wade.

Among elders serving were J. F. Groves, H. F. Shugart, L. W. Roy, W. A. Ramsey, Chas. Henderson and J. W. Creswell.

COHUTTA CUMBERLAND PRESBYTERIAN CHURCH AND PRESBYTERIAN CHURCH OF U. S. A.*

The Cohutta Cumberland Presbyterian church was organized by the Reverend Hiram Douglass about 1842, at the residence of James Johnson two miles east of Cohutta, then Murray county and now Whitfield county, Georgia. It was soon after located at Flint Springs, Bradley county, Tennessee. Soon after its location at that place, for the convenience of the members on the Georgia side of the state line, the congregation was divided and the members were organized as a separate congregation. The new church was located about two miles south of Cohutta on the farm of Wilson Norton, and took the name of Pleasant Grove.

About the time that the Southern railway built the Ooltewah cut-off and located the Cohutta Station, the Reverend A. R. T. Hambright moved to the community and preached his first sermon in a grove near the center of the village.

In about 1886 he gathered the scattered members together —thirty-six in number—as the Cohutta Cumberland Presbyterian church. This congregation erected the first house of worship of any order in the place. The other two churches located here used this building while their buildings were being erected."

Among the charter members of the Cumberland Presbyterian church were: S. H. and Emily Parker, Nancy A. Huffaker, Joseph E. and Sarah Stockburger, Benj. D. and Thirza Leonard, Wm. J. and Mary Lowe, A. R. T. and Martha I. Hambright, Wm. and Sarah J. McGaughy, Mary C. McGaughy, John A. Pickens and family, Sarah Armstrong, Catherine and Polly Stancill and W. M. Hackney.

Pastors who served this church were A. R. T. Hambright, J. B. Wilhoit, S. M. Bennett, J. H. Miller and Frank Burns.

In 1906 this church joined in the union of the Cumberland Presbyterian and the Presbyterian Church of the United States of America, since which time a number of members have been added. The old building has been sold, a central location

---

*History of this church written by Rev. A. R. T. Hambright. List of charter members taken from his autobiography now in possession of Mrs. Fannie Hambright Boyd.

bought, and a modern house of worship erected.

The pastors who have served since this union are J. M. Wooten, Marvin Murphy and S. G. Frazier.

MOUNT OLIVET METHODIST CHURCH

Official records of Murray county show that on August 6, 1845, John B. Maston deeded to John Pitner, James H. Huff, M. P. Varnell and Seaborn Span, trustees in trust for the Methodist Episcopal church at Mt. Olivet one acre of land. The consideration was five dollars.

Whitfield records of 1858 list the trustees of Mt. Olivet as T. H. Pitner, B. F. Prater, T. Lawrence, Wm. McCaughy and James H. Huff.

Mt. Olivet was the strongest rural Methodist church in Whitfield county. The trustees of this church assisted in establishing three other Methodist church in nearby sections.

The circuit rider who served Mt. Olivet also served the following churches: Red Clay, Varnell, Mt. Zion, Pleasant Grove, Mt. Pleasant and Tunnel Hill.

COHUTTA BAPTIST CHURCH

The Cohutta Baptist church was organized in 1906 with the following charter members: Mr. and Mrs. W. C. Haddock, Mr. and Mrs. T. J. Bagby and son, Fred, Mr. and Mrs. Thomas Williamson, Mr. and Mrs. J. H. Bridges and Mr. and Mrs. W. H. D. Haddock.

On April 28, 1908, Mrs. Malinda Piner deeded one-half acre of land to the Missionary Baptist church, and on this land the members erected the building in which they have since worshipped.

The pastors have been W. C. Haddock, P. D. Longley, W. E. Grey, Wm. Rhymer, Charlie Maples, R. L. Austin, W. H. Bridges, B. H. Hunt, W. F. Huffaker, W. F. Henesley and W. M. Kelly.

DAWNVILLE BAPTIST CHURCH

According to tradition, Macedonia is the oldest church of the North Georgia Baptist association, preceding in date Poplar Springs church, which was organized before 1836.

The first pastor of whom there is any record was Rev. John

M. Wood, who went west long before the War between the States and who wrote back during the sixties for a copy of his credentials which he had lost. Rev. Wood was an uncle of Rev. Joe T. Nichols.

County records show that on December 6, 1855, Jordan Webb deeded Edward McAbee, Lorenza Wood, William Wiggins and David Williams land on which to erect Macedonia church and right of way to water.

Among early members of the church were William Wiggins and wife, Cynthia, Lazarus and Rebecca Wood, Mrs. Betty Wood Dycus, Mrs. Elvira Wood Ray, Kimzy, Isaac, Joe and Pierce Wood, Mrs. Elizabeth Williams, Etheldred Tarver and wife, Jane McNair.

Among the pastors of Macedonia were J. M. Gambrell, —. —. McAbee, Joe T. Nichols, J. C. Parrott, J. J. Gilbert, Charlie Maples, J. O. Dantzler, J. N. Dooly and W. E. Roberts.

DAWNVILLE METHODIST CHURCH

Mount Zion Methodist church was organized near Meredith Camp ground in the Meredith home about 1860. The members worshiped in an old log building about one and one-half miles northeast of Dawnville for several years until the site of the present church building was purchased.

The original deed states that on February 9, 1874, E. F. Dawn deeded three-fourths acre of land to Wm. McNabb, Geo. P. Fraker, A. S. Dean, H. D. Keith and J. M. Poag, said land to be used for Mt. Zion M. E. church, south. The consideration was thirty dollars. The deed is signed by E. F. Dawn and Mary Dawn.

A second deed made on November 27, 1886, by Thos. Caldwell and Margaret Caldwell grants an additional acre to the trustees named, Wm. McNabb, George P. Fraker, A. S. Dean, H. D. Keith and F. L. Lane.

The purchase price was thirty dollars. Each deed specifies that there are to be no burials on the lot.

The church building erected in 1874 served the congregation until 1925, when it was replaced by the larger building now in use.

Among the first members of Mt. Zion were the Meredith

family, Jackson Davis and wife Jane, James Crouch and wife Lavinia, George P. Fraker and wife Evaline, Andrew Fraker and wife Margaret, Wesley Fraker and wife Sallie, Nathan Jones and wife Violet, Alexander Dean and wife Elizabeth.

Among pastors at Mt. Zion were ———— Hamilton, Thomas Pledger, J. R. Speck, A. J. Hughes, G. L. Chastain, W. E. Kennedy, E. M. Stanton, W. T. Hamby, W. R. Kennedy, Henry D. Pace, J. F. Tyson, J. W. Bailey, A. J. Mann, J. M. Hawkins, N. A. Parsons.

DAWNVILLE

The Cumberland Presbyterian church at Dawnville was organized in 1869 by Rev. S. R. Henry and the members were invited to hold their services in Macedonia Baptist church. In appreciation of this privilege they assisted in the remodeling of the church.

Among the charter members were James F. Miller and wife Rebecca, Henderson Renfroe and wife Nancy, William D. King and wife Susan, Calvin Whitener and wife, Mrs. Hardcastle and Thomas Caldwell.

In 1886 a site was purchased and a church building erected by the members. The trustees who signed the purchase deed were David King, Columbus Varnell, Henderson Renfroe, William Combee and A. J. Miller.

Pastors of this church were S. R. Henry, ———— Dale, John Whitener, ———— Humphries, Z. M. McGhee and J. H. Miller.

DEEP SPRINGS BAPTIST CHURCH

The following sketch is from "A Brief History of Deep Spring Church" written by Rev. W. A. Henry in 1922.

"In the year 1851, in a sparsely settled community about ten miles northeast from Dalton, Georgia, in the county of Whitfield, near a large and deep spring, and located on the Dalton and Benton public road was built a log school house for the mutual benefit of all concerned. The teacher during 1852 and 1853 was James S. James.

"Not long after this, the exact date not known, a Baptist church was constituted and a permanent shed built for the better accommodation so much needed.

"A title to five acres of land was granted by P. M. Routh to the deacons of the church, which has been used for building site and ground and burial ground.

"Numbers went out from this church. Rev. Robert Routh, son of P. M. Routh, preached in the West many years. Rev. E. C. Routh, grandson of P. M. Routh, is editor of The Texas Baptist Standard. Henry and John A. James, sons of James S. James, served in the ministry of song as teachers and directors of music.

"Among early pastors were Elders McNut and Hawkins, Giles Dunn and his son, Billy Dunn, and James Gambrell.

"Camp meetings were held, families coming and camping on the church grounds.

"The cruel Civil war with its blighting influence came—strife and antagonism developed. The church had no pastor and failed to keep up regular meetings and records prior to 1872." We copy the following from minutes of September, 1872:

"Deep Spring church during a protracted meeting held by Bro. Levy Dunn and Elder D. B. Cunningham—agreed to come together and keep house for the Lord."

"A frame house built during Elder Cunningham's pastorate was destroyed by fire in 1899.

"Elder Martin Isbill was pastor following Elder Cunningham. The North Georgia Baptist Association was held at Deep Springs in 1878. It is said that Martin Isbill has been moderator of the same for a number of years."

The minute book shows that among early pastors were James Gambrell, H. D. Gilbert, B. F. Foster, W. H. Boyd, E. C. Hudson and W. A. Henry.

DUG GAP BAPTIST CHURCH

Dug Gap Baptist church was organized in 1860. Buildings on three different sites have been used, the present building having been erected in 1912.

Rev. J. T. Nichols, who was pastor in 1887, gives the following names as early members: Mr. and Mrs. James Longley, Mr. and Mrs. Lewis Longley, Mr. and Mrs. Bowdry, Mr. and Mrs. Jasper Longley, Mrs. Martha Poole, Mr. and Mrs. Jasper

Oxford, Mr. and Mrs. LaFayette Oxford and Joseph, Richard, John and Coleman Williams and Miss Annie Williams.

County records show that on February 1, 1912, L. C. Babb deeded to the Church of Christ of Dug Gap for one dollar and love and esteem for the Church of Christ, slightly less than one acre of land.

Among pastors serving Dug Gap have been B. F. Foster, J. T. Nichols, Will Dawn, Charlie Maples, J. H. Cargal, E. O. Davis, J. O. Dantzler, W. E. Roberts and S. P. Chitwood.

GOOD HOPE

The church records give September 27, 1879, as the date of its organization. The Presbytery consisted of Z. T. Clark, J. T. Huffaker, J. W. Patty and W. M. Cash. Charter members were: Alfred J. Neal, Howard Cagle, John Cole, A. W. Tate, J. C. Crow, D. D. Willis, J. C. Johnson, John C. Manis, Martha Manis, W. A. Manis, Mary Creasman, and others. Among the early pastors were W. D. Davenport, B. F. Foster, W. E. Dawn, W. B. Bridges, Lee Taylor, W. G. Darnell and H. A. Winstead.

HARMONY

A revival meeting was held beneath a brush arbor at Harmony in 1890, and at the close of this meeting, Harmony Baptist church was organized by F. D. McConnell, J. O. Ragsdale and ———— O'Kelly.

The charter members were J. W. Langston, W. T. Moore, S. A. Cash, J. M. Cash and Berry Gladden.

On September 17, 1898, L. B. Duckett deeded a plat of land to Harmony for a consideration of twenty-five dollars. On this land was erected the church building now in use.

Among pastors of Harmony church have been A. B. Nucholls, Joe Four, B. F. Foster, J. M. Stone, J. M. Cash, Charlie Maples, Joe Maples, Walter Bennett, J. O. Dantzler, R. C. Rooney, J. W. Dooley and George Fletcher.

HOPEWELL BAPTIST CHURCH*

This church was organized in 1858 on a site one mile north of the present site, just over on the Tennessee side of the state

---

*T. J. Cooper gave this information.

line. The first building was a log structure. The present building was erected about 1865. The first deacons were W. H. Wilson, Samuel Read, Strander Raines and Albert Varnell.

Early members of Hopewell were Henderson and Catherine Wilson, James C. and Elizabeth Wilson, Achilles and Margaret Webb, Thomas and Minerva Wilson, John A. and Mary Wilson, Frank and Martha Wilson, J. Augustus and Minerva Wilson, Josiah Felix and Haseltine Ford Wilson, Samuel and Jane Reid, John and Jane Rose, Matthew and Cornelia McCraw, Mrs. Sarah Bagby, Matthew Johnson and wife, James P. Whitten, Richard Wheat and wife.

Pastors of Hopewell church have been H. P. Holland, Martin Isbill, H. D. Gilbert, Isaac Watkins, H. P. Stokes, W. C. Tallant, Lee Burch, Charlie Wright, W. C. Rymer, W. E. Gray, B. F. Foster, Samuel Melton, W. M. Kelly and W. F. Huffaker.

McGAUGHY'S METHODIST CHURCH

This church was organized about August 15, 1882, with Riley Barnes, W. C. Kirby, W. M. Wilson, F. M. Swinny and W. Headrick among its organizing members. (Book L. P.—116.) Services were at first held in a log school house while the church was being erected on two and one-half acres of ground, deeded for this specific purpose by R. B. McGaughy for the consideration of fifty dollars. The first church was built by F. M. Swinney. The first pastor* was H. Triplette, who was followed by Fidella Carroll, —— Boyd, Ferdy Cochran, Ware, Pitt, Earnest, Chastain, Posey, Allen, Hurley, Frank Cook, Henry Mitchell, George Ridley, Parsons and Hampton.

LITTLE PROSPECT BAPTIST CHURCH

In 1870 a group of men including Jesse Huffaker, Anderson Mathis, W. C. Haddock and Will Autry organized the members of their faith into a church which they named Prospect. The name Little Prospect came to be used to distinguish between the new church and an older Prospect in Murray county.

The church has been served by the following pastors:* W. C. Haddock, H. P. Holland, Jesse T. Huffaker, —— Cunning-

*List of pastors given by T. J. Cooper.

ham, P. D. Longley, ——— Ensley and W. M. Lowry, ———
Stokes, Arnold Breeden and Wm. Boyd.

MOUNT PLEASANT

Numbered among the oldest Methodist churches of North Georgia is Mount Pleasant in the northeast section of Whitfield, near the Murray county line. It is served by the pastor of the Varnell Circuit. The first church building, which was on a site adjoining the cemetery, was destroyed by fire. The present building was erected on a nearby lot a short time later. Among the early members of Mount Pleasant were Robert H. and Mary Foute Baker, Alonzo and Mahala Earnest, George Click and family, James and Irene Cooper, Elbert Dean and wife, Mrs. Mary Earnest, Joseph Bandy and family, James Cook and family, and Peter Messemer and family.

MILL CREEK BAPTIST CHURCH

Mill Creek Baptist church was organized February 27, 1853, with the following charter members: David Kenemer, James Boyd, Jerry Bridges, Sarah Bridges, A. J. Bridges, Sarah Clark, Elizabeth Calhoun, Sarah Montgomery.

The following pastors have served the church: Lampkin Vandiver, Jack Bell, Zachariah Clark, M. S. Clonts, J. C. Head, C. Chastain, F. M. Roebuck, B. F. Hunt, B. F. Foster, J. H. Blalock, W. H. Boyd, J. T. Nichols, Henry Cordell, J. H. Cargal, T. A. Burgess, J. E. Hudson, Sam Hair, J. A. Smith and J. O. Dantzler.

The clerks who have served this church from its beginning to this time are:

Jerry Bridges, C. A. Harris, F. M. Babb, E. A. Cox, W. G. Morris, W. H. Parson, J. E. Sisk, J. L. Morris, A. M. Ward, J. L. Morris, Jesse Montgomery, E. W. Babb.

MT. VERNON METHODIST CHURCH

On August 23, 1895, Dr. E. C. Cochran, C. T. Williams and W. W. Jordan, elders of the Chatoogata Presbyterian church in Cherokee Presbytery, deeded to R. W. Ault, N. G. Henderson, H. J. Head, I. H. Harlan, and G. M. Christian, trustees of the

Mt. Vernon M. E. church, one acre and sixty-two rods of land. (Book P, page 339).

The markers in the old cemetery bear names of members of Presbyterian families.

Among early members of the Methodist congregation, other than trustees, were Thomas Spriggs, Joshua Harlan, Joe Dobson, Arch Austin, G. M. Easley, ——— Sebastian, M. G. Harris.

MINERAL SPRINGS

The one acre lot was given to the Methodists for a building site by Harvey McHan, July 31, 1873. The trustees were Moses Collins, Wm. Odell, Jesse Fincher and Wm. H. Lasseter.

Among the early members were William Lasseter and wife, and Joseph Fincher and wife Lucinda.

PINE GROVE BAPTIST

This church was organized before 1870. County records list the granting of a deed by R. J. Keith on April 27, 1896, to the deacons of Pine Grove church for the consideration of ($12.50) twelve dollars and fifty cents. (Book P, p. 339).

Early members were Mr. and Mrs. Samuel Keith, Mr. and Mrs. Dyer Keith, Mr. and Mrs. Bailey Keith, Mr. and Mrs. Edward Hill, Mr. and Mrs. Richard Hill, Mr. and Mrs. Augustus Hill, Mr. and Mrs. Perry Bradley and Mr. and Mrs. Nathaniel Thomas.

Pastors were B. F. Foster, Joe T. Nichols, W. R. Lackey, H. D. Gilbert, Charlie Maples, J. O. Dantzler, J. M. Dooley and W. M. Kelly.

POPLAR SPRINGS*

In 1836 Thomas Crow cleared land and built a house (which is still standing and occupied) near the Poplar Springs church which was already established.

During a battle of the war between the states, Poplar Springs church was burned, presumably by shell fire. The present building replaced the one burned.

---

*The information for this sketch was furnished by Mr. J. L. Murphy, who is a grandson of the pioneer, Thomas Crow.

Early members of the congregation were Mr. and Mrs. Thomas Crow, Mr. and Mrs. Silas King, Mr. and Mrs. Jerry Kettles and Mr. and Mrs. S. R. Murphy.

Thomas Crow was a charter member of the North Georgia Baptist Association and suggested its name. Two of the three churches which composed the association were Macedonia church at Dawnville and Poplar Springs.

Among pastors of Poplar Springs were A. B. Nuckols, T. A. Higdon, J. T. Fincher, J. M. Stansberry, W. H. Davenport, Wm. Clonts, Joe Padgett and Charlie Maples.

RED CLAY

The records of Whitfield county show that on February 17, 1874, James H. Huff conveyed to the Methodist Episcopal church, South, "For and in consideration of the love I bear for the cause of Christ and from an earnest desire to promote His heritage on earth—land whereupon is to be erected a house for public worship and also to be used as an academy of learning."

Among those forming the congregation at Red Clay were the Huff families, the Weatherly families, the Leonard family, the Huffaker family and the Parker family.

A parsonage there was used by the circuit rider of the Varnell circuit for a number of years.

RIVER BEND BAPTIST CHURCH

River Bend Baptist church* was constituted the fourth Sunday in August in 1898. Charter members were I. B. Teasley and family, E. B. Holland and family, D. C. Henton, Sr., J. L. Henton, Miss Belle Henton, W. L. Brown and family, C. G. Caldwell and family and A. L. Caldwell and family.

The first pastor was Rev. J. M. Cash, who organized the church with nearly fifty members, including twenty-six who entered by profession and baptism.

River Bend church was reestablished in August, 1931, with Reverend George Fletcher serving as pastor. The present membership numbers sixty-eight.

---

*This information was supplied by J. L. Henton.

ROCKY FACE BAPTIST CHURCH

Rocky Face Baptist church was organized in 1873. Presbytery was composed of the following ministers: Reverend Clonts, John Gilbert and J. C. Stansbury. The deacons ordained were J. W. Bridges and Henry King; clerk, M. L. McDonald. Charter members were J. M. Bridges, J. W. Bridges, Henry King, M. L. McDonald, Mrs. M. L. McDonald, Mrs. Henry King, Mrs. J. W. Bridges. First members received by baptism were Mrs. W. N. Russell, Bennie Young, Mrs. Hamp Young and Mrs. Harriet Bridges.

The church was organized in a building where the Rocky Face school house now stands. At that time the Methodist and the Baptist used the same building which was also used for a school house. The building burned, and the Baptist and Methodist then moved their place of worship to an old log house which stood where the home of H. H. Russell now stands. They decided to build a community church. Each man in the community furnished a log; some two. This new church was built on the site of the present Baptist church. Two of the members were turned out of the church and threatened to take out their logs. Other members remarked that the building would be rather queer looking with a log missing out of one end and one side.

About this time the Methodists decided to rebuild the church which had burned. County records show that on July 8, 1879, Berry Smith deeded land to Anthony Green and Thomas McClure as trustees of Rocky Face Methodist church. One hundred dollars was received from the church extension society. Michael Hassler, with a little help from neighbors and the hundred dollars received, built this church for the Northern Methodists. He furnished the greater part of the material and labor.

This church was used by the Methodists about eighteen years. Many of the members eventually moved away, and the church was discontinued. This building, with a few additional changes, is the present school building at Rocky Face.

The only church at Rocky Face at present is the Baptist church, which was built in 1883.

SHADY GROVE

It is recorded (Record Book A, p. 203) that on August 19, 1852, Stephen A. Cady deeded 2½ acres to "William Callahan, Rudd Morgan and John Morgan, Trustees, for a meeting house and school house to be called Shady Grove."

On this property a large log building was erected which served the community several years, Methodist and Baptist preachers alternately addressing the union congregation.

After the membership had increased in numbers the two denominations—Baptist and Methodist—assumed responsibility for separate church buildings nearby, which have since been known as Grove Level and Pleasant Grove, each church retaining a part of the original name.

GROVE LEVEL

The Baptist members of the Shady Grove congregation had organized their church one day previous to the date of the deed made by Dr. Stephen Cady to the community church, as the church records now list Grove Level's organization as October 18, 1852. However, they worshiped in the community church of Shady Grove until August 11, 1874, when Duke Richardson by gift and donation deeded a portion of land lying immediately in the forks of the Cleveland and Benton roads to the Grove Level Baptist church (Book I, p. 134).

Here was constructed their building. On June 9, 1906, Victor C. Richardson deeded to Jos. G. Robertson, A. P. Dantzler and W. H. Isbill, deacons, one-half acre lying east of one acre already purchased for the consideration of six dollars (Book T, p. 335).

The first members* of Grove Level were Duke Richardson and wife Emily, Henry Brooker and wife Jane, Jacob Dantzler and wife Susan, William Sapp and wife Sarah, Martin Workman and wife Nancy Ann, William Russell and wife Cyntha Ann, Eliza Ann Moore, R. Morgan and Matilda Morgan.

Among pastors who served Grove Level are: Wm. A. Wright, J. M. Brittain, J. M. Gambrell, J. M. Stansberry, Martin Isbill, H. D. Gilbert, W. C. McCall, I. M. Roebuck, H. M. Jones,

---
*Names of members given by Mrs. Joseph Robertson and Mrs. Joseph E. Spann.

M. L. Clontz, Isaac Watkins, J. M. Stone, J. T. Nichols, Lee Taylor, Charlie Maples, J. A. Maples, J. E. Morgan, H. A. Winstead, J. O. Dantzler, J. W. Sosby and W. E. Roberts.

PLEASANT GROVE

The Methodist members of Shady Grove purchased land and erected a building on the Cleveland highway south of the original structure. The first acre of the new location was deeded by Anthony Bolander for the consideration of fifteen dollars to Martin P. Berry, Isaac N. Hair, Thos. A. Tye, John Lewis Bender and S. C. Swan. This was on July 26, 1873.

The second deed records that on March 31, 1876, John D. Williamson gave five and one-fourth acres "for the cause of Christianity" to M. P. Berry, S. Swan, J. M. Bailey, J. L. Bender and L. W. Quillian.

An additional grant of one and three-fourths acres was given by Cephus Stradley on September 7, 1885, to J. L. Bender, James Kirk and T. A. Tye.

In the deed made by John D. Williamson to M. P. Berry et al one acre of land was reserved ("to be selected and measured by said party of the first part") for the purpose of erecting a cottage and stables to be used at the camp meetings held annually at Pleasant Grove.

A church and a school building were erected on these grounds, also a huge arbor where the Whitfield County Sunday school convention has been held for about sixty years.

In addition to the trustees named in the deeds were others prominent in the development of the church's history. Among them were the Brooker family, the Jewell family, the Cady family and the Kirk family.

This church is one of a group comprising the Varnell circuit. (For list of pastors, see Varnell Methodist).

SHILOH METHODIST CHURCH

Shiloh church was organized about 1870 on a plot of ground about a mile west of the new Shiloh in the Mill Creek Valley. It was known as an independent protestant Methodist. New Shiloh church was erected a few years later on the Mill Creek road, about one mile south of Mill Creek cemetery, where divine wor-

CHURCHES AND SCHOOLS

ship was held until 1901, when this church merged with the M. E. Church, South. Then a building was erected, two miles south, on the same road. This church was dedicated in memory of the late Thomas Griffin and wife, Lucinda Kenemer Griffin.

Dr. George Harlan was the beloved pastor of Shiloh from 1870 to 1890. Reverend William Cator also served as pastor and was highly esteemed by the people in that community.

Charter members of old Shiloh were Mr. and Mrs. Adolphus Williams, Mr. and Mrs. David Lowry Kenemer, W. E. Love, Mr. and Mrs. Geo. Walker, Mr. and Mrs. Thos. Hall, Professor George Christain, Mr. Thomas Lowry, Miss Lissie Lowry, Newt Kinsey, Needham Griffin and others.

From this church two members answered the call to the ministry. Reverend Reece Griffin who is now serving as presiding elder in the South Georgia conference, and Reverend Felton Williams, who is a prominent minister in the North Georgia conference.

TILTON METHODIST

Whitfield county records show that Susan A. Brown deeded to F. W. Elrod, James Leak, John S. Hogan, L. W. Thomasson and W. H. Coker, Jr., three-fourths acre of land on which to build a Methodist church. The date was October 8, 1897, the consideration was five dollars. Previous to this time the members had worshipped in the Cumberland Presbyterian church erected by Mr. Wm. Brown.

TILTON BAPTIST CHURCH

A deed to one acre of land was made April 23, 1874, to the Building committee of the church, H. H. Green, J. Simmons, W. M. Fain and the Tilton Lodge of F. & A. Masons No. 291.

VARNELL METHODIST

In 1860 Mitchell P. Varnell deeded to Ch. Rauschenberg, James H. Huff, M. P. Varnell, Ben F. Prater, T. H. Pitner, T. Lawrence and John C. Barnett an acre of land on which to erect a Methodist church. The consideration was fifteen dollars.

The parsonage now used by the pastor of the Varnell circuit was deeded by Mrs. Baniel for this specific purpose.

Among the charter members of Varnell Methodist church were Mr. and Mrs. Mitchell Varnell, Mr. and Mrs. Leonard Speer, Mr. and Mrs. J. C. Barnett and Robert Baniel and mother.

Among the pastors who have served the Varnell Church and the Varnell Circuit are: ＿＿＿＿＿＿Hamilton, Thomas Pledger, J. R. Speck, A. J. Hughes, G. L. Chastain, W. E. Kennedy, E. M. Stanton, W. T. Hamby, Henry D. Pace, J. F. Tyson, J. W. Bailey, A. J. Mann, J. M. Hawkins, N. A. Parsons, H. G. Garrett, W. H. Spear, J. E. Russell, John Foster, W. F. Walden, L. G. Hendricks, and W. B. Mills.

TUNNEL HILL

Mrs. Lula J. Chester, daughter of Major Joseph Guthrie, very kindly supplied the information concerning Tunnel Hill churches.

In 1894 the trustees of the Methodist church listed as W. H. Foster, I. H. Harlan, C. P. N. Harris, J. L. Heggie and T. Jeff Smith, gave a deed to the F. & A. Masons, and in this transaction they refer to the original deed as having been made in 1858, naming Clisbe Austin as the original trustee.

This brick building which was built by Mr. Austin was used for stables by Federal troops during the War. The store building of Major Guthrie and the home of W. H. Foster were used as hospitals for the ill and wounded. Dr. Wyble was the physician in charge.

Early members of this church were Dr. and Mrs. Emerson, Mr. and Mrs. Dave Morelock, Mr. and Mrs. James Ault, Mrs. Judith Hardy, Mrs. W. H. Foster, Mr. and Mrs. Bearden, Emma and Tina Rogers and Joseph Rogers.

TUNNEL HILL PRESBYTERIAN CHURCH

Before the War Between the States this congregation was composed largely of county families. Among them were the Green family and the Wilson family. The Cherry family was prominently identified with early activities of the church and town. Able assistance was given by the McGill family of Stone church, who attended regularly.

Members who later were staunch supporters of the church were Dr. and Mrs. E. C. Cochran, W. W. Jordan, Mrs. Jennie Wyatt, Mrs. May Fielder, Mrs. Florence Foster, W. S. Jordan,

Mrs. James Headrick, Mrs. Will Emerson, Mrs. L. Q. Howden, Dr. and Mrs. Word and Elijah Laymance and family.

TUNNEL HILL CUMBERLAND PRESBYTERIAN

Among the first members of this denomination were Mrs. J. T. Kirkpatrick, Mr. and Mrs. W. M. Headrick, Mrs. Laymance, Mrs. John Whitton, Franklin and William Gillian, Joe Rogers, Miss Addie Rogers and Haynie Fox and family.

BAPTIST CHURCH

The Baptist church of Tunnel Hill was organized before the War Between the States. Worship was conducted monthly at the school house. After the war the members accepted the invitation of the methodists to worship in the war-wrecked building.

Later the Cumberland Presbyterians built a church and the Baptists were invited to hold services there one Sunday each month. This they did for several years. (The invitations were extended in appreciation of the help given by Baptist members in the erection of both the Methodist and the Cumberland Presbyterian churches.)

County records show that on May 14, 1887, W. H. Foster sold to Deacons George W. Head and L. S. Flemister a site for a church building for a consideration of fifty dollars.

In response to the steady urging of Reverend Stansberry to build a church of their own, a building was erected in 1888 and was dedicated by Dr. Robert B. Headden of Cartersville.

Among the early members were Major and Mrs. Joseph Guthrie, Mrs. L. J. Chester, Mrs. Rufus Foster and family, the Whitten family and the Bowman family.

VARNELL BAPTIST

This church was organized before 1860 and a building was erected on land given by M. P. Varnell.*

Among the charter members were Charles B. and Elizabeth Ann Kirkpatrick, Sylvanus and Hannah Kaneaster, Joseph and Hannah Spann, George and Abigail Fagala, Mr. and Mrs. Hiram Cox, Mr. and Mrs. Jesse Crow, Mr. and Mrs. Joseph Blair.

---

*This information was given by Mrs. Fannie Kirkpatrick Webb.

Among the early members were John and Sarah Fagala, Mrs. Cooksey, Mrs. Alma Eslinger, Mrs. Susan Bare, Miss Sarah Hartsfield, Miss Mary Whittle, Mrs. Sarah Cox, Misses Mary, Luvenia and Sarah Kirkpatrick and Martin Houston.

Reverend J. A. R. Hanks and Reverend J. M. Stansberry were among the first pastors of the church.

COLORED CHURCHES OF DALTON

Burning Bush, A. M. E., Matilda Street; Bethel, A. M. E., Spring Street; New Hope Baptist Church, McCamy Street; Liberty Baptist Church, Pentz Street; Mt. Ridge Baptist Church, Matilda Street; Antioch Presbyterian Church, McCamy Street.

SCHOOLS

"All the possibilities of a democracy rest squarely upon education."—Franklin D. Roosevelt.

The first school of any consequence in Dalton was conducted in the old Methodist church frame building which stood on the lot directly opposite the present Methodist church.

Mr. and Mrs. Cooledge came here about 1870 and opened a larger school in the basement of the old Baptist church. Later on Dalton issued bonds to the value of $20,000.00 to build the Dalton Female College and the Crawford High School (for boys), the female college to be under the care of Wesleyan College at Macon, and Crawford High under Mercer, also at Macon.

The female college was the first to be ready for occupancy. Reverend W. A. Rogers was president, being followed by Rufus W. Smith, John A. Jones, A. A. Jones, ____ ____ Warwick, J. G. Orr, G. J. McLellan, Miss Mabel Head, Thomas L. Bryan and ____ ____ Summitt.

Mrs. Fannie C. Lester was in charge of the preparatory department of this institution for more than thirty years. Many hundreds of women all over Georgia owe the foundation of their education to her splendid training. The religious instruction and spiritual guidance given to her pupils by this consecrated teacher meant much toward the character building of these women.

It was mainly by the efforts and influence of the First Baptist church that Mercer University, through its trustees, secured land on Fort Hill and promoted the first boys' school there under the name of Crawford Academy.

In 1883 the trustees of Mercer University proposed to turn the property over to the City of Dalton for school purposes. The proposition was accepted, but before the consummation of the transaction a plan was proposed which was thought to be a happy solution of the educational question for all times to come.

The plan was for the Methodists to conduct a school for girls at the present location of City Park school, and the Baptists to have a school for boys on Fort Hill. This being agreeable to everybody, Mercer University deeded the Fort Hill property to the First Baptist Church for school purposes; thus the church assumed charge of the school. The name was changed to Brown University in honor of Governor Joseph E. Brown, who contributed a considerable sum to put the school on a good foundation. But this school, also, like the Crawford Academy, failed to be self sustaining, and so after a time the property was conveyed back to the town, and the boys joined the girls on the west side until the whole work was taken over by the city under the present school system.

DALTON PUBLIC SCHOOLS*

"The Public School is the most democratic and distinctly American institution that we have, and on its success depends in a large measure the future of our country. As long as the bells from twenty-five thousand or more school houses ring out every morning from Maine to Mexico, and twenty-five million bright faced children march off to school to be trained and molded into intelligent citizens, we may rest pretty well assured that America is going to make no very serious mistakes which America cannot rectify. The solemn compact, signed in the cabin of the Mayflower, that the 'little brown school house' should be one of the first buildings erected in the new free land to which they were going was typical of the mighty spirit of that little band, as someone has so aptly said, 'The first row of pot hooks scratched across their copy books by New England urchins was the preamble to the Declaration of Independence.'

*This article was written by Mr. Frank Manly, who was for many years chairman of 'tre Board of Education of the Dalton public schools of Dalton. The article was written for a special edition of The Citizen.

CITY HIGH SCHOOL

CITY PARK SCHOOL BUILDING

"The history of the Dalton Public Schools, with one hectic exception, is but the 'short and simple annals of the poor.' Born in 1886-87 under the mayoralty of Colonel W. H. Pruden, the city took over the Joseph E. Brown Institute (formerly the Crawford High School) on Fort Hill, electing Colonel W. K. Moore as first Chairman of the Board, his associates being John Black, W. T. McCarty, Joe Kenner and D. K. McKamy.

"Among the first teachers were Mrs. B. M. Thomas, Misses Allie Moore, Agnes Morris, Minnie Field, Nell Barrett, Carrie Bitting and Laura Kelly, a faculty of brilliant women whose high character and fine ability did much to insure the success of the new venture.

"After the grammar school became well established efforts were made from time to time, without much success, to establish a two or three grade High school as part of the public school system. Little was accomplished until under the chairmanship of Paul B. Trammell in 1909 a determined resourceful campaign for an accredited High School was successfully put through in the face of strenuous and bitter opposition. In the meantime the city had taken over the building of the old Dalton Female College, converting it into a High School which was used until the new High School was built.

"The first superintendent of the Dalton schools was Wm. Harper, who was succeeded by General B. M. Thomas, J. W. Weatherly, T. S. Lucas, C. D. Meadows, J. H. Watson, J. T. Duncan, U. J. Bennett, M. O. McCord, J. I. Allman, W. C. Jones and J. W. Williams.

"Since the public schools were organized, forty-six years ago, there have been eight Chairmen of the Board of Education: Colonel W. K. Moore, Dr. C. P. Gordon, Walter Jones, Sherry McAuley, C. D. McCutchen, Paul B. Trammell, Frank Manly, and Paul B. Fite, Sr.

"In connection with the Dalton Public School system it is an interesting fact that three members of the board have given twenty-five years of service—one of whom, P. B. Fite, is still serving. The othess were Frank Manly and W. C. McGhee.

"In all these years our children have had the guidance of many splendid, noble women, a goodly number of whom are still with us, and whose lives have been, and are, a light and a joy

FORT HILL SCHOOL BUILDING

NORTH DALTON SCHOOL BUILDING

and an inspiration and a benediction to thousands of boys and girls who have come under their good and kindly influence."

COUNTY SCHOOLS*

The first county board of education of which there is any record is that of 1872. The members appointed by the grand jury in April of that year were W. C. Richardson, T. H. Pitner, W. H. Kenner, C. D. McCutchen and W. K. Moore. Several members of the board have given many years of service to the county school system, and W. C. Martin has served as chairman of the board for twenty-nine years.

The past superintendents, beginning with Martin Berry and arranged chronologically, are: Martin Berry, J. C. Sapp, J. J. Copeland, J. D. Fields, Miss Phoebe Broadrick and Alvin White.

Its educational facilities growing space with its industrial development, Whitfield county now has one of the most modern and complete public school system in the State of Georgia.

While the number of schools in the county is decreasing, owing to consolidation and hence to increased efficiency, the enrollment increases yearly.

The mill schools, part of the county system, are model educational plants. They are the Crown Point school at the Crown Cotton Mills, the Atcooga school at the American Thread Company, and the Boylston Crown school at the Boylston Crown Mill.

The school program of Whitfield county has been made possible by the co-operation of the various local districts with the county school authorities, and at the present time there is an excellent consolidated school within the reach of every child in Whitfield county, which gives complete high school opportunities.

All the consolidated schools have modern brick buildings which were financed jointly by the county and local districts, and in the case of Varnell and Pleasant Grove the Federal government aided to the extent of thirty per cent. In no case has the building of a school been through the efforts of any individual, but these schools have been made possible through the combined efforts of the county and district school authorities, with the co-operation of the patrons and citizens of the different districts, and in some cases the Federal Government.

*By Alvin White, Whitfield County School Superintendent.

Plans are approved to build teacherages at all consolidated schools, and it is believed that these buildings will be completed before the end of 1935.

There are also four colored schools in the county system.

The consolidated schools of the county are:

DAWNVILLE CONSOLIDATED SCHOOL

Dawnville was the first consolidated school. In 1928 the

DAWNVILLE SCHOOL BUILDING

school districts of Liberty, Temperance Hill, Harmony, Bunker Hill, and Dawnville formed the Dawnville consolidated school and erected the present school building. Miss Phoebe Broadrick was County School Superintendent and trustees were Homer Boyles, Gordon Foster and Luther Bonds. The County Board of Education at that time was: W. C. Martin, Chairman; S. R. Hassler, L. M. Babb, W. C. Bryant, and V. B. Pullen.

In 1931 electric power and a water system was installed, and the grounds landscaped. In 1932 a home for the principal was built, and in 1934 the building was enlarged for the purpose of taking care of a boys' work shop and a home economics department for the girls.

A community cannery has been established where the surplus vegetables of the farmers may be canned on a profitless basis. Plans are under way for the building of a combination auditorium and gymnasium, as the present auditorium is not adequate.

In 1934 Beaverdale school district combined with this school, and in 1935 Deep Springs district was added. Tentative plans

COHUTTA SCHOOL BUILDING

for the consolidation of Union Point and Pine Grove with the Dawnville school are now under consideration.

COHUTTA CONSOLIDATED SCHOOL

In 1929 this school, composed of Keeler, Hopewell, McGaughey and Cohutta school districts, was organized and the present school building erected. Its trustees were: P. O. Parker, M. Q. Brackett and W. W. Seaton.

The grounds have been landscaped, shrubbery planted and an electric power and water system installed.

In 1934 a home economics cottage was built, and a gymnasium is now under construction. This school also has a community cannery where surplus farm products may be canned.

It is hoped that during 1935 Tuckers and Mount Pleasant school districts will be added to this school.

The Cohutta Consolidated School and all subsequent consolidated schools were organized under the County Board of Education composed of W. C. Martin, chairman; S. R. Hassler, L. M.

VARNELL SCHOOL BUILDING

Babb, W. C. Bryant and W. W. Seaton, with Alvin White as County School Superintendent.

VARNELL CONSOLIDATED SCHOOL

This school, comprising Varnell and portions of Good Hope, McGaughey, Broadacre and New Hope school districts, was organized in 1933 with the following trustees: W. O. Wilson, T. J. Manis, J. R. Wheeler, Robert Crow, and W. A. Hayes. The present school building, equipped with electric power and a water system, was erected. The grounds were landscaped and shrubbery was planted.

VALLEY POINT CONSOLIDATED SCHOOL

This school had its beginning in 1929 with the school districts of Five Springs, Center Point and Dug Gap; in 1930 Carbondale was added, and in 1931 Redwine Cove became a part of it. Union was added in 1935, and it is planned that Tilton, Oak Grove and Antioch become a part of this organization.

VALLEY POINT SCHOOL

In 1934 with H. H. Ezzard, J. W. Godfrey, H. S. Huston, C. E. McCollum and J. W. Sims as trustees the present building was erected. At that time it was the largest rural consolidated school building in the state, consisting of nineteen rooms. The building is equipped with electric power and a water system; the grounds have been landscaped and shrubbery has been planted.

In 1935 a cannery and home economics cottage was added.

PLEASANT GROVE CONSOLIDATED SCHOOL

Pleasant Grove School with J. B. Hill, C. H. Felker, John Hasty, C. O. Richardson and Guy Bryant as trustees, erected its present building in 1934. This school is also equipped with electric power and a water system, its grounds landscaped and shrubbery planted.

It is composed of the following school districts: Broadacre, Cedar Valley, Good Hope, Pleasant Grove and a portion of Deep Springs. It is planned to add the Waring school district in the near future.

PLEASANT GROVE SCHOOL BUILDING

WEST-SIDE CONSOLIDATED SCHOOL

Plans for this, the newest of the consolidated schools in the county, were perfected early in 1935 and the building erected in time for the August school session. Plans are now made to enlarge the building by the addition of an auditorium and three class rooms.

This school comprises the Salem, Gordon Springs, Mill Creek, Mount Vernon, Fairview and Rocky Face school districts, with the following trustees: Carl Loner, Bart Wallace, H. P. McArthur, E. W. Babb and W. M. Dobson.

WEST SIDE SCHOOL BUILDING

TUNNEL HILL DISTRICT

The Tunnel Hill school district has a bond election pending for the purpose of building and equipping a consolidated school. If the results of this election are favorable, the districts of Tunnel Hill, New Hope, Trickum, Houston Valley and Ridge Grove will unite, thus completing the plans of the County Board of Education that all sections of the county shall have adequate, well equipped schools, with school bus lines making them reasonably accessible to all the children of Whitfield County.

TUNNEL HILL SCHOOL BUILDING

CHAPTER VI

Organization of Clubs and Societies

"This is the place, stand still my steed,
Let me review the scene,
And summon from the shadowy past,
The forms that once have been."

THUS Longfellow expressed the emotions which come to us all. Whitfield county has been featured in song and story, yet, each successive generation finds pleasure in a review of the times, events and lives of "Auld Lang Syne"—we delight to thrum the harp chords of the yester-years.

Whitfield is rich in historical lore, and her unsung heroes loom large on the horizon of the unforgotten past. Heroes? Yes! Each played well his or her part in the drama, comedy or tragedy which we call life.

There passes in review a procession in which faces and forms may be seen, long since gone but not forgotten. Time and space will not permit an inclusion of all who have nobly done their part, but each district has had its leaders, and, without disparagement as to the others, a few of the outstanding characters in each district may be mentioned:

COHUTTA (Formerly known as Red Clay): J. G. W. Mills, T. H. Pitner, James Huff, Henry Shugart, J. F. Wilson and Wm. Chambers.

UPPER TENTH: W. M. Lowry, S. G. Shields, V. B. Pullen and W. M. Tucker.

VARNELL: F. A. Rauschenberg, John W. Brooker, Pearce Horne, George W. Sapp, B. F. Prater, J. A. Wilson, D. Bare, D. Eslinger, D. Speer and W. H. Isbill.

LOWER TENTH: Daniel Cline, S. H. Routh, A. J. Warmack, A. J. Larmon and Edmond Creekmore.

NINTH: William McNabb, R. M. Tarver, George Mitchell, J. S. Rollins, George McNair, John Broadrick, Otis M. England, Addison P., Lemuel N., Rowan F. and Jacob Dantzler and Joseph G. Robertson.

FINCHER: Dyer P. Keith, William Carder, Joseph

ORGANIZATION OF CLUBS AND SOCIETIES   131

Fincher, E. O. Herndon, J. A. Britton and Sam Glass.
   TILTON: B. B. Turner, R. B. Maynard, L. W. Thomason and Berry Turner.
   CARBONDALE: John M. Redwine, A. J. Barnett, N. A. Bradford, Anse Grasshoff and Henry Redwine.
   MILL CREEK: J. A. Griffin, Francis Babb, William Evans, Needham Kenemer and J. J. Montgomery.
   TRICKUM: J. T. Deck, Charles Harlan and James S. Richardson.
   ROCKY FACE: Hamilton Young and James H. Wood.
   TUNNEL HILL: George W. Head, W. S. Jordan, E. C. Cochran, F. J. Flemister, Haney Fox, Dr. Kirkpatrick, William Headrick, W. W. Calloway, Joe Moore and C. D. Hunt.
   DALTON: A. P. Roberts, S. B. Felker, J. P. Freeman, W. H. Brooker, Sam P. Maddox, T. J. Bryant, George Glenn, W. C. Glenn, Jesse Glenn, H. C. Hamilton, W. K. Moore, George W. Hamilton, Frank T. Reynolds, and many more from every nook and cranny in the county who lived well their parts to do in the affairs of life; it would take volumes to record their virtues and accomplishments.

The thought of oblivion is obnoxious, and we abhor its contemplation; men in all ages and climes have endeavored to perpetuate their memories in various ways. In addition to the few mentioned in each district of Whitfield county, many more could be added who are just as outstanding, the descendants of whom yet reside in these various localities to enjoy the rich heritage which is theirs by inheritance from noble forebears.

Let us ever remember:

> "Full many a gem of purest ray serene,
>   The dark unfathom'd caves of ocean bear;
> Full many a flower is born to blush unseen,
>   And waste its sweetness on the desert air."

It would require a library to contain all the worthy names, many of whom appear elsewhere in this volume, but, sufficient is it to say, they wrought well in their day and generation, and literally, "their works do follow them."

FRATERNAL ORGANIZATIONS

The fraternal organizations in Whitfield county have been many and varied. A list would include Masonry in all of its branches, Odd Fellows, Rebekahs, Junior Order United American Mechanics, Daughters of America, Eastern Star, Maccabees,

Woodmen of the World, Red Men, Elks, Civitans, Junior Chamber of Commerce, Lions, Patriotic Sons of America and Knights of Pythias.

With the advent of good roads and rural free delivery, many of these organizations passed out of existence and joined company with the small post offices and cross-roads stores.

In 1935, Masonry is represented in the county by lodges located at Cohutta, Dawnville, Tunnel Hill, Rocky Face, Gordon Springs, Tilton, and Dalton. One lodge of Odd Fellows, located in Dalton; one chapter of Eastern Stars located in Dalton. There are three councils of Junior O. U. A. M., located respectively at Cohutta, Tunnel Hill and Dalton; one council of Daughters of America at Dalton; one lodge of Rebekahs at Dalton; Civitan Club, and Junior Chamber of Commerce, located at Dalton; one tent of Maccabees, Woodmen of the World, Modern Woodmen of America and others, located at Dalton. All colored organizations of Whitfield county are located at Dalton.

DALTON LODGE NO. 72, I. O. O. F.

Dalton Lodge, No. 72, Independent Order of Odd Fellows, was instituted June 12, 1901, with the following members: J. R. Fallis, T. B. Goodwin, F. A. Hamilton, E. C. Harris, P. S. Henderson, Samuel Pyle, J. T. Taylor, and others. Since that time the following have served as Noble Grands:

J. W. Brown	M. A. Keister
G. H. Hightower	C. H. Fraker
C. C. Maples	Thomas Cowart
Tom Hill	C. A. Kreischer
L. N. Shahan	C. L. Cowart
T. D. Ridley	C. B. Houston
F. F. Baker	G. C. Hill
J. E. Goddard	W. H. Houston
Buell Stark	J. E. Routh
T. E. Roberts	M. B. Davis
J. L. Buchanan	C. A. Black
Frank Mitchell	J. H. McCoy
J. L. Wallace	M. F. Caldwell
W. A. Ault	S. F. Armstrong
R. R. Gilliland	E. H. Wofford
B. P. Bishop	J. W. Brumlow
B. H. Hill	J. R. Poteet
Guy W. Keister	F. A. Hamilton
J. E. Sandiford	J. P. Smith

ORGANIZATION OF CLUBS AND SOCIETIES 133

Arthur Bramlett	G. A. Bennett
W. A. Johnson	H. M. Marney
J. W. Reynolds	H. H. O'Briant
J. T. Wills	W. W. Coffee
H. G. King	C. E. Wood
Landon Huffaker	M. V. Bradley
H. D. Thompson	J. E. Hannah
W. W. Metcalf	R. H. Sapp
Frank Daniel	W. C. King
P. P. Clement	Lofton C. Ward

The present officers are Lofton C. Ward, noble grand; J. A. Blevins, vice-grand; M. A. Keister, secretary; W. W. Metcalf, treasurer.

Since the dispensation was granted the lodge has never failed to have a quorum each Friday night, regardless of weather conditions or any other cause.

This lodge has furnished two Grand Masters to the state in Hon. J. E. Bodenhamer and the late Hon. T. D. Ridley, the former also serving as Grand Treasurer for a number of years. The Rev. C. C. Maples served as Grand Chaplain of the state.

Dalton lodge is now counted among the "Big Three" of the state in membership, and is second to none in impressiveness in its degree work. It has at present members in five states besides Georgia, viz.: Alabama, Florida, Illinois, South Carolina and Tennessee. Only one of the original charter members is still a member—Mr. F. A. Hamilton; one who became a member soon after its founding—Mr. J. E. Goddard.

The lodge had all its effects destroyed in the big fire of 1911, but soon was in good condition again, and has been in its present location for more than 20 years.

When America entered the great conflict between the nations in 1917, this lodge bought liberally of Liberty Bonds and Savings stamps, purchasing almost $2,000.00 worth.

Ten of its members joined the forces of Uncle Sam in the World War: G. W. Albertson, M. A. Albertson, Henry Bailey, R. Q. Boyles, W. M. Garrett, J. G. Jordan, C. A. Kreischer, Anderson Phillips, Joseph Rackley and Lawson Rackley.

Nineteen members have a continuous membership of twenty-five years, which entitles each of them to wear a veteran's jewel. They are: R. L. Anderson, W. C. Bowen, John Collins, C. H. Fraker, J. E. Goddard, B. H. Hill, Fred W. Hix, Thomas Kirk,

Guy W. Keister, M. A. Keister, H. L. McEntire, W. H. Orr, R. L. Palmer, John W. Reynolds, T. D. Ridley, J. E. Routh, N. W. Sims, W. S. Thompson, J. L. Wallace.

REBEKAHS IMPORTANT PART OF ODD FELLOWSHIP

The ladies' auxiliary, known as the Rebekah division, has always played an important part in Odd Fellowship throughout the nation. There have been two lodges of Rebekahs organized in Dalton. The first organization was instituted on November 4, 1922, and functioned only a very short time.

The present organization, known as Dalton Rebekah Lodge No. 38, was instituted April 7, 1931, by Mrs. H. H. Hardin, of Decatur, special deputy, with a charter list of thirty-two members. It is in a flourishing condition, maintaining an efficient degree team under the direction of H. G. King, team captain. This team puts on its own ritualistic work.

The first lodge was instituted by Mrs. M. C. Strickland, grand secretary of the Rebekah Assembly of Georgia.

This organization, like the Odd Fellows, is democratic in its mode of government, yet non-political—and universal in its scope. The major claims of the society are for aid of the orphans' home at Griffin, and relief of members in distress, educational activities, visiting the sick and the fitting burial of the dead.

The present officers are as follows: Mrs. Clara Smith, Noble Grand; Miss Agnes Clore, Vice Grand; Mrs. W. W. Coffee, Secretary; Mrs. Carl Finley, Treasurer.

LAUREL CAMP NO. 24, W. O. W., DALTON, GEORGIA

This organization has a membership which literally believes that: "He that provideth not for his own is himself worse than an infidel."

During its existence it has been the medium through which thousands of dollars in insurance and relief have been distributed to worthy members in sickness and to dependent ones upon the invasion of the Grim Reaper.

The present corps of officers consists of the following: R. M. Hill, Council Commander; F. S. Goad, Advisory Lieutenant; M. C. Cox, Banker; Henry Lee Roy, Escort; T. N. Peeples, Watchman; H. Deitch, W. H. Cole, J. B. Hill, Auditors; John W. Ray, Secretary.

The camp holds bi-monthly meetings.

FORT HILL CAMP NO. 16945, MODERN WOODMEN OF AMERICA
Chartered February 13, 1917

Consuls: C. P. Hannah, 1917-24; J. H. Neely, 1924-28; V. E. Burdette, 1928-29; Fred White, 1929-30; M. C. Cox, 1930-31; John Ault, 1931-32; W. W. Coffee, 1932-33; C. D. Pedigo, 1933; Erwin Self, incumbent.

Clerks: C. F. Palmer and McAfee Bates Davis, and W. W. Coffee, present incumbent; Morris Hill, Banker; John R. Grove, Advisor; T. L. Williams, Conductor.

The charter members were: Barney Anderson, Joe L. Buchanan, A. S. Carter, F. J. Flemister, W. C. Griffin, C. P. Hannah, J. B. Hill, L. B. Hubbs, J. H. Neely, A. N. Parker, Matt Deck, J. W. Carter, M. B. Davis, W. J. Bankston, B. E. Counts, R. W. Smith, E. L. Anderson, Frank Mitchell, Frank Short, Hardee Hill, E. H. Walston and R. M. Hill.

Since its organization, the camp has lost nine members by death: W. L. Cole, B. E. Counts, Frank Mitchell, W. F. Manning, George A. Dick, Floyd Rittenhouse, W. T. Neely, Frank Short and F. J. Flemister.

The present membership of the camp is composed of about one hundred adults and eight juniors. The minimum amount of insurance which may be carried is $500.00, and the maximum is $10,000. Total assets of the order are $40,000,000, and over one billion dollars of insurance in force.

The Modern Woodmen of America maintain a sanitarium near Colorado Springs, Colorado, at the foot of Pike's Peak, where over fourteen thousand members of the order have been treated free of charge. Over ten thousand of these have been successfully treated, restored to health and loved ones.

DALTON COUNCIL NO. 30, JUNIOR O. U. A. M.
DALTON COUNCIL NO. 15, D. OF A.

Officers, Junior Order U. A. M.: H. G. King, Councilor; Landon Huffaker, Recording Secretary; P. P. Clement, Financial Secretary; R. H. Sapp, Treasurer.

Officers, Daughters of America: Mrs. Glennie Bramblett, Councilor; Mrs. Lillie Burch, Vice-Councilor; Mrs. Bessie Faith, Junior Past-Councilor; R. H. Sapp, Treasurer; Oba Gravitt, Financial Secretary; Mrs. Kirk Lindsey, Recording Secretary.

Together the councils have a membership of over four hundred.

The Junior O. U. A. M. Council has been honored by having one of its members, the late T. D. Ridley, elevated to the position of State Councilor; the D. of A. Council has furnished two state councilors in the persons of Mrs. Lona Jones and Mrs. May Combee; and the Councils have otherwise been signally honored in committee and other appointments. Collectively these councils have paid out nearly twenty-five thousand dollars in death benefits, and many dollars as sick benefits.

The "Liberty Tree," ornamenting the post office grounds, was planted under the auspices of these Councils during the state convention held in Dalton, August, 1924. The soil placed beneath this tree was procured from every state in the union, the District of Columbia, and every county in Georgia, and was deposited with befitting ceremonies by representatives of each of these political divisions, who were welcomed in pageantry by Uncle Sam and Miss Columbia and Miss Georgia.

The idea of planting the Liberty Tree was originated by W. M. Sapp, and through his efforts the soil was procured from the various divisions.

During a subsequent remodeling of the post office the tree, together with the sacred soil beneath it, was moved to a new location, where it continues to "nod and bend in the breezes."

These Councils have presented numerous Bibles and flags to various schools throughout this section, and at all times they contribute their best endeavors to anything pertaining to their cherished principles.

COHUTTA LODGE NO. 64, F. & A. M.

This lodge meets on Saturday before the full moon in each month. During its years of existence it has moved forward in the even tenor of its way in true Masonic conduct.

The present master is C. R. Wilcox, its secretary is W. M. Rogers.

It has a membership of twenty.

Among the masters who have served this lodge may be mentioned: R. A. McCoy, T. M. Frazier, E. W. Bagby, F. J. Dantzler, W. H. Isbill, J. D. Wallace, W. M. Rogers, and others.

TUNNEL HILL LODGE NO. 202, F. & A. M.

Meets Saturday before full moon.

The present officers are: J. H. Morgan, Worshipful Master; W. C. Griffin, Secretary.

TILTON LODGE NO. 291, F. & A. M.

Meets first and third Saturdays.

The officers are: D. H. Carder, Worshipful Master; J. H. Gentle, Secretary.

GORDON SPRINGS LODGE NO. 463, F. & A. M.

Meets second and fourth Saturdays.

John Reed, Worshipful Master; B. L. Wallace, Secretary.

ROCKY FACE LODGE NO. 678, F. & A. M.

Meets second Wednesday.

J. C. Lynch, Worshipful Master; Carl Roach, Secretary.

DALTON CHAPTER NO. 65, O. E. S.

On March 4, 1908, there was a call meeting of the wives, widows and daughters of the Masons of Dalton, for the purpose of considering the advisability of organizing an Eastern Star chapter.

The meeting was called to order by F. F. Baker, Master of Dalton Lodge, No. 105, and, after an explanation by Mr. Baker and Mrs. Jennie L. Newman, the names of those present who desired to become members of the order were enrolled as follows:

F. F. Baker, J. M. Longley, Mrs. C. E. Longley, E. W. Petty, J. A. Land, Mrs. Eliza Petty, Mrs. R. H. McFarland, R. H. McFarland, R. R. Gilliland, F. A. Hamilton, J. P. Godwin, Mrs. J. P. Godwin, Miss Irene Hunt, W. C. Cornelison, Mrs. W. C. Cornelison, Mrs. J. R. Risner, Mrs. Mary Griffin, Miss Daisy Hamil-

138   HISTORY OF WHITFIELD COUNTY

ton, C. C. McCamy, Miss Laura Griffin, Miss Jessie Gilliland, Miss Pearl Daves, Mrs. H. B. Farrar, H. B. Farrar, Mrs. Nola Connally, Rev. Pryce E. Gatlin, Mrs. Pryce E. Gatlin, Miss Lucile Gatlin, Joseph Buchanan, Mrs. J. A. Land, W. M. Sapp, T. S. Carr, Mrs. T. S. Carr, R. A. Shatzer, Mrs. R. A. Shatzer, W. L. Steed, Mrs. J. A. Longley, W. G. Tankersley, J. L. Farnsworth, Mrs. J. L. Farnsworth, J. B. Wallace, P. A. Roberts, Mrs. R. R. Gilliland, Miss Susie Hightower, Mrs. Georgia Talley, W. Petty and Miss Sadie Sapp.

The election of officers resulted as follows: Mrs. P. E. Gatlin, Worthy Matron; F. F. Baker, Worthy Patron; Miss Sadie Sapp, Secretary.

Upon motion the Chapter agreed to meet Wednesday evenings following to complete the organization by appointing and installing the other officers.

On March 11th, the organization was completed by the installation of the above-named officers, and the following: J. P. Godwin, Treasurer; Miss Lucile Gatlin, Conductress; Mrs. H. B. Farrar, Associate Conductress; Mrs. J. P. Godwin, Associate Matron; Miss Irene Hunt, Ada; Mrs. Georgia Talley, Ruth; Mrs. J. C. Longley, Esther; Mrs. W. C. Cornelison, Martha; Mrs. Eliza Petty, Electa; Miss Susie Hightower, Marshal; H. B. Farrar, Chaplain; Robert Gilliland, Sentinel; T. S. Carr, Warder.

The time for meeting was fixed to be held on the second and fourth Wednesday evenings of each month, and a fee of fifty cents for each member was fixed as annual payment. By-laws were adopted. Thereafter, officers have been elected as follows as to Worthy Matron and Worthy Patron:

    1909—Mrs. Jennie L. Newman
    1910—Mrs. Jennie L. Newman, J. P. Godwin
    1911—Mrs. Jennie L. Newman, J. P. Godwin
    1912—Mrs. Dollie Spencer, T. D. Ridley
    1913—Miss Daisy Hamilton, H. B. Farrar
    1914—Mrs. John Hutchinson, John Humphries
    1915—Mrs. Mary Brown, J. P. Godwin
    1916—Mrs. J. L. Newman, J. W. Hutchinson
    1917—Mrs. Mae Finley, John Hutchinson
    1918—Mrs. Georgia Lochridge, T. D. Ridley
    1919—Mrs. Bessie Smith, W. M. Sapp
    1920—Mrs. Bessie Smith, W. M. Sapp
    1921—Mrs. J. L. Newman, J. W. Hutchinson
    1922—Mrs. Jennie L. Newman, J. W. Hutchinson

ORGANIZATION OF CLUBS AND SOCIETIES 139

1923—Mrs. Lizzie Hyer, J. W. Hutchinson
1924—Mrs. H. J. Wood, Richard Hill
1925—Mrs. Bessie F. Smith, T. D. Ridley
1926—Mrs. Pearl Hardy, T. D. Ridley
1927—Mrs. Lou McFarland, T. D. Ridley
1928—Mrs. Onie Neal, W. M. Sapp
1929—Mrs. C. F. Springer, W. M. Sapp
1930—Mrs. C. F. Springer, W. M. Sapp
1931—Mrs. Carolyn Griffin, W. L. Denson
1932—Mrs. C. P. Hannah, W. L. Denson
1933—Mrs. V. D. Parrott, W. C. Griffin
1934—Mrs. Lena Denson, W. L. Denson
1935—Mrs. Alice Daves, John Whiteside
1936—Mrs. Mattie Hunsucker, John Whiteside

The Chapter has been signally honored by the Grand Chapter of Georgia in the selection of its Grand Officers: Mrs. Jennie L. Newman, Grand Secretary, 1909-1916; Past Worthy Grand Matron, 1916; T. D. Ridley, Worthy Grand Patron, 1913-1914; Frank F. Baker, Worthy Grand Patron, 1917-1918, 1918-1919; W. M. Sapp, Worthy Grand Patron, 1920-1921; and otherwise, honored by the appointment of Star Points, Grand Representatives and Committee assignments.

W. M. Sapp was appointed Chairman of the committee on foreign relations of the General Grand Chapter, and served in that capacity at the meeting of the General Grand Chapter at San Antonio, Texas, November, 1931.

DALTON LODGE NO. 105, F. & A. M.

From the best available sources, Dalton Lodge, No. 105, F. & A. M., was constituted by authority of the Grand Lodge of Georgia in 1849, since which time it has enjoyed a continuous existence, without interruption except during the period of the Civil War, when the membership was engaged in military service or was forced to refugee.

The charter members included Mark Thornton, P. T. Canter, A. P. Wade, R. P. Zimmerman, Rev. William A. Simmons, W. D. Fulton, William L. High, R. L. Graves, E. W. Allen, W. W. McCoy, S. W. Batey, Rev. Levi Brotherton, Rev. Elisha Trimble, M. P. Varnell, J. Beeman, Charles W. Linton, and the following who served as the first officers of the lodge: F. W. McCurdy, Worshipful Master; T. B. Daniel, Senior Warden; P. L. Wade, Junior Warden; C. Hiberts, Treasurer; J. N. Cates, Secretary;

W. J. Hailes, Senior Deacon; James Lynan, Junior Deacon; R. L. Cook, Tyler, all of whom were pioneer citizens and prominently connected with the early history of this section.

At that time, Dalton was located in Murray county, this being just prior to the constitution of Whitfield county, in 1852. Beginning with F. W. McCurdy, agriculturist, who served as Master, 1849-56, his successors who have wielded the gavel over the destinies of Dalton Lodge have been as follows: Rev. M. A. Clonts,* 1857; W. P. Chester,* 1858; W. T. Stancell,* 1859; D. J. Haney,* 1860; Mayor E. S. Bird,* 1861; (1862-3-4, no return, Civil War); James H. Bard,* merchant, 1865; David Weir,* contractor, 1866; William A. Henderson,* farmer, 1867-8; (1869, no return under seal); I. E. Shumate,* lawyer, 1870; David Bukofzer,* capitalist, 1871-2; Charles P. Gordon,* physician, 1873-1883-1885-1890; Jacob A. Blanton,* contractor, 1884; J. A. Longley,* 1891-92; Sam P. Maddox,* lawyer, 1893-4; S. E. Berry,* merchant and educator, 1895-6, 1900-01, 1904-5; J. W. Brown,* textile manufacturer, 1897-98; George W. Hamilton,* textile manufacturer, 1899; M. D. Smith,* manufacturer, 1902-03; F. A. Hamilton, textile superintendent, 1906; Frank F. Baker, Grand Secretary, 1907-08; T. D. Ridley,* banker, 1909; W. M. Sapp, lawyer, 1910-1930; Frank T. Hardwick,* banker and financier, 1911; Henry B. Farrar,* lumberman, 1912-13; Eugene Hardin, postal clerk, 1914; James P. Godwin, jeweler, 1915-22-25; C. C. McCamy,* superintendent city water and light commission, 1916-17; William F. Manning,* contractor, 1918; John F. Williamson, printer, 1919; Guy W. Keister, City Clerk, 1920; Joseph E. Whitson, merchant, 1921; Charles P. Hannah, merchant, 1925-1932; M. A. Keister, printer, 1924; Sam M. Easley, dentist, 1926-27; Horace J. Smith, capitalist, 1928; Walton C. Griffin, postal clerk, 1929; W. E. Dellinger, manufacturer, 1931; C. P. Hannah, merchant, 1932; W. L. Denson, textile, 1933; M. Westbrook, clerk superior court, 1934; Devine Hubbs, merchant, 1935-6, present incumbent.

Dalton Lodge has been signally honored in the recognition of its members by the Grand Lodge of Georgia. Dr. Charles P. Gordon served as Deputy Grand Master; Samuel E. Berry was honored with many important appointments; Frank F. Baker

---
*Deceased. Dimitted to Celestial Grand Lodge.

has served for a long period of years as Grand Secretary; W. M. Sapp is the present Junior Grand Warden of the Grand Lodge, and others have been recognized by the Grand Lodge whose names are not available.

The Lodge room of Dalton Lodge has been destroyed at least twice by fire, once by the soldiers of General Sherman and again in 1911; the Lodge has occupied various quarters throughout Dalton, including the old hall at the northwest intersection of Hamilton and Waugh streets; the third story of the Showalter building on Hamilton street, where it was forced to move on account of the fire which destroyed so much property here in 1911. For a short time, the Lodge was domiciled in the Cumberland Presbyterian Church, at the southwest intersection of Gordon and Pentz streets. For ten years the lodge met in the Holland building at the intersection of Hamilton and Gordon streets. The Lodge erected and moved into its present quarters in 1925, the building being dedicated that year and the corner stone laid with impressive ceremonies conducted by the late Hon. W. S. Richardson, Grand Master.

The present Masonic Hall is the home of the other branches of Masonry, including the Chapter, Council and Commandery, and the Order of the Eastern Star.

Commemorative of the lives and characters of the Past Masters who have been called from earthly labors to eternal rest in the celestial Grand Lodge above by the Grand Master of the Universe, it may be truly said:

> *Each well the lessons of Masonry taught,*
> *With diligence, too, as workmen they wrought;*
> *True, since Eighteen Hundred and Forty-nine,*
> *Marked with zeal and labor, has been the line.*
> *Silent the gavel and vacant the chair,*
> *Their earthly race is completed and run;*
> *Their work has been tried by Time's level and square,*
> *And they have heard the plaudit, "Well done!"*

DALTON POST NO. 112, AMERICAN LEGION

The Dalton Post No. 112, of the American Legion, was organized and chartered in 1920.

Gordon Mann was elected the first Commander, since which time the following have served as commanders: Dr. J. H. Steed,

Sr.., Clayton Ault, L. A. Weems, G. D. Wright, J. C. Mitchell, Walter L. Single and Claud E. Miller.

The Post occupies commodious quarters, owned by itself, located on Pentz street. The building cost about $1,400.00, which sum was contributed by its members. This is one of the largest posts in the Seventh Congressional District, having about one hundred fifty members.

The present officers are: W. H. Lumpkin, Commander; Judson Manly, Vice Commander; G. T. McDonald, Adjutant; John Ratcliff, Financial Officer.

The officers of Dalton Unit No. 1, Post 112, Auxiliary, are: Mrs. Olivia Kenemer, President; Mrs. Harry O'Cain, First Vice President; Mrs. Jesse Bates, Second Vice President; Mrs. Milton Ryman, Secretary; Mrs. William Britton, Treasurer; Mrs. Mary Hardin ("Gold Star Mother"), Chaplain; Miss Ione Springer, Historian. The Unit has been organized about three years and has a growing membership.

DALTON'S CIVIC ORGANIZATIONS

Civitan Club

The Dalton Civitan Club was organized in 1922, since which time it has been a material factor in the progress of Dalton.

In the community, it is identified with civic progression and education; it inculcates civic pride, builds business through Civitan contact, fellowship and friendship; it coordinates civic forces for collective civic achievement and improves and maintains health, and aligns its co-operative force with every laudable endeavor. In the state, it maintains aggressive interest in good roads, develops interest in increasing prosperity of the state as a whole, and is the medium to bring new business within its borders; it co-operates in and encourages all phases of agricultural and horticultural improvement.

In the nation, it instills in the youth a love for our country and respect for its flag; it develops a knowledge of higher concepts and ideals in the attainment of an intelligent voting citizenship; it trains the youth in the necessity of discipline and awards citizenship medals. It impresses the alien with the necessity of becoming good citizens and inculcates respect for all law. It joins forces in the prevention of disease by dissemination in the knowledge of hygenic education and in securing curative agencies. Civitan selects her membership upon the classification basis, accepting one man from each business and profession who is genuinely interested in civic welfare. It, therefore, represents within its ranks a true cross-section of the community life. It knows no religious bounds or political lines, but all its members are pledged to live and practice the Golden Rule. Its creed includes a pledge to the highest endeavors in life and its motto is "Builders of Good Citizenship."

Paul B. Fite was the first president, and it is largely through his efforts and means that the club has progressed. He was succeeded by J. A. McFarland, prominent attorney, who in turn was succeeded by Walter M. Jones, John P. Neal, and H. L. Smith, the present incumbent. The secretaries have been T. S. McCamy, Frank Sims, Jr., W. M. Sapp, Sam M. Easley, and Clark Jones, the present incumbent. T. D. Ridley served as treasurer of the organization of the club until his death. He was succeeded by Sam Head, present incumbent.

The present membership includes fifty-eight business and professional men of Dalton and bi-monthly meetings are held on the first and third Fridays.

Thomas D. Ridley, of the Dalton club, served as Governor of the district of Georgia, Civitan International, and W. M. Sapp as state secretary.

Junior Chamber of Commerce

The local Junior Chamber of Commerce was organized in 1926. Frank Sims, Jr., was elected its first president, and on April 13, 1926, the Atlanta Junior Chamber of Commerce formally presented the charter from the national order.

The accomplishments of this civic organization during the first year of its existence were as follows:

Sponsored a "trade at home" campaign; was instrumental in getting the merchants to close their stores one afternoon each week during the summer months; sent a representative to the national convention at Jacksonville, Florida; sponsored the first Fourth of July celebration that Dalton had put on in several years; broadcast a program over radio station WSB advertising Dalton to the world; assisted in raising the "Empty Stocking Fund" which has now become a community chest. Many of these activities have been carried on in the succeeding years.

The presidents succeeding Frank Sims and the order in which they have been elected are: Judson Manly, Oliver R. Hardin, Bob McCamy, John Lake Brooker, the first six months of 1930 and C. P. Hannah was chosen to succeed him and then was re-elected the first half of 1931.

To Warren Sims fell the lot to lead the organization during 1931-32. During his administration the club has successfully sponsored and co-operated with the other clubs in putting across the community chest, merchant's cotton week, editors' state convention, golf tournament with Civitans, and many other worth while projects. Two highway signs were suspended over Thornton avenue directing tourists through the business section of town. He was succeeded by Pete Lumpkin, Henry Nevin and W. M. Jones, Jr.

During March the Jaycees celebrated their seventh anniversary. At the annual election of officers in June, the following officers were elected: Carlton McCamy, President; Bob Neal, first vice president; Donald McFarland, second vice president; Edward Davis, secretary; John B. McCarty, treasurer; Walter Jones, Jr., Clarence Archer and W. L. Roberts, Jr., directors.

WOMEN'S ORGANIZATIONS

The Lesche Woman's Club

The Lesche Woman's Club was organized on September 19, 1890, by Mrs. Gertrude Manly Jones. It was primarily a study club, and has, during these forty-six years, done much for the cultural and intellectual life of Dalton. It is the oldest federated club in the state.

When Georgia entered the General Federation of Women's clubs in 1896, the Lesche joined the state federation at that time, and the general federation in 1899. It is the oldest literary club in the State of Georgia, having been organized in September, 1890.

Outstanding work has been done in community service in

co-operation with the Red Cross and helping the needy and unemployed. Each year Lesche sponsors the sale of tuberculosis seals in the city.

The Lesche is joint owner with the U. D. C. of the handsome Central club house.

The club now has eighty-nine members, with the following officers for the year 1934-1935: President, Miss Martha Lin Manly; Honorary Vice President, Miss Alice Moore; First Vice President, Miss Fannie McLellan; Second Vice President, Mrs. O. R. Hardin; Recording Secretary, Miss Sarah McGhee; Treasurer, Miss Laura Harris; Historian, Mrs. Lee McWilliams; Librarian, Mrs. G. M. Cannon; Parliamentarian, Miss Ethel Sapp; Scrap Book Custodian, Mrs. W. C. Martin.

The past presidents of the organization include: Miss Agnes Morris, Miss Alice Moore, Miss Blanche Bivings, Mrs. Grace Gardner McCamy, Mrs. Ella Lewis Martin, Mrs. Flora Lester Blevins, Miss Mabel Head, Miss Kate Hamilton, Miss Jennie Hamilton, Miss Mattie Lee Huff, Mrs. May Gordon Curtis, Mrs. Nell King Davis, Miss Elizabeth Hamilton, Miss Elizabeth Denton, Mrs. Lula Felker Chipley, Miss Lucy Kirby, Mrs. Belle McCarty Reeder, Miss Lois Morse, Mrs. Marcia Buchholz Ellington, Miss Willie Stewart White, Miss Grace Flemister, Mrs. Carolyn Kirby McGhee, Miss Carrie Green, Mrs. Ruth Allen Thomas, Miss Mary Louise Horan, Mrs. Ellen Wortly Jones, Mrs. Nita Miller Fraker, Miss Ethel Sapp, Miss Olivia McCarty and Miss Eugenia Sapp.

The Dalton Woman's Club

This club was organized August 12, 1921, the interests of which were to be civic, social, philanthropic ond educational. Mrs. M. E. Judd was elected president, and in all of these lines of endeavor the club has made a notable record. It has sponsored many activities for the upbuilding of the town and county. The club has sponsored successfully two cooking schools and many plays and entertainments. They have held annual flower shows and have planted many trees and shrubs.

Many notable speakers have appeared on their programs.

The club's most outstanding achievement is the establishment of a free public library as a memorial to Robert Loveman.

Dalton's well known poet. The Robin's nest, the house which is ever reminiscent of the Georgia poet, now houses the library, and the Dalton Woman's Club. This was made possible by the generosity of the Loveman family.

Another achievement of this club was the organization of the Junior Woman's club.

Present officers are: Mrs. M. E. Judd, president; Mrs. F. K. Sims, first vice-president; Mrs. C. L. Hamilton, second vice-president; Mrs. G. H. Rauschenberg, third vice-president; Miss Kate Freeman, recording secretary; Mrs. C. M. Hollingsworth, corresponding secretary; Mrs. W. M. Sapp, treasurer; Mrs. W. M. Sapp, historian; and Mrs. H. J. Smith, parliamentarian.

Mrs. M. E. Judd has been president of this organization since its beginning.

The Dalton Junior Woman's Club

The Dalton Junior Woman's Club was organized in March, 1933, by Mrs. Luther Thomas Mann, who was elected first president of the organization. The organization meeting took place at "Oneonta" the home of Mrs. M. E. Judd, founder and first president of the Dalton Woman's Club. The Dalton Junior Woman's club has been exceedingly active since its organization and ranks among the best clubs in Georgia. Its objectives have been the maintaining of a milk fund, the monthly contribution to the Robert Loveman Memorial Library, home of the Dalton Woman's Club and the Dalton Junior Woman's Club, the maintaining of a book case in the library, the offering of the club's services at any and all times to assistance in worthy causes.

The charter members of the Dalton Junior Woman's Club are: Mrs. Luther Thomas Mann, Mrs. Fred Westcott, Mrs. Warren Sims, Mrs. Joseph Wrench, Mrs. Kincaid Thomas, Mrs. O. R. Hardin, Mrs. Frank Innis, Mrs. Frank Raines, Mrs. Gayle Kenner, Mrs. Walter Kenner, Jr., Mrs. Glenn Looper, Mrs. R. G. Bush, Mrs. Milton Ryman, Mrs. J. K. Dickson, Mrs. Hubert Judd, Mrs. Harold Ayers, Mrs. H. W. Nevin, Mrs. G. D. Wright, Mrs. Joseph Barrett, Mrs. John Newton and Miss Eloise Harlan.

The present officers of the Dalton Junior Woman's Club are: President, Mrs. Milton Ryman; first vice-president, Mrs. O. R.

Hardin; second vice-president, Mrs. Doss Bare; third vice-president, Miss Eloise Harlan; recording secretary, Mrs. Carlton McCamy; treasurer, Mrs. Ben Strain; corresponding secretary, Miss Johnnie Roberts.

Bryan M. Thomas Chapter, United Daughters of the Confederacy

The local chapter of United Daughters of the Confederacy is the outgrowth of the Soldiers Aid Society, an association composed of patriotic Southern women who banded together for the purpose of caring for wounded soldiers, burying the dead, and for securing hospital supplies during the war between the states.

The Ladies Memorial Association was formed shortly after the war, in 1866, for the purpose of caring for the graves of the Confederate dead and erecting monuments in honor of them. It was but natural that after the formation of the Daughters of the Confederacy the Dalton Ladies Memorial Association was merged into the Bryan M. Thomas Chapter United Daughters of the Confederacy. The local chapter was organized in 1898 by Mrs. Scylla Hamilton, with twenty-five charter members. It has now become one of the largest chapters in the state, with a membership of about one hundred fifty. It has met every obligation and is doing all within its power to carry forward the work of this noble organization.

Among the many achievements of the local chapter are the marble markers which have been erected for the three hundred confederate dead, who are buried in the soldiers' cemetery, enclosing the well-kept grounds with a fence of iron and stone, bestowing hundreds of crosses upon the Confederate veterans, and bestowing crosses of service on the World War veterans, who are descendants of the Confederate veterans, thereby bringing the two more closely together.

The only monument ever erected in honor of Joseph E. Johnston, one of the South's greatest leaders, was unveiled by the Bryan M. Thomas chapter. The erection of this monument is one of the outstanding pieces of work done by the organization, and was done at the cost of six thousand dollars. It has also taken an active part in the marking of historic points of interest along the Dixie highway.

Those who have served as president of the local chapter are: Mrs. D. C. Bryant, Mrs. Paul B. Trammell, Sr., Mrs. R. M. Herron, Mrs. W. C. Martin, Mrs. H. J. Smith, Mrs. F. W. Elrod, Miss Kate Hamilton and Mrs. Walter McGhee.

The officers for the ensuing year are: Mrs. W. C. Martin, president; Mrs. W. C. McGhee, first vice-president; Mrs. W. K. Moore, second vice-president; Mrs. Amos Gregory, recording secretary; Miss Grace Bogle, corresponding secretary; Mrs. W. A. Black, treasurer; Mrs. W. M. Sapp, registrar; and Mrs. R. M. Herron, historian.

The Central Club House

In 1926, the Central club house was built jointly by the Lesche woman's club and United Daughters of the Confederacy at a cost of $25,000.00. It is a modern and convenient building of cream colored brick, containing not only a spacious club room but also a stage and dressing rooms, a kitchen, and a lovely and unique "memory room" of pink Georgia marble on which the names of one hundred seventy-five of Whitfield county's pioneer citizens are carved.

It is one of the handsomest club houses in the state and one of the few built originally for a club house.

The building committee was as follows: Mrs. W. C. Martin, Mrs. John S. Thomas, co-chairman, Mrs. G. M. Cannon, Mrs. W. C. McGhee, Mrs. W. K. Moore, Mrs. R. M. Herron.

Daughters of the American Revolution

The Governor John Milledge Chapter, Daughters of the American Revolution, was named for one of Georgia's most noted statesmen, Governor John Milledge, and the chapter may well point with pride to its record since it was organized in 1912, having taken its place at once as a force to be reckoned with in city and state.

Mrs. C. M. Hollingsworth was appointed as organizing regent by the state authorities and the chapter was chartered with twelve members and now numbers sixty-four.

CENTRAL CLUB HOUSE

The regents who have served the chapter during the twenty-four years of its life are Mrs. C. M. Hollingsworth, Mrs. R. M. Herron, Mrs. Paul B. Trammell, Mrs. H. L. Smith, Mrs. B. A. Tyler, Mrs. W. E. Mann, Mrs. Porter G. Walker, Mrs. Clarence Fraker, and Mrs. C. L. Bradley.

In educational work, the chapter gives prizes for history work done in high schools, medals and scholarships. The perpetual loan scholarship fund, a memorial to, and named for Mrs. Paul B. Trammell, is a loan fund of five thousand dollars which has been placed in the perpetual custody of this chapter, where the fund started.

Shortly after the war was over, memorial trees were planted in honor of the Whitfield county soldiers who died in the service. Funds were raised for the erection of a monument to the soldier dead of Whitfield county. This monument is on the post office grounds. A memorial book case was placed in the Dalton public library in memory of the life historian of the chapter, Mrs. Warren Davis, who passed away in 1925.

The marking of historic spots has been an especial work of the chapter. The graves of three revolutionary soldiers and the graves of a daughter of a revolutionary soldier have been located and two of them marked. A marker was also placed at Tennga to mark the place where General Andrew Jackson first entered Georgia territory in 1818.

A handsome granite marker with a bronze plate, commemorating the establishment of the Moravian mission to the Cherokees was placed near Spring Place on the one hundredth anniversary of the mission house.

The present officers are: Miss Mattie Lee Huff, regent; Mrs. C. L. Bradley, 1st vice regent; Mrs. Shelly McWilliams, 2nd vice regent; Mrs. Janice Kreischer, corresponding secretary; Miss Rebecca Ruth McWilliams, recording secretary; Mrs. R. D. Higgins, treasurer; Mrs. Clarence Fraker, registrar; Mrs. R. M. Herron, Sr., historian; Mrs. W. R. Cannon, librarian; Miss Carrie Green, chaplain; Miss Maud Hamilton, curator.

Service Star Legion

The local chapter, called the Whitfield county Service Star Legion, was organized in Dalton, March 31, 1925, with the following officers: Mrs. C. M. Hollingsworth, president; Mrs. J. A. McFarland, vice-president; Mrs. L. P. Smith, recording secretary; Mrs. Hubert Judd, corresponding secretary; Mrs. H. C. Hamilton, treasurer; and Mrs. H. L. Smith, historian and registrar.

The work of this organization is honoring the memory of the dead, and promoting the interests of the living men who sacrificed much for their country. And after eleven years this chapter is still enlisted in loyalty and co-operation, honoring the memory of the dead, rendering service to the living and working together for the betterment of our beloved country.

The local chapter provides comforts for the men in the government hospital No. 48, in Atlanta. It also assists the American Legion in caring for the needy soldiers in Whitfield county.

Present officers: President, Miss Carrie Green; first vice-president, Mrs. W. E. Mann; second vice-president, Mrs. H. A. Howard; corresponding secretary, Mrs. Ruth Babb; recording secretary, Mrs. Sanford Carr; treasurer, Mrs. De Witt Miller; registrar, Mrs. H. L. Smith; historian, Mrs. C. A. Deakins.

The American Legion Auxiliary

In July, 1932, The American Legion Auxiliary, the youngest of Dalton's women's organizations, was organized by Mrs. J. M. Toomey, of Atlanta, state president, with ten members and the following officers: Mrs. J. C. Mitchell, president; Mrs. T. W. Kenemer and Mrs. C. F. Springer, vice-presidents; Mrs. W. H. Lumpkin, secretary; Mrs. W. M. Whiteside, treasurer; Mrs. J. E. Catlett, sergeant at arms; Mrs. Clarence H. Hill, historian; and Mrs. Mary E. Hardin, chaplain.

The chapter now has nineteen members and is affiliated with both State and National organizations.

The present officers are: President, Mrs. T. W. Kenemer; vice-president, Mrs. Harry O'Cain; second vice-president, Mrs. J. T. Bates; secretary, Mrs. Milton Ryman; treasurer, Mrs. William Britton; historian, Miss Ione Springer; chaplain, Mrs. Mary Hardin; sergeant at arms, Miss Arrie Wood.

Parent Teachers Association

The Parent Teachers Association was organized in 1932,

with the following officers: Mrs. A. Wollenweber, president; Mr. Frank Taylor, first vice-president; Mrs. Frank Innis, second vice-president; Mrs. Varner Neal, secretary; and Mrs. B. J. Bandy, treasurer.

The organization has done a splendid work during the short time it has been organized. It has established a cafeteria at Fort Hill school and has promoted a class in home economics in the colored school.

It has bought books for pupils in the schools unable to buy them, has cared for under nourished children, and has paid for improvements on the school buildings and made liberal donations to the school library.

Present officers are: President, Mrs. C. L. Bradley; vice-president, Mrs. R. B. Higgins; second vice-president, Mrs. H. A. Howard; secretary, Miss Anne McCamy; treasurer, Mrs. B. J. Bandy.

Dalton Garden Club

The Dalton Garden Club was organized April 12, 1933, by Mrs. Kincaid Thomas, who was elected first president of the organization. The charter members of the club are Mrs. Kincaid Thomas, Mrs. Luther Thomas Mann, Mrs. O. C. Alley, Mrs. Joseph Barrett, Mrs. Robert Hamilton, Mrs. Blair Cannon, Mrs. Clark Jones, Mrs. William Lumpkin, Mrs. Robert Gardner McCamy, Mrs. Donald McFarland, Miss Annie Laurie McCutchen, Mrs. John McLellan, Mrs. Fred Westcott, Mrs. Dewey Wright, Mrs. Judson Manly, Miss Martha Lin Manly, Mrs. Joe Wrench, and the following associate and honorary members: Mrs. Donald Hastings, of Atlanta, Mrs. M. E. Judd, Mrs. C. W. Moore, Mrs. Howard Motley, Mrs. John S. Thomas, Miss Mary Baker McGhee, Miss Charles Chester and Mrs. John B. McCarty. The present officers of the Dalton Garden Club are: President, Mrs. John McLellan; vice-president, Mrs. Pete Lumpkin; secretary, Mrs. John McCarty; treasurer, Mrs. Clark Jones; scrapbook custodian, Miss Charle Chester.

The Cherokee Chapter, Georgia Society, Daughters of the American Colonists

The Cherokee Chapter, Georgia Daughters of the American

Colonists, was organized in Dalton December, 1934, with sixteen charter members, with the following officers:

Mrs. W. E. Mann, organizing regent; Mrs. C. L. Hamilton, first vice regent; Mrs. Grace McCamy, second vice regent; Miss Margaret Gavitt, recording secretary; Mrs. C. W. Moore, corresponding secretary; Miss Annie Horne, treasurer; Mrs. Charles Kreischer, registrar; Mrs. L. J. Allyn, chaplain; Miss Mary Hamilton, historian; Mrs. B. J. Bandy, auditor.

Other charter members include, Mrs. Henry Hamilton, Miss Zeph Pate, Miss Irene Gavitt, Mrs. Luther Mann, Mrs. J. G. Jernigan, Mrs. G. W. Hamilton.

The objects of this society are patriotic, historical and educational; to make research as to the history and deeds of the American colonists and to record and publish these accomplishments; to commemorate deeds of colonial interest; to inculcate and foster the love of America and its institutions by all its residents; to obey the laws and venerate the flag, the emblem of the Union's power and civic righteousness.

CHAPTER VII

Modern Whitfield

WITH the dawning of the new century, the modern history of Whitfield county and Dalton may be said to have had its real beginning. In the city, modern lighting, water and sewer plants were installed. Many of the manufacturing plants that have made Dalton prosperous had been long established and several new ones were well under way. There were no paved streets, no sidewalks except rough brick on Hamilton street, but the citizenry was becoming alive to the need of modern improvements and the copies of "The Dalton Citizen" of the years immediately after the beginning of the century were full of projected changes and it was not long before many of the improvements advocated became things accomplished.

It is impossible to tell of the many enterprises attempted which are no more, but while some business houses have faded into oblivion and many have changed their names with changing owners or merged with others into larger enterprises, there has never been a time that Dalton and the county have taken a step backward or removed their hands from the plow.

One of the most helpful forward steps taken was the employment of a county demonstrator and a county agent as soon as the state law made this possible. A general improvement in agriculture in the county has been the result and while Whitfield can never compete in quantity production with the level stretches of land along the river bottoms in some other portions of the state, the fact remains that the prize for the best farmer in the state, given under the direction of the State College of Agriculture, went to Hillard Seaton of this county in 1929. The county demonstrator by the promotion of the 4-H clubs, poultry raising, good vegetable gardens and contests in home decoration, house furnishing and flower growing has added immeasurably to the comfort, plenty and beauty of our country homes.

The 4-H club of Whitfield county is part of a nation-wide organization, designed to interest the growing girls of rural communities in home building, and to instruct them in the domestic arts. For some years the girls belonging to this organization in the county have made an annual exhibit of their work, always creditable, and in many cases surprisingly so.

Another important innovation was the organization in 1913 of the Whitfield County Medical Society by Doctors Ault, Erwin, Harris, Kennedy, McAfee, Rollins and Sams. It was chartered by the Medical Association of Georgia in 1915.

At present the following doctors compose its membership: Doctors Ault, Bradley, Broaddrick, Easley, Erwin, Kennedy, McAfee, Rollins, Shellhorse, Starr, Steed and Wood, of Dalton, and W. J. Green, of Ringgold, Georgia.

An extension of the health work of the county was made by the employment of a county nurse in 1925. It was her first duty to come to the rescue of the many cases of tuberculosis which could not otherwise have had proper care. Funds for this work were supplied jointly by the national government under the provision of the Shepherd-Towner bill, the City of Dalton and the county. Miss Beulah Carrington was the first county nurse, and when she gave up the work to take a similar position with the Westcott Hosiery Mills, she was succeeded by Miss Kate Wright.

HAMILTON MEMORIAL HOSPITAL

An institution that has been of the greatest service and comfort to the people of Dalton and vicinity is the Hamilton Memorial Hospital, built in 1920 as a memorial to the late George W. Hamilton, president of the Crown Cotton Mills at the time of his death.

The stock of the hospital association is all owned in Dalton, much of it by the Crown mills and the several physicians of the city. Various organizations furnished many of the rooms as memorials.

The building is of cream stucco in Spanish style and has twenty rooms, including four wards, making it possible to take care of thirty-two patients. There is a fully equipped X-ray room, operating room and all the conveniences and facilities for comfort and sanitation found in the largest city hospitals. The

HAMILTON MEMORIAL HOSPITAL

building within is sanitary to the last degree and the management is proud of spotless corridors, the almost sound-proof rooms, and the beautifully arranged and equipped kitchens, as they have every reason to be.

On November 1, 1935, the Dalton Civitan Club leased the hospital from its owners and it is now operated by a Civitan Hospital Board, Inc., composed of Dr. F. K. Sims, president, Paul B. Fite, vice-president, O. C. Alley, treasurer, T. S. McCamy, G. L. Westcott and John A. Looper. Miss Dorothea Thompson, R.N., is superintendent.

The Charles C. Maples Memorial Association made it possible, by donation of part of the necessary funds, for the Board to erect as an addition to the hospital an emergency room which has been named "The Charles C. Maples Memorial Emergency Room."

Among the health work and charitable institutions of Dalton, none has done better work for more people than the Empty Stocking Fund. This fund was begun by Dr. F. K. Sims and T. S. McCamy then local editor of The Dalton Citizen, and was sustained for a number of years by purely voluntary contributions.

Later a substantial sum was bequeathed by the late Herman Fox, long a respected and charitable business man of the city, the interest to be used to relieve distress among the poor. This sum has been increased and is yearly augmented by large sums for immediate distribution. The fund has been administered for twenty-five years by Dr. Frank K. Sims, pastor of the First Presbyterian church.

The Red Cross organization and the county nurse also have funds for relief at their disposal.

The following is culled from an article written by Harlee Branch, then a reporter on the Atlanta Journal, and appeared in the issue of December 12, 1924:

"Dalton is destined to be one of the principal industrial cities of Georgia, and that at no distant day. Already it has taken its place in the forefront of the small industrial centers of the state and is making such strides that one can very easily visualize it as a city of 25,000 within the next twenty years.

"However, Dalton is not a 'factory town' as one understands that term. It is a city of fine homes, beautiful churches, parks and thoroughly creditable improvements. In its population of more than 10,000, ninety per cent of which is white, it numbers scores of outstanding civic leaders and its public-spirited citizens run into the hundreds.

"Thus Dalton has a spirit that one senses as soon as he gets near the corporate limits. This spirit translates itself into tireless and enthusiastic activities which perpetually proclaim the city's progress and virtues and which go out after new citizens and new industries.

"On every hand can be heard the hum of wheels. People are busy and happy and prosperous. No wonder they have the utmost confidence in the present and future of their town.

"Among the important industries located here and which are now paying nearly $3,000,000 a year in wages and salaries are the following:

"Crown Cotton mills, 50,000 spindles, manufacturing duck; Dalton Hosiery Mills, manufacturing 750 dozen pairs of silk hose a day and shipping a large part of its output to Cuba and South America, Duane Chair company, which ships its products to Chicago and other western furniture centers; Dalton Brick and Tile company, which manufactures shale face brick and building tile. Four big lumber manufacturing concerns, Farrar Lumber company, Cherokee Manufacturing company, Brooker Lumber company and Acme Lumber company; Smith Tent and Awning Manufacturing company; two ice plants; Barrett, Denton & Lynn company, flour mills; and the A. J. Showalter company, commercial printers, binders and publishers, which is one of the largest concerns of its kind in this part of the country.

Another distinctive and extensive manufacturing plant here is that of the Monly Jail Works. This concern specializes in jail cells and convict cages, but also actually builds jails. It sells its products in all parts of the country. Some of the other industries are: Three foundries and machine shops, two marble and granite works, two cotton gins, three steam laundries, two bottling works, etc.

"The list of industries and pay roll distribution does not include the plant of the American Thread company, a very large plant, but only one-third the size it will be when completed.

"Excellent sites are offered new industrial plants. Plenty of cheap hydro-electric power and plenty of industrious, intelligent native labor can be had. The main supply lines of the Georgia Railway and Power company run through the city.

"On top of Mount Rachel, which is in the outskirts of the city, is located the big municipal waterworks reservoir. The city owns its gas plant and electric system, although it buys its current from the Georgia Railway and Power company.

"Dalton is situated 778 feet above sea level; it has annual rainfall of 57 inches, a mean temperature of 61.5 degrees; highest temperature in summer, 93 degrees; lowest in summer, 50 degrees; highest in winter, 65 degrees; lowest in winter, 12 degrees; birth rate 29.41 per 1,000; death rate, 11.17 per 1,000; 2,500 factory workers, three banks with deposits of $3,000,000; annual postoffice receipts, $50,000.00; motor fire department; two miles of paved streets, 15 miles paved sidewalks, a white way, a hospital with forty beds, costing $85,000, and a new and modern hotel with 50 bedrooms, six stores and a barbershop, that was erected at a cost of more than $200,000.

"This hotel, known as Hotel Dalton, was sponsored by the Civitan club which is the leading civic organization here, and the stock was all sold to local people. H. J. Smith, a leading and public-spirited citizen, was chairman of the hotel committee, and not only looked after the sale of the stock, but also supervised the construction and furnishing of the building. W. C. Bowen is now president.

"The county of Whitfield, with the sympathetic and hearty co-operation of the business interests of Dalton, is making rapid progress with its agriculture, dairying, cattle, hog and poultry raising, and with improvements to its roads and schools.

"Fifteen years ago the normal cotton crop was 3,000 bales. Before the boll weevil came the normal cotton crop was 6,000; then it went as low as 4,900. In 1933 the crop was 7,500 bales, which is a high record.

"The farmers of Whitfield county are also engaged extensively in the growing of hay, grain, potatoes, strawberries, tomatoes, corn and other crops. Hay, potatoes, tomatoes and corn are shipped to various markets in quantity, and 80 cars of peaches were shipped this year from Cohutta orchards.

"Dalton was the home city of the late Will N. Harben, noted

author; the late Robert Loveman, famous poet, and the late A. J. Showalter, who was one of the country's leading sacred song composers."

Other authors that Dalton can claim are Mrs. Frank K. Sims, Jr., now of Charlotte, N. C., and Mrs. Sylla W. Hamilton, of Athens, Georgia. The late Mrs. Gertrude Manly Jones was another writer, whose negro dialect songs and stories gained for her a reputation as an author. Mrs. Lilian Whitman Carter has written many short stories and is a well-known contributor to many periodicals. Miss Jessie Baxter Smith, another writer whom Dalton can claim, contributes regularly to papers.

One of the industries not mentioned by Mr. Branch deserves a paragraph of its own, partly because it is distinctively a Whitfield county industry, and partly because in these lean recent years it has brought a steady stream of outside money into the county. This is the tufted bedspread industry which is carried on in a large way by a number of firms which ship the spreads and bath-mats in quantity, and by at least a dozen other firms which ship to a limited and exclusive clientele.

Originally all the spreads were made on unbleached sheeting with natural colored yarn, but later interior decorators began asking for spreads tufted in colors. This brought new problems to those engaged in the business, but they were successfully met and connections were made with reliable firms to dye the yarn any desired shade.

While many men are now engaged in the industry, it is woman's work, and commercializing it has brought to hundreds of county women a financial independence thoroughly enjoyed.

Reliable figures show that receipts for spreads shipped from Whitfield county in 1933-34 exceeded the total value of the county's cotton crop which ran into large figures.

Colonial hooked rugs are also made in the county and shipped by hundreds. These are in most cases made from the old designs our grandmothers loved, hand-hooked into a burlap background, and in their lovely texture and color harmonize perfectly with the early American furniture now so much used. The industry also brings a handsome sum yearly into the county.

THE DISASTROUS FIRE OF 1911

In April, 1911, Dalton experienced her first major catastrophe in a fire which devastated the heart of the city and swept away property to the value of a quarter of a million dollars. These included the old Hotel Dalton, the Opera House, the A. J. Showalter company and the Dalton Buggy Company buildings. In the hotel building there were several retail stores, the stocks of which were a total loss. From this shocking catastrophe the city was quick to recover and within the week most of the firms burned out were doing business elsewhere. The Opera House has never been replaced. Two modern picture shows have taken its place. During the war years no attempt was made to replace the hotel, but in 1923 the present modern building of the new Hotel Dalton was erected on the site of the old one.

Dalton's reaction to the war alarm in 1917 was what might be expected. The classes for the first training camp were hardly announced before there were applications for membership from three Dalton boys, including James A. McFarland, R. M. Herron, Jr., and W. B. Farrar, all of whom finished the course with credit and were duly commissioned officers. Later training camps also had several Whitfield county boys; twelve officers in all being commissioned from this county. At the first call, numbers of boys enlisted so that the first draft quota for the county was only six men, the remaining number of the quota were already in service. In all Whitfield county sent six hundred eighty-three men to wear their country's uniform and follow her flag, and there is no record that any one of them failed in his duty. Many "fought the war" in cantonments in this country, but that does not detract from the fact that they did their best, and it is written that "They also serve who only stand and wait." The first casualty among the county's quota was John F. Slaton, killed by shrapnel while on sentry duty on the night of April 13, 1918, and buried at Rourvois the following day. Sixteen other Whitfield county boys gave their lives in the service and in their honor the Governor John Milledge Chapter, D. A. R., assisted by other organizations, erected a monument on the post office grounds shortly after the war was over. It is a granite block with a handsome bronze marker, standing under the flag they died to protect, and bears the following inscription:

Whitfield County pays tribute to these, her sons, who
died for Liberty

John F. Slaton

Elmer Chester	Lewis Hopkins
Spartan Crow	Robert Lanham
George Cupp	James E. McDougal
Melvin Dill	Aaron Pangle
Roy Eslinger	Scott Prothro
Guy Felker	Adlai Stephenson
Samuel Frazier	Claude Richardson
Clarence Grant	William Wear
Amos Hardin	John Wimpey

And to those others who served with the colors during the World War.

The list of all the soldiers who gave Whitfield county as their residence at the time of enlistment is given in the appendix. There were many others, natives of the county, who enlisted elsewhere but their names cannot be obtained.

Of the civil service rendered by the citizens of the county, too much cannot be said. The Red Cross was the first of the organizations formed though many women had been knitting for the Navy League under the direction of Mrs. George P. Mills some weeks before the Red Cross formally began work. This first knitting consisted largely of sweaters made for the sailors on the battleship, Georgia, but when they were supplied, all later knitting was done through the Red Cross by the request of the Secretary of the Navy.

THE RED CROSS

The work of the Red Cross chapter is best shown in the report made at the close of the first year, as follows:

"The chapter showed a membership, including both senior and junior memberships, of 5,216, and 51,499 different articles have passed through the ladies' workroom. Officers for the year were elected as follows:

"W. C. Martin, chairman; Mrs. M. E. Judd, vice chairman; Miss Kate Hamilton, secretary; T. D. Ridley, treasurer; Mrs. R. M. Herron, director of woman's work; F. K. Sims, chairman membership and extension; W. C. McGhee, chairman war work and finance; T. S. McCamy, chairman publicity; Mrs. Alfred Brown, workroom instructor; F. F. Farrar, chairman home service; Mrs. Julian McCamy, chairman canteen; B. A. Tyler, chairman conservation; J. J. Copeland and J. H. Watson, chairmen county and city Junior Red Cross; W. C. Martin, Mrs. M. E. Judd, Mrs. R. M. Herron, Mrs. P. B. Trammell, Mrs. W. C. Martin, F. F. Farrar, B. A. Tyler, H. J. Smith, C. C. Maples, J. D. Hammond, Josiah Crudup, F. K. Sims, Mrs. Julian McCamy, Mrs. G. P. Mills, Miss Willie White, J. G. McLellan, T. S. McCamy and H. L. Erwin, executive committee."

Classes were held for making surgical dressings at the work room on Crawford street, and three groups of women qualified as instructors, and worked throughout the summer. These were under the supervision of Mrs. Alfred Brown, instructor, and Mrs. R. M. Herron and Mrs. W. C. Martin, executive chairmen.

When the campaign for War Savings Stamps was initiated, Mr. E. P. Davis,* vice president of the First National Bank, was made chairman for the county, and under his efficient leadership the committee so thoroughly organized the work that by July 4th, the total amount of the quota of $339,400 was raised, this being one of the first ten counties in the state to report "over the top."

The Whitfield County Liberty League was organized in July, 1918; all members pledged themselves to do any kind of war work when called upon. The plan followed was that under which Mr. E. P. Davis had conducted the War Savings Stamps campaign to such a successful issue.

J. G. McLellan* was president of the organization and F. S. Pruden, secretary.

Another organization that did valuable service was the local branch of the American League for Women's Service, organized by Mrs. M. E. Judd. This group specialized in making clothing to be sent to France and Belgium for the relief of the civilian population of those war torn nations. Thirteen hundred garments are of record but many more were made later.

The war over, the citizenry settled down to rehabilitation work; the Dixie Highway claimed much attention. This highway extends the length of the county, and is a link in the road connecting Chicago and Detroit with Miami. Agitation and influence were brought to bear and the concrete highway is now complete in the county.

---
*Deceased.

The public library, founded by the Dalton Woman's Club, deserves mention. This is housed in the old Robert Loveman home, "The Robin's Nest", which is the home of the club, and is maintained as a memorial to the poet. The library is supported by private subscription and the county board appropriates a certain sum for children's books regularly. Some four

THE DALTON LIBRARY—MEMORIAL TO ROBERT LOVEMAN

thousand volumes are in circulation and Miss Cora Henderson is the librarian.

Dalton boasts two trees of unusual significance; the John Eason oak which owns itself, a magnificent forest tree of unknown age but certainly antedating the expulsion of the Cherokees in 1838. And the Liberty tree standing on the post office lawn which was planted in 1924 as a war memorial, with the assistance of the local council of the Junior Order of American Mechanics and the Daughters of America, an affiliated order of women.

At the ceremony of planting, each state was represented by a young lady and each county of Georgia by a boy or girl, appropriately dressed, who were received by Uncle Sam, Miss Columbia and Georgia. In many cases the soil sent for the planting was from some place that has a part in the history of the locality sending it, such as Stone Mountain, the grave of Alexander Stephens and Faneuil Hall. The soil from Vermont was sent by the father of President Coolidge, Judge John Coolidge. This plan was originated by Honorable W. M. Sapp, then senator, and all the detail of securing earth from each state in the union was arranged by him.

Dalton's retail stores of every kind deserve appreciative

BANK OF DALTON

mention. Hamilton Street, the main business street, has four blocks of business buildings and others are on the various cross streets intersecting Hamilton.

There are six thriving drug stores of which Fincher & Nichols antedates all the others, having been in the drug business since 1882. The furniture business is also represented by three firms. Of general merchants and dealers in groceries and meats, there are a generous number, and both the privately owned groceries and the chain cash-and-carry do a thriving business. The drygoods trade of the city and county is thoroughly well cared for by a dozen or more clean, bright stores carrying not only the usual staples, but also ready-to-wear and millinery of satisfactory quality and price. Dalton boasts of three novelty stores which carry a wide range of nickel and dime items though none of them are restricted to articles of that price. The Routh store is the oldest and has branches in several near-by towns. There are four hardware stores also. Three seems to be the favorite number in Dalton's retail district as

HARDWICK BANK AND TRUST COMPANY

there are that number of cleaning establishments also. The city boasts of three modern steam laundries, an adequate ice plant, and at least a dozen restaurants, all doing a thriving business.

Dalton is particularly proud of the fact that there has never been a really bad business failure during its history. This is in a large part due to the three strong banks that handle finances for this and surrounding counties.

The first of these in point of time is the Hardwick Bank

and Trust Company, established by the late Frank T. Hardwick in 1873 as a private bank, with a capital stock of $15,000 and under his fostering care it became one of the strong financial institutions of this section. Mr. Hardwick died in October, 1921, and was succeeded as president by his son, W. M. Hardwick. The late T. D. Ridley, who was cashier for several years, remained at that post, and in February, 1922, the bank was reorganized as a state bank and continued to flourish. The bank became an associate of the Hamilton National, of Chatta-

FIRST NATIONAL BANK

nooga, in September, 1930, with the late Mr. Ridley as president. The bank is housed in a beautiful modern building, erected in 1925. Their capital stock is $100,000.00 and the surplus $200,-000.00. The slogan adopted years ago: "Safe, Sound and Constructive Banking" continues to be their guiding star.

The First National Bank was organized in 1888, as told elsewhere. Paul B. Trammell re-organized it and became president under the new regime, which office he held until his death in 1925. Associated with him were W. C. Martin, first vice-president,* E. P. Davis, second vice-president, and J. G. McLellan, cashier. On Mr. Trammell's death, Mr. Martin was made president, Mr. Davis, first vice-president, and

Mr. McLellan succeeded him as second vice-president. After Mr. Davis' death in 1925, Mr. McLellan succeeded him as first vice-president and three years later, S. J. Head was made cashier. This office he held until the death of Mr. McLellan in 1932, when he succeeded to the office of the first vice-president, which office he still holds. Lee Jones is now cashier and trust officer, Walter Jones, Jr., and John B. McCarty, assistant cashiers. The bank has a force of ten persons including officers; a capital of $100,000.00 and a surplus of $125,000.00 and resources in excess of $2,000,000.00. It is a member of the Federal Reserve System. The bank is housed in a beautiful marble bank building which is one of the handsomest buildings in the South. The men who have made the First National have wrought well and the work of their hands stands as a monument to their sane and conservative ability.

The Bank of Dalton was organized as a state bank in 1911 by Buell Stark and Dennis Barrett. After some years, in 1918, it was reorganized with W. C. Martin as president, J. C. Copeland as cashier and Arthur Broadrick as assistant cashier; all continue to hold these offices. The capital is $50,000; the surplus, $10,000, and the bank has resources in excess of a quarter of a million dollars and serves more than one thousand five hundred customers, owning its own building adjoining the post office, and fills a real place in the financial structure of the county.

Several years ago civic pride bestirred itself and the jail, which adjoined the court house on one of the most prominent streets in the city, was moved to a less conspicuous location. The new jail is built of Dalton brick and last year was mistaken by a party of tourists for a hotel. The court house was rebuilt at the same time, and modernized in various ways, and standing as it does, in a whole square of lawn, with beautiful forest trees surrounding it, is a building of which any county may well be proud.

DALTON BUILDING & LOAN ASSOCIATION

The Dalton Building & Loan Association is the oldest and one of the largest Building & Loan Associations in Georgia, founded in 1889, and is now larger than ever in its history. Its chief purpose is and has been to stimulate savings and assist in the building of houses, and in both it has been an important agency. During its existence it has paid out to its stockholders in matured stock and divirends over a half million dollars. Its present officers are—W. C. Martin, President; W. C. Bowen, Vice-President; S. J. Head, Secretary and Treasurer, and John McCarty, Assistant Secretary-Treasurer. Directors: W. C. Martin, W. C. Bowen, J. S. Thomas, S. N. McWilliams, Lee Routh, S. J. Head, W. M. Jones, Jr., John B. McCarty, and John McLellan.

THORNTON AVENUE LOOKING NORTH

MARKING HISTORIC SITES

In 1933 the Civitan Club appointed a committee to locate and mark in a suitable manner some of the most noted historic places on the Dixie Highway in Whitfield County. John S. Thomas was appointed chairman of this committee, assisted by Frank Manly, Walter Jones, George Hamilton, Miss Willie White, Mrs. R. M. Herron, Mrs. Clarence Fraker, Mrs. W. C. Martin.

Handsome bronze markers were placed on the following sites, the Huff house on Selvidge street, headquarters of General Joseph E. Johnston; Tibbs house on North Hamilton street, at one time headquarters of General Joseph E. Johnston; Dug Gap battlefield marker placed on South Thornton avenue; home of Drowning Bear on the creek of that name.

Battle of Mill Creek Gap; at the intersection of Cleveland and South Thornton avenue, marking site of Indian race track, and the Indian ball ground nearby; Battle of Resaca in South

Whitfield County, erected by Dr. H. L. Erwin in memory of his father, Lieut. H. C. Erwin, 4th Georgia cavalry, who fought and was wounded in that famous battle.

The Whitfield county of today with its American born population, its healthful climate, its beautiful valleys and rugged mountains, its winding streams, its diversified soil, its splendid schools, its many churches, its fraternal orders, its efficient officers and its spirit of peaceful progress, is a great county.

NEGRO POPULATION

From the days before the war the negro population of Whitfield county down to the present day has been exceptionally good. During those trying times in the war between the states they showed loyalty and devotion to their "white folks."

The two races have lived side by side through the ensuing years in peace and harmony. No friction or racial troubles that have occurred in other sections of the south have been known here. Some splendid types of the negro race have lived in this county, respected by both white and colored.

CHAPTER VIII
Greater Whitfield County

WITH all the splendid forces mentioned in preceding chapters at work together with the wonderful progress that has been made in the last ten years, all these assure a greater future for the county.

The advancement in every line of endeavor has given the county a momentum that will project its progress into the years to come. The vast amount of constructive work done in the past few years has been a powerful factor in the tremendous strides that the county has taken and the gains that have been made in taxable wealth, even during the years of the depression, have been considerable.

ROAD BUILDING

About the middle of the year 1925 a plan originated by W. C. Martin was presented to the Civitan Club for the paving of five county roads all centering in Dalton. The estimated cost of this road building plan was $1,600,000 and the cost was to be borne one-fourth by the State of Georgia, one-fourth by Whitfield County and one-half by the Federal Government.

The plan was promptly sponsored by the Civitan Club and at their request, it was presented by W. C. Martin to the Board of Roads and Revenues of Whitfield County, and adopted by it and an election was called in October, 1925, for a bond issue of $400,000. At the election the vote was practically solid in favor of bonds. Soon after that the bonds were issued and from time to time sold as the funds were needed to pay the county's part.

The roads are now all paved under this plan. It was only necessary to use $350,000 of the county's bonds. The county has on hand $265,000 in highway certificates and approximately $35,000 sinking fund, making a sum sufficient to pay the entire bond indebtedness thus leaving the county free of debt.

Thus it will be seen that all paved roads in Whitfield county have been built since 1925. The county maintains these roads and is well equipped with modern road-building machinery and maintains an average of fifty convicts on the roads all the time.

These roads penetrate a beautiful and picturesque country, crossing clear streams spanned by concrete bridges, then winding around mountains bringing the traveler suddenly to green meadows and rich farming lands. There is no highway in the county that will not repay the tourist with wonderful mountain scenery, views of smiling valleys with here and there springs of pure sparkling water.

INDUSTRIAL LOCATION

The county is located in the busiest industrial zone of the south on the main Dixie highway with two great trunk lines of railways leading northward and southward.

It is close to raw material of almost every kind and has abundant labor.

It has unlimited electric power and is in the district of the Tennessee Valley Authority and will receive the benefits of this gigantic development.

The county has a rare all-the-year-round climate, pure mountain water, splendid drainage, scenic surroundings and a wholesome moral and religious atmosphere.

EDUCATIONAL FACILITIES

The entire county outside of Dalton is organized into seven consolidated school districts—each being provided with a modern up-to-date school building, readily accessible to all the children with the aid of about 30 school busses. The advance in facilities for education has been notable and the system of schools is equal to that of any county in the state.

The erection of the consolidated school buildings and the large amount of money spent on education is an index of what Whitfield county will continue to do along that line. The teachers are always paid promptly and the schools are rated A-1 in scholastic standards.

DALTON, THE COUNTY SEAT

The city is situated in the northern extremity of a triangular plain with just enough undulations to give good drainage and a fine variety of scenic beauty.

On the west is a towering range of mountains, many of the peaks having palisades extending for many miles.

On the east in the distance there rises the tall peaks of the Cohutta mountains.

From the summit of Mount Rachel immediately north of Dalton and almost within the corporate limits, there may be seen a picturesque valley, through which a number of streams wind their way.

The city, too, has steadily advanced in the last few years. The extension of water, gas and electric lighting facilities have gone forward with vigor, as have street paving, sidewalks, and sewer extensions.

Large numbers of new houses have been constructed in city and county in the last few months and many others are being planned for in the near future. A new city hall is in the process of building which will be a credit to the city, and a new school is being erected on Fort Hill as a part of the city system of schools.

Business houses almost without exception report substantial gains in volume and profits during the past year. The banks show largely increased deposits. And the city's increasing population, estimated now at 14,000 including the immediate surrounding territory, is looking and working toward ever greater fulfillment of Dalton's destiny as one of Georgia's leading cities.

WHITFIELD CITIZENRY

The population of Whitfield County is approximately 20,000 and more than nine-tenths of pure Anglo-Saxon lineage.

Sound economical government has made the tax burdens of city and county unusually light.

Those who feel most interested in the county's welfare and who think most of her future growth and development are men and women of moral worth and high intellectual standing and their reputation for hospitality, friendliness and courtesy is known far and wide.

No city or county in the south can boast of public-spirited men that are more zealous advocates of every measure that looks to the moral, physical and financial betterment of the people.

Looking the entire nation over, it may be confidently stated that no better place can be found anywhere to make a happy home than here in Whitfield County.

Census of 1850 of Murray County, Georgia

(Of which Whitfield County was then a part)

HEADS OF FAMILIES ONLY
Copied from original records in Census Bureau, Washington, D. C., by Mrs. R. M. Herron

Census taken by Absolem Holcombe

Absalom Holcombe
Peter Gosnell
James Cox
Rebecca Howard—w
William Cochran
Wylie Nichols
James W. Hall
Catherine Springfield
—w
William Russell
Malone Cox
William Burk
Sarah Workman—w
D. T. Fulton
William B. Robertson
Nathan Ward
Robert Pool
William White
John Wade
Lewis Mathis
Absalom Foster
Mary Baker
Johnson Warmack
Martha Ward
John P. Smith
Henry Tyler
Eugene Hill
Richard H. Mobley
Nathan Daugherty
E. M. McGuire
Thomas Cleary
Thomas Ramey
Volentine Abernathy
Malinda Coley
Stephen Pace
Mary P. Martin
Sarah Sutton—w
Christopher Cornish
J. D. Gray
David Powers
James Coragan
James Neenan
James Kinney
Edward Cochlin
Hugh Flood
William Kelly
Peter Stackpole
Hugh Gathey
James Lima
C. W. Waddle
John Waddle
Andrew Fletcher
Robert Rogers
Michael White
James Gilman
John Wilson
Alexander Morrison
Johy Doyle
Jas. F. Prator
Alsa Peeper

Robert Rhinehart
James Currin
Michael Griffon
George W. Jewel
Chas. Carroll
Patrick Gardner
Terreen McKinny
Hugh Milligan
Patrick Meeren
Peter Colly
John Griffon
Sarah Correll
Mary Coragan
Chas Linton
Marshall McFearson
Isaac Cloud
Reuben Carter
John Michael
G. R. Harris
Susan Harris
Jas. M. Cloud
L. Lee
Isaac Swanson
J. M. Bell
George Horne
William Dunn
John Thomas
John Hartnett
Clisbe Austen, Sr.
Stokely Shugart
Jas. Squires
Edward Green
John Hayne
William Grees
  (Agt. Tunnel Ry.)
Richard Marchal
John Thomas
William Gold
D. H. Eledge
Lewis D. Cade
Thomas Jinks
Elizabeth Bell, Sr.
Reuben Herndon
Smith Treadwell
Henly Snow, Sr.
John M. Wood
Diadnea Ware
C. I. Emerson (Dr.)
L. P. Wood
John B. Bell
J. D. Buffington
Peter Mason
William Mathis
Melgin Smith
Geo. H. Ramey
Thos. C. Davis
William Pool
John Thomas
William Wood
Jeremiah Clark

S. A. Rogers
Aaron Cantrell
Thomas Morris
Jehu Hall
William Cleary
Andrew J. Copeland
Franklin Smith
Jas. Peterson
Wm. Hall
Lucinda Wood
Jas. Miller
Joseph Miller
John Kincaid
Wm. Pressley
David Hall
Jemima Hall
Gillam Long
Jas. Burk
Jeremiah Ray
Enoch Herndon
Daniel Andoe
John Jordan
John Gordon
Mary Jane McPheeters
John Hall
Solomon Darnel
Isaac George
Jas. Morrison
Adam Calhoun
Jas. Boyd, Sr.
Jas. Boyd, Jr.
Samuel Linder
Jas. D. Justice
William N. Bishop
Jehu Trammell
Jas. Roach
John Robertson
Green B. McAlla
Elizabeth Haywood
Thomas Gardner
Anderson Lemon
James Cantrell
William Freeman
Isham Freeman
Abraham Neighbours
Ervin Dishroon
Isaac Dishroon
Jas. N. Stewart
William Conolly
Beatty Perin
William J. Love
John H. Love
Jas. Gossett
Patrick Reily
Geo. Chappell
Abraham Chappell
John L. Sansom
William A. Mote
Sam. P. Bridges.
Cornelius T. Cunning-

ham
Frederick Cox (Sheriff)
Jacob Cox
William Gossett
William Crow
Noah Roberts
Alexander Fleming
A. Walkley
William Cook
A. B. Gurley
Jas. Isbel
Thos. T. Christain
Geo. Chestnut
M. D. Warmack, Esq.
A. H. Farnsworth
Reuben R. Dobbs
Francis R. Rouche
Chas. Sellers
Joseph McJunkin
P. B. Nichols
John Gavin
Timothy Magurty
Richard W. Jones
Jane Davidson
E. A. Wood
Thos. Flynn
William Cox
David Wear
Wm. Dunn
E. W. Allen
Julius Deadman
John W. Wells
John Snow
John Natt
Clark Beggarly
Wm. Burk
Cicero Allen
John Elsman
Jas. Coleman
Coley Beavers
Callaway Dobbs
John Fulton
Thomas Brown
Edward H. Edwards
Thos. C. Henry
Henry Davis
A. E. Blount
J. M. Wright
William L. High
P. M. Craigmiles
Jas. M. Craigmiles
David Stewart
Sanford L. Bell
Christopher McCrary
Robt. S. Rushton
Richard L. Cook
L. W. Earnest
J. S. Waugh (Dr.)
Sam S. Bailey (Dr.)
Robert McCall
Green B. Hardin
Henry Young
S. Floerch
Chas. H. Wilson (Dr.)
Silas Mote
Joshua Wuman
Linsey Fortune
Alex A. Simmons
Jas. Holland
Chas. G. Muller
M. G. Jolly
Wm. H. Cox
Jesse Holland
Wm. P. Hackney
Jas. T. Sitton
La Fayette Powell
John Nelson

Chas. Baker
Thos. Hancock
Stoddard Russel
Daniel J. Haney
John W. Graves
Christain Rauschenberg
Gustavus Heerlain
Chas. Schwab
John McGee
Henry Taylor
Jonathan N. Cate
Wm. P. Chester (Hotel)
Wm. T. Lowe
J. H. Gudger
W. H. Stancel
G. W. Selvidge (Bap. Minister)
Richard Cross
George Comstock
A. J. Lane
I. R. F. Dantzler
Lorenza McNalb
J. A. Carden
Franklin Ware
Wm. Ellard
Geo. Pratt
Benhamin Wilson
Jas. S. Bryant
Andrew S. Holder
H. W. Hargroves (Agt. Sta.)
Jesse C. Hooper
W. Pierce
N. A. Milner
Jas. Thompson
John H. Thompson
John Keenan
Cornelius Hebberts Supt. R.R.)
Abner J. Parks
Jas. Pyron
Hiram B. Perkins
Joel Thacher
Lucinda Brown
Susan Clark
Matilde Ross
John Goetz
August Kanz
Ferdinand Schrann
Julius Dittrick
Abner Tweedy
F. M. C. Riley
Joseph England
Bodwell IE. Wells
Jabez P. M. Pitman
Nancy L. Prinel
John P. Love
Daniel Stroup
J. A. Fergerson
Chas. Beruff (Artist)
Otta Lentz
Henry H. Talley
Leopold Merkel
Geo. Weeker
Wm. B. Cone
Wm. R. Berner
Georgia A. Stafford
Elizabeth A. Martin
Chas. Knorr (Bavaria)
Christopher Dreoksell
Edward White
William H. Fonerdon (Dr.)
William Gordon
John W. Evans
T. C. McOwen
Reuben Carver
Archibald G. Johnson

(Pres. Minister)
H. A. Wrench (England)
Drury R. Smith
John Newman
Rufus H. Ford
Elizabeth Manes
C. W. Smith
Docia Cook
Chas. Riley
John Anderson
Ernestine Schaefer
Elizabeth Harben (Oldest son, Oliver W., age 15)
Jas. R. Allison
A. E. Firestone
Robt. G. Hague
Dr. Winston Gordon
F. M. Tillotson
L. L. Tillotson
Margaret Sherwood—w
B. C. Morse
Wiley Prince
Richard Dodd
Jacob Moore
John Oneal, Sr.
James Murphy
John Davis
C. Gordon
Fredric W. Fischer
Jean Florr
Solomon Graham
Gilbert Long
Wm. Bell
John Hamilton
Levi Brotherton (Meth. Preacher)
Gustav Buber
F. T. Boceman
Michael Brown
Robt. Squires
Jacob Kemp
Joseph Johnson
Washington Rowe
J. F. Carden
David Blalock
Obediah Able
Nancy Center
Edwai B. Hathaway
Thos. H. Sparks
Wm. J. Underwood
Barbary Kelly
Geo. Couch
David Wrinkle
Nancy S. Hill
Edward S. Hill
Moses G. Collins
Sam W. Hoss
Christopher C. Hammond (Dr.)
Gustavus Heerline (R. R. Agt.)
John Odell
Jas. M. Morgan
Susannah Evans
John McGill
Leonard Pace
Thornton Burgiss
Talitha Herren—w
John W. Odell
Armel Clark
John F. Sutherland
William Odell
William Richardson
Zachariah D. Clark (Bap. Minister)
Jeremiah Roberts
Russell Smith

Census of 1850 of Murray County

Johnson Smith
Delila McCurdy
L. K. Crawford
Wade H. Harris
Jas. W. Toney
P. T. S. Black
Martin Strawn
David Strawn
Thos. McCune
Henry B. Robbins
John L. Rodgers
Francis W. McCurdy
John M. McCurdy
J. C. Creekmore
Mumford Lee
Allison McHan
  (Meth. Preacher)
Abraham Chastain
Sam. H. Magar
Wm. Harris
Isaac Atchley
Jas. M. Richardson
Miller Richardson
Benjamin Copp
John Reeves
Drewry Johnson, Sr.
  (Bap. Minister)
Wm. P. Stone
Jas. Smith
Edward McAbee
  (Baptist Minister)
Wm. Hess
Geo. W. Webb
Benjamin Wiggins
Wm. Wiggins
Geo. W. Suttle
Griffin C. McMichael
A. B. Dycus
Jas. Creekmore
Henry P. Heald
Elias C. Shelton
Solomon McMurray
Malinda Winkler
Wm. A. Robbins
John Thornbery
Elizabeth McElroy
Wm. Stephenson
Thos. Walker
Silas W. Bell
Chas. Cook
Chas. Bull
Thos. Nelson
Wm. Johnson
Lavina Fry
Augustus G. Black
Abner Seets
Francis Bailey—w
John P. Railey
Thos. C. Black
Hesekiah Inman
Griffin Heath
Jehial Helton
John F. Black
Singleton Jones
Wm. Hammond
Wm. H. Ketchum
Duke Richardson
Henry Smith
John Divers
Peter McElroy
Benj. Gazaway
John Hany
Mary Ann Butler
Jesse C. Creekmore
Martha Dycus
Lician Clinger
Jas. McDonald
Elisabeth Gaddis—w

Wylie Pierce
Pleasant Rosse
Alfred B. Plummer
John Godard
Martin Frolic
William Heerlein
Absolem Bradley
Gideon Smith
Thos. W. Patrick
Peter Miller
Anderson McDonald
Pleasant Slay
Wm. E. Cox
J. R. Sweatman
J. C. Caler
Abel Fulks
Sarah Jones—w
Harrison Fulks
Wm. Lawson
Robt. H. Campbell
Stephen Phillips
Abraham Steele, Sr.
A. K. Steele
Isaac Noblet
Wm. Callahan
Davis Stockton
Micajah Sanson
Orran M. Sansom
William Sansom
Thos. Pope
Wm. Day
Lewis Rice
Wm. Murphy
Jos. T. Williams
Ira Coffee
Drury Woodall
David H. Shealds
Alphonsa S. Vandevere
Lampkin Vandevere
  (Bap. Minister)
William S. Williams
Jas. Millirons
William Masters
Benj. L. Parks
Geo. B. Campbell
David W. Mitchell
Wiley D. Morgan
Wm. D. Hancock
Charlotte Hancock—w
Robert R. Edwards
James Bardem
Frances Lockerd
Mansel D. Coker
Noah Pearson
Joseph E. Morgan
John Oxford
William McCarell
John P. Bryson
G. T. Tate
Oliver P. Owens
Eliot Lacey
Joseph C. Looney
Robt. Coker
Claborn Jackson
Nanc Faith
Benjamin Jacison
Jesse Whittaker
Thos. Chappell
Rufin Ginn
William B. Malone
Henry Bowman
William Bucaloo
Pleasant M. Ship
Dr. F. Kinman
Garrison Creamer
Edward Bagby
S. H. Chambers
Thos. B. Mitchel

Jas. B. Tate
Nancy Brumbelo—w
Jas. Mitchell
John P. Gilbert
  (Baptist Minister)
Claborn Perry
Joseph Mote
Elijah Cates
Jas. Forsythe
Elijah Langford
George W. Keith
Amos. L. Sutherland
Thos. G. Morgan
Calvin Brumbelo
John Parks
Jas. R. Bradberry
Mark Thornton
John Calahan
Wm. G. McCarson
Elijah M. Chapman
Wills W. Mote
Anderson A. Mote
William Sweatman
Thomas Davis
Jas. L. Wilson
Joseph Vandergrif
Geo. G. McCay
Michael Howell
Sherwood Whitlock
Jacob L. Cobb
Stephen C. Cady
Andrew Mauldin
Tillotson Gray
John I. Hendricks
Daniel May
Absolem Carpenter
Jas. Seay
C. C. Money
Charner Adams
William Worthy
William Rader
William Jones
Jonathan Oxford
Joshua Boatwright
Elizabeth Cheek—w
Geo. W. Ramsey
Francis M. Hegwood
Nathan L. Bennett
William H. Seay
Jesse Snow
Philip Manis
Elizabeth A. Snow
Mitchell Bennett
Benj. Nealy
Arthur Bridgers
Juda Bradley—w
Levie Snow
William I. Tate
William A. Boling
Alfred Spangler
Jeremiah Bridges
Jonathan Bridges
Peter Kreischer
  (Germany)
William P. Haslet
Gabriel McCook
Jas. L. Wilson
Elizabeth McDonald—w
Jordan Batson
B. B. Whaley
Elisha Ivie
John Heath
Carter Pope
Jackson Turner
Geo. W. Thompson
John McNabb
William McNabb
John Martin

Peyton Mobley
Benj. F. Hurst
Warren I. Bradley
Mary McGhee—w
Eliza Compton—w
Elizabeth Glover
Jackson Glover
Wiley Glover
Jas. Wrenn
Henry Clemens
Thos. Harper
David A. Cline
John Webb
Howard Cash
Henry S. Patterson
John Bookout
Andrew Fraker
Milton Strickland
Wm. Kirk
Malachi Strickland
Marshal Strickland
Robert King
Andrew Watt
Burrell Jordan
John Hackney
Joseph Hackney
Jas. B. Hackney
Wm. H. Brock
Jacob B. Dansler
James Jewel
Alexander M. Cahoon
Robert Brock
John Morgan
Franklin Shelley
Rudd Morgan, Sr.
Jordan Morgan
Robert Chanler
William Dooly
Silas F. Morgan
C. N. Caster
William Belk
Henry Brooker
William Russell
George Fagala
John Shelton
Hamilton H. Moore
William Cole
Isaac Davis
Andrew Cummins
Jas. A. Callahan
Jeremiah Plummer
Joseph Vandergrif
Robert Bohannon
Alfred M. Turner
Dauson A. Walker
  (Atty.)
John C. Burch
John A. Tyler
Geo. S. Jones
Sam I. Dwight (M.D.)
John H. Williams
Solomon L. Stow
S. H. Sterling
J. M. Teague
Hugh Shannon
Balis Donaldson
Adison I. Jarnagan
Mary McClain
Richard Couch
James Edmondson
William Anderson
Thos. Montgomery
Andrew M. Norris
  (P. M. Spring Place)
John S. Beall
Joseph McDowell
  (M. D.)
James A. R. Hanks

  (Atty.)
Jas. Morris
Thomas Crews
Anderson Farnsworth
  (Atty.)
Abel Johnson
Chas. E. Broyles
  (Atty.)
Nathaniel L. Baxter
Franklin B. Morris
Britain C. Tyler
J. A. W. Johnson
  (Atty.)
John O'Conner
Wm. B. Brown
  (Pres. Minister)
Jas. Ramsey
Jacob Shoopman
Ralph Ellison
  (Clerk of Court)
Jane E. Cheek
G. W. Whitecotton
Thos. F. McMulleen
Jones Henderson
Benjamin Henderson
Jas. M. McGhee
Joshua D. Stafford
Jas. Whittenberg
Perry Shields
Alfred Monell
Jas. Anderson
Alexander Officer
Rebecca Weaser
Aulden Tucker
William Tucker
Jas. Tucker
Robert Isbel
Thos. Sutliff
Baxter B. Brown
  (M. D.)
William E. Laughmiller
Byron Hargrove
  (Clerk in Depot)
Wm. B. Hunter
Geo. M. Brown
Jas. Buchanan (Sheriff.)
Dickinson Taliaferro
John O. Ellis
C. B. Tucker
Abel Jackson
Garland A. Hooper
William McCamey
Chas. W. Bond
Jos. P. McElrath
Thos. I. Farmer
John Oats
Thos Hames
Owen H. Kenan (Atty.)
Ambrose H. Blackwill
  (Atty.)
Jas. C. Loughridge
William P. Stanfield
Jacob Ware
John Pendley
Jas. C. Hill
Jacob Pearce
Gideon Garner
C. L. Vining
Hillsman Stancel
Allen Griffin
John H. Butler
Calvin Rollins
Wm. Lowry
Solomon Kinnery
Thos. J. Pritchard
Bennett Springfield
William E. Brown
Nathaniel Connally

William Carter
Geo. C. Cleveland
Jesse Hishop
Catherine Hosler
Stephen Crow
Jas. M. Anderson
Andrew J. Rollans
Elizabeth Waggoner
Henry J. Wilson
Uriah Hunt
Geo. W. Millborne
Abraham B. Wilson
Carswell Ramsey
William McGill
Wm. H. Stead
Alfred Wheat
John Shea
Lemuel Garner
R. H. L. Buchanan
  (Atty.)
John Brown
J. A. Black
E. S. Bird
Lewis McKinney
Joseph Ruble
Hugh Goddard
Richard S. Morriss
David Whitener
Benjamin Clark
Elijah W. Bond
Martha Meredith
Wm. C. McDonald
Jordan Webb
John W. Webb
Littleton Strawn
Joel Shelton
Wm. East
Wm. Holcombe
J. M. Self
John C. Bales
Joseph J. Davis
Robert Crumley
John Broaddrick
Alexander Paul
Lewis Green
Asa May
Jane Dyke
Leonard Pace
Daniel Newman
John Bowman
Benjamin Taleferio
Wm. Chambers
David Fry
Josiah Jones
Frederick Tankersley
Wm. Bohannon
Wm. Stinson
Mizely Williamson
Joseph Bailey
John Burk
John Bohannon
Thos. Bohannon
Jas. M. Keener
Michael Varnell
Asa Hodges
Joel Coffee
Willis Copper
John S. James
Richard S. Shields
James Verner
H. E. Cowan
William M. Cowen
Abraham Crew
Martha Mitchell
W. C. Day
Peter Etter
John Stockberger
Jacob Stockberger

CENSUS OF 1850 OF MURRAY COUNTY   179

Edward Scott
Philip Hefs
Chas. Hefs
John Parker
Nancy Carter—w
David Boles
L. G. Haskins
Nancy White—w
William Allen
William S. Harris
John Thomas
Thos. C. Wilson
John Harris
Asa Keith, Jr.
Robert Carter
Richard H. Stewart
Littleton J. Logan
Joseph Haskins
Jas. Everett
Wm. Rose
Jas. H. Huff
William McGaughey
Jacob Rose
William Rose
Rachel Carter
Moses A. Cop
Samuel McGaughey
McKinney Rose
Allen M. Rose
Thos. Lawrence
Henry Cowdon
Augustus J. Jones
Jocepher Miles
Davie Smith
Augustus W. Hutchin-
    son
Manly Nations
Benj. T. Lee
Joseph W. Gamblin
Chas. McKinney
Wm. Prestwood
John Burk
Benj. Ellis
Bacharah P. Ellis
W. E. Price
Thos. Eldridge
John Reed
Francel Anderson—w
Zachariah Aken
Samuel A. Torbet
Jeremiah Plumer
Robert C. Evans
Lewis Blanton
Moses Glaze
John Lancaster
Lewis Parker
Ann Rogers—w
Jane McCoy
John Mackey
Henry Ault
Jason Kerby
Daniel Boles
Joel M. Foster
    School Teacher)
Chas. B. McAlister
Anthony Heartsell
Rodman Deavers
Thos. Crow
Jas. Strawn
    (Bap. Minister)
Samuel Barien
Thos. Wiley
Jas. Henson
Wm. Neal
Hugh Burk
Elijah Harris
Robt. M. Williamson
Martin E. Eslinger

Joseph W. Blair
H. M. Ward
Thompson Barfield
Israel Nations
Chas. F. Ore
Robt. Brookshear
Jas. Garner
Bazel A. Johnson
Jacob Messamore
Jas. Hambleton
Jas. Elledge
Sarah Fulbright
Elias Hutchinson
John Hutchinson
Benj. Baxter
Jas. M. Williams
Josiah Turpin
Wm. M. Nance
Joseph Gamblin
M. M. Trammell
Winniafred Hargreve
Wm. Lamance
Robert McCamy
Thos. Seay
Jas. Conley
Isaac Rutherford
    (Meth. Minister)
John Rutherford
Reuben Truman
John Davis
Spencer Davis
Shannon Nelson
Noah Nelson
Hutson B. Parl
L. D. Parl
Levi M. Henderson
Hardy Pate
William I. Bowman
James Park
John McMullin
L. D. Buchanan
David Humphreys
David Hawkins
John Cahoun
Sam Rogers
Wm. Bailey
Wm. Hunter
Levi Timmons
John H. Hawkins
Sarah Arnold
Slex Nix
Thos. C. Christain
Geo. Black
Levi W. Hall
John Williamson
Joab Humphreys
John Davis
Isaac Roberts
Palmore Deam
John Freeland
Isaac M. W. Roberts
Wm. G. Field
Jade Carter
Aclep. Martin
Wm. Hall
John Morrison
Jesse Morrison
William M. McEntire
Amus Bright
Joseph A. McEntire
Nathan Miller
Joseph Black
Farish Carter
Thomas B. Simmons
Geo. W. Simmons
Jas. Swann
Joseph Swann
Elisha Randolph

Jas. S. Hampton
Wm. McGugey
Elizabeth Coley
Nathan Howard
Elias S. Raimes
Sam Rogers
Mary Kinknan
Wm. Bailey
James Black
George Black
Moses Black
Sam McJunkein
Elizabeth Dean—w
Daniel Taylor
John Naler
Wm. Connally
Jas. Couch
Wiley Bramblet
Thos. Connally
Joel T. Miller
John Connally
Thos. T. White
Alex Mauldin
Robt. S. Carr
John Timmons
Thos. G. Carr
Warren Fleming
Jas. T. Trent
Tabither A. Beaty—w
Jas. M. Kent
William Kent
Gulfred Martin
Alexander Martin
Henry Johnson
Moses Johnson
William Davis
Stangemon Johnson
William Williams
Elisha Tremble
    (Meth. Minister)
Sam Gentle
Wm. A. Ellis
Permelia Moore
Chas. Hames
Jas. Mallay
Edward I. Bunyard
John J. Smith
Sam Waldrup
Robt. Hawk
Elijah Rowland
Adam Bowlan
Jacob Rowland
Kinnay Johnson
Jesse Nations
Arthur Gilbert
Seaborn Read
Elias Jackson
John W. Strawn
James M. Oyen
Drewry R. Hall
Drewry F. Hall
Fenton J. Hall
Anderson Dover
William Martin
Allen Daves
Larkin C. Daves
William A. Daves
Henry S. Daves
Sam C. Fain
Isaac Benton
Jas. W. Denton
Ferdinand Bailey
L. B. Gazaway
William McBrayer
John McClure
Nancy McBrayer—w
Hugh McBrayer
Wiley Roberts

Jas. Gazaway
David C. L. Shaw
Mary Harden—w
Perry Harden
Wm. Montgomery
Thos. Montgomery
Levi Ellrod
John Ellrod
Sam Woody
Jeremiah Ellrod
Wm. W. Anderson
Wm. E. Wilson
David Jones
Andrew Hips
Enoch Humphrey
William Brown
Jacob Cox
John McCaslan
Joseph Tremble
John M. Jackson
Sarah Cox
S. R. Kelly
Alex Strickland
Matthew Thompson
Jas. Crane
Jas. Suggs
Sara Wright
Geo. H. Hogan
William W. Haskins
John Wilson
Calvin Wilson
John Wilson
Jehu Noblett
John A. Hogan
Geo. Peoples
John Baxter
Henry Cagle
Eli Cagle
Nancy Johnson
Sarah Smellwood
Elijah Whitemore
John B. Brunnely
Anderson Hemphill
Wm. B. McCrary
Robert Dillard
Isaac Edwards
Isaac Harris
Geo. Thomasson
Jas. Johnson
Dean W. Chase
Jas. Baxter
Robt. Smith
Thomas Christam
Christopher McCrary
Isaac Gilbert
Isaac Pledge
Asa Pledger
Hiram Montgomery
Ann K. James
John Davis
Ransom Gaines
Jacob Hegar
Adam Sanders
Geo. Gilbert
Elisber Lewis
William E. Wellborn
Edith Kimbro
Caroline Coley—w
Jesse Coley
Osburn B. Johnson
David S. Coley
Jas. Gilbert
Westley Johnson
Edmund Phillips
Joseph B. Hannes
Mansfield Ganis
Robt. Neal
Adam Neal

Thos. Elrod
Robt. J. Sanfield
Benj. F. Stanfield
Stephen White
Thos. Jackson
Wilson Fossett
Thos. S. Green, Jr.
Henry Yager
Lewis Bender
Fritz Bender
Chapleigh Denman
Sarah Wubey—w
Susan Adkisson
Jas. W. Neal
Harrison Cowley
Joel Barrett
Wm. C. Davis
Rebecca Rice
John McGrew
Benj. Mullinax
William Floyd
Ralph Jackson
John P. Johnson
Jas. Ketchem
Wm. Manis
John W. May
James May
Leonard Tinsley
Wm. James
Thomas Dickson
Henry Wilkinson
Joseph Meredith
Seaton East
Drewry East
Wm. Creekmore
Willis Morgan
William R. Morgan
Pleasant M. Routh
Jas. Yarberry
Jacob J. M. Peek
Benj. Orear
Daniel Boatright
Lewis B. Orear
Jas. Boatright
Joshua B. Boatright
Shadrach Ogilsby
William Horner
Henry McKinsy
John Stanton
Joshua Cahoon
M. T. Fullerton
John Stancel
James T. Tracy
Willis Carrell
Geo. McNabb
John Ferguson
John T. Holden
Jas. Johnson
Albert Varnell
Wiley Potts
Wiley Templeton
Sam H. Parker
Godfrey Ishell
Chas. Dawtry
Jas. H. Norton
Peter Mesamore
John T. Stewart
Dixon Naler
Stephen Hillis
Pleasant Rudel
Seaborn Spann
Geo. W. Prater
John Kanester
Jacob Bare
Jesse Davis
Jesse Hammontree
John Cithell
Melvin J. Smith

John Pettigrew
William Gamblen
Jesse Harris
Hillary Stoker
Jonas Fagala
Elizabeth Paul
Robt. Reed
Harris Hammontree
J. S. P. Powell
(M. E. P. M.)
Peter Greenfield
Sampson Williams
Geo. Whittle
Jas. N. Thatch
John B. Marston
Caswell Williams
Andrew H. Garner
Geo. Raines
John T. Mathis
Patrick Whittle
Carrack Whittle
David Roach
Caleb Johnson
Tarpley Jones
Hugh Montgomery
Allen Edgeman
Bailey Leverton
John Leverton
David McNair
Price McNair
Francis Williams
Andrew McDonald
Jas. Mathace
Thos. Thomasson
Geo. King
Franklin Hughes
James Longley
James Purkey
George Longley
Jordan Harris
Alex Williams
David Fagala
Theophlus Poham
Jacob Bolton
Jas. L. Hughs
Peter Bolton
Britain Williams
John Campbell
Rebecca A. Smith
Christopher Nations
Geo. W. Merk
Jno. Wigginton
Robt. McCrarry
Silas Leverton
Jas. H. Johnson
Allison T. Blair
John M. Combs
Jas. Merk
Silvanus Kanester
Hiram H. Blanton
Cleverly Phillips
Cleverly Hughes
Jesse Wade
Jas. Anderson
Raleigh Cupp
Thos. J. Burns
Galaway Pitner
Wm. F. Burns
Sam R. McCamy
Wm. Alexander
Iverson Triplett
Wilton Crouch
William Norton
Andrew Harris
Carter Harris
Bertley Crewell
Elijah Cagle
Wilson Norton

Census of 1850 of Murray County

John King
John Pitner
Elizabeth Singleton
Joseph Henderson
Wm. Naber
Dixon C. Naber
Jas. Fulks
Daniel Harrison
Amos Ford
Americus M. Ford
David May
John Couch
Robt. B. McGaugey
Richard Elder
Pinkney Elder
Thos. Cupp
Hugh McCord
Jacob Wilson
Wiley Smith
Colman C. Harwell
Louisa Harwell—w
John Moody
Jas. S. Moody
Collins Smith
George A. Jenkins
William Murray
Riley Horne
Jas. Perry
Hannah Perry
Sherwood Baity
Barty M. Smith
Benson Werldem
John W. Smith
Ales Smith
John Smith
James White
Henry Martin, Sr.
Martha E. Springfield
Gilbert Reeves
Francis A. Williams
Harden Marchand
Thos. B. Gurtman
Jas. Crow, Sr.
Jas. Crow, Jr.
Thomas Crow
Lemuel Hamby
Torrence Byran
John Elrod
Sam Burnes
Hugh McYord
Christopher Wilson
Nancy Byram—w
Jefferson Goins
Isaac Lamance
Wm. C. Wheat
John Bryant
Jas. A. Bryant
Mulberry Grier
Drewry Wheat
Wm. Campbell
Chas. Scoggin
Wm. Falkner
John E. Wilson
Clarence L. Cox
Sam Stafford
Benj. Stafford
David Waddell
Robt. B. Davis
William Saxon
John Page
Jacob Hedrick
William Hedrick
Jeremiah Crowson
Daniel Kalor
Wm. Harden
John Anderson
Joseph Anderson
A. S. Hansard

Ephraim Miller
L. D. Gordon
John Gordon
Joshua Gordon
Adam May
John Towns
Euclid Waterhouse
Thos. Hill
Wm. Phariss
Robt. Phariss
P. M. Pharis
Rachael Anderson
Elisha Coffee
L. E. B. Young
Lewis Montgomery
Elisha Thomas
D. E. Cole
Anderson Putnam
William Williamson
Wiley Jones
Abraham Graves
Stephen E. Lee
Voilus Bell
Absolem Ledford
John Cockburn
Leonard Corinth
Jacob Hollofield
Percy J. Cleary
Martin Harper
Alvin Logan
Benj. Francisco
Willman Muncucker
Jonathan Whitten
Jas. H. Barnet
W. K. Davis
John C. Head
J. P. Garner
McFalls Ledford
William Glass
James Ragan
William J. Ray
Sarah Lemons
Levina Wilson
S. B. Reed
Campbell Carver
Thos. Slipp
Jas. S. James
Jas. Horn
Nicholas Voiles
David Voils
Margaret Campbell
Chas. F. Cullenton
Rucker Mauldin
Franklin Carder
Nathan Barnes
John Brakebill
Pete Brakebill
John Voils
Andrew J. Martin
Peter Brakebill, Jr.
Eliza Goad
Humphrey Hembre
William H. Hembre
Peter Vangergrift
Hugh McDonald
Isaac Nichaelson
John Nichaelson
James Nichaelson
  (Bailiff)
J. D. Isenhower
Sam'l W. Dorgan
Ruth Campbell
John Pritchard
William N. White
Griffith Cummins
Woodford Whittle
James Julian
Elias Bates

Lawson Carpenter
Sam'l Cate
Jorden Goodess
Elizabeth Phillie
Joseph Rorex
John Palmer
Jacob Gullipy
Solomon Sanders
L. H. Davis
John W. Loggins
Peter Loggins
William Lackey
Mary Moseley—w
William Turk
William Worley
Hiram Couch
Elijah Coffee
Buford Wright
H. B. B. Huffsetter
Geo. O. Black
Edward Galt
Francis W. Galt
Wm. B. Harris
Wm. Strickland
Albert P. Early
Calvin Reynolds
Jas. Hampton
E. F. M. Long
Ephriam Ledfore
McLin Carr
Thos. L. Ray
Nancy Atchley
Isaac Gooden
Rollins Bodin
Thos. Hall
Durrett Mangumn
Benj. Griffin
John N. Harris
Elijah King
John Mattox
M. I. Murphey
Elijah Hickes
Wm. Garner
W. W. McCoy
Wm. Whitten
Joseph Thompson
Chas. W. Head
Henry Whisenant
Thos. Carver
John Harris
Jacob McManus
Jacob Everett
Wm. Johnson
Joseph H. Manus
John Morelock
Joseph Jarrett, Jr.
Joseph Jarrett, Sr.
Allen Arnold
Sam'l B. Blair
Jas. K. Payte
John W. Stanton
William Pullian
A. L. Hitson
John M. Lance
Wm. A. Chaffin
Mary Brown—w
Lemuel Brown
Geo. Cox
John Jarrett
Dan'l White
Jas. Pate
John V. Short
John Duncane
Robert Duncan
Giddathy Cook
Mary Earnest—w
Thos. Whitten
Hiram Reese

HISTORY OF WHITFIELD COUNTY

Shadrach Cash
Geo. W. Clark
Andrew J. Barnett
Nathaniel Moreland
Lilbern Grigsby
Carrady Cooper
Benj. F. Smith
Frederick Short
Wm. Richardson
Elias H. Berry
Marcus L. Barnett
Rebecca Dunn
John Palmer
Thos. Scoggin
Isaac Cook
Mary Wayne
Wm. Prince
Rufus McClelland
Caroline Glover
Demay Rice
Fila Oliver
Barnard Poteet
Joseph Turner
Caswell Shields
Solomon Fouts
Sarah Foutt
Noah L. Foutt
Geo. A. Coxey
John Moore
Wm. Lowrey
Geo. Watson
Elizabeth Carter
William A. Raines
Eadon White
Whittain White
Shadrach Inman
Jonathan Lasater
Robt. Harris
Mack Mann
Joel Waggoner
Isaac Groves
John McClung
John Johnson
Samuel Meroney
Abraham Hendrix
Manly Johnson
John Glatson
Robt. Pendergraft
Robt. McCanis
Allen Dunn
Jacob Graves
Alexander McCamy
John S. Lee
Wm. Galt
Leonard Cline
Jonathan Parsons
Chas. Adair
William Sisk
Collin McDoland
Robert Cochran
Thomas Henry
William McDonald
Edward Adair
John Adair
Benj. F. Adair
Nathan Harrison
Clark Wright
John C. Knotte
Paulhill Thompson
William Terry
Levi Brotherton
Wm. Rogers
David Westfield
Nathan Harrison
Joseph Moreland
William Cleveland
David F. Mooney
Geo. Edmonson

Izaia Phipps
John Beaver
Wm. Smith
William Hassler
John Latch
Abner Phipps
Philip Swanson
Benj. Burgin
Ranson Hall
Wiley Ledbetter
Simpson Barefield
Wm. Ellard
Ales McDonald
Mary Latch—w
John King
Thos. Duckett
Julius Bales
Cornelius Anderson
Wm. Bales
Madison Bales
Francis Queen
Elizabeth Chatham
Hughs Queen
Jas. Angell
Gideon Jackson
John Bates
Rice B. Bates
John Jackson
Uriah H. Duncan
John Johnson
Joseph Coker
Sam W. Connally
Westley Sullivan
Isaac Roberts
Jacob Matthews
Wm. Walker
Palmer Deam
Joseph Slipp
Ransom Turner
Ezekiel Stafford
Roland Wimpey
Jackson Fincer
Benj. Willbanks
Hugh Springfield
Benson Gordon
Reuben Emery
Woody Sullivan
Joseph J. Richardson
Henry J. Johnson
Wm. Payne
William B. Keith
Thos. Payne
Sam'l Keith
Dan'l H. Burgin
Wm. Roads
Jas. Harkins
Nancy Harkins—w
Jane Mansfield—w
Lewis Terry
Thos. Carder
Abner Chastain
Philip Swanson
Alex Black
Madison Lotch
Jas. Black
Thos. Yearwood
John W. Latch
William P. Swanson
Luke B. Strawn
Chas. W. Keith
Wm. Hogue
Jas. Strawn
Wm. Hougue
Flemon Pace
Wm. Latch
Wm. A. Swanson
Jas. Stewart
Barnabus Steward

Jesse Jackson
Harrison Johnson
Joseph Terry
Abel Johnson
Isham B. Mealer
Jas. McFarlin
Alex Campbell
Isaac M. Newton
Dan'l C. W. Higginbotham
Rufus Christian
Duncan Terry
Harton Sumney
Mores Yates
David Duncan
Geo. Rollins
Wm. Willbanks
Neilson Groves
John W. Leonard
Richard Jenkins
Isaac T. Leonard
Wm. Jackson
Wm. Peoples
Elias F. Peoples
Wm. C. Harrison
Thos. Officer
Jas. D. Vann
Jesse Thompson
Seaborn Youngblood
Isaac Gooden
Mores W. Robertson
Stephen Butterworth
Warren G. Bell
Benj. Loughridge
John H. Oneill
Joseph Smith
Robt. McCliver
Noah Longley
Jas. L. McEntire
Johnson Clement
Martin Keith
Robert Hitt
Chileon Pachare
Alfred Davis
Sam'l Waddle
Isaac Ballew
Thos. Banks
L. B. Jackson
Thos. W. Jackson
Ralph Jackson
Jesse Gilreath
Joel Henry
Chalap Davis
Benj. Carpenter
L. P. Carpenter
Geo. Ray
Wm. T. Tyson
John G. Hammock
Barney Freeman
Caleb Holand
Asberry Edwards
Jeremiah Harrison
William Campbell
Jasper Grier
Jas. M. Boatright
John D. Orr
Jas. S. Teasley
Wm. Wellborn
Amy Bridges—w
Geo. A. Tilley
Jas. Holder
Floyd Farrington
John Hutson
Minnyard W. Harris
Jesse Fulyum
Alexander Sisk
Turner Floyd
Wm. Garner

CENSUS OF 1850 OF MURRAY COUNTY 183

Silas Stovall
Girrard Johnson
Alexander Strickland
John Cromby
Isaac McLain
Benj. West
John J. Robertson
Cornelius Patterson
John W. Beck
Wm. A. Beck
Mack Blacke
Samuel Money
Elias D. Lewis
B. J. Thompson
Jas. Kenny, Sr.
John Gamble
Loisa Carden—w
Job Tye
Geo. McCulloch
Sam'l Tye
Gibson Hix
John S. Moore
Jas. F. Davis
Jesse Holbrook
Michael O'Conner
Clemmas Quillian
Thos. Cleveland
Lewis Edmondson
Wm. C. Edmondson
Willis Waldrup
John J. Robins
J. B. Robins
Sam'l H. Robins
Mary Turner
Vinyard Harris
R. R. Keith
G. N. Harris
Isaac Jernigan
John Buster
John Fulkes
Wm. Gardner
Wiley Childers
Abraham Burger
Jas. Fox
John S. Childers
Matthew Black
John Crumly
Elinder Crumly
Thos. Bagby
Albert G. Vining
Nelson Ball
Geo. W. Howard
Joshua Yates
Nathan Ellis
Benj. Partain
Minnyard Harris
Geo. C. McLane
Thos. Donaldson
Eliza J. Sain
Allen Officer
Sarah Ables
Wm. E. Cleveland
Susan Calaway
Jas. A. Chandler
Nathaniel McGhee
John H. Miller
Frances Wright
Webster Coffee
Dan'l Ballew
John C. Anderson
William E. Cleveland
Jas. Helton
Daniel Smith
William Edwards
Denson M. Lewis
Sam'l Miller
Catherine Smith
Henry Wrinkle

John Wrinkle
Robt. Mann
Patrick Burdon
Hugh Clement
Dan'l Ballew
Edward Harris
Jonathan Rogers
Ransom Johnson
Moses Neal
Jasper Stone
Oliver Crawford
Daniel Martin
Osborne Love
Caswell Johnson
John Love
Wm. B. Gass
Kenney Pate
Jess Bookout
Elizabeth Edwards
John Black
Chas. Reed
Elihu Coward
John Ellis
Geo. W. Ellis
Moses Ellis
Mahala Ellis
Chas. Lane
John Hill
Alphe Buttiff
Morgan Hampton
David Davis
John Miller
Benj. Miller
John Malone
Martha F. Anglin—w
Joshua T. Steel
Jas. Brewer
Augustus Williams
Henry Kinnamman (M. D.)
John Miller
David Miller
Floyd Steward
Doctor B. Malone
Andrew Brock
Nathaniel Beauchamp
J. B. Copelin
Almarine E. Vandever
B. T. Mercier
Caleb Taylor
John Taylor
Isaac Brock
Wm. Miller
John H. Harper
Thos. Haly
David Lutz
J. F. McCutchun
G. H. Stephenson
Wm. M. Pasley
Smith Jones
Jesse Miller
A. B. Echols
Wm. Cooper
Washington Head
John Shipp
Abel Greeson
Abern Jester
B. F. Freeman
Jas. Russell
John T. Warren
Strawberry Reaves
Alfred Baringer
John Moore
Thos. Copelin
Richard Wyley
S. W. Wyley
Jas. B. Crumly
Henry M. Crumly

Wm. W. Kilpatrick
Blair R. Mayse
Precious Blackburn
Josiah Sisk
Sion Wheat
John A. Everett
Alfred Henry
Archibald Gilmer
Bertrand Zachary
Isaih Davis
John Mackey
Chas. Johnson
Wm. A. Spence
Y. F. W. Tate
P. O. Pittman
Jas. Eubanks
Wm. P. Eubanks
Richard Sly
Joseph Holcombe
Geo. Bandy
A. J. Wells
Jesse N. Miller
Henry Dunn
Sam'l Hollinway
Jame Standric
Simpson C. Wingo
John Vanderford
Elizabeth Moneyham
James Stone
Alven Eubanks
Joseph Campbell
Arthur George
Thaddeus Owen
Jesse K. Widener
George Sailors
Andrew Widener
Willey Massengill
Jas. McNeal
Sarah Hughey—w
Austin P. Tidwell
Thos. Nations
James B. Ruker
Matthew Patrick
Wm. B. Holcombe
John Hughey
Sam'l Holcomb
Absolem J. Holcomb
Elias Hughey
Kelley Pepper
John Faith
Nany Faith
Richard Helton
John J. Bartlett
Nathaniel Strickland
Wm. Sloan
Henry Strockland
Jonathan McLane
Jas. Masters
John Masters
Nathaniel W. Phillips
Eli Cannon
Harrison Rogers
John O. Nean
Geo. A. Shields
M. H. Pitman
Wiley Bartett
William Redwine
Thos. Jones
Anthony Smith
Henry Wilson
Peter Fright
Marcus Morrison
John Jones
Littleton Widener
Gideon Jackson
P. L. Smith
Isaac N. Buckner
Sam'l Matthews

Harrison P. Timms
John Hayes
M. H. Luffman
Jeremiah Elrod
James M. Wilson
Isabella Hicks—w
Absalom Wright
Wm. F. Wacarer
LaFayette Williamson
James Jones
Lavina Pendlam
Job S. Swift
Abraham E. Widener
Moses Perry Widener
Louisa Couch—w
Archibald Sloan
John Sloan
Wm. McAbee
Waddy Thomas
Elijah Horn
John F. Green
Giles Widener
Williamson Gaddy
Hiran Widener
Jas. Hite
Francis M. Widener
Moses Widener
John Monroe
William Sisk
John H. Stewart
Thos. O. Auston
  (Post M.)
Pleasant E. Barber
John Worthy
Thos. Johnson
Jas. M. Creekmore
F. M. Upton
L. B. Hunt
John Silk, Sr.
John Sisk, Jr.
Archibald Eaves

Wm. Eaves
B. H. Vaughn
Martha Echols
Thos. Norton
Wm. A. Monroe
Archibold Offut
Jethro O'Shields
Wm. McMilion
Luch Tidwell
Elbert Autry
Geo. W. Collins
Catherine Collins—w
John W. Smith
Jeffrey Pittman
B. F. Miller
Wm. Bownsan, Sr.
John Warren
Ellis Sloan
Mountain H. Geeson
Christopher Wheeler
Thos. B. Wade
Aniss Cox
J. B. Sloan
Sherwood Adams
Pesley Huff
Southern Leaptrott
Pinkney F. Howell
Wiley Jones
Wiley Hite
Dan'l Smart
Austin Henderson
Thos. Haney
John M. Wright
James Morgan
James R. Morris
William Wright
Milton Worthy
Joseph B. Robertson
Chas. Thompson
  (Bap. Minister)
Alfred Hicks

Jesse Millirons
Alfred Collum
David Delk
John Howard
Ann Dupree—w
Jas. McElrath
Jesse Jones
Wm. B. McGuire
Jas. Montgomery
John T. Holdron
Paschal Wilson
Oswell Wilson
Jas. Blackwell
Henderson Hopkins
William W. Green
Oliver Cowart
David Osborn
Richard R. Couch
William Shipp
Vann Tate
Thomas Owen
Jas. Landers
Jas. Robertson
Benj. W. Robertson
Orman L. Morgan
Asa Keith
Ezekiel Norris
John Brock
Isham C. King
Jas. Jones
William Jones
J. M. Williams
W. M. Stone
Michael Redwine
Sam'l D. King
John Kilpatric
Nicholas Masters
B. J. Johnson
John Waeaser
Peter Whisonant
James McEntire

Whitfield County, Georgia
(OFFICERS)

House Bill, No. 64, providing for a new county in the galaxy of counties of Georgia, was introduced and passed at the regular session, 1851, of the General Assembly of Georgia, and the following is a synopsis of the passage of the bill, and the establishment of the county:

In the Senate: Read first time December 9, 1851; read second time December 15, 1851; read third time and passed December 24, 1851.

At this time James A. Merriwether was Speaker of the House, and Thaddeus Sturgis was Clerk; Andrew J. Miller was President of the Senate, and Luther I. Glenn was Secretary.

Honorable Howell Cobb, as Governor, approved the Bill December 30, 1851.

On roll call in the House December 8, 1851, House Journal, 1851, Page 287, at 3:00 o'clock, P. M., the bill received fifty-three years and fifty-one days, S. S. Bailey, representative from Murray county, voting for the passage of the Bill.

In the Senate, Senate Journal, 1851, Page 314, the Bill received fourteen votes favoring its passage, and twelve votes in opposition, on Wednesday, December 24, 1851, when it was passed.

OFFICERS OF WHITFIELD COUNTY

The word: "Whitfield" was inserted in the bill at the last moment, as appears in the following part of the bill:

"Be it enacted: That the new county described in the first Section of this Act, shall be known by the name of WHITFIELD, and be attached to the Cherokee Judicial Circuit."

The new county was taken largely from Murray county with a small strip on the western side carved from Walker county.

To Whitfield, an associate of the Wesleys, is attributed the honor of having the county named for him.

Whitfield county is located just south of the 35th parallel, north latitude; 85th degree, west longitude; has an average altitude of about seven hundred feet, and an area of two hundred eighty-one square miles.

The first election for county officers was held in January, 1852.

The first settlers of Whitfield county were of the purest Anglo-Saxon blood, many of whom came here from North Carolina.

Whitfield county has made its reasonable contribution to the body politic, and, practically without exception, its officers and representatives have acquitted themselves as persons who literally regarded public office as being a public trust.

The following lists contain the names of those who have served Whitfield county, and, while there may be some omissions, in the whole the roster may be regarded as approximately correct.

"He's true to God who's true to man."

Originally, there were not so many districts, but in 1933, the following are the voting precincts and militia districts, given by name and number:

Dalton district, 872nd District G. M., vote at Dalton; Cohutta, 1278th District G. M., vote at Cohutta; Upper Tenth, 1294th District G. M., vote at Tucker's school; Varnell, 628th District G. M., vote at Varnell; Lower Tenth, 629th District G. M., vote at Deep Springs; Tunnel Hill, 1049th District G. M., vote at Tunnel Hill; Ninth, 631st District G. M., vote at Dawnville; Fincher, 1305th District G. M., vote at Keith's Mill; Mill Creek, 1233rd District G. M., vote at Mill Creek; Rocky Face, 1433rd District G. M., vote at Rocky Face; Trickum, 863rd District G. M., vote at McCutchen; Carbondale, 1298th District G. M., vote at Carbondale; Tilton, 627th District G. M., vote at Tilton.

Whitfield county is located in the following divisions: Seventh Congressional District; Forty-third State Senatorial District; Cherokee State Judicial Circuit; Northern District of Georgia, Rome Division, United States District Court.

The following have served as congressmen from this district since the creation of Whitfield county:

Thomas C. Hackett	William H. Felton
John H. Lumpkin	Judson C. Clements
Augustus R. Wright	John W. Maddox
John W. H. Underwood	Gordon Lee
Pierce M. B. Young	Malcolm C. Tarver

JUDGES SUPERIOR COURT
Cherokee Circuit

1832-35	John W. Hooper	1849-50	John W. Hooper
1835-38	Owen Kenan	1850-53	John H. Lumpkin
1838-42	Turner H. Trippe	1853-59	Turner H. Trippe
1842-43	Geo. D. Anderson	1859-60	Leander W. Crook
1843	John A. Jones	1861-66	Dawson A. Walker*
1843-49	Augustus R. Wright	1866-68	James Milner

*Resigned.

186 HISTORY OF WHITFIELD COUNTY

1868-72	Josiah R. Parrott	1889-97	Thomas W. Milner
1872-81	C. D. McCutchen	1897-1917	A. W. Fite
1881-88	Joel C. Fain*	1917-27	Malcolm C. Tarver
1888-89	Sam P. Maddox	1927	Claude C. Pittman

JUSTICES OF THE INFERIOR COURT WHITFIELD COUNTY
Created December 30, 1851

John Hamilton	2/ 6/1852—1/ 8/1853
Winston Gordon	2/ 6/1852—1/ 8/1853
Francis W. McCurdy	2/ 6/1852
James Robinson (Robison)	2/ 6/1852—1/ 8/1853
Hughs (Hughes) Burk	2/ 6/1852—1/ 8/1853
Edward H. Edwards	9/18/1852—1/ 8/1853
Archibald Sloan	1/ 8/1852—1/12/1857
Edward H. Edwards	1/ 8/1853—1/12/1857
Francis W. McCurdy	1/ 8/1853—1/12/1857
John Hamilton	1/ 8/1853— 1854*
Philip Minis	1/ 8/1853— 1854
Harrison Rogers	1/24/1854—1/12/1857
Joshua Harlan	8/10/1854—1/12/1857
William Hammond	1/12/1857—1/10/1861
Ethelred J. Tarver	1/12/1857—1/10/1861
James Green	1/12/1857—1/10/1861
William J. Underwood	1/12/1857—1/10/1861
William P. Chester	1/12/1857—1/10/1861
William J. Underwood	1/10/1861
F. B. Morris	1/10/1861
Thomas C. Davis	1/10/1861
W. T. Campbell	1/10/1861
Baxter B. Brown	1/10/1861
Lawrence W. Earnest	2/17/1864—1/23/1865
Baxter B. Brown	1/23/1865—1/23/1868
L. W. Earnest	1/23/65
J. H. King	1/23/65
S. B. Sloan	1/23/65
T. A. Jackson	1/23/65— 9/ 8/66
W. J. Underwood	9/ 8/66

JUDGES CITY COURT OF DALTON

1905-09	J. A. Longley	1913-17	G. G. Glenn
1909-13	G. G. Glenn	1917-21	G. G. Glenn

STATE SENATORS REPRESENTING WHITFIELD COUNTY

1853-54	S. E. Bailey	1886-87	James A. McKamy
1855-56	C. B. Wellborn	1888-89	Samuel E. Fields*
1857-58	Smith Treadwell	1889	Paul B. Trammell
1859-60	Wm. R. Moore	1890-91	James M. Harlan
1861-62	J. M. Jackson	1892-93	E. W. Rembert
1863-65	C. D. McCutchen	1894-95	Trammell Starr
1865-66	J. A. W. Johnson	1896-97	O. N. Starr
1868-70	Joel C. Fain	1898-99	C. N. King
1871-72	L. N. Trammell	1900-01	B. Z. Herndon
1873-74	L. N. Trammell	1902	W. P. Dodd**
1875-76	R. E. Wilson	1903-04	O. N. Starr
1877	R. E. Wilson	1905-06	C. N. King
1878-79	Joel C. Fain	1907-08	W. C. Martin
1880-81	S. G. Treadwell	1909-10	Logan R. Pitts
1882-83	Thos. R. Jones	1911-12	C. T. Owens
1884-85	W. R. Rankin	1913-14	M. C. Tarver

*Died 1888.
**Resigned.

OFFICERS OF WHITFIELD COUNTY 187

1915-16	T. W. Harbin	1925-26	W. M. Sapp
1917-18	E. H. Beck	1927-28	A. B. David
1919-20	George G. Glenn	1929-30	V. C. Pickering
1921-22	A. B. David	1931-32	Buell Stark
1923-24	Thos. E. Green	1933-34	J. H. Paschal

WHITFIELD COUNTY'S REPRESENTATIVES

1853-54	F. W. McCurdy	1892-93	Riley Giddens***
1855-56	R. H. Sapp	1894-95	J. A. Longley
1857-58	Dickinson Taliaferro	1896-97	S. E. Berry
1859-60	Chas. E. Broyles	1898-99	Will A. Black
1861-62	W. J. Underwood	1900-01	W. H. C. Freeman
1862	John Thomas	1902-03	Geo. G. Glenn
1863-64	W. J. Underwood	1905-06	W. W. Seymore
1864	T. F. B. Jackson	1914	George G. Glenn
1865-66	J. A. Glenn	1909-10	M. C. Tarver
1866	M. P. Quillian	1911-12	M. C. Tarver
1868-69	I. E. Shumate	1913-14	S. E. Berry****
1871-72	C. J. Emerson	1914	George G. Glenn
1873-74	J. Rodgers	1915-16	N. A. Bradford
1875-76	J. P. Clements	1917-18	Dennis Barrett
1877	W. C. Richardson	1919-20	N. A. Bradford
1878-79	J. A. R. Hanks	1921-22	N. A. Bradford****
1880-81	C. E. Broyles	1922	W. M. Sapp***
1882-83	C. E. Broyles	1923-24	W. M. Sapp
1884-85	B. Z. Herndon	1925-26	Buell Stark
1886-87	Wm. C. Glenn	1927-30	O. R. Hardin
1888-89	Wm. C. Glenn	1933	Clarence Keown
1890-91	P. B. Trammell*	1934	Kelly McCutchen
1892-93	P. B. Trammell**		

ORDINARIES

1852-56	William Gordon	1889	J. C. Norton
1856-59	Winston Gordon	1893	Joseph Bogle
1859	Jesse P. Freeman	1912	Harlan J. Wood
1868	Henry Brooker	1925-28	J. C. Black
1873	William J. Underwood	1929-32	O. M. Stacy
1885	J. P. Freeman	1933	J. C. Brooker

SOLICITORS GENERAL SUPERIOR COURT, CHEROKEE CIRCUIT

1832-35	William Ezzard	1881-88	J. W. Harris*
1935-41	Henry L. Sims	1888-97	A. W. Fite
1841	John H. Lumpkin	1897-1909	S. P. Maddox
1841-43	Thomas C. Hackett	1909-15	T. C. Milner
1843-47	Richard Jones	1913-15	S. P. Maddox
1847-55	John J. Word	1915-24	Joseph M. Lang
1855-61	James C. Longstreet	1925-27	C. C. Pittman
1868-72	Charles E. Broyles*	1927	J. C. Mitchell
1872-81	A. T. Hackett*		

CITY COURT OF DALTON SOLICITORS

1909-13	F. K. McCutchen	1917-21	F. K. McCutchen
1913-17	F. K. McCutchen		

SHERIFFS OF WHITFIELD COUNTY

1852-54	Frederick Cox	1862-64	D. W. Mitchell
1854-56	John L. Martin	1866-67	W. L. Kincannon
1856-58	Joseph T. B. Jackson	1866-67	J. W. Longley
1858-60	Moses Collins	1867	W. W. West
1860	Frederick Cox	1868	D. A. Mitchell

*Speaker Pro Tem.
**First Session.
***Second Session.
****Died in office.

---

*Resigned.

History of Whitfield County

1871	Felix G. Horne	1902	J. M. Johnson
1873	A. P. Roberts	1908	J. H. Gilbert
1879	Frederick Cox	1912	Thos. R. Glenn
1883	Sampson D. Poarch	1914	Charley Connally
1889	S. A. Frazier	1920	T. N. Peeples
1895	J. M. Johnson	1925-28	W. C. Cleckler
1900	Lake Quillian	1929	J. T. Bryant

WHITFIELD INFERIOR COURT CLERKS

1852	Britton C. Tyler	1860	Samuel B. Sloan
1856	Agrippa P. Roberts	1866	K. McDonald
	(Office Abolished)		

WHITFIELD SUPERIOR COURT CLERKS

1852	John W. Anderson	1887	D. Sholl
1860	L. W. Earnest	1898	H. A. Russell
1862	J. E. Cox	1900	W. M. Sapp
1864	T. H. Pitner	1920	C. L. Isbill*
1868	T. K. McDonald	1924	Mrs. Belle Isbill**
1871	Henry C. Hamilton	1925	M. Westbrook

CLERK CITY COURT OF DALTON

1905	W. M. Sapp

WHITFIELD COUNTY TAX RECEIVERS

1852-53	Clement Quillian	1879	H. A. Wrench
1855-56	Joseph T. Williams	1881	W. H. Wilson
1856-58	John J. Gilbert	1885	Joseph Bogle
1858	Hugh McDonald	1887	L. W. Thomason
1859	John J. Gilbert	1902	William Thompson
1860	James Roberts	1906	R. A. Williams
1862	Timothy Ford	1910	W. A. Broadrick
1864	A. J. Weaver	1916	C. C. Maples
1868	T. O. Shayess	1919	Charley Deck
1871	John Rollins	1924	John Hill
1873	Jesse P. Freeman	1933	C. W. Watters

WHITFIELD COUNTY TAX COLLECTORS

1852	Joseph Ford	1893	D. W. Mitchell
1854	William Sally	1898	T. J. Bryant
1855	Thos. G. Morgan	1904	B. R. Bowen
1858	Timothy Ford	1906	H. D. Keith
1868	James Morgan	1910	J. H. Smith
1871	Richard N. Varnell	1912	J. T. Nichols
1873	Robert Varnell	1916	J. M. Johnson
1875	A. J. Barnett	1918	A. E. White
1879	Warren R. Davis	1920	Wayland Calloway
1881	J. P. Freeman	1925	Frank Rollins
1885	J. W. Fincher	1929	John Sansom
1891	J. C. Head		

WHITFIELD COUNTY TREASURERS

1860	L. W. Earnest	1887	L. W. Barrett
1862	R. L. Cook	1893	L. H. Calloway
1864	J. P. Love	1900	J. S. Richardson
1866	M. R. Bunner	1902	C. S. Carey
1871	Warren Davis	1908	R. S. Green
1875	L. W. Barrett	1910	A. J. Calhoun
1877	R. P. O'Neil	1912	T. D. Ridley*
1879	W. S. Murray	1912	Sam Thomas
1881	Newt Wood	1914	J. T. Coker
1883	M. V. Wood		(Office Abolished)

*Died in office.
**By appointment.

*Served five months.

OFFICERS OF WHITFIELD COUNTY

WHITFIELD COUNTY SURVEYORS

1852	E. J. Tarver	1873	Thomas Hamilton
1854	William B. Malone	1875	E. J. Tarver
1856	Elijah King	1877	Samuel E. Street
1858	James H. Hamilton	1881	James H. Hamilton*
1860	J. H. Bitting	1883	W. H. Boyd
1862	E. J. Tarver	1885	Fred W. Moore
1864	R. D. Coxe	1896	H. C. Hamilton
1866	John Bitting	1912	Peck Worthy
1868	Thomas Hamilton	1920	Robt. E. Smith

WHITFIELD COUNTY CORONERS

1852	Asa Keith	1896	W. A. Black
1862	James Holland	1898	Lake Quillian
1864	A. J. Holder	1900	J. M. Rudolph
1871	S. M. Barrett	1904	J. R. Tarver
1873	Richard Warren	1912	J. A. Ault
1875	A. L. Sutherland	1916	T. N. Peeples
1877	Richard Warren	1920	A. W. Hill
1879	A. L. Sutherland	1925	J. A. Ault
1887	T. W. Chastain	1932	S. R. Brooke**
1889	John R. Tarver	1933	S. F. Armstrong
1895	B. B. Brown		

SUPERINTENDENTS OF COUNTY SCHOOLS

1886-1904	Martin P. Berry	1920-1924	J. D. Field
1904-1917	Judson C. Sapp	1925-1928	Miss Phoebe Broadrick
1917-1918	James J. Copeland	1929	Alvin White

JUSTICES OF THE PEACE AND NOTARIES PUBLIC AND JUSTICES OF THE PEACE

Carbondale
(1298th District G.M.)

	J. P.		J. P. and N. P.
1877-81	S. W. Adams	1868	A. J. Barnett
1885-97	Silas W. Mote	1878-80	S. W. Mote
1893	John B. Yaeger	1881	W. L. Thomason
1893	William A. Davis	1881-85	Leander W. Thomason
1899	G. W. Redwine	1887	Paul B. Trammell
1900	H. S. Huston	1891-1915	Newton A. Bradford
1905	W. T. Masters	1922	William F. Thacker
1909-13	H. T. Redwine		
1917	S. A. Borders		
1918-21	J. H. Bowman		
1926	J. W. Godfrey		

Cohutta
(1278th District G.M.)

	J. P.		J. P. and N. P.
1876-77	W. H. Wilson	1876	John W. Jones
1881	W. M. Lowry	1877	George D. Hoskins
1883	Samuel Reed	1879-87	J. G. W. Mills
1885	W. M. Chambers	1891-1903	W. H. Wilson
1889	F. A. Rauschenberg	1907-24	J. F. Wilson
1890	John W. Creswell	1927	G. L. Groover
1893-05	J. G. W. Mills	1933	J. C. Dulin
1906-09	J. C. Parrott		
1907	T. L. Williamson		
1913-21	W. S. Johnson		
1924	C. W. Wheeler		
1933	H. H. Bridges		

*Appointed March 23, 1881.
**Appointed to succeed A. W. Hill, Deceased.

Dalton
(872nd District G.M.)

J. P.

1856	Vredenburg Thompson
1857	Vredenburg Thompson
1857	Jesse P. Freeman
1858	Wesley H. Stansell
1861	W. J. Walls
1861	V. Thompson
1874	John M. Jones
1866-69	John P. Love
1866	Thomas Renfroe
1869	Jesse A. Glenn
1873	J. F. Trevitt
1877	H. L. Sams, Sr.
1885-93	J. A. Longley
1897	W. T. Lowry
1900-17	S. B. Felker
1919	T. C. McBryde
1921	T. J. Bryant

N. P. and J. P.

1868	Robert Battey
1872-76	Baxter B. Brown
1879-81	Jesse P. Freeman
1881	J. F. Trevitt
1885-89	J. A. R. Hanks
1892	Robert H. Baker
1896-1914	A. P. Roberts
1917-21	R. A. Williams
1925	Chas. Deck.
1929	J. R. Whitener

Fincher
(1305th District G.M.)

J. P.

1881	J. M. Fincher
1885	S. A. Keith
1888	William W. West
1889	Josiah Perkins
1893	James Britton
1897	T. T. Smith
1905	Terrell T. Smith
1909	T. T. Smith
1913-17	J. A. Britton
1921	W. E. Caldwell
1926	L. E. Hollinger
1926	J. T. Fincher
1930	Jesse Brock

N. P. and J. P.

1878	Jesse C. Fincher
1879-91	Henry F. Turner
1895-1904	R. A. Williams
1907-18	R. B. Hill

Lower Tenth
(629th District G.M.)

J. P.

1853	Joseph Garner
1853	Martin P. Berry
1854	Raleigh Cupp
1857	Hugh McDonald
1857	Raleigh Cupp
1858	William Cole
1861	E. S. Dean
1861	J. P. Anderson
1866-89	C. R. McAllister
1873	John H. Hackney
1877	J. C. Wilson
1877	E. Creekmore
1881	N. B. Mitchell
1882	John Farmer
1885	J. W. McAllister
1889	W. H. Bryant
1893	W. H. Bryant
1897-1901	Samuel H. Routh
1905	M. H. Hackney
1909	W. C. Crow
1913-21	E. F. Jarrett
1926	J. L. Morgan
1933	O. E. Crow

N. P. and J. P.

1872-76	Raleigh Cupp
1881-96	Daniel L. Cline
1900	J. N. Crow
1901	Jeff D. Brackett

OFFICERS OF WHITFIELD COUNTY   191

Mill Creek
(1233rd District G.M.)

J. P.
1861	William J. Love
1861	G. W. L. Freeman
1866	A. Harris
1866	R. Lanier
1869-71	Robert S. Carr
1873	J. J. Williams
1876-77	R. S. Carr
1881	Francis M. Babb
1885-89	R. S. Carr
1893-1901	B. C. Chase
1905-09	M. C. Kenemer
1913-15	E. W. Babb
1921	W. M. Dobson

N. P. and J. P.
1872-73	Thomas King
1873	Philip E. A. Cox
1877-80	Edwin C. Chapman
1880	Elisha Lowry
1885-97	Francis M. Babb
1889	James E. Sisk
1892	David S. Hall
1901	George W. Sisk
1901	Neeham Griffin
1909	W. M. Dobson
1913-21	R. A. Truelove

Ninth
(631st District G.M.)

J. P.
1853	Sherwood W. Battey
1853-57	William East
1857-61	Benjamin Wiggins
1861	R. H. Fraker
1869	E. T. King
1872-81	W. M. McNabb
1885	R. M. Tarver
1889	A. M. Richardson
1893-97	W. M. McNabb
1900	W. E. Dawn
1905-17	J. H. Gilbert
1909	R. B. Palmer
1913	Sam Hair
1921	Sam King
1930	W. C. Palmer

N. P. and J. P.
1872	H. H. Green
1872-76	John R. Tarver
1876	J. A. Maddox
1876-88	J. L. Farnsworth
1880-82	N. N. Davis
1882-85	Alexander S. Dean
1886-90	William McNabb
1888-93	David W. Mitchell
1893	R. H. McHan
1895-99	R. M. Tarver
1903-11	R. M. Tarver
1915-17	Parker Warmack
1917	H. F. Hair
1918-22	A. D. Strickland

Rocky Face
(1433rd District G.M.)

J. P.
1890-97	R. W. Ault
1893-94	W. W. Calloway
1897-1900	R. W. Ault
1905	John Kenemer
1909-11	J. J. Wood
1911-21	J. F. Roberson
1924	O. P. Wood
1926	H. H. Russell

N. P. and J. P.
1868	Hamilton Young
1891-99	W. N. Russell
1895-1901	W. B. Head
1903-08	Harlan J. Wood
1909	T. D. Bates
1914	Grover C. Roach
1916	I. S. Morgan

Tilton
(627th District G.M.)

J. P.
1853	M. C. Martin
1853	Robert S. Smith
1856	Sherwood Adams
1857	Jachariah N. Davis
1857	Z. N. Davis
1857	John D. Farrow
1859-61	Joseph J. Martin
1861	W. D. Hancock
1865	S. W. Adams
1865	J. R. P. Cudd
1866	J. J. Martin
1866	John Faith
1869	Wm. W. Sebastain
1873	S. W. Adams
1877-81	A. J. Green
1885	John S. Rollins
1889-97	B. B. Turner
1900-03	J. W. Owens
1905-13	B. B. Turner
1917-21	John L. Henton
1922	M. L. Pinson

N. P. and J. P.
1872	John R. Tarver
1872-80	H. H. Greene
1882	F. Mc. F. Moore
1886-90	Frank Moore
1890-98	F. W. Elrod
1902-06	John D. Townsend
1907-14	Robert B. Maynard
1914-18	J. S. Parker
1922	M. L. Pinson

Trickum
(863rd District G.M.)

J. P.

1854	Joseph Dobson
1854-7-89	James L. Capehart
1857-61	John W. Cain
1861-73	Joseph Rodgers
1866	James T. Deck
1869	George W. Green
1881	Lewis G. Crawford
1877	S. M. Easley
1885	M. A. Reed
1893	A. M. Tate
1897-10-21	W. C. Pangle
1900	E. D. McArthur
1905-09	W. L. Keown
1913	J. G. Tate
1925	A. M. Reed

N. P. and J. P.

1868	James L. Capehart
1868	W. H. C. Freeman
1872-1904	James T. Deck
1908	Robert Deck
1910-22	J. Williford Hammontree
1912-21	A. M. Reed

Tunnel Hill
(1049th District G.M.)

J. P.

1852	Peter Mason
1852	James A. Ault
1854	Richard Bearden
1857-63	Robert W. Ault
1857-60	George W. Lacey
1860-63	J. J. Trammell
1861-69	S. J. Ward
1871-73-77	S. J. Ward
1871	H. H. Porter
1873	James A. Ault
1881-89	D. C. P. Clark
1893	R. H. Fox
1900	J. R. Foster
1905	D. C. Clark
1906	O. W. Harbin
1909	S. H. Baldwin
1913	S. M. Prothro
1917	A. F. Williams
1918	G. W. Head, Jr.
1921	Grady Head
1924	S. M. Hair
1930	B. C. Epps

N. P. and J. P.

1872-73	Lewis P. Headrick
1878-80	Morgan Head
1884	Newton Russell
1891-99	D. C. P. Clark
1903-07	Wm. Moody
1912-13	Geo. W. Head
1913	W. C. Moody
1922	S. M. Frothro

Upper Tenth
(1294th District G.M.)

J. P.

1877-84	J. C. Wilson
1884-90	Wm. M. Lowry
1900-04	Wm. M. Lowry
1889	S. W. Norton
1905	R. G. Shields
1909-12	P. G. Shields
1911-13	C. V. Earnest
1914-21	T. S. Wilson

N. P. and J. P.

1877-80	J. H. Anderson
1884	William Pullen
1888-90	H. M. Stonecipher
1890	Peter K. Messimer
1893-94	Z. T. Plemons
1894	Columbus V. Earnest
1898-1902	J. L. Wear
1906	James Webb
1910	J. C. Webb
1914	Thomas E. Brown
1917-22	W. P. Newman

Varnell
(628th District G.M.)

J. P.

1853	James A. Ault
1853	Joseph Guthrie
1853	John S. Martin
1853	William Whitten
1854	C. Russell McAllister

1856	Griffin A. McAllister
1857	Albert Varnell
1857	John S. James
1858-61	Jesse Wade
1861	Jonathan Green
1868	Albert Varnell

OFFICERS OF WHITFIELD COUNTY

1866-69	Frederick A. Rauschenberg	1909-17	A. L. Meers
1868	Leonard N. Speer	1921	George Powell
1868	R. N. Varnell	1922	E. Kerr
1872	George W. Sapp	1924	E. K. Caylor
1873	B. C. Headrick	1926	Albert Varnell
1877-80	E. H. Martin	1872	George W. Sapp
1881-85	F. A. Rauschenberg	1876	F. A. Rauschenberg
1886	E. H. Martin	1880-84	B. C. Hendrick
1887-88	George F. Mulkey	1888-96	John A. Wilson
1888-93	John Fagala	1897-1901	John Fagala
1897-1905	W. H. Isbill	1904	Thomas M. Seymour
		1907-19	John W. Eslinger

COMMISSIONER

The last Board of Commissioners of Roads and Revenue to serve in Whitfield county was composed of:

J. A. Thomason   Sam H. Wilson
Troy G. Kirk   Grover C. Stafford

Under legislative enactment, the Board of Roads and Revenue was abolished and the affairs of the county were placed in charge of a sole commissioner for which place Harlan J. Wood was duly elected and qualified. He entered upon his service as commissioner January 1, 1933.

EARLY DEEDS OF RECORD IN WHITFIELD COUNTY

GRANTOR	GRANTEE	DATE
Willis Jones	D. T. Fulton	2-4-1852
E. M. & F. W. Galt	James Edmondson	1-7-1852
Alexander Williford	Jesse H. Nelms	8-15-1851
Lucas Upson of Southington, Conn.	Amon Headley and Rool Gridley	9-2-1851
Charles Schwab	John McGhee	10-31-1851
S. R. Harris	Susan A. Lee	10-23-1850
Shelby McCalla	Joseph Guthrie	1-3-1852
Thomas A. McGraw	Robert Anderson	12-10-1857
S. S. Bailey	John McGhee and Chas. Rauschenberg	
John M. McGhee	Sam'l Rauschenberg	2-10-1851
John Vandiford	Martin Pitman	4-10-1851
John Hamilton, Chas. Schwab and Gotleib Blumenstock	Christian Rauschenberg	1-3-1852
John Hamilton, etc.	Gotleib Muller	3-24-1852
Elizabeth Martin	Cozzy Martin	3-24-1852
James R. Rice	Newton F. Heath	3-18-1852
Edward White	Peter Patterson of Gilmer County	6-27-1850
		11-7-1848
Edward White	Robert Abell	
Starkey J. Sharp	Drury Corker and J. W. Reynolds	8-20-1851
		2-5-1833
James M. Reynolds, Admr. of Joseph S. Reynolds and Drury Corker	Wm. A. Robins	2-9-1847
Wiley Fricks	Peter Patterson of Gilmer County	3-8-1849
Henry Tolson	John C. Waters	9-10-1835
James N. Causey	James R. Bradberry	3-15-1852
Richard Cross	David Weir	1-3-1852
S. S. Bailey	Patrick McOwen	8-2-1852
Patrick McOwen	James Lynan and David Weir	2-2-1852
James McCulley	Jeremiah Plummer	3-1-1851
Stephen Mays	James Dobbs	3-23-1852
James Morris	James Whittenburg	3-22-1851
John Moody	Hiram Blanton	9-28-1841
H. H. Blanton	Jacob Schliger	1-7-1842

Jacob Schliger	Robert King	9-6-1843
Robert King	Wm. McCulley	4-3-1844
Wm. Tate	Michael Scheck	2-10-1852
F. W. McCurdy	Giudrat & Co., of Montgomery, Ala.	4-9-1852
James Edmondson	W. J. Underwood	4-7-1852
Thomas Walker	Martin Workman	3-27-1852
David Shields	Martin Pitman	4-15-1852
C. M. McCalla & Co.	Wm. B. Quinn	1-6-1852
A. M. Wallace	R. S. Rushton	4-14-1852
Edward White	Wm. H. Cox	7-9-1851
C. J. McDowell	Wm. Pace	11-2-1850
Wm. Pace	Raleigh Cupp	11-3-1850
J. H. Gudger & Co. and N. M. Foster	Joseph H. Gudger	2-7-1852
Wm. Stevenson	Julius Langheld	1-17-1852
Chas. Schawb	Henry Yeager	1-7-1852
Joseph Barett	Joseph Corles	2-5-1851
Chas. Schawb	Henry Yeager	1-7-1852
Henry Yeager	Wm. Hurlein	4-3-1852
E. J. Tarver	Dennis C. Johnson	5-19-1851
Solomon Strickland	Barnabas Strickland	4-12-1847
Fred Cox, Sheriff	John Hamilton and W. J. Underwood	5-7-1852
Lewis F. Harris and McPherson B. Millon, Chatham, Ga.	Peyton L. Wade, Scriven, Ga.	2-26-1852
James M. Wood	Benj. Wiggins	12-31-1851
Ison C. King	Wm. Stevenson	6-1-1852
John Vandiford	Martin H. Pittman	6-18-1852
Jacob L. Cobb	M. J. & J. F. Murphy	6-19-1852
Chas. Hess	Allen Floyd	5-18-1852
Willis Noles and Susan Nones (wife) Lottery Land		
A. M. Cousins	A. M. Cousins	12-22-1851
Wm. Gray	James T. Tracy	12-22-1851
James Waters	James Tracy	12-22-1851
James B. Simmons	James Tracy	1-26-1852
Samuel Moore	Wm. McKlesoy	6-18-1834
Wm. McKlesoy	Rufus K. Ford	4-30-1851
Edward Smith	Edward Smith	12-20-1836
John T. Riley	Rufus K. Ford	2-4-1852
Edward White	Edward White	4-3-1852
Geo. W. Thompson	Mayor & Council John Anderson in trust for Frances Thompson (negro)	7-5-1852
Elizabeth Tenesson, Bulloch County	John McMurrain	1-7-1838
Wm. McMurrain	Wm. Driscoll	5-10-1850
Wm. Driscoll	G. R. Harris and Smith Treadwell	8-22-1850
Dalton City Co., (Ben E. Green, C. W. Selvidge, Gustavus Hurlein)	Lynan & Weir	7-16-1852
F. W. McCurdy	Joseph Taylor, Jr.	3-25-1852
Francis W. McCurdy	John McCurdy	8-18-1852
J. A. W. Johnson (for Roderick L. Bane)	John N. Harris	3-18-1852
Isaac Dickerson	Erwin Dickerson	7-24-1851
Isaac Dickerson	Erwin Dickerson	2-7-1852
John N. Harris	J. Florish	3-30-1852
Robert Gray	Gilliland & Howell	4-12-1852
Barnett Malcolm	Micajah C. Martin	1-21-1852
Thomas D. Johnson, James S. Jones and Jonathan Peck	M. C. Martin	1-23-1851
F. W. McCurdy	B. D. Hargrove	12-31-1857
W. J. Underwood	Wm. R. Long	7-11-1849
Wm. R. Long	Stoddard Russell, Laurence W. Earnest, Lafayette Powell, Bodwell E. Wells (Dalton Leather & Shoe Mfg. Company)	1-1-1851
L. W. Earnest	S. Russell, L. F. Powell, B. E. Wells and L. W. Earnest	1-11-1851

OFFICERS OF WHITFIELD COUNTY 195

W. J. Underwood
S. J. Lazzenby
Charlotte Reid, of Abbeville Dist., Widow of Rev. Henry Reid
John Newman
John Gavin
Oramil Clark

Dalton Leather & Shoe Mfg. Co.   2-27-1852
A. L. Sutherland   10-23-1851

Ethelred J. Tarver   11-1-1851
A. J. Tweedy   12-30-1850
Robt. Johnson, Jr.   5-28-1852
John Frederick Sutherlin   7-22-1851

WILL BOOK I, BEGINNING MARCH 1, 1851

Thomas Wilie
Wm. Sloan
James Anderson
Seborn J. Spann
George Chappell
Valentine Harlan
George R. Harris
Jacob Deck
John McGhee
Isaac Roberts
Hugh Burk
John Stancil
John Pitner
Martha Octavia Manes, (Widow)
James Tate
John Brown
John McCutchen
Ezra W. Green
John L. Henton
Margret Wilop
Williams Crook
Samuel McCalla
Richard Bearden
Mary Hudson
John Henderson

Jeremiah Roberts
Elihu Williams
John Wilson (1856)
Jane Lynder
Gotleap Miller (signed in German script)
Owen W. C. Kenan
Greenville Fuller
Joshua S. Carpenter
Adam Motts
William East
Micajah C. Martin
Robert C. Cox
Barney B. Whaley
James B. Alexander
Leonard J. Deck
Elizabeth Keenan
Archibald Sloan
Mary S. Wilson
James Morris (44)
A. E. Blount
John M. Jackson
Jeremiah Roberts
Robert Bohannon
David W. Humphreys
F. W. Fischer (August, 1867)

Officals Who Have Served the City of Dalton

The city has been particularly fortunate in the personnel of the officials that have served as officers of the city government. They have been men of high integrity and have given loyal service to the community. Prior to 1882 there is no record that is available but the files of the Dalton Argus furnish in part the names of the officials of the city government from 1882 and till 1892 from that date the files of the clerk's office have been open to us through the courtesy of the present clerk, Guy W. Keister.

The first mayor was Ainsworth E. Blount. The mayor during the War Between the States was Judge Elbert Sevier Bird.

1882 and 1883
Fred Cappes, Mayor; no record of councilmen.

1884
Fred Cappes, Mayor; S. E. Berry, W. H. Pruden, John Black, A. W. Lynn, S. E. Finley, James Herron, Sr., Aldermen.

1885
Sam P. Maddox, Mayor; Fred Cappes, S. E. Berry, Jim Coleman, John Black, Joe H. Kenner, J. P. Swick, Aldermen.

1886
Sam P. Maddox, Mayor; J. R. McAfee, W. H. Pruden, Joe H. Kenner, Aldermen; no record of the others.

1887
W. H. Pruden, Mayor; I. S. Finley, S. M. Clemmons, J. H. Kenner, O. P. Gordon, Joseph Bogle, Aldermen; no record of others.

1888
Fred Cappes, Mayor; John Black, Joe H. Kenner, S. D. Poarch, S. E. Berry, W. H. Pruden, Warren R. Davis, Aldermen.

1889
Cal Bryant, Mayor; John Black, J. H. Kenner, J. C. Riley, Sam E. Berry, Sam P. Maddox, Warren R. Davis, Aldermen.

1890
John Black, Mayor; W. H. Pruden, Sam P. Maddox, J. C. Riley, John Townley, Warren R. Davis, Aldermen.

1891
John Black, Mayor; Aldermen same as in 1890.

1892
John Black, Mayor; Warren R. Davis, J. G. McAfee, W. H. Pruden, Aldermen.

1893
John Black, Mayor; Warren R. Davis, J. G. McAfee, W. H. Pruden, J. C. Bivings, Sherry McCauley, S. B. Felker, Aldermen; B. C. Bivings, Clerk; D. K. McKamy, Treasurer; J. C. Fincher, Marshal.

1894
Sam P. Maddox, Mayor; W. H. Pruden, S. B. Felker, Sherry McCauley, J. C. Riley, W. F. Summerour, J. C. Bivings, Aldermen; B. C. Bivings, Clerk; D. K. McKamy, Treasurer; J. C. Fincher, Marshal.

1895
Sam P. Maddox, Mayor; Fred Cappes, Sam Loveman, Sam W. Farnsworth, J. C. Riley, W. F. Summerour, W. H. Pruden, Aldermen; B. C. Bivings, Clerk; D. K. McKamy, Treasurer; J. C. Fincher, Marshal.

1896
J. G. McAfee, Mayor; T. A. Berry, D. M. Peeples, W. R. Davis, Fred Cappes, Sam Loveman, T. J. Bryant, S. W. Farnsworth, Aldermen; B. C. Bivings, Clerk; D. K. McKamy, Treasurer; R. D. Ralston, Marshal.

1897
J. G. McAfee, Mayor; H. P. Colvard, J. H. Bender, F. A. Hamilton, D. M. Peeples, T. A. Berry, T. J Bryant, Aldermen; B. C. Bivings, Clerk; D. K. McKamy, Treasurer; R. D. Ralston, Marshal.

1898
W. H. Pruden, Mayor; John Black, Sherry McCauley, Sam Farnsworth, T. J. Bryant, H. P. Colvard, F. A. Hamilton, Aldermen; W. M. Hannah, Marshal; B. C. Bivings, Clerk; D. K. McKamy, Treasurer.

1899
W. H. Pruden, Mayor; R. W. Weatherly, H. J. Smith, J. K. Farrar, Sherry McCauley, John Black, Sam Farnsworth, Aldermen; B. C. Bivings, Clerk; D. K. McKamy, Treasurer; W. M. Hannah, Marshal.

1900
Sherry McCauley, Mayor; B. D. Leonard, B. R. Bowen, J. M. Sanders, R. W. Weatherly, H. J. Smith, J. K. Farrar, Aldermen; B. C. Bivings, Clerk; D. K. McKamy, Treasurer; J. C. Fincher, Marshal.

1901
Sherry McCauley, Mayor; Sam Loveman, Walter R. Davis, R. W. Weatherly, B. D. Leonard, J. M. Sanders, B. R. Bowen, Aldermen; B. C. Bivings, Clerk; D. K. McKamy, Treasurer; J. C. Fincher, Marshal.

Officials Who Have Served the City of Dalton

1902
Julian McCamy, Mayor; J. L. Grigsby, B. R. Bowen, G. H. Hightower R. W. Weatherly, Sam Loveman, Walter R. Davis, Aldermen; B. C. Bivings, Clerk.

1903
Julian McCamy, Mayor; Jacob Wrinkle, D. J. Bearden, H. J. Herron, J. L. Grigsby, B. R. Bowen, G. H. Hightower, Aldermen; B. C. Bivings, Clerk; J. G. McAfee, Treasurer; A. E. White, Marshal.

1904
Sherry McCauley, Mayor; J. H. Robinson, R. W. Weatherly, W. E. Wood, Jacob Wrinkle, D. J. Bearden, H. J. Herron, Aldermen; B. C. Bivings, Clerk.

1905
Sherry McCauley, Mayor; D. A. McLain, W. H. Stroup, W. C. Fincher, J. H. Robinson, R. W. Weatherly, W. E. Wood, Aldermen; F. S. Pruden, Clerk; J. R. McAfee, Treasurer; J. C. Fincher, Marshal.

1906
H. P. Colvard, Mayor; J. N. Caylor, J. K. Farrar, Charles Wood, D. A. McLain, W. H. Stroup, W. C. Fincher, Aldermen; F. S. Pruden, Clerk.

1907
H. P. Colvard, Mayor; W. C. Fincher, D. A. McLain, W. A. Leslie, J. N. Caylor, J. K. Farrar, Chas. Wood, Aldermen; F. S. Pruden, Clerk; J. H. Stanford, Treasurer; J. C. Fincher, Marshal.

1908
W. E. Wood, Mayor; F. A. Hamilton, Tom Hill, I. S. Finley, W. C. Fincher, D. A. McLain, W. A. Leslie, Aldermen; F. S. Pruden, Clerk; J. H. Stanford, Treasurer.

1909
W. E. Wood, Mayor; S. J. McKnight, L. L. Bishop, J. M. Rudolph, George C. King, D. J. Bearden, I. S. Finley, F. A. Hamilton, Tom Hill, Aldermen; W. M. Carroll, Clerk; J. H. Stanford, Treasurer; J. A. Longley, Recorder; J. C. Fincher, Marshal.

1910
Paul B. Trammell, Mayor; John T. Wills, J. S. Thomas. W. E. Mann, George C. King, D. J. Bearden, S. H. McKnight, L. L. Bishop, J. M. Rudolph, Aldermen; W. M. Carroll, Clerk; J. H. Stanford, Treasurer; J. C. Fincher, Marshal; J. A. Longley, Recorder.

1911
Paul B. Trammell, Mayor; F. E. Shumate, J. J. Duane, W. A. Buchanan, L. H. Elkins, John T. Wills, W. E. Mann, J. S. Thomas, George C. King, Aldermen; W. M. Carroll, Clerk; J. H. Stanford, Treasurer; J. C. Fincher, Marshal; J. A. Longley, Recorder.

1912
J. F. Harris, Mayor; S. F. Bell, W. E. Wood, W. M. Smith, J. S. Thomas, F. E. Shumate, J. J. Duane, W. A. Buchanan, L. H. Elkins, Aldermen; W. M. Carroll, Clerk; J. R. Tarver, Recorder; J. C. Fincher. Marshal.

1913
J. F. Harris, Mayor; J. H. Robinson, Joseph Bogle. T. F. Pierce, E. F. Hamilton, S. F. Bell, W. E. Wood, W. M. Smith, J. S. Thomas, Aldermen; W. M. Carroll, Clerk; J. H. Smith, Treasurer.

1914
B. R. Bowen, Mayor; J. L. Holland, David Stewart, W. D. McNally, J. B. Hill, J. H. Robinson Joseph Bogle, T. F. Pierce, E. F. Hamilton, Aldermen; W. M. Carroll, Clerk; J. H. Smith, Treasurer.

1915
B. R. Bowen, Mayor; T. F. Pierce, J. H. Robinson, W. H. Kenner, J. W. N. Bray, J. L. Holland, David Stewart, W. D. McNally, J. B. Hill, Aldermen; W. M. Carroll, Clerk; C. H. Smith, Treasurer.

HISTORY OF WHITFIELD COUNTY

1916
W. E. Wood, Mayor; J. B. Hill, W. D. McNally, David Stewart, J. A. Owens, T. F. Pierce, J. H. Robinson, J. W. N. Bray, W. H. Kenner, Aldermen; W. M. Carroll, Clerk; C. H. Smith, Treasurer; J. R. Tarver, Recorder.

1917
W. E. Wood, Mayor; Henry Hill, J. D. Puryear, W. F. Summerour, C. L. King, J. B. Hill, W. D. McNally, J. A. Owens, David Stewart, Aldermen; W. M. Carroll, Clerk; R. L. Catlett, Treasurer.

1918
J. H. Robinson, Mayor; Byron Smith, Farish C. Black, L. J. Allyn, W. D. McNally, Henry Hill, J. D. Puryear, W. F. Summerour, C. L. King, Aldermen; W. M. Carroll, Clerk; R. L. Catlett, Treasurer.

1919
J. H. Robinson, Mayor; Henry Hill, J. N. Caylor, C. L. King, J. D. Puryear, Carter Stacy, Byron Smith, L. J. Allyn, W. D. McNally, Aldermen; W. M. Carroll, Clerk; G. F. Springfield, Treasurer.

1920
W. E. Wood, Mayor; Carter Stacy, Ben Staten, Van F. Kettles, David Stewart, Henry Hill, J. N. Caylor, C. L. King, J. D. Puryear, Aldermen; W. M. Carroll, Clerk; G. F. Springfield, Treasurer.

1921
W. E. Wood, Mayor; J. W. Williams, J. N. Caylor, W. T. Kenner, F. D. Percy, Carter Stacy, Ben Staten, Van F. Kettles, David Stewart, Aldermen; W. M. Carroll, Clerk; G. F. Springfield, Treasurer.

1922
J. G. McAfee, Mayor; Ben Staten, John A. Shope, C. L. King. F. D. Percy, Aldermen; W. M. Carroll, Clerk; G. F. Springfield, Treasurer.

1923
J. G. McAfee, Mayor; Lee H. Elkins, N. N. Robertson, Ben Staten, C. L. King, Aldermen; W. M. Carroll, Clerk; G. F. Springfield, Treasurer.

1924
J. G. McAfee, Mayor; R. H. McFarland, R. M. Hill, L. H. Elkins, N. N. Robertson, Aldermen; W. M. Carroll, Clerk; G. F. Springfield, Treasurer, J. T. Bryant, Marshal.

1925
J. G. McAfee, Mayor; F. J. Flemister, W. H. Graves, R. H. McFarland, R. M. Hill, Aldermen; W. M. Carroll, Clerk; G. F. Springfield, Treasurer; J. T. Bryant, Marshal.

1926
J. A. McFarland, Mayor; W. J. King, F. E. Watkins, F. J. Flemister, W. H. Graves, Aldermen; W. M. Carroll, Clerk; G. F. Springfield, Treasurer; J. T. Bryant, Marshal.

1927
J. A. McFarland, Mayor; H. F. Hamilton, David Stewart, W. J. King, F. E. Watkins, Aldermen; Guy W. Keister, Clerk; G. F. Springfield, Treasurer; J. T. Bryant, Marshal.

1928
J. A. McFarland, Mayor; J. L. Renfroe, Byron Smith, H. F. Hamilton, David Stewart, Aldermen; Guy W. Keister, Clerk; G. F. Springfield, Treasurer; J. W. Ray, Recorder; T. N. Peeples, Marshal.

1929
J. A. McFarland, Mayor; H. F. Hamilton, J. P. Smith, J. L. Renfroe, Byron Smith, Aldermen; Guy W. Keister, Clerk; G. F. Springfield, Treasurer; T. N. Peeples, Marshal.

1930
J. G. McAfee, Mayor; J. L. Renfroe, Byron Smith, H. F. Hamilton, J. P. Smith, Aldermen; Guy W. Keister, Clerk; G. F. Springfield, Treasurer; W. A. Britton, Marshal.

OFFICIALS WHO HAVE SERVED THE CITY OF DALTON

1931
J. G. McAfee, Mayor; H. F. Hamilton, J. P. Smith, J. L. Renfroe, Byron Smith, Aldermen; Guy W. Keister, Clerk; G. F. Springfield, Treasurer; W. A. Britton, Marshal.

1932
J. G. McAfee, Mayor; W. M. McDonald, Byron Smith, H. F. Hamilton, J. P. Smith, Aldermen; Guy W. Keister, Clerk; G. F. Springfield, Treasurer; W. D. McNally, Recorder; W. A. Britton, Marshal.

1933
J. G. McAfee, Mayor; H. F. Hamilton, C. A. Connally, W. M. McDonald, Byron Smith, Aldermen; Guy W. Keister, Clerk; G. F. Springfield, Treasurer; W. A. Britton, Marshal.

1934
J. G. McAfee, Mayor; F. E. Watkins, J. M. Love, H. F. Hamilton, C. A. Connally, Aldermen; Guy W. Keister, Clerk; G. F. Springfield, Treasurer; W. A. Britton, Marshal.

1935
J. G. McAfee, Mayor; H. F. Hamilton, J. P. Smith, F. E. Watkins, J. M. Love, Aldermen; Guy W. Keister, Clerk; G. F. Springfield, Treasurer; W. A. Britton, Marshal.

WATER, LIGHT AND SINKING FUND COMMISSION

The City of Dalton voted bonds for $30,000 on November 13, 1886, for the purpose of building a water system for the City. The contract was let April 11, 1888. Fred Cappes was the Mayor.

The first commissioners of the Water, Light and Sinking Fund Commission were J. R. McAfee, John Townley, George W. Hamilton. The following men have served the city as commissioners:

	Elected		Elected
D. C. Bryant	Sept. 17, 1894	W. C. McGhee	Jan. 1, 1911
J. W. Barrett	Jan. 1, 1901	H. B. Farrar	Jan. 1, 1911
Sherry McAuley	Jan. 1, 1902	P. B. Trammell, Chmn.	Jan. 1, 1912
W. H. Prater	Jan. 1, 1904	T. D. Ridley	Jan. 1, 1914
C. G. Spencer	Jan. 1, 1905	J. S. Thomas, Chmn.	Jan. 1, 1916
H. J. Smith, Chmn.	Nov. 16, 1906	T. B. Wright	Jan. 1, 1923
J. M. Sanders	Jan. 1, 1908	W. C. Bowen, Chmn.	Feb. 15, 1926
J. P. Herndon, Chmn.	Jan. 1, 1928		

FORMER MEMBERS OF BOARD OF EDUCATION
Dalton, Georgia
Organized 1886

John Black
Joe Kenner
D. K. McKamy
S. E. Berry
W. K. Moore
W. T. McCarty
W. H. Pruden
G. W. Hamilton
Walter Jones
J. G. McLellan
B. D. Leonard
C. P. Gordon
W. M. Jones
Sherry McCauley
P. B. Trammell
W. E. Wood
C. D. McCutchen
Dennis Barrett

Frank Manly
T. D. Ridley
W. E. Mann
G. W. Orr
J. F. Whitson
T. S. Shope
S. B. Felker
H. L. Smith
W. C. McGhee
J. J. Copeland
Paul Fite
Floyd Farrar
Walter Davis
F. S. Pruden
P. E. Stone
Judson Manly
O. C. Alley

MUNICIPALITY OF DALTON
1936
Oliver R. Hardin, Mayor

Councilmen

J. M. Love
Pleas Smith
Hugh F. Hamilton
W. M. McDonald

W. H. Souther, Chief of Police
Guy Keister, Clerk
Land Norris, Treasurer.

Water, Light & Sinking Fund Commission

W. C. Bowen, Chairman
Dr. J. G. McAfee

T. B. Wright
John Black, Acting Agent

BOARD OF EDUCATION

Paul Fite, Chairman
Judson Manly

J. J. Copeland, Sec. & Treasurer
Phil Stone

Ogburn Alley

REVOLUTIONARY SOLDIERS

There could be found only a few names of Revolutionary soldiers buried in this county, but there are doubtless others whose names could not be secured:

John Stevenson   Jesse Cox

SOLDIERS OF THE WAR OF 1812

Thomas Simmons*   Benjamin Clark**

SOLDIERS OF MEXICAN WAR

D. F. H. Walker*   Geo. W. Towers***

SOLDIERS OF INDIAN WARS

Dr. George Harlan****   Geo. W. Towers***

State Capitol Records of Confederate Soldiers

Copied by Mrs. W. M. Sapp, Mrs. Clarence Fraker,
Mrs. R. M. Herron, Mrs. B. A. Tyler

NOTE: The following lists of records of Confederate soldiers from Whitfield county were copied from papers in the State Capitol, Atlanta, Georgia. These included only the names of the men who enlisted from Whitfield county. There were many others from the county who enlisted elsewhere in the state, but these could not be secured.

AUTHORITY:
*J. C. Barnett.
**Lucian Knight, Memorials and Landmarks.
***Mrs. Alice Cruce.
****Sam'l H. Kennedy.

THE DALTON GUARDS
Excellent and Daring Record of Our Famous Company of Militia

"In the year 1861, when the tocsin of war sounded, Dalton was found with a well drilled and finely equipped military organization composed of the very flower and chivalry of our county called, 'The Dalton Guards.' This company had perhaps been in existence a year or two, and numbered one hundred and ten men.

"The officers were:

Captain: R. T. Cook, June 11, 1861	2nd Sergeant: John H. Bitting
1st Lieutenant: J. F. B. Jackson	3rd Sergeant: William Hamilton
2nd Lieutenant: John Norris	4th Sergeant: R. P. O'Neill
2nd Lieutenant: Thomas Hamilton	1st Corporal: O. S. Higgins
1st Sergeant: James J. Byers	4th Corporal: M. G. Hill

"In the spring of 1861, the Guards rendezvoused at Camp McDonald near what was then known as Big Shanty, and were there mustered into Phillips' Legion for three years or during the war. The Guards went to Virginia in August, 1861, November following were sent to West Virginia under General Floyd. Had several sharp skirmishes with General Rosecran's troops in December at Hawk's Nest and Sewell Mountain.

"They went to the coast in South Carolina in January 1862, and did picket duty all winter. They returned to Virginia in the spring of 1863 for the campaign around Richmond and Chickahominy. From there they went to Manassas, thence into Maryland to the battles of South Mountain and the bloody battle of Sharpsburg, after which they recrossed the Potomac.

"The Dalton Guards had among their volunteers several mere boys of sixteen or seventeen years of age, who fought like Trojans during the entire war. Three of them I now recall. They were Warren Davis, Nick Bitting, Tom Wells. In one or two instances Mr. Davis was conspicuous for his bravery."*

The following list contains the names of the men who formed the Dalton Guards:

MUSTER ROLL, COMPANY B, PHILLIPS' LEGION, GEORGIA INFANTRY,
June 11, 1861
Privates

Adams, John	Davis, Warren R.	Glover, D. P.
	Davis, C. C.	Griffin, Thomas H.
Baker, R. H.	Dunn, Samuel	Griffin, T. W.
Blanton, G. J.	Dyer, S. M.	
Bridges, W. M.		Hinton, J. H.
Bard, H. H.	Edwards, W. R.	Hill, William
Bridges, W. L.	Edwards, A. B.	Henderson, S. J.
Boyles, W. D.	Edwards, A. M. V.	Hawkins, J. W.
	Edwards, J. H.	Hooper, W. J.
Carson, John T.	Edwards, J. L.	Howells, J. F.
Carter, W. T.	England, J. C.	Hammond, A. H.
Carter, Richard	Eldridge, F. M.	Headden, R. B.
Cline, Daniel		
Carroll, W. M.	Fields, J. H.	Jackson, W. W.
Cureton, J. C.	Fields, W. T.	Jolly, T. B.
Cowan, William	Fincher, Jesse C.	
	Ford, F. M.	Kincannon, William
Ducket, E. J.	Freeman, J. H. G.	Kingsley, E. T.
Davis, H. O.		
Davis, John A.	Gambril, B. O.	Lockard, William

---

*Article prepared for the Bryan M. Thomas Chapter, United Daughters of the Confederacy by the late Miss Laura Kelly, Historian.

Lynn, A. W.
Mayfield, J. W.
Mitchell, J. F.
Mitchell, W. F.
Mercer, J. A.

Owens, Daniel
Odell, J. A.
Odell, James W.

Pittman, A. J.

Quinn, Charles

Rauschenberg, A.
Robbins, H. A.
Reed, E. F.
Russell, H. L.

Small, A. B.
Small, C. J. B.
Stone, Richard P.
Stone, H.

Shumaker, T. J.
Summers, William
Samples, J. W.

Tarver, J. E.

Whittaker, T. F.
Wilson, Paschal
Wills, T. P.
Williams, C. C.

LIST OF DALTON GUARDS
By R. H. Baker

Published in the Dalton Citizen many years after the war. This contains the names of some not listed in the roster at the State capitol in Atlanta. It was probably made at a later date. Copy furnished by Mrs. J. F. Alexander, daughter of Mr. Baker.

Abraham, A.

Barry, John
Barry, Joe
Blanton, J. A.
Brown, Geo. E.
Broyles, Marcellus
Broyles, Water
Bryant, William
Byers, Jas.

Callahan, John
Carroll, Frank
Chapman, Lyman

Davis, Van

Edwards, Joshua

Gambril, Ed
Glover, Gus

Hawkins, Marion
Hill, Gus

Kline, Dan

Lynch, William
Lynch, Stephen

Mercer, Robert
Mitchell, Wash

Owens, Thaddeus

Pitman, William

Richardson, Dave
Richardson, Robert
Richardson, Ben

Tarver, R. M.
Turner, Frank

Varnell, R. H.

Wells, Thos.
Willis, Miller
Worthy, William
Worthy, Henry
Worthy, Hal

MUSTER ROLL, COMPANY I, FIRST REGIMENT, GEORGIA STATE TROOPS
Combined Rolls of May, 1863, through January, 1864

Colonel E. M. Galt, Commanding
Captain: Robert H. Morris
1st Lieutenant: Andrew J. Keith
2nd Lieutenant: Joe R. Garner
3rd Lieutenant: John W. Whitner
4th Lieutenant: J. T. Lynch

5th Lieutenant: E. W. Miller
1st Corporal: Jacob R. Miller
2nd Corporal: McAfee Bates
3rd Corporal: Marcus Maxwell
4th Corporal: A. D. Kendrick

Privates

Agnew, John S.
Amos, John E.

Bates, Andrew
Bates, Napoleon B.
Bates, McAfee B.
Batey, Andrew
Bray, Jas. T.
Bradley, Jno. A.
Berry. Chas. W.
Bearden, Wm. C.
Black, Jno. S.
Bridges, Jeremiah
Bowman, Elijah A.
Bradley, Jack H.
Brewer, Franklin
Brindle, Doctor C.

Cameron, Robert A. B.
Carter, Reuben
Chastain, Miles R.
Chapman, Thos. L.
Clement, Jno. A.
Cavender, Joseph W.
Cox, James
Cochran, Coleman C.
Cochran, Jas. W.
Caldwell. John
Craig, John G.*
Clardy, John I.
Crow, John C.
Cunningham, M. M.

Davis, Spencer B.
Dantzler, Lem M.

Dowdy, Jasper P.

Earnest, Marcellus B.
Esskew, Wm. I.
Edge, Cicero W.
Eads, C. A.

Fagala, Lewis
Fant, or Faut, Enoch M.
Farnsworth, Wylie P.
Fitzgerald, Edw. C.

Gaines, Aaron N.
Gamer, Francis
Gassaway, E. G.
Green, Jas. P.
Green, Jas. P.

Greeson, Green
Greeson, Abraham
Griffin, Adam
Grice, Wm. J.
Glimp, John B.

Haddock, David C.
Hardcastle, Wm.
Harris, Moses
Harlan, Joshua
Haynes, Virgil H.
Hayes, V. H.
Helton, Thomas
Hodge, Robert G.
Holcomb, Jno. M.
Holland, Wm. K.
Hopper, Zacheriah
Howell, James C.
Howell, Martin S.
Hunsucker, Bayless C.

Johnson, John J.

Keith, Jno. M.
Keith, Vincent D.
Keith, John B.
Keith, Sam'l A.
Keown, Henry C.
Key, Baron L.
Keys, John M.

Lance, Madison
Langford, Aaron A.
Laday, John P.
Lanier, Madison
Leonard, Berry

Longly, Wm. C.
Lyard, John P.

Malone, Wm. B.
Major, Edwin G.
Mann, Young A. B.
Mashburn, Jackson B.
Maxwell, Caldwell
Maxwell, William
Mauldin, Andrew J.
Mauldin, Alex
McLain, Hugh
McGhee, Hugh
Miller, James F.
Mims, Geo. W.
Morgan, Pleasant N.
Moore, Robt. M.*
Morris, Geo. W.
Morris, J. C.
Mote, John I.
Murphy, Sam'l F.

Nations, Thomas
Nelson, Walter T.

Owens, John M.
Osborn, Wylie
Offutt, Robt. A.
Oxford, Calvin F.
Orr, Wm.

Parks, James H.
Pender, Henry N.
Pullen, Thos. N.
Pendergrass, Hugh

Rees, Christopher
Redwine, M. M.
Rhodes, Madison E.
Roberts, Andrew J.
Rhodes, John W.
Rollins, John D.
Richardson, John R.
Richardson, H. L.
Richardson, Lee C.
Robertson, Robert
Reynolds, John W.

Staten, Wylie P.
Staten, Samuel
Simmons, Jas. B.
Small, Jas. C.
Sturdivant, John P.
Strickland, Henry F.
Swift, T. G.

Talley, John H.
Tolliaferro, Wylie P.
Thomas, Richard T.
Treadwell, John
Thompson, J. K. P.
Turpin, Josiah

Verhine, Richard T.
Verhine, Henry

Waddell, Alfred
Ware, Robert N. C.
Wetzell, Benj. C.
Wright, J. W.
Whitfield, Benj. F.

MUSTER ROLL, COMPANY H, EIGHTH REGIMENT, THIRD BRIGADE, GEORGIA STATE TROOPS
Camp Jackson

Lieutenant Colonel: Jno. S. Fain
Captain: John W. Walker
1st Lieutenant: R. M. Fleet
2nd Lieutenant: G. W. Duncan
3rd Lieutenant: S. W. Johnson
1st Sergeant: M. S. Riddle
2nd Sergeant: A. J. Sitton

3rd Sergeant: C. D. Ford,
4th Sergeant: D. N. Gibson
5th Sergeant: J. W. Ford
1st Corporal: W. R. Davis
2nd Corporal: B. J. Sitton
3rd Corporal: H. Fitzgerald
4th Corporal: H. A. Wrench

Privates

Abraham, A.

Bowman, A. D.
Beevers, G. G.
Bohanan, J. T.
Bohanan, R.
Bostick, C. H.
Brown, L. W.

Collins, M.*
Chester, H. A.
Crawford, W. S.
Christian, John R.

Davis, E. W.

Evans, H.

Futton, G. S.
Fisher, H.

Harden, E. R.
Harden, W. H.
Hammond, A. W.
Hamrick, Wm.
Harris, N. L.
Hill, J. F.

Jones, J. T.

Lewis, W. J.
Love, R. R.

Mitchell, J. B.
Masters, J. A.
Maloy, John
Mauldin, A.
Mooney, J. P.
Mauldin, C. H.
Mobley, R. H.

O'Neill, James

Roberts, J. M.

Smith, J. R. W.
Sam, R. J.
Siner, W. W.
Snow, J. H.
Snow, John
Swift, Edward

Wilson, R.
Williamson, G. A.
White, W. J.
Ward, W. N.
Warmack, J. W.
Warmack, Jesse
Wright, Joe P.
Wilson, Daniel

*1st Corps.

*3rd Corps.

*3rd from February 1st to 22nd.

MUSTER ROLL, COMPANY H, THIRTY-SIXTH REGIMENT, GEORGIA VOLUNTEER INFANTRY, ARMY OF TENNESSEE, C. S. A.

Captain: Agrippa P. Roberts
1st Lieutenant: William G. Harris
2nd Lieutenant: Jeremiah Smithey
2nd Lieutenant: Thos. B. McIntire*
1st. Sergeant: William J. Beck
2nd Sergeant: Samuel H. Harris
3rd Sergeant: Thos. K. Bates

4th Sergeant: William A. Hall
5th Sergeant: Robt. A. Smithey
1st Corporal: S. M. Dye
2nd Corporal: John J. Ballard
3rd Corporal: G. W. Webb
4th Corporal: John W. Kooksey**

Privates

Anderson, A. J.
Arnold, John
Arrowood, B. C.

Baker, John F.
Ballard, John
Beck, William A.
Benton, J. S.
Boles, G. W.
Brookshire, Vardery
Burkett, Wm. Anderson

Clegg, John P. W.
Combee, Wm. L.
Compton, Arthur
Compton, Marshall
Cooksey, John W.***
Creekmore, Geo. T.
Cross, Garrison

Crouch, Joseph Larkin
Crouch, Wm. A.

Devers, Rowland
Dunn, Joseph P.
Dunn, William

Ellis, James H.
Ellis, John M.

Gordon, John
Grant, Richard W.

Hall, Harris
Hall, Thos. J.

Owens, F. C.

Peterson, J. H.

Phillips, J.

Ray, J.
Richardson, R.
Richardson, D.
Ruth, R. J.

Turner, Allen
Thrailkill, Henry
Tarver, J. R.

Varnell, W. E.

Underwood, W.

Wood, John H.
Wright, A. F.
Winfree, M. F.
Wrinkle, E.

MUSTER ROLL, COMPANY A, THIRTY-FOURTH REGIMENT, GEORGIA VOLUNTEER INFANTRY, C. S. A.

Captain: Jno. M. Jackson
1st Lieutenant: L. N. Tinsley
2nd Lieutenant: W. T. Crow
2nd Lieutenant: Thomas W. Morris*
1st Sergeant: W. F. Routh
2nd Sergeant: John Hopper

3rd Sergeant: Thomas W. Worthy
4th Sergeant: Oliver L. Keith
5th Sergeant: John R. McDonald
1st Corporal: J. H. Bohannon
2nd Corporal: Geo. W. Jackson
3rd Corporal: Geo. W. Mayfield
4th Corporal: Jas. C. Riley

Privates

Ables, Jeremiah
Arthur, Joseph

Bailey, J. R.
Bates, Nelson
Beck, Solomon
Beck, Jas.
Bests, W. L.
Bohannon, Robert
Brown, Lemuel
Burnes, Geo. H.
Burns, W. H.
Burns, Jefferson

Cameron, Joseph
Claiborn, Wesley
Coffee, John G.
Cleveland, David
Collins, Martin
Davis, W. Z.

Dover, C. M.
Dover, Henry S.

Fowler, C. S.

Garner, John
Gantt, Simeon
Glass, J. W.
Goode, Abram
Goode, Michael
Goodwin, Chas. J.
Goodwin, Simeon G.
Grubb, Francis M.

Hambrick, N. M.
Hamilton, Jas. H.
Harris, Jasper
Harris, John P.
Hays, William H.
Horne, Peter M.

Horne, William J.

James, John
James, Pulaski
James, Patrick
Jiles, William P.
Jones, Chas. D.
Jones, John T.
Jordan, James W.

Keister, Ravarrus
Kelly, Jeffra L.
Kelly, William S.

Looney, B. F.

McClure, William A.
Mansill, Jas. A.
Martin, M. C.
Mayfield, D. J.

*Junior 2nd Lieutenant.
**Kooksey or Cooksey.
***See 4th Corps.

*Jr. Second Lieutenant.

Meade, John
Melton, W. C.
Mooney, Jackson, R. B.
Morgan, J. M.
Morris, D. W.
Mullins, LaFayette J.

Nance, Larkin R.
Nance, W. T.
Neal, A. J.
Neal, W. J.

Payne, Samuel C.

Roberts, W. Bryson
Routh, Rice J.
Sebastian, E. J.
Shannon, John
Shepherd, John M.
Shepherd, M. L.
Shipp, J. J.
Summerman, J. C.
Sinor, William W.
Smith, Arthur C.
Smith, Edward
Stephenson, G. H.
Suggs, John C.
Suggs, Loring

Swinney, Francis M.
Swinney, Haden

Thomas, Henry
Thomas, William M.

Waite, J. W.
Weaver, Simeon
Wheat, D. A.
Wheeler, G. W.
Wheeler, Riley
Whisenant, D. H.
Whisenant, Nicholas

MUSTER ROLL, COMPANY B, THIRTY-SIXTH REGIMENT, GEORGIA VOLUNTEER INFANTRY, ARMY OF TENNESSEE, C. S. A.

February 1, 1862

Captain: Geo. A. Cooper
1st. Lieutenant: Wm. A. Hill
2nd Lieutenant: Ephraim Holland
2nd Lieutenant: John Edwards*
1st Sergeant: Anthony A. Sarratt
2nd Sergeant: James J. Holden
3rd Sergeant: Andrew J. Moody

4th Sergeant: Isaac P. Thrailkill
Thomas K. Clarke
1st Corporal: Warren D. Peterson
2nd Corporal: James M. Dempsey
3rd Corporal: James S. (or L.) Dyer
4th Corporal: Abraham M. Head

Privates

Alton, James M.
Babb, Francis M.
Beshires, James
Blanton, Joseph W.
Boatwright, J. D.
Boyd, Martin Y.
Boyd, Thomas R. (or K.)
Bratton, William M.

Calhoun, Andrew J.
Calhoun, J. P.

Campbell, W. S.
Carder, Thomas
Carr. R. S.
Couch, R. B.
Couch, Thomas
Couch, William
Craig, James
Craig, Robert M.
Craig, Thomas
Cullens, James A.

Daniels, Apollos Bonnell
Davis, Joseph
Dempsey, Edmond F.
Dempsey, James
Dunbar, James P.
Duncan David N. (or C.)
Dunn, Jesse

Edwards, Edward H.
Elrod, Samuel
Evans, Augustus Sydney

Helton, Joseph
Holland, Andrew
Howard, E. H.
Farmer, John
Franks, Jackson A.
Gasney, J. W.

Gudger, Joseph H.

Hackney, Alexander
Hackney, LaFayette
Hambree, Hampton
Harris, Oliver R.
Hayes, Albert
Helton, Jahyle M.
Howard, James T.
Howard, Stephen J.
Howard, W. L.
Howard, Wm. W.
Howell, Daniel D.

Jennings, E.
Jennings, George W.
Jones, W. M.

Kendley, James C.
King, E. T.
King, Isaac N.
King, Thomas K.

Lacy, William
Larmon, A. J.
Latch, Wesley
Lenon (or Lemon), Henry L.
Loggins, Absalom B.
Loggins, George R.
Loggins, J. N.
Loggins, S. B.
Loggins, William W.
Loner, William M.
Looney, Jeptha C.
Lyons, Jeremiah (Jerry)

Massengale, A. Jeremiah
Massengale, R.
Metts, Hugh C.

McCrary, James M.
McCurry, Thomas
McDaniel, M. Lewis (or McDonald)
McDaniel, Stephen J. (or McDonald)

Nations, James L.
Nations, Thomas

Ortum, James
Owens, Obediah

Patrick, Peter
Pernell, L.
Peterson, James H.
Peterson, Warren D.
Phillips, James W.
Phillips, Jesse J.
Phillips, John
Phillips, William T.
Pook, Jackson A.
Price, George W.
Price, John
Prince, John
Prince, Wyley

Ratteree, James W.
Reese, Jarrett
Richey, Joseph G.
Roberts, John R.
Robinson, J. A.
Rogers, John W.

Sarrett, L. (or S.) A. J. or Seratt
Setzefant, Leopold
Smith, Elias
Smith, J. Graham
Smith, Mark L.
Snow, J. H.

Sparks, John S.
Sparks, Samuel
Stafford, Joseph D.
Stroup, Joseph
Sullivan, Frank M.
Sullivan, John
Sullivan, Warren M.
Sullivan, William

W.
Talley, Dock
Tate, William J.
Thomas, James J.
Thomas, John M.
Thrailkill, Isaac P.
Turner, Henry

Turner, John C.
Wadkins, Lemuel
Wheeler, James H.
Woody, Jonathan
Word, Charles B.
Wrinkle, Jacob
Wrinkle, Wiley H.

MUSTER ROLL, COMPANY C, THIRTY-SIXTH REGIMENT, GEORGIA VOLUNTEER INFANTRY, ARMY OF TENNESSEE, C. S. A.

Captain: B. B. White
1st Lieutenant: F. M. Dwight
2nd Lieutenant: John R. Griffin
2nd Lieutenant: E. S. Hill
1st Sergeant: Jesse James Suttle
2nd Sergeant: Wm. H. Lassiter
3rd Sergeant: Hendrix Willis
4th Sergeant: Fair Kersey
5th Sergeant: Jasper Bradley
1st Corporal: Elijah McGinnis
2nd Corporal: William Masters
3rd Corporal: L. H. Drum
4th Corporal: John S. McNabb

Privates

Bentley, J. A.
Blackstock, J. L.
Bond, G.
Bond, Jas. Larkin
Bond, John G.
Bradley, Crayton
Brannon, J. C. (or Branan)
Brannon, Thomas S.
Brasil, Richard L.
Braswell, F. M.
Brook, Jas. W.
Burass, William

Chastain, A. M.
Chatham, Jas. I. (or J.)
Chatham, S. M.
Chatham, J. T.
Compton, H. M.
Davis, Daniel T. (or F.)
Drum, Abrum
Donaldson, James G.
Drum, L. H.

Ellard William M.
Estes, Emory
Estes, Hudson
Estes, N. M.
Estes, Wesley
Evans, A. N.
Evans, M. D.

Freeland, W. J.

Galloway, Robert M.
Garner, John H.
Griffy (Griffin) G. W.

Hall, William P.
Hardy (or Hardee) Jasper N.
Haygood, James L.
Hendriks, F. G. D.
Higgins, J. L.
Higgins, Sam'l Gilmore
Holbrook, W. C.
Holland, J. G. (or S. J.)

Johnson, Henry

Keith, Geo.
Kennamor, David L.
Key, A. W.
Kirksey, A.
Kirksey, William H.
Kreischer, Adam
Kreischer, W. M.

Lamb, John E.
Lamb, Larry L.
Lamham, Charles
Lassister, J. B.
Lasssiter, William H.
Loughridge, Jacob
Love, J. A.

Major, Enoch B.
Masters, William
McBrayer, S. R.

Nealy, Berry

Odell, Jas. A.
Ogle, J. L.

Parsons, R. H.
Phillips, Geo. W.
Phillips, Jas. W.
Pope, M. L.
Pugh, J. P.

Rider, Martin V.
Rollins, Jas. A.

Samples, Jas. Thomas
Sexton, Reuben T.
Shurdury, C.
Smith, Wm. H.
Snow, Fielding
Stephens. John
Suttle, Robt. G.
Suttle, Thomas K.
Suttle, William A.

Thomas, Elisha P.
Thompson, J. K.
Tribble, James
Tribble, Stephen D.

Vaughn, Andrew G.
Vaughn, James M.

Whaley, W. A.
Williams, William
Woodall, ———

MUSTER ROLL, COMPANY G, THIRTY-SIXTH REGIMENT, GEORGIA VOLUNTEER INFANTRY, ARMY OF TENNESSEE, C. S. A.

Captain: D. H. Elledge*
1st Lieutenant: Jas. P. Smith
2nd Lieutenant: J. M. Rogers
2nd Lieutenant: R. T. Bridges**
1st Sergeant: Sam'l L. Rogers
2nd Sergeant: Martin P. Gentry
3rd Sergeant: William R. Sumner
4th Sergeant: John C. Huffaker

*Jr. Second Lieutenant.

STATE CAPITOL RECORDS OF CONFEDERATE SOLDIERS 207

1st Corporal: Simeon D. Howell
2nd Corporal: Carrick W. Whittle
3rd Corporal: John Nations

H. H. Davis, Musician
S. M. Roach, Musician

Privates

Aldridge, Geo. W.

Bartlett, Burrell
Bearden, A.
Bellew, Jas.
Black, James N.
Bolton, G. W.
Bostick, Caswell H.
Bridges, Henry P.
Bridges, Joseph
Bridges, Robert T.
Broom, F. C.
Broom, J. L.

Cadle, James
Caudell, Jas. W.
Carlisle, Benj. H.
Clarke, Alfred W.
Combs, W. H.

Davis, Oscar T.
Davis, Sampson C.
Deadman, Joseph
Deadman, J.
Denton, T. A.
Dickson, D. M. C.
Dooley, Jas. P.
Dooley, M. C.
Douglas, J. R.
Duckworth, G. W.

Fagan, W. T. (or W. S.)
Fisher, Sam H.
Freeman, John C.

Garner, Jas. Daniel
Garner, John H.
Garner, J. W.
Gentry, C. T.
Gentry, James O. A.
Gentry, Wm. J.

Gordy, J. W.

Harris, Richard
Horne, William H.
Howard, W. D.
Howard, W. L.
Howell, Andrew J.
Huffaker, Ignatius H.
Huffaker, Isaac A.
Hughes, Henry W.
Hurt, E. S.
Hurt, Wm. J.

Jones, Geo. W.

King, W. A.

Langford, Zebedee
Langley, B. M.
Leatherwood, Edmund N.
Leroy, M. C.
Love, Geo. W.

Marsh, J. J.
Messemer, John D. (or Messimer)
Michael, George
McKinney, S. James

Nations, Christopher
Nations, John
Nations, Joseph, Jr.
Nations, J. A.
Nations, J. M.
Nichols, W. H.
Nicholson, J. H.
Nicholson, William

Peterson, John D.
Patterson, Joseph
Patterson, Joseph W.

Pelfrey, Dapid J.
Pelfrey, Thomas
Perkins, Benj.
Phillips, Jas. W.
Plumer, F. M.
Pope, S. C.
Price, J. M.

Roach, Jas. H.

Smith, A.
Smith, Jas. G.
Smith, John H.
Smith, T. Jefferson
Smith, Wm. H.
Stevenson, A. B.
Stewart, N. S.
Stokes, E.
Stokes, Henry
Stokes, Richard H.
Sumner, Wm. R.

Thatch, Andrew J.
Toney, W. T.
Trague, (or Teague) John
Tyler, Caleb
Tyler, Pinckney J.

Vincent, G. T. (or Vinant)

Ward, Ervin A.
Ward, Russell Hunter
Williams, Edward J. (or Edwin)
Wilson, Richard
Woolbright, Jas. T.
Woolbright, M. P.
Workman, John W.
Workman, M. L.

MUSTER ROLL, COMPANY D, NINTH REGIMENT, THIRD BRIGADE GEORGIA STATE TROOPS
December 11, 1861

Captain: William K. Moore

1st Lieutenant: R. Fleming*
2nd Lieutenant: W. J. Keith
2nd Lieutenant: A. N. Center**
1st Sergeant: Hugh Springfield
2nd Sergeant: J. T. Lynch

3rd Sergeant: Jacob Wrinkle
4th Sergeant: M. C. Hooper
5th Sergeant: Thomas Black
1st Corporal: P. L. Byron
2nd Corporal: A. N. Wrinkle
3rd Corporal: Jesse Powell
4th Corporal: J. Q. A. Mote

Privates

Brooker, J. W.
Brown, G. E.
Bennett, Henry L.
Black, Thomas
Barnett, W. F.
Bennett, Wm.
Bard, Thomas D.

Babb, F. M.
Babb, James

Cate, J. N.
Clark, T. J.

Duckett, E.

Ellison, E. B.

Guyer, William
Glimps, J. B.
Gore, E.

Hamilton, J. H.

*The name of Jasper J. Trammell appears on a roll made by survivors of this company as the original captain.
**Junior 2nd Lieutenant.

Hicks, B. K.
Haralson, W. H.
Hackney, A.
Henderson, J. J.
Helton, J.

Jones, H. L.

Keith, A. J.
Keith, W. A.
Keith, J. L.
Kendrick, W. B.
Ketchum, William
Ketchum, John
King, J. W.

Lyon, J.

Martin, M. C.
McCune, John
McIntyre, F.
Mack, James

Norton, J. C.

Hampton, Hugh
Hampton, William
Hardcastle, John R.
Harden, Geo. W.
Harden, Isaac W.
Hartley, Samuel
Harris, Andrew
Harris, John R.
Hayes, Henry C.

Hayes, J. B. (or B. J.)
Hayler, Abney M.
Higdon, Wm. L.
Hill, James F.
Holland, Sam'l N.
Hooper, Monroe C.

Kayler, Eli
Keith, Reuben R.
Keith, Wm. A.
Kile, Newton
Kile, William
King, James W.
King, Whitten
Kooksey, John W.

Lackey, Thos. J.
Lane, James
Lane, John T.
Lane, L. M.
Lane, Thos. H.
Lemons, W. J.
Lowery Wm. M.

Mauldin, Alexander
Mantooth, Doctor H.
Mantooth, Hugh
Mantooth, Thos.
Martin, David H.
Masters, Jas. A.
Mitchell, N. B.
Moody, Andrew J.
Moore, Martin B.

Mullinax, Benson J.
McDonald, A. J.
McAfee, A. C.
McDonald, Wm. B.

Peterson, John H.
Phillips, Robertson
Poteet, B. A.
Poteet, J. B.

Rambeau, John N.
Ray, Wm. A.
Rider, Martin V.
Ridley, Henry
Roberts, aJmes M.

Simmons, Jno. E.
Simmons, Thos. J.
Sims, Joseph G.
Smithey, James
Sparks Thos. W.

Tarver, John R.
Tye, Samuel Miller

Watzell, B. C.
Webb, G. W.
West, Sam'l P.
Wood, John H.

Yarborough, Edw. W.
Yarborough, Elias

MUSTER ROLL, COMPANY I, THIRTY-SIXTH REGIMENT, GEORGIA VOLUNTEER INFANTRY, ARMY OF TENNESSEE, C. S. A.

Captain: Jacob L. Morgan

1st Lieutenant: L. R. Willis
2nd Lieutenant: Robert R. Grant
2nd Lieutenant: V. D. Liles*
1st Sergeant: Wm. R. Russell
2nd Sergeant: John F. Morgan
3rd Sergeant: Dan'l Beachamp
4th Sergeant: L. F. Holcombe

1st Corporal: A. M. Chastain
2nd Corporal: J. M. Scott
3rd Corporal: B. M. Longley
4th Corporal: Henry C. Plemons
5th Sergeant: Andrew Grant

Jackson McManis; Musician
Levi Silver: Musician

Privates

Barnes, M. R.
Beachamp, Jackson
Boyd, J. A.
Brackett, Daniel
Brackett, Jas. R.
Burch, James
Burgan, Kinsley S.
Burgan, Leander W.

Carroll, Andrew J.
Carroll, John H.
Chastain, A. M.
Cowart, James
Cochran, Starling

Dover, G. L.
Dover Martin L.

Edwards, A. J.

Fitzsimmons, Patrick W.
Franks, Jackson

Grant, Thomas J.

Head, Henry W.
Hensley, Andrew J.
Hire, Chase
Holmes, C. W.
Horton, John
Hubbard, Isaih
Hutchins, C. Arvil

Jones, Jas. C.
Jones, John C.

Kelly, A. W.
Kelly, R. S.

Kelly, William C.

Langston, W. F. H.
Liles, Augustus S.
Liles, L. G.
Liles, Napoleon B.

McElreath Thomas
Manning, John C.
Mannning, John L.
Manning, T. P.
Morgan, John

O'Kelley, Solomon

Parker, John
Perkins, E. R.

Walls, Jesse

*Resigned March 22, 1862.
**Junior Lieutenant.

State Capitol Records of Confederate Soldiers   209

Roach, Henry
Rice, John C.
Robertson, Benj. F.
Simms, J. J.
Silver, Sam'l
Smith, Edward
Stephens, G. W.

Stokes, John
Stokes, Thos. G.
Townsend, W. H.
Waters, Columbus C.
Wicket, John
Williams, William Anderson

Willis, G. W.
Willis, Thos. Jefferson
Willis, William W.
Wilson, Samuel
Young, William
Young, W. A.

MUSTER ROLL, COMPANY C, THIRTY-NINTH REGIMENT, GEORGIA VOLUNTEER INFANTRY, ARMY OF TENNESSEE, C. S. A.

February 28, or March 10, 1862.

Captain: Timothy Ford

1st Lieutenant: John F. Senter
2nd Lieutenant: Wm. H. Brotherton
3rd Lieutenant: Augusta McHan
1st Sergeant: James M. Brotherton
2nd Sergeant: Andrew J. Weaver

3rd Sergeant: Alexander S. Hill
4th Sergeant: Caleb S. Fraker
5th Sergeant: M. Manning
1st Corporal: Addison Jewell
2nd Corporal: Spencer G. Beavers
3rd Corporal: Amos C. Williams
4th Corporal: Benjamin F. Ferrell

Robert A. Matheny: Musician

Privates

Alexander, Frank C.

Black, John F.
Black, Thomas K.
Bridges, John H.
Bridges, W. M.
Bowman, E. J.
Bowan, W. A. T.
Box, William B.
Broadrick, Drury
Bell, R. M.
Bowman, William, Sr.
Bowman, William, Jr.

Caldwell, David L.
Cardin, C. H.
Cardin, Russell S.
Cardin, A. W.
Cantrell, Jeremiah J.
Cleghorn, John S.
Cady, Edward V.
Creekmore, Jesse C.
Compton, John J.
Clarke, J. F.
Carter, Caleb A.
Cardin, Andrew J.
Chastain, A. M.

Dunnigan, Ezekiel J.
Deck, Leonard J.
Dantzler, Addison P.
Dantzler, J. N.
Dilliard, T. P.
Doke, J. E. J.

Ferrell, Charles A.
Freeman, William C.
Ferrell, Benjamin F.
Faith, James A.
Fraker, John A. M.
Fraker, Hilliam M. H.
Faith, Samuel A.
Fielder, John G.
Fraker, C. S.
Ferrell, D. T.
Fraker, G. D. M.

Griffin, William
Glover, Eli J.
Glover, James N.
Griffin, Allen
Griffin, Edward
Gray, R. W.

Howell, Marion
Head, Isaac N.
Hill, Edward M.
Herndon, T. D.
Herndon, John F.
Head, John C.
Head, J. C.
Houston, David J.
Holly, John B.
Haynes, Charles G.
Hill, Marion W.
Hair, George W.
Hix, J. B.
Hix, B. K.
Hayward, C. G.
Haynes, J. M.

Jones, John R.
Jones, Thomas M.
Jones, William
Jewel, Marshall C.
Jackson, Jasper N.

Keown, M. J.

Lavender, Hardy B.
Longley, Jasper
Longley, Wm. J.
Lane, Gideon
Lloyd, Benjamin

McCutchen, Wm. P.
McArdle, James
McKein, James
McIntyre, Frank
McIntyre, Felix
McYork, Henry
McAbee, James E.
Matheny, Grier B.

Mitchell, John F.
Morris, Leander C.
Massengale, E.
Malone, George Elwood

Neal, Robert P.

Pollard, Joshua J.
Plumer, J. W.
Pepper, John
Pritchett, Anderson
Pepper, A. J.
Plemons, John M.

Queen, James M.
Queen, William J.

Redwine, James N.
Redwine, L. S.
Roberts, Isaac M.
Robinson, James A.
Routh, James C.

Sloan, Robert B.
Seay, Alexander M.
Small, George W.
Stone, James
Strickland, Wilson

Thornton, Alexander N.
Thompson, William

Vining, Casby L.
Vining, C. T.

Wilson, W. G.
Wilson, Reuben
Whaley, John
Whaley, Ambrose V.
Wright, Jos. P.
Wilson, D. N.
Williams, A. C.
Wilson, J. K.
White, John
Wilson, James
Williams, Wm. J.

*Junior 2nd Lieutenant.

THIRTY-NINTH REGIMENT, GEORGIA INFANTRY

No official list of Companies A, B, D, E, F, and G could be found of this regiment, but the two that are listed below, while unofficial, contain the names of many Whitfield county men who served in this Regiment.

The Dalton Argus of August 20, 1887, contained the following account of a reunion of this regiment giving the names of a few men who served with the regiment:

"Reunion of the 39th Georgia Regiment was held in Dalton, Georgia, in August, 1887. At this meeting a communication was read from Captain S. Percy Green, of Fort Worth, Texas, in which he stated that he had returned to the survivors their old colors which were rent and torn from the effects of many battles. Capt. Green stated that when he received orders to surrender, that he could not find it in his heart to give up the old flag, so he took it from the staff and wrapped it around his body under his clothing, and so carried it out and had preserved it.

"The following list contains the names of the survivors of the 39th Georgia Regiment attending this reunion:

J. F. B. Jackson, Colonel
T. H. Pitner, Major
W. H. Brotherton, Captain

A.C.S.
F. A. Rauschenberg, Physician
L. N. Trammell, A.I.M.

Company A

Lieutenant: Wm. G. Field
Sergeant: B. B. Hemphill
Sergeant: M. L. Keith
Sergeant: Amos L. Keith

Privates

Adams, John

Black, John
Black, Wm. R.
Bramlett, Harrison
Coffee, A. E.

Gordon, C. P.

Kilgore, F. M.

Rollins, John S.

Tyson, W. R.

Welch, Milus M.
Williams, Henry

Company B

Captain: John H. King
Lieutenant: John W. Brooker
Lieutenant: Jesse Crow
Sergeant: E. A. Fincher
Sergeant: J. C. Norton

Privates

Collum, P.
Collum, S. C.
Cagle, J. H.

Duckett, E. A.
Denton, J. F.

Fagala, R. A.

Green, Drury

Kaneister, H. R.
Kaneister, Joseph

Martin, W. H.
McGaughy, H. C.

Powell, Geo. W.

Ray, James E.
Redwine, Henry T.

Stephenson, John

Wilson, John

Company C

Captain: Timothy Ford
Lieutenant: W. H. C. Freeman
Lieutenant: Robert P. Neal
Lieutenant: A. V. Whaley
Ensign: M. W. Hill

Privates

Bowman, William
Bridges, John H.
Black, T. H.

Dilliard, Thos. P.
Dantzler, A. P.

Hix, B. K.
Hair, Geo. W.

Longley, W. J.

Mitchell, J. F.
McKeon, John

Redwine, J. M.

Strickland, Wilson
Stone, James

Williams, A. C.
White, John

STATE CAPITOL RECORDS OF CONFEDERATE SOLDIERS 211

Company D

Sergeant: J. L. Sutton
Sergeant: M. A. B. Tatum

Privates

Bryant, J. F.
Morehead, G. W.

Company E

Private: J. B. Hill

Company F

Captain: J. H. Anderson
Sergeant: D. E. A. Anderson

Privates

Conley, Charles
Fox, R. H.
Gillilan, D. W.
Harris, G. P.
Keys, W. A.
MaGill, L. L.
Smith, C. A.
Smith, R. F.
Smith, J. W.
Taylor, T. H
Wells, B. F.

Company H

Sergeant: John Williams
Corporal: H. G. Baker

Privates

Evans, H. T.
Halcomb, A. G.

Company K

Lieutenant: T. J. Foster
Lieutenant: W. A. Weaver
Sergent: A. L. Alexander
Sergeant: S. A. Brice
Sergeant: M. G. Clements
Corporal: W. H. Chapin

Privates

Duncan, Hugh L.
Evitt, T. M.
Keith, Joel M.

ADDITIONAL LIST OF 39TH GEORGIA REGIMENT

Brooker, John W.	Co. B.	Hill, W. W.	
Black, John	Co. A.		
Bowman, William	Co. C.	Keys, Isaac	Co. F.
Black, Hamilton		Keys, W. A.	Co. F.
Brooker, W. C.	Co. B.		
Bridges, John H.	Co. C.	Longley, Jasper	Co. C.
Collum, Charles	Co. B.	Messimer, Peter K.	Co. D.
Duckett, E. A.	Co. B.	Norton, J. C.	Co. B.
Denton, John F.	Co. B.	Neal, Robt. P.	Co. C.**
Dillard, Thos. P.	Co. C.	Nix, William	Co. B.
Field, Wm. G.	Co. A.	Parrott, Josiah C.	Co. G.
Freeman, W. H. C.	Co. C.**	Price, O. D.	Co. G.
Fox, Haney	Co. F.	Rollins, John	Co. A.
		Redwine, Henry T.	Co. B.
Gillian, D. W.	Co. F.		
		Smith, Charles A.	Co. F.
Hair, George W.	Co. C.	Stone, James	Co. C.
Hix, B. K.	Co. C.	Strickland, Wilson	Co. C.
Hammontree, W. R.	Co. F.		

*List furnished by Mrs. W. M. Sapp.
**Captain.

THIRTY-NINTH GEORGIA INFANTRY****

Colonel: J. T. McConnell
Colonel: J. F. B. Jackson
Major: J. H. Randall
Adjutant: Wm. McAllister
Captain, Co. A: L. W. Crook
Captain, Co. B: T. H. Pitner
Captain, Co. C: Timothy Ford
Captain, Co. D: J. W. Cureton
Captain, Co. E: C. D. Hill
Captain, Co. F: Jas. H. Anderson
Captain, Co. G: B. J. Brown
Captain, Co. K: J. W. Brady
Captain, Co. I: John D. Hayes
Captain, Co. H: Wm. H. Edwards

MUSTER ROLL, COMPANY B,*** SIXTIETH REGIMENT, GEORGIA VOLUNTEER INFANTRY, ARMY OF NORTHERN VIRGINIA
Evans' Brigade, Gordon's Division

Captain: Walter B. Jones*****
1st Lieutenant: John W. McGhee
2nd Lieutenant: C. D. Birks
2nd Lieutenant: Geo. W. Wood***
1st Sergeant: John C. Fuller
2nd Sergeant: Geo. W. Fuller
3rd Sergeant: Thos. J. Hardy
4th Sergeant: Benj. M. Gates

5th Sergeant: Thos. C. Neal
1st Corporal: John J. Ransom
2nd Corporal: S. H. Satterwhite
3rd Corporal: Benj. H. H. Gates
4th Corporal: John Bailey

John Donald, Drummer

Privates

Adams, Wm. A.
Adams, James
Adams, Wm. F.
Adams, E. S.
Allen, H. C.

Bailey, Hinton C.
Boon, Jesse T.
Boon, James P.
Butts, Wm. J.
Beeland, Leroy N.
Baker, A. T.
Brantley, John
Brantley, Robert R.
Brewer, Alfred
Brewer, Hilliard
Belt, John W.
Boles, P. B.

Caudle, Thos. A.
Caudle, D. P.
Caudle, Robt. F.
Cleveland, John O.
Cleveland, Joseph H.
Cleveland, E. P.
Cox, Barney C.
Cox, W. C.

Dennis, H. S.
Duke, Wm. B.
Davis, Wm. H.
Durham, W. H.
Duke, J. A.

Fuller, Green
Fuller, James D.
Ferguson, Robt. Hill
Floyd, T. F.
Floyd, H. D.
Fuller, Croff

Fuller, A. J.
Forrester, R. R. S.
Floyd, J. D.

Gorham, Henry H.
Gorham, Wm.
Gray, Jacob
Gilbert, Wm. F.
Glanton, W. E.
Green, Charleston H.
Griggs, A. J.
Gore, J. F.

Hale, W. C.
Hardy, Wm. L.
Herndon, Jesse H.
Hardy, John R.
Hall, Pleasant B.
Hardy, W. B.
Hicks, Amos E.
Hunter, J. D.
Hale, John
Hardy, J. C.
Hardy, J. R.
Hill, A.
Hunter, W. A.
Hardy, J. D.

Ingram, W. T.

Jones, T. G.
Johnson (or ston), Thos. L.
Johns, William
Jones, J. M.
Johnson, J. S.
Jones, W. H. C.

McCurry, John T.
McCauly, William

McCutchen, T. P.
McDonald, Robert
McKee, W. M.
McGhee, T. W., Sr.
McGhee, T. W., Jr.
McFarland, R. S.
McAlister, A. P.
McKinley, W. P.
McGhee, Mack
Mobley, W. D. A.
Marsh, John
Marsh, Thos. T.
Mallory, Wm. J.
Moore, Wm. A.
Mervin, A. F.
Mallory, J. N.
Middlebrook, Wiley J.
Mallory, J. D.

Neal, Nathan H.

O'Neal, Jas. R.
Oliver, Joseph H.
Oliver, T. J.
O'Neal, Rouse
O'Neal, W. H.
O'Neal, Augustus

Piper, J. H.

Rutldege, Wm.
Ransome, Erwin B.
Rogers, Seaborn J.

Sevils, John
Sample, John T.
Smith, Wm. M.
Smith, J. W.
Smith, J. J.
Smith, J. M.

***Junior 2nd Lieutenant.
**Promoted to Major.

***Originally Company B, Fourth Georgia Batallion, enlisted July 17, 1861; made Company B, Sixtieth Georgia Regiment, January or June 5, 1862.
****List taken from Avery's History of Georgia.
*****Later promoted to major.

STATE CAPITOL RECORDS OF CONFEDERATE SOLDIERS 213

Sevills, J. Samuel
Satterwhite, S. H.
Spears,
Sturdivant, J. J.
Simmons, A. F.
Smith, J. M.
Strong,

Talley, Leon F.
Thompson Wm.
Traylor, Wm. P.
Thrash, Geo. W.

Varner, Wm.

White, Jno. T.
White, Elipah V. H.
White, Milledge W.
Williams, Henry W.
Wilson, Thos. F.
Wright, Columbus, G.
Wills, Wm. D.
Williams, Wm.
Wise, Walton J.
Warner, Jas. H.
Wade, Henry
White, A.
White, W. M.
White, J. W.

White, G. A.
White, R. A.
Watts, John T.
Wyche, Jefferson W.
Watts, Robert
White, A.
Williams, D. F.
Williams, J. W.
White, C.
Watts, Levi E.
Yancey, Linton W.

MUSTER ROLL, COMPANY C, SIXTIETH REGIMENT, GEORGIA VOLUNTEER INFANTRY, ARMY OF NORTHERN VIRGINIA
Evans' Brigade, Gordon's Division
September 18, 1861

Captain: J. Wardlaw
1st Lieutenant: M. Russell
2nd Lieutenant: F. Napier
2nd Lieutenant: D. F. Myers*
1st Sergeant: H. H. H. McWhorter
2nd Sergeant: A. J. Blackwell
3rd Sergeant: D. F. Hale
4th Sergeant: H. A. Maddox
5th Sergeant: William Foster
1st Corporal: G. B. Carroll
2nd Corporal: C. W. Taylor, Jr.
3rd Corporal: W. R. Jones
4th Corporal: J. W. Blackwell
J. D. Taylor: Musician

Privates

Allen, C. P.
Alexander, J. A.
Arnold, Jacob
Arnold, James
Atkins, J. F.
Atkins, W. J.
Atwood, John
Alexander, H. N.
Alexander, J. F.

Bailey, W. B.
Bird, J. H.
Bird, P. J.
Brookout, J. C.
Butler, William
Brewer, G. W.
Bird, W. B.
Bird, J. M.
Carroll, H. H.
Cason, Andrew
Chastain, J. N.
Caudell, E. C.
Caudell, S.
Caudell, M.
Collins, G. B.
Collins, W. P.
Crutchfield, J. H.
Cooper, J. M.
Cooper, T. A.
Calhoun, R. G.
Cooper, Robert

Denton, J. A.
Dedmond, J. T.
Dunn, W. F.
Day, T. M.
Day, James
Day, J. B.

Edwards, C. M.
Ellis, R. A.
Edge, John
Edge, R. D.

Lambert, Daniel
Lambert, John
Lively, Augustus
Lanier, R. M.
Lowry, V. S.
Lansford, G. E.
McCurdy, William
McWhorter, I. M.
McDonald, J. C.
McDaniel, T. C.
McCutchen, A. R.
McCutchen, J. T.
McWhorter, L. R.
McKinney, A. D. (F)
McArthur, A. R.
McWhorter, W. D.
McWhorter, W. F.
McClure, W. J.
McClure, S. D.
McClure, W. C.
Maddox, W. P.
Moore, N. W.
Murray, D. A.
Myers, G. B.
Mack, J. W.
Myers, E. J.

Porter, John
Pendley, B. M.
Poe, T. C.
Pendley, S. S.
Pendley, A. P.
Pendley, B. F.
Pendley, A. F.
Payne, W. R.
Rutledge, J. H.

Spraggins, William
Surratt, H. A.
Strickland, W. C.
Swift, J. A.
Self, J. A.
Smith, J. H.

Ellis, Cyrus H.

Farnsworth, J. W.
Farnsworth, L. R.
Fletcher, L. R.
Farnsworth, G. W.

Gilliam, James M.
Gannt, J. S.
Gray, W. R.
Gillian, J. H.
Gillian, M. A.

Hale, G. H.
Hall, J. A.
Hall, S. M.
Hall, J. M.
Hall, J. E.
Hall, G. W.
Hendon, J. A.
Hendon, L. M.
Hendon, T. B.
Harris, M. C.
Hall, David
Hall, G. H.
Hall, W. S.
Hall, W. A.
Howell, T. G.
Haish, M.
Hall, G. W.

Ireland, William

Jackson, Edward
Jackson, D. C.
Jones, H. H.
Jay, J. C.
Jay, William
Jay, James
Jackson, Thos. N.

Keown, N. A.
Kirkes, J. W.

*Junior 2nd Lieutenant.

Taylor, John
Taylor, C. W., Sr.
Terrell, Edward
Thomas, Daniel
Tipton, G. W.
Thurman, B. F.
Tucker, W. H.
Tipton, C. C.
Wilson, H. H.
Wilson, W. W.
Wilson, George R.
Williams, W. R.
Williams, J. N.
Williams, H. H.
Welden, W. M.
Wardlaw, J. F.
Wardlaw, J. F.
Ward, E. A.
Wilson, J. L.
Williams, J. F.
Wall, William T.

MUSTER ROLL, COMPANY D, SIXTIETH REGIMENT, GEORGIA VOLUNTEER INFANTRY, ARMY OF NORTHERN VIRGINIA
Evans' Brigade, Gordon's Division
C. S. A.

D. Taliaferro: Captain Sept. 19, 2861; resigned Aug. 15, 1863.
J. E. Norris: 1st Lieutenant Sept. 19, 1861; promoted to Captain Aug. 15, 1962; resigned 1863.
T. J. Jackson: 2nd Lieutenant Sept. 19, 1861; resigned April, 1862.
George A. Cooper: Junior 2nd Lieutenant Sept. 19, 1861; resigned Feb. 13, 1862.
A. G. Owens: 1st Sergeant Sept. 19, 1861; elected 2nd Lieutenant April, 1862; promoted 1st Lieutenant June 10, 1863; mortally wounded Sept. 2, 1864.
W. J. Ault: 2nd Sergeant Sept. 19, 1861; reduced December 14, 1862; discharged Feb. 1, 1863 furnishing W. Hollifield as substitute.
J. A. Huffaker: 3rd Sergeant Sept. 19, 1861; reduced to ranks July, 1862;
J. M. W. Christain: 4th Sergeant Sept. 19, 1861; promoted to 1st Sergeant December, 1862; elected 3rd Lieutenant June 10, 1863; promoted 1st Lieutenant Sept. 2, 1864.
E. H. Martin: 5th Sergeant Sept. 19, 1861; elected Junior 2nd Lieutenant February 28, 1862; promoted 1st Lieutenant 1864.
H. M. Jones: 1st Corporal September 19, 1861; captured 1864; in prison close of war.
J. K. Spann: 2nd Corporal Sept. 19, 1861; discharged Jan. 25, 1865, disability.
A. H. Bohannan: 3rd Corporal Sept. 18, 1861; died Richmond, Va., July 19, 1863; buried Hollywood dcemetery.
T. K. McDonald: 4th Corporal Sept. 19, 1861; promoted 3rd Corporal 1862.
Robert Hawks: Fifer September 19, 1861.

Privates

Ault, Henry C.

Bandy, George M.
Bridges, W. L.
Bridges, J. W.
Brock, N.
Burke, James
Bohannon, W. L.
Bohannon D. J.
Boatwright, John
Bowen, W. M.
Bowler, Robert
Brumbow, W. F.
Burgess, William
Bowen, T. H.
Brown, Jos. T.

Crow, C. M.
Coffee, T. D.
Clark, D. J.
Clark, B. B.
Christian, F. A.
Christian, J. W.
Christian, J. H.
Dean, Thomas H.
Dowdy, J. A.
Davis, William

Guyse, G. H.
Greenwood Wiley
Gassaway, David

Hicks, J. W.
Hawkes, S. M.
Hawkes, S. F.
Hawkes, P. L.
Hardy, W. C.
Hicks, J. M.
Hicks, J. J.
Haigler, A. S.
Holden, H. R.
Hollifield, Wiley
Haigler, Adam
Hammett, W.

Ivey, G. W.

Jones, G. E.
Johnson, A. A.
Johnson, C.
Johnson, N.
James, F. F. (or E.)
Jackson, F. (or E.) C.

King, B. C.
King, S. H.
Kyle, J. C.

Lanier, W. N.
Lanier, H. Y.
Lanier, Bartley
Lanier, Robert
Lother, William

Landers, H. A.
Lane, Granville B.

Montgomery, James H.
McAbee, J. W.
McAbee, W. F.
McDonald, A. P.
Mastin, N. B.
Martin, J. B.
Morgan, W. M.
Mulkey, F. M.
Murdock, S. P.
Miller, S. T.
Milliron, A. J.
Moore, E.
Mote, S. M. P.

Oglesby, W. B.
Oliver, Reuben
Pruits, Isham
Pryor, P. W.
Potts, G. J.
Potts, W. J. G.
Potts, D. L.
Perry, J. M.
Potts, J. A.
Potts, W. M.

Regan, James C.
Rollins, J. F.

STATE CAPITOL RECORDS OF CONFEDERATE SOLDIERS 215

Shaw, J. G.
Sloan, W. A.
Strickland, F. (or E.) P.
Stone, L. S.
Sloan, F. W.
Stroup, J. M.

Tate, W. W.
Taliaferro, W. F.
Tate, A. C.
Tate, W. J.
Thomas, Wm. M.
Townsend, H. M.

Wright, A. H.
Wright, William
Webb, J. F.
Wilson, L.
Wilson, Pleasant

MUSTER ROLL, COMPANY E, SIXTIETH REGIMENT, GEORGIA VOLUNTEER INFANTRY, ARMY OF NORTHERN VIRGINIA
Evans' Brigade, Gordon's Division
C. S. A.

September 19, 1861

Captain: John W. Beck
1st Lieutenant: Robert J. McCamy
2nd Lieutenant: W. W. Wilkins
2nd Lieutenant: W. T. Cleveland*
1st Sergeant: J. L. Beck
2nd Sergeant: S. S. McCamy
3rd Sergeant: P. M. Teasley

4th Sergeant: D. Nix
5th Sergeant: R. H. White
1st Corporal: J. S. Loftin
2nd Corporal: Henry Hogue
3rd Corporal: M. M. Earnest
4th Corporal: W. P. Gamble

Privates

Beck, R. T.
Box, J. M.
Bagwell, T. J.
Bruce, H. K.
Brown, Jas. M.
Blackritter, J. R.
Burkett, J. M.
Beck, R. T.

Cleveland, Thomas
Cleveland, J. O.
Cain, W. F.
Couch, J. B.
Cox, W. S.
Curtis, Joshua
Cook, Neverson
Cardin, W. M.
Curd, Benjamin
Cooper J. G.
Cook, J. M.
Coffee, James
Campbell, John
Cain, J. H.
Cain, J. C.

Dover, James E.
Dover, S. Z.
Dobbins, Lewis
Dover, A. E.

Earnest, S. F.

Floyd, W. A.

Goodwin, James
Goodwin, John
Gilbert, C. D.
Gamble, J. W.
Gaines, A. M.
Green, D.
Henson, Loyd
Harris, R. G.
Harris, Robert
Hackett, John

Hall, G. W.
Hembree, J. P.
Hembree, D. G.
Hopper, James C.
Henry, A. A.

Ivie, Milton

Jones, B. Henderson
Johnson, T. D.
Kettle, W. C.
King, J. M.
Kile, Jasper

Landers, T. L.
Logan, J. H.
Ledford, Ephriam
Lackey, W. C.
Langford, John
Lents, J. K. P.
Lents, Willis
Logan, J. P.
Landers, H. A.

McCamy, James
Miller, Joseph
Moats, A. J.
McCulloch, G. T.
Mack, T. H.
Mack, John
McIntyre, J. C.
Mackey, J. W.
McDonald, Collins
McClerg, W. D.
McCormik, H.
McClain, D. C.
McClain, Thomas
McClain, Jones

O'Neill, W. J. T.
Osborne, John

Price, H. C.
Palmer, R. H.

Plemons, J. M.
Plemons, Z. T.
Parker, J. H. H.
Palmer, Thomas.
Page, T. J.
Pullen, Green
Palmer, J. R.
Plemons, W. E.
Plemons, Z. T.
Pullen, G.
Rosey, J. T.
Rosey, J. W.
Roberson, J. M.
Ray, David J.
Reagan, J. T.
Roberts, Thomas
Roberts, M.
Reagan, J. E.
Reed, William
Routh, K. L.

Smith, J. G.
Shelton, Robert
Sparks, G. W.
Stanton, John W.
Sims, E. T.
Smith, J. L.
Satterfield, B.

Tarver, E. L.
Thompson, J. W.
Thompson, G. H.
Terry, Champ
Thomas, G. W.

Umphrey, John

Vining, Thos. B.

White, F. M.
Wagner, S. D.
Webster, Martin

Zachary, C. W.

216   HISTORY OF WHITFIELD COUNTY

MUSTER ROLL, COMPANY F, SIXTIETH REGIMENT, GEORGIA VOLUNTEER INFANTRY, ARMY OF NORTHERN VIRGINIA
Evans' Brigade, Gordon's Division
C. S. A.

Captain: W. P. Jarrell
1st Lieutenant: W. W. Elder
2nd Lieutenant: W. R. Jenkins
2nd Lieutenant: T. L. Rogers*
2nd Lieutenant: William M. Jones
2nd Lieutenant: S. B. McCamy
2nd Lieutenant: B. F. Keller*
1st Sergeant: A. E. Dover
2nd Sergeant: O. W. Penie
3rd Sergeant: Jas. M. Rogers
4th Sergeant: William T. Ash
5th Sergeant: S. A. Plemons
1st Corporal: T. H. Bennett
2nd Corporal: Elam Orr
3rd Corporal: A. J. Fore
4th Corporal: Allen Martin
Jas. H. Montgomery, Drummer

Privates

Bass, John
Brooks, H. P.
Bryan, L. F.
Bennett, R. B.
Brown, B. W.
Bennett, J. A.

Cole, J. W.
Clark, J. K.
Clark, J. W.
Cross, W. W.
Corbin, Hamilton
Corbin, L.
Carlisle, L.
Canote, Robert
Corbin, M. C.
Carroll, M.
Carroll, W. M.
Carroll, John
Cooper, A. W.
Cooper, William

Douthit, Silas
Deffer, Martin
Dover, James
Davis, T. J.
Douglas, Calvin
Densmore, A.
Deffer, W. J.
Dover, H. J.
Douglas, J. T.
Davis, Wm.
Dover, Killen
Dover, Bailey
Dover, D. M.
Dover, Jesse

Eason, J. F.
Elder, H. T.
Elder, J. S.

Flanigan, John
Fullbright, A. C.
Fullbright, H. W.
Hipp, W. M.
Hill, M. R.
Higgins, James
Harris, D. H.

Ivie, L. C.
Ivie, J. O.
Ingram, M. C.
Ingram, J. M.
Inman, G. W.

James, J. S.
James, W. H.
Jones, Gilbert
Jones, G. W.

Kilpatrick, C. L.

Lusk, W. R.

McKinney, A.
Master, W. W.
Maddox, John H.
Moreland, W. E.
Moreland, J. F.
Moreland, J. L.
Moreland, J. W.
Moreland, W. D.

Nelson, A. E.
Nelson, J. E.

Orr, James

Parkes, T. M.
Painter, M. A.
Pritchett, J. M.

Pritchett, N. R.
Pritchett, Jasper
Penn, Leroy
Perry, C. B.
Pankey, Wm. E.
Plemons, W. M.
Painter, W. J.
Pritchett, J. M.
Plemons, J. L.
Plemons, T. M.
Pankey, Wiley
Payne, J. T.

Rutledge, J. R.

Spears, D. F.
Stroup, L.
Souther, J. W.
Souther, John J.
Smart, M. L.
Spears, W. B.
Spivey, L. D.
Sluder, John
Sluder, J. C.
Sharp, J. M.
Spears, J. M.

Tatum, P. M.
Terry, J.
Turner, Jas.
Talley, B. B.

Welch, A. S.
Wells, Thos. J.
Williams, Jas. J.
West, Henry
Wooding, John
Wayne, W. R.

FOURTH GEORGIA REGIMENT OF CAVALRY

"The first organization of the Fourth Georgia Regiment was a scouting company called the Georgia Mountain Dragoons. Its officers were, I. W. Avery, Captain; W. L. Cook, 1st Lieutenant; D. J. Owens, 2nd Lieutenant and H. H. Burk, 3rd Lieutenant.

"This independent company was raised mainly in Whitfield county, but some of its members were from the adjoining counties. Before they left the state, the ladies of Dalton made them a beautiful stand of colors of the Southern Cross, which Miss Anna Harden in a most happy

*Junior 2nd Lieutenant.

manner presented to them.

"August, 1862, the Twenty-third Georgia Batalion consisting of five companies, was organized and in a short time thereafter they were ordered to join the arrmy in Tennessee. November, 1862, near Fayetteville, Tennessee, the Fourth Georgia Regiment was formed with I. W. Avery as Colonel, W. L. Cook as Lieutenant, D. J. Owens as Major, W. K. Moore Quartermaster, Columbus Waddle, Commandant, Dr. Edelin, Surgeon, Thos. L. Kelly, Assistant Surgeon and B. H. Newton, Adjutant.

"The Fourth Georgia Cavalry was with General Braxton Bragg through the entire campaign in middle Tennessee. They fought gloriously at Chickamauga, Dalton, Resaca, Oostanaula, Kennesaw, Atlanta, Jonesboro on to Savannah, through the Carolinas to Bentonville.

"May 26, 1864, Colonel Avery was desperately wounded at New Hope Church. He raised and led fifteen hundred men, surrendering fifty-eight under General Joseph E. Johnston in North Carolina, all that were left after participating in more than one hundred battles and skirmishes. It also took part in the capture of General Stoneman, near Macon. It was called the 'Charging Regiment' of General Crewe's Brigade.

"The late Judge, C. D. McCutchen, and Colonel W. K. Moore were officers in the Fourth Georgia Regiment. Dalton furnished a number of men to the Fourth Georgia Regiment of Cavalry, who represented 'All that was lofty in principle, pure in patriotism and dauntless in courage'."*

Officers Fourth Georgia Cavalry

Colonel: Isaac W. Avery
Lieutenant Colonel: W. L. Cook
Major: D. J. Owen
Major: J. R. Stewart
Adjutant: B. H. Newton
Adjutant: J. W. Ramsay
A. C. S.: Jos. M. Stones
Captain (A): R. A. Keith**
1st Lieutenant (A): G. D. Hancock
2nd Lieutenant (A): G. A. Sloan
Captain (B): G. B. May
1st Lieutenant (B): T. S. May
2nd Lieutenant (B): J. C. McIntyre
2nd Lieutenant (B): J. W. Ramsay
2nd Lieutenant (B): J. Hill
Assistant Quartermaster: W. K. Moore
2nd Lieutenant (B): Dave May*
Captain (C): Jeff Johnson
1st Lieutenant (C): H. C. Erwin
2nd Lieutenant (C): D. A. Holland
2nd Lieutenant (C): A. R. Bates
Captain (D): Wm. J. Rogers
1st Lieutenant (D): J. C. Hartman
2nd Lieutenant (D): J. M. Boydston
2nd Lieutenant (D): J. Readdick
Captain (E): W. L. Cook
Captain (E): Olin Wellborn
Captain (E): B. C. Waddell
1st Lieutenant (E): J. Johnson
2nd Lieutenant (E): J. J. Johnson
2nd Lieutenant (E): A. H. Jones
Captain (F): C. D. McCutchen

Captain (F): Jos. E. Helvingstone*
Captain (F): J. D. Allen
Captain (F): J. W. O'Neal
Captain (F): J. R. Sloan
Captain (G): Wm. R. Logan
Captain (G): R. E. Kingsley
1st Lieutenant (G): R. E. Creekmore
2nd Lieutenant (G): W. J. Dean
2nd Lieutenant (G): W. M. C. Parkinson
Captain (H): G. H. Graham
1st Lieutenant (H): J. T. Freeman
1st Lieutenant (H): Wm. T. Arnold
1st Lieutenant (H): W. M. Martin
Captain (I): I. W. Avery
Captain (I): D. J. Owen
Captain (I): H. H. Burk
1st Lieutenant (I): D. J. Owen
1st Lieutenant (I): H. H. Burk
2nd Lieutenant (I): J. Shehan
2nd Lieutenant (I): A. C. Guntz
2nd Lieutenant (I): G. W. Mitchell
2nd Lieutenant (I): R. Sutherland
Captain (K): J. R. Stewart
1st Lieutenant (K): P. W. Stewart
2nd Lieutenant (K): W. O. Cain
2nd Lieutenant (K): F. A. Eubanks
Captain (L): L. B. Anderson
1st Lieutenant (L): J. C. N. Foote
2nd Lieutenant (L): W. B. Chappell
2nd Lieutenant (L): W. A. Nolan
Captain (M): John D. Ashton

---

*This article was prepared for the Bryant M. Thomas Chapter, United Daughters o the Confederacy by the late Miss Laura Kelly, Historian of the Chapter

**Killed.

*Killed.

HISTORY OF WHITFIELD COUNTY

Privates in Colonel W. K. Moore's Regiment

———Hamilton, Chaplain
Rufus Fletcher
George P. Fraker

———Worley
———Crumley
Lee Burse

Other Officers of Fourth Georgia Cavalry Regiment (Second) 867

Colonel: Duncan L. Clinch
Lieutenant Colonel: John L. Harris
Major: J. C. McDonald
Captain (A) J. S. Wiggins
Captain (B): W. M. Hazzard
Captain (C): N. A. Brown
Captain (D): Jno. Raddick

Captain (E): R. N. King
Captain (F): J. P. Turner
Captain (G): A. McMillan
Captain (H): T. S. Wylley
Captain (I): J. C. Nichols
Captain (K): D. Crum

MUSTER ROLL, CAPTAIN JOSEPH GLENN'S COMPANY, COMPANY A, 36TH GEORGIA VOLUNTEERS
Station, Mount Vernon
January 15, 1862
Copied from original muster roll now in the possession of Mrs. Thomas Glenn

Colonel Jesse A. Glenn, Commanding
Dr. J. R. McAfee, Acting Surgeon
1st Lieutenant: Samuel H. Baker
2nd Lieutenant: Daniel Connor
3rd Lieutenant: John Sanson
1st Sergeant: Isreal Hallman
2nd Sergeant: S. W. Pile (or Pike)

3rd Sergeant: C. B. W. Buece
4th Sergeant: S. T. Mote
5th Sergeant: Thomas Ring
1st Corporal: Jackson Couch
2nd Corporal: Alfred North
3rd Corporal: F. M. Jennings
4th Corporal: H. D. Lymance

Privates

Beuce, W. F.
Brown, L. E.
Blackston, Henry
Blanks, Joseph
Bryce, Alexander
Baker, E. P.
Bradley, J. J.
Brown, L. W.
Barber, W. C.

Cox, Philip
Connor John
Cruse, F. W.
Cronan, J. W.

Dyer, Wm. E.
Drennan, J. C.

Etheridge, Bryant
Etheridge, John
Ezzard, George W.

Ezzard, J. T.
Ezzard, Thomas W.
Fowler, James
Frazier, John
Fortner, C. D.

George, L. C.
Green, Isaac
George, Silas
Green, M. J.

Hilton, James
Holcomb, R. R.

Kincannon, L. S.
Kincannon, Aaron
Karr, Jesse W.
Karr, Greenberry
Ketchum, J. S.

Larman, J. B.

Mauldin, C. H.
Morgan, John F.
Mayfield, G. B.
Montgomery, W. H.

Norrell, Samuel A.
Norrell, Robert

Roper, J. H.
Roper, P. B.
Roberts, R. W.

Stephens, L. H.
Stewart, J. W.
Samples, W. C.
Thomas, J. R.
Thomas, O. P.
Yancey, Charles
Williams, J. J.
Wadkins, Lemuel
Wood, Robert

Return of 36th Regiment Georgia Volunteers July 31, 1862, stationed at Camp Hatton, East Tennessee.

Company A, Joseph Glenn, Capt. .... 112 Men
Company B, George A. Cooper, Capt. .... 109 Men
Company C, F. M. Dwight, Capt. .... 90 Men
Company D, John Loudermilk, Capt. .... 113 Men
Company E, J. E. Gilbert, Capt. .... 97 Men
Company F, C. L. Martan, Capt. .... 98 Men
Company G, D. H. Elledge, Capt. .... 88 Men
Company H, A. P. Roberts, Capt. .... 82 Men
Company I, J. L. Morgan, Capt. .... 72 Men
Company K, A. Dyer, Capt. .... 71 Men

STATE CAPITOL RECORDS OF CONFEDERATE SOLDIERS

OFFICERS OF COMPANIES OF 36TH GEORGIA VOLUNTEERS, JULY 31, 1862

Company A—
  Jesse A. Glenn, Colonel
  Dr. J. R. McAfee, Acting Surgeon
  Samuel H. Baker, 1st Lieutenant
  Daniel Connor, 2nd Lieutenant
  Johnson Sanson, 3rd Lieutenant
  Isreal Hallman, 1st Sergeant
  S. W. Pile, or Pike, 2nd Sergeant
  C. B. W. Buece, 3rd Sergeant
  S. T. Mote, 4th Sergeant
  Thomas Ring, 5th Sergeant
  Jackson Couch, 1st Corporal
  Alfred North, 2nd Corporal
  F. M. Jennings, 3rd Corporal
  H. D. Lymance, 4th Corporal

Company B—
  G. A. Cooper, Captain
  Wm. H. Hill, 1st Lieutenant
  E. Hollin, 2nd Lieutenant
  James A. Edwards, 3rd Lieutenant

Company C—
  F. M. Dwight, Captain
  J. B. Griffin, 1st Lieutenant
  E. S. Hill, 2nd Lieutenant
  J. J. Suttle, 3rd Lieutenant

Company D—
  John Loudermilk, Captain
  John Davis, 1st Lieutenant
  Willis Martin, 2nd Lieutenant
  Henry Young, 3rd Lieutenant

Company E—
  J. D. Gilbert, Captain
  L. E. Jefferson, 1st Lieutenant
  W. B. Hilhards, 2nd Lieutenant
  J. J. Leonard, 3rd Lieutenant

Company F—
  E. L. Morton, Captain
  C. M. Jones, 1st Lieutenant
  G. B. Hudson, 2nd Lieutenant
  W. E. C. Wilson, 3rd Lieutenant

Company G—
  D. H. Elledge, Captain
  J. B. Smith, 1st Lieutenant
  J. N. Rogers, 2nd Lieutenant
  R. T. Bridges, 3rd Lieutenant

Company H—
  A. P. Roberts, Captain
  W. G. Harris, 1st Lieutenant
  J. Smither, 2nd Lieutenant
  T. B. Kelptyne, 3rd Lieutenant

Company I—
  Jacob L. Morgan, Captain
  L. R. Willis, 1st Lieutenant
  R. R. Grant, 2nd Lieutenant
  V. D. Lyles, 3rd Lieutenant

Company K—
  A. A. Dyer, Captain
  J. C. Carroll, 1st Lieutenant
  T. J. Curier, 2nd Lieutenant
  N. L. Wallace, 3rd Lieutenant

Captain B. B. White, Company C, of Whitfield, resigned July 8, 1862. D. F. M. Dwight promoted July 8, 1862 to captain; Lieutenant J. B Griffin to First Lieutenant; Lieutenant E. S. Hill to Second Lieutenant, and J. J. Suttle from First Sergeant to Third Lieutenant.

Roster of Joseph E. Johnston Camp, No. 34, United Confederate Veterans, Dalton, Ga.

There are doubtless few who know that Camp Joseph E. Johnston, No. 34, United Confederate Veterans, was the first camp ever organized in the South, but such is a fact. While the camp is designated No. 34, it is rreally entitled to first place. It came about in this way: The camp was organized August 18, 1891, and on January 11, 1892, together with thirty-three others at New Orleans, received its charter, or permit, from General John B. Gordon and the quotation, "The first shall be last" was literally verified.

The following were the first officers: A. P. Roberts, Commander; B. M. Thomas, Vice-commander; W. K. Moore, Vice-commander; J. A. Blanton, Adjutant; Fred Cappes, Treasurer. There were about thirty-five charter members, among them were: C. D. McCutchen, John R. Tarver, R. J. McCamy, L. H. Tinsley, J. W. Barrett, J. F. Denton, A. W. Lynn, Jesse A. Glenn, Judson C. Clements, John W. Brooker, W. H.

Brooker, J. G. McAfee, C. P. Gordon, John Black, Geo. W. Anderson, James H. Hamilton, Geo. W. Hamilton, H. C. Hamilton, R. P. O'Neill, Thomas Jolley, Warren R. Davis, T. H. Pitner, W. H. Pruden, B. K. Hix, John Sansom, and T. H. Pitner.

Captain A. P. Roberts was the initial organizer, and for years was the chief executive, and was untiring in his efforts to build up the camp.

The selection of the name was a most happy one, and very appropriate, on account of Dalton having been headquarters, at one time, of General Johnston, the great strategist of the sixties.

MEMBERS*

Albertson, Sam W.	Co. D, 27th Ga. Reg. Inf.
Anderson, G. W.	Co. —, Tenn. Inf.
Baker, R. H.	Phillips' Legion
Barnett, Andrew J.	Co. D, 22nd Ga. Reg.
Barrett, Lank W.	Co. E, 29th Tenn. Reg.
Batey, W. W.	Co. F, 20th Tenn.
Bazemore, R. M.	Co. E, 6th Ga. Reg. Inf.
Bearden, D. J.	Co. D, 65th Ga. Reg.
Bogle, Joseph	Co. I, 40th Ga. Reg.
Bogle, John W.	Co. I, 1st State Line Troops
Bowen, T. H.	Co. D, Ga. Bat.
Bowman, William	Co. C, 39th Ga. Reg.
Bowie, John W.	Co. B, Cobb's Legion
Black, Hamilton	Co. B, 39th Ga. Reg.
Black, John	Co. A, 38th Ga. Reg. Inf.
Black, Thomas	Co. C, 3rd Ga. Reg.
Blackburn, B. F.	Co. G, 11th Ga. Reg.
Blackburn, B. F.	Co. G, 10th Ga. Reg.
Blanton, J. A.	Co. B, Phillips' Legion
Bramblett, Harrison	White's Bat.
Bramblett, W. H.	White's Bat.
Bradford, N. A.	Co. C, Cobb's Legion
Bridges, J. W.	Co. D, 4th Ga. Bat.
Bridges, J. H.	Co. C, 39th Ga. Reg.
Britton, W. A.	Co. E, 4th Ga. Cav.
Brooks, John	Cain's Tenn. Bat.
Brooker, John W.	Co. B, 39th Ga. Reg.
Brooker, William H.	Co. G, 39th N. C. Reg.
Brown, J. H.	Co. H, 4th Tenn. Cav.
Brown, A. T.	Gibson's Bat., Cheatham's Div.
Bryson, W. H.	Co. B, Thirty-ninth Ga. Reg.
Burroughs, W. W.	Co. I, Palmetto Sharpshooters
Cannon, G. M.	Co. G, 2nd Tenn. Cav.
Calhoun, A. J.	Co. B, 36th Ga. Reg.
Calhoun, J. K. P.	Co. B, 36th Ga. Reg.
Callahan, John S.	Co. B, Phillips' Legion
Cappes, Fred	Tenn. Battery (Cain's)
Carder, W. H.	Co. A, 3rd Confederate
Carder, Kimsey	Co. C, 11th Ga. Reg.
Carr, R. S.	Co. B, 36th Ga.
Cash, J. M.	Co. H, 3rd Tenn. Inf.
Cates, W. N.	Co. K, 7th Ga. Reg.
Cator, W. M.	7th Ga. Regiment
Chapman, I. N.	Co. F, 1st Maryland Cav.
Clark, Geo.	Co. A, 36th Ga. Reg.
Clark, L. F.	Co. K, 1st Reg. S. C. State
Chester, John S.	Railroad Service, W. & A.
Clements, J. P.	
Clements, Judson C.	Co. I, Ga. State Line
Collum, Chas.	Co. B, 39th Ga. Reg.
Cooper, J. G.	Co. E, 60th Tenn. Reg.
Cochran, Dr. E. C.	Surgeon 31st Tenn.
Coker, Barney	1st S. C. Cav.
Cox, Capt. Fred	Q. M. 36th Ga. Reg.
Clinton, D. P.	Co. I, 42nd Ga. Reg.
Crawford, O. A.	Co. A, 4th Ga.
Crawford, W. H.	Co. C, 11th Ga. Bat.
Crow, F. C.	Bugler Calloway's Battery

STATE CAPITOL RECORDS OF CONFEDERATE SOLDIERS 221

Crump, F. L. .... Co. F, Ga. Reg.
Crump, F. L. .... Co. F, 11th Ga. Inf.

Darnell, W. H. .... Co. C, 40th Ga. Inf.*
Dantzler, L. N. .... Co. I, State Line
Davis, Warren R. .... Co. B, Phillips' Legion
Davis, A. R. .... Co. H, 23rd Ga. Reg.
Denton, J. F. .... Co. B, 39th Ga. Reg.
Deveral, J. H. .... Co. B, 16th Ga. Reg.
Dill, T. H. .... Co. —, 3rd Tenn.
Dimsdale, W. D. .... Co. A, 16th Ga. Reg.
Dowling, John D. .... Co. E, 1st Confederate Inf.
Duckett, E. A. .... Co. B, 3rd Ga. Reg.
Dudley, J. L. .... Co. F, 37th Ga. Inf.
Dillard, T. P. .... Co. C, 39th Ga.

Echols, B. W. .... Co. B, 3rdr Confederate Cavalry
Echolson, C. S. .... Co. E, 3rd Ga. Cav.
Echols, C. S. .... Co. G, 2nd Ga. State Troops
Edwards, Lewis .... Co. I, Glenn's 36th Ga.
England, O. M. .... Co. H, 2nd Ga. Reg. Inf.
England, J. C. .... Co. B, Phillips' Legion
Eubanks, Thos. .... Co. C, 7th Ga. Reg.
Erwin, Henry C. .... Co. C, 4th Ga. Cav.*

Fann, Dr. J. P. .... Co. I, Thomas' Legion (Tenn.)
Farnsworth, J. L. .... Co. I, 29th Tenn. Reg.**
Farrar, C. H. .... Co. H, 18th Va. Reg.
Franklin, A. G. .... Ga. Militia
Felker, S. B. .... Co. D, 2nd Ga. Cav.
Fletcher, R. L. .... Co. G, 4th Ga. Cav.
Ferguson, S. H. .... Army of Virginia
Freeman, Thos. P. .... Co. I, 1st Ga. State Line
Freeman, W. H. C. .... Co. C, 39th Ga. Reg.
Freeman, Jesse P. .... Ga. State Service***
Field, John L. .... Co. D, 6th Ga. Reserves
Field, W. G. .... Co. A, 39th Ga. Reg.
Fincher, Oliver .... Co. H, 4th Ga. Cav.
Finley, W. H. .... Co. C, 1st E. Tenn. Cav.
Finley, Isaac .... Ga. Reserve State Troops
Ford, Timothy .... Co. C, 39th Ga. Reg.*
Fox, Haney .... Co. F, 35th Ga. Reg.
Foster, W. H. .... Co. K, 1st Confederate

Gaffney, Jas. .... Co. F, 13th Ga. Reg.
Gardner, Wm. .... Co. B, Phillips' Legion
Graham, J. D. .... Co. E, 43rd Ga. Inf.
Gramling, Jno. F. .... Co. A, 9th Ga. Batt.
Graves, J. B. .... Co. I, 43rd Tenn. Reg.
Graves, S. G. .... Co. I, 43rd Tenn. Reg.
Glenn, Jesse A. .... 36th Ga. Reg.***
Gregg, A. B. .... Co. F, 39th Tenn. Reg.
Gilbert, N. J. .... Co. K, 4th Ga. Reg. Cav.
Gillilan, D. W. .... Co. F, 39th Ga. Reg.
Godfrey, A. C. .... Co. —, State Reg.
Groves, J. J. .... Co. I, 4th Ga. Cav.
Goodwin, J. T. .... Co. D, 2nd Rifles (S. C.)
Gunz, A. C. .... Co. I, 4th Ga. Cav.

Hair, Geo. W. .... Co. C, 39th Ga. Reg.
Hall, William .... Co. C, 29th N. C. Reg.
Hamilton, Jas. .... Q. M. 34th Ga. Reg.
Hamilton, G. W. .... Co. G, 3rd Ga. Reserves
Hamilton, H. C. .... Co. G, 3rd Ga. Reserves
Hamilton, Thos. .... Co. B, Phillips' Legion
Hammontree, W. R. .... Co. F, 39th Ga. Reg.
Hartley, B. A. .... Co. B, 29th Tenn. Inf.
Hawkins, Wm. .... Co. I, 24th Ga. Reg.
Henderson, Perry .... Co. H, 56th Ga. Reg.
Hendricks, G. W. .... Co. A, 64th Ga. Inf.
Henley, A. J. .... Co. I, 25th N. C. Reg.
Henton, John .... Co. B, Phillips' Legion
Hicks, H. H. .... Co. A, 1st State Line Troops
Hickman, Rev. J. Q. A. .... Co. E, 18th Ga. Reg.

*1st Lieut.

Hickman, M. Fortune .... Co. E, 40th Ga. Reg.
Higgins, J. M. .... Co. —, 60th Ga. Reg.
Hill, W. W. .... Co. C, 39th Ga. Reg.
Hill, John H. .... Gen. W. B. Bates' Escort.
Hix, B. K. .... Co. C, 39th Ga. Reg.
Hooper, Jas. .... Bates' Escort
Hopkins, Jacob .... Co. F, Tenn. Reg. Cav.
Hord, A. J. .... Co. K, 18th Tenn.
Howell, A. H. .... Co. A, 41st Miss. Reg.

Johns, D. C. .... Co. E, 1st Reg. Confederates (Navy)
Johnson, W. W. .... 1st Ga. Reg.
Johnson, L. B. .... Co. B, 25th Ala. Reg.
Johnson, Isaac .... Co. D, Phillips' Legion
Jolly, Thos. ....
Jones, W. F. .... Co. A, 38th Ala. Reg.
Jordan, W. W. .... Co. —, 31st Tenn. Reg.
Jones, H. Melvin .... Co. D, 4th Ga. Bat.

Kelley, Pat .... Co. C, 12th S. C.
Kenner, William H. .... Co. G, Tenn. Cav.
Kennemer, D. L. .... Co. C, 36th Ga. Reg.
Keys, W. A. .... Co. F, 39th Ga. Inf.
Keys, Isaac .... Co. F, 39th Ga. Inf.
King, Thomas .... Co. B, 38th Ga. Reg.
Kirby, T. M. .... Co. H, 14th Tenn. Inf.

LaFitte, J. V. .... Co. I, 5th Ala. Reg.
Lane, J. A. .... Co. G, 28th Ga. Inf.
Lankford, W. C. .... Co. C, 11th Ga. State Cav.
Long, Gilbert .... o. E, 9th Ga. Reg.
Long, Wylie M. .... Co. C, 21st Ga. Reg.
Long, H. P. .... Co. D, 11th Ga. Reg.
Longley, Jasper .... Co. C, 39th Ga. Reg.
Lowry, John A. .... Co. A, 4th Ga. Bat.
Lowry, Esquire W. ....
Lynch, John .... Co. I, 1st Ga. State Line
Lynn, Alex W. .... Co. B, Phillips' Legion
Lynn, Rev. J. C. .... Co. D, 15th Ga. Reg.

McAfee, Dr. J. R. .... Surgeon 36th Ga. Reg.
McBryde, T. C. .... Co. C, 44th Ala. Longstreet Corps
McCamy, S. B. .... Co. F, 60th Ga.*
McCamy, R. J. .... 4th Ga. Bat., 60th Ga.
McCutchen, C. D. .... Co. C, 4th Ga. Cav.*
McEntyre, Chas. .... Co. E, 5th Ark. Reg.
McKinney, Lee .... 1st Ga. State Troops
McKnight, S. J. .... Co. B, Taylor's Tex. Cav.
McNabb, Rev. William .... Co. C, 11th Ga. Reg.
Main, Dr. H. K. .... Co. A, 36th Ga. Reg.
Masters, Jas. A. .... Co. H, 36th Ga. Reg.
Messimer, P. K. .... Co. B, 39th Ga. Reg.
Millirons, W. J. .... Co. H, 2nd Ga. Reg. Inf.
Mitchell, J. F. .... Co. B, Phillips' Legion
Moore, W. K. .... Q. M. 4th Ga. Reg. Cav.**
Moore, L. N. .... Co. F, 11th Ga. Reg.
Moore, Joseph H. .... N. B. Forrest's Command
Morgan. J. F. .... Co. I, 36th Ga. Reg.***
Moss, W. A. .... Co. B, 56th Ga. Inf.
Motes, Silas .... Co. G, 28th Ga. Reg.
Mullinax, Geo. W. .... Co. H, 1st Ga. Reg.
Mulkey, F. M. .... Co. D, 60th Ga. Reg.

Nations, R. H. .... Co. I, 12th La. Reg.
Nations, J. M. .... Co. A. 1st Ga. Cav.
Neal, R. P. .... Co. C, 39th Ga. Reg.*
Nichols, Wash P. .... Co. E, 4th Ga. Cav.
Nix, William .... Co. B, 39th Ga. Reg.
Norris, James .... Co. I, 24th Ga. Inf.

---

*Captain.
**Colonel.
***2nd Lieutenant.

---

*Lieutenant Colonel.
**Captain.

State Capitol Records of Confederate Soldiers

O'Briant, Sam .... Co. H, 3rd Confederate Cav.
O'Neill, R. P. ....
Oxford. J. L. .... Co. E, 9th Ga. Reg.

Painter, W. J. .... Co. F, 3rd Ga. Cav.
Parrott, Rev. J. C. .... Co. I, S. C. Reg.
Pearce, Jesse M. .... Co. E, 37th Ga. Reg.
Pelfrey, D. J. .... Co. G, 36th Ga. Reg.
Perkins, Josiah .... Co. F, 1st S. C. Rifles
Plemmons, J. L. .... Co. F, 60th Ga. Reg.
Plemmons, Z. T. .... Co. E, 60th Ga. Reg.
Phillips, G. W. .... Co. F, 4th Ky. Cav.
Phillips, J. N. .... Co. I, 45th Ga.
Phillips, W. W. .... Co. I, 28th N. C. Reg.
Price, O. D. .... Co. G, 39th Ga. Reg.
Polk, K. R. .... Co. H. 2nd Ga. Reg.
Pool, A. J. ....   11th N. C. Reg.
Pruden, W. H. ....   32nd Ga. Reg.*

Quinn, John W. .... Co. G. 1st La. Cav.

Redwine. Henry T. .... Co. B, 39th Ga. Reg.
Renfro, W. A. .... Co. A, 62nd Tenn. Reg.
Renfrow, Henderson .... Co. G. 2nd Tenn. Cav.
Richardson Robert .... Co. B, Phillips' Legion
Riggs. W. B. ....
Risner, J. N. .... Co. F, 4th Ala. Inf.
Roach, J. E. .... Co. A, 52nd Ga. Reg.
Roach, W. L. .... Co. G. 36th Ga. Reg.
Roberts, A. P. .... Co. H. 36th Ga. Reg. Inf.**
Roberts, M. .... Jeff Davis' Legion
Rodgers, Joseph .... Co. I, 1st Ga. State Line
Rollins, John .... Co. A, 39th Ga. Reg.
Russell, H. A. .... Co. G, Fifth Reg. Ga. Cav.
Roach, Joshua .... Co. I, 18th Ala. Reg.

Sanfor, J. H. .... Co. H, 23rd Ga. Inf.
Sanson, John .... Co. A, 36th Ga.
Sapp, Geo. W. .... Co. D, 2nd Ga. Reg.
Saylors, Jordan H. .... Co. H, 23rd Ga. Reg.
Simpson, R. A. .... Pendleton's S. C. Inf.
Sykes, J. J. .... Co. G 1st Ga. Reserves
Shannon J. C. .... Co. C. 37th Tenn. Reg.
Stacy, Thomas B. .... Co. C. 39th Ga. Reg.
Stafford, Geo. W. .... Co. H, 2nd Ga. Reg. Inf.
Stanford, J. H. .... Co. F, 4th Ga. Reg.
Stark, John W. .... Co. C, 39th Ga. Reg.
Stephens, W. A. F. .... Co. G, 2nd Tenn. Cav.
Stephenson, B. F. .... Co. I, 4th Ga. Reg. Cav.
Smith, J. L. .... Co. E. 60th Ga. Reg.
Smith, Joe H. .... Co. H. 4th Ga. Reg. Inf.
Smith, C. A. .... Co. F, 39th Ga. Reg.
Smith, T. Jeff .... Co. G, 36th Ga. Reg.
Smith, Geo. F. .... Co. H. 1st Ga. State Troops
Smithy, Robt. .... Co. H. 36th Ga. Reg.
Strickland. Wilson .... Co. C, 39th Ga. Reg.
Stocks, J. W. .... Co. C, 37th Ga. Reg.
Stokes, J. W. .... Co. C, 37th Ga. Reg.
Stone, James .... Co. C. 39th Ga. Reg.
Shumate, I. E. .... Q. QM. State Line

Tarver, John R. .... Co. H. 36th Ga. Reg.
Tate. W. J. .... Co. I, 4th Ga. Reg. Cav.
Tate. A. M. .... Co. A. Ga. State Troops
Tibbs, John I. .... Co. G, Tenn. Cav.
Townsend, J. J. .... Co. E. 4th Ga. Cav.
Touchstone. S. .... Co. A, Roswell Bat.
Thrailkill, J. P. .... Co. B, 36th Ga. Inf.
Thrailkill. Isaac .... Co. B. 36th Ga. Reg.
Thomas, J. G. .... Co. F, 25th Va. Reg.
Thomas, Gen. B. M.** ....
Thomas, J. G. .... Co. —. 25th N. C. Reg.

*This list was compiled from the minutes of the Joseph E. Johnston Camp for 1900 et seq. and is the most accurate one now available.
**Brigadier General.

224　　　　　　History of Whitfield County

Thomas, Jas. J. .... Co. B, 36th Ga. Reg.
Thomasson, L. W. .... Co. A, 1st S. C. Reg.
Thompson, W. H. .... Co. B, 53rd Ga. Reg.
Trippe, W. B. .... Co. F, 3rd Ga. Cav.

Vance, C. N. .... Post. Q. M. Dept., Greenville, Tenn.

Wade, Ramey A. .... Co. A, 52nd Ga. Reg.
Wailes, W. E.*** .... Jos. E. Wheeler, Cav.***
West, J. N. .... Co. G, 43rd Tenn. Reg.
Wood, W. T. .... Co. C, 9th Ky. Reg. Cav.
White, John .... Co. C, 39th Ga. Reg.

Young, Jno. C. .... Co. K, 1st Ark. Inf.
York, A. J. .... Co. G, 11th Ga. Reg.

***Adjutant General for Joseph E. Wheeler.

World War Soldiers of Whitfield County

A complete list of names of men who gave Whitfield county as their place of residence when they entered the service of our country during the World War.

List furnished by War Department, U. S. A.

OFFICERS

Brown, Locke
Carr, James Homer
Dortch, Robert L.
Farrar, William B.
Herron, Robert McKissen, Jr.
Hollingsworth, Joe Latimer
McFarland, James Archie
McKamy, William Edwin
Reiter, Ralph Louis
Speck, Luther Zirkel
Steed, John Henry

Privates

Abanathy, Ben
Albertson, Geo. W.
Albertson, Marion A.
Anglin, Lee
Anderson, Barney J.
Anderson, Carl R.
Anderson, Fletcher L.
Anderson, Martin L.
Anderson, Paul Jackson
Arwood, Kyle L.
Arnold, Jay
Armstrong, Hubert
Ault. Thomas A.
Austin, West (col.)

Babb, Vaugn Albert
Bagby, William C.
Bagby, Thomas Lee
Bagby, Lon W.
Bagby, James L.
Baggett, James
Bailey, Henry W.
Bailey, James E.
Bailey, Talmer L.
Bailey, William Oscar
Baker, Ernest Clinton
Baker, Oscar
Baldwin, Isaac L.
Bankston, William J.
Barksdale, Reese (Col.)
Barnes, Howard D.
Bartenfield, Charlie A.
Bartenfield, Carl

Beach, Pat
Bearden, Ernest C.
Beaver, Judge
Bell, George C.
Bennett, Charlie
Bennett, James F.
Berry, Samuel E.
Bevil, James Franklin
Bishop, Charley
Bishop, Paul L.
Black, Charles W. (col.)
Black, Charles F.
Boatwright, Deedie A.
Boyd, Henry F.
Boyd, James L.
Boyd, Sank
Boyles, Charles S.
Boyles, Richard Q.
Bradley, James Fred
Bramblett, Vernon
Brazelton, Frank (col.)
Bridges, James M.
Bridges, Horace Hutchison
Bridges, Rastus
Bright, Dewey B.
Britton, Hobart M.
Britton, William A.
Brooks, Perry C.
Broome, Olin J.
Brown, John S.
Bryson, Charlie W.
Bryant, Homer D.
Bryant, Robert L.

Buchanan, James F.
Burch, Bill
Burch, Jim
Burch, William
Burns, Jefferson Brisco
Burrough, Harold J.
Burse, Cicero (col.)

Cade, Cicero (col.)
Cade, Durham (col.)
Cade, Earnest (col.)
Caldwell, Charles H.
Caldwell, William M.
Calhoun, William E. (col.)
Callahan, George
Callahan, William
Campbell, Albert E.
Campbell, Andrew P.
Campbell, William C.
Cannon, Elbert C.
Cantrall, Willie D.
Carder, John H.
Cargal, Archie J.
Carpenter, Frank
Carr, Carl E.
Carr, Sam T.
Carr, Sanford P.
Carroll, Will G.
Carter, Cecil W.
Carter, Charles L.
Carter, Wood
Caylor, James P.
Caylor, William H. F.

STATE CAPITOL RECORDS OF CONFEDERATE SOLDIERS   225

Center, Andrew J.
Chadwick, William O.
Chambers, Burl (col.)
Chambers, James (col.)
Chambers, James (col.)
Clark, Berney L.
Clark, DeForrest
Clark, Martin
Clark, William A.
Clemons, Bonie L.
Clemon, George H.
Clemons, Paul
Cline, Grover C.
Cline, Joe H.
Cochran, Frank Nathaniel
Cochran, Willis
Coffey, James Harris
Cogdill, Benjamin J.*
Coker, Tren F.
Coker, Vester
Collier, Wm. (col.)
Collins, Hobart C.
Collins, Samuel Layette
Collins, Tom
Combee, Paul Frederick
Cook, Guy (col.)
Cooley, John (col.)
Cooper, Ernest F.
Cooper, Edgar A.
Cooper, John E.
Copeland, Robert E.
Counts, Charles W.
Cox, Ernest
Cox, William Thomas
Coyle, Ed
Crow, Spartan L.*
Cucksee, Alfred M.
Cupp, George M.*
Cullins, Frank
Cummings, Olie D.
Curtis, Henry A.

Daffron, William Granville
Deakins, Robert H.
Deck, Charles
Dempsey, Thomas Jacob
Densmore, William
Dills, Melvin O.*
Drum, Arthur P.
Dunn, Charley A.
Dupree, Walter
Earnest, Charles B.
Easley, Sam M.
Edwards, Arthur Lester
Edwards, Gordon
Eidson, Joel A.
Ellison, James F.
Elzy, Fletcher (col.)
Epps, James F.
Eslinger, Roy L.*
Eslinger, John William
Evans, Charlie N.
Ewton, Otis B.
Ezzard, Henry S.
Faith, Abe
Faith, Curtis Henry
Faith, Talmadge L.
Felker, Fletcher D.
Felker, Fort F.
Felker, John C.
Felker, Quillian
Felker, Raymond Wallace
Fitts, Lloyd David
Flemister, Linton H.
Foster, Philip H.

*Deceased.

Foster, Roy
Franklin, Aberham T.
Frazier, John P.

Gaddis, Luther H.
Gallman, Spain
Gasaway, Luther C.
Gay, Clinton ((col.)
Gay, Floyd
Gilbert, Thomas E.
Gilstrap, Trenver W.
Givens, George W.
Gordon, Lawrence (col.)
Graham, Buford F. (col.)
Graham, Edward D. (col.)
Grant, Charles C.*
Grant, Price B.
Grant, Ulysses S.
Gravitt, Oba
Green, Paul (col.)
Green, Robert (col.)
Greeson, Jasper J.
Greeson, Jesse
Greeson, Smith
Griffin, Noyce Lovic
Gryder, Sam S.

Hackney, Charley B.
Hackney, Harve
Hackney, Wesley L.
Hall, Richard (col.)
Hall, Thomas L.
Hambright, Jack (Col.)
Hamilton, James A.
Hamilton, Sherry M.
Hammontree, Herman H.
Harden, John
Harden, John J.
Hardin, Amos*
Hardin, James M.
Hardin, Walton
Harlan, Lum (col.)
Harland, Harse (col.)
Harrison, Henry
Head, Samuel J.
Heath, Lessley
Hegwood, Alfred
Helton, Martin T.
Henderson, Ferman C.
Henderson, John G.
Henderson Robert P.
Henry, Clarence
Henry, William
Hewett, Ames B.
Hicks, Joseph Winston
Hicks, Robert T.
Hill, Arthur Augustus
Hill, Charlie (col.)
Hill, Clarence C.
Hill, George (col.)
Hill, Roy T.
Hix, Edward
Hix, William K.
Hodges, Frank
Holder, Fred William
Holland, Troy Augustus
Hopkins, Jesse James
Horne, Lon L.
Huguley, Oscar (col.)
Hunsucker, Ira N.
Hunsucker, William C.
Hyde, Jim
Hyer, Willie Howard

Isbell, Clarence W.

Jackson, Henry H. (col.)
Jackson, Hugh (col.)
Jackson, Lee R. (col.)
James, Henry L.
Jefferson, Samuel L. (col.)
Johns, Oscar (col.)
Johns, Robert (col.)
Johnson, Calvin (col.)
Johnson, Curt H.
Johnson, James F.
Johnson, John B.
Johnson, Robert Edward
Johnson, Rob
Johnston, John C.
Johnston John L.
Jones, John (col.)
Jordan, Henry L.
Jordon, James A.

Keeler, William
Keen, Victor E.
Keith, George H.
Kelley, Loring S.
Kenemer, Carl. H.
Kenion, Eugene (col.)
Keown, Clarence B.
Keys, Charles Eugene
Kidd, Willie C.
Kinamon, Frank
Kimsey, Fred I.
Kimsey, George C.
Kinnamon, William N.
King, John N.
Kirk, Paul D.
Kitchings Doyle B.
Kittle, Harry R.

Lacewell, Zeek T.
Landen, Thomas J.
Lankford, Jim M.
Land, Carlton A.
Land, Harvey L.
Lanier, Henry
Lasater, Horace Clark
Leach, Edward
Ledford, Charlie F.
Lewis, John H.
Lindsey, Thomas W.
Longley, Houston M.
Longley, John L.
Long, Evans T.
Long, James B.
Long, John
Looper, Glenn
Looper, John W.

McCarty, William B.
McCollum, Virgie R.
McDaniel, Fra..k R.
McDaniel, Robert A.
McDonald, Joseph P.
McDonald, William B.
McDougal, James E.*
McEntire, Walter E.
McFalls, Elmer
McFarland, Edward S.
McKeehan, Benjamin F.
McKeehan, George W.
McLellan, John Mac
McNally, John
Maddox, Swift R.
Maeger, Herschel
Maeger, Lige
Mallett, Joseph A.
Manis, John W.

Manis, Thomas W.
Mann, William G.
Martin, Dennis L.
Martin, William C.
Mason, Dulie (col.)
Matthews, Horace, N.
Mathis, Joe
Mathis, Sidney J.
Mauldin, Anderson
Mayes, Roy L.
Miles, Charles
Miller, Edward W.
Miller, James Dewitt
Miller, Samuel P.
Mills, Jesse
Mincher, Harvey
Mitchell, Douglas W.
Montgomery, Walter
Moody, Allen M.
Moody, John T.
Moody, Monroe J.
Moore, Ben (col.)
Moore, John (col.)
Moore, Wylie (col.)
Morgan, Frank N.
Morris, Clifford (col.)
Morris, Earl T.
Morris, Mitchell F.
Morrison, Thomas A.
Mullins, Am
Mullins, Tillmon

Nations, Henry T.
Neighbors, Thomas J.
Nelson, Sam
Nelson, William E.
Newman, Louis
Nix, Bearden W.
Nunn, Dallas C.

Oakes, Charles J.
O'Neal, Will (col.)
Orr, Luther S.

Painter, Charles C.
Pander, Oscar
Pangle, Aaron L.*
Page, Willard W.
Palmer, Carleton G.
Parsons, Laborn
Patten, Lee F. (col.)
Patton, Jud
Phillips, Anderson
Phillips, Emmett
Phillips, James T.
Pickens, Charlie E.
Pinson, John C.
Piwell, Noah O.
Pitts, Guy
Pitts, Joseph W.
Platt, James L.
Pool, Floyd
Porter, Schafter (col.)
Powell, Robert D.
Powell, William C.
Pryor, Elic F.
Pryor, John R.

Quinn, Arthur J. (col.)
Quinn, Ross P.

Rackley, Henry L.
Rackley, Joe B.
Rann, Hugh
Ray, Carl
Reed, William T.
Richardson, Claud E.*
Richardson, Claude
Richardson, Guy C.
Richardson, William B.
Ridley, Wyley V.
Roberts, Alton R.
Roberts, Charley
Roberts, Thomas P.
Robertson, Aldine I.
Roy, Charles (col.)
Robbs, Willie (col.)
Rogers, John L.
Rollins, John Henderson
Runyan, Oscar C.
Runyan, Sam

Sansom, Earl
Segers, Clayton L.
Seay, Frank (col.)
Shepherd, Bird
Shields, William E.
Shugart, James G.
Shugart, Cooksey
Shults, McKinley
Shumaker, Marion W.
Silvers, Joe
Slaton, John F.*
Sloan, Melvin
Smith, Arthur
Smith, Benjamin F.
Smith, Fred S.
Smith, Howard L. (col.)
Smith, Horace J.
Smith, Headrick D.
Smith, Lawrence P.
Smith, Olin L.
Smith, Paul Lee
Souther, William H.
Spann, Charles O.
Speer, Charles L.
Stacy, Henry P., Jr.
Stacy, Oliver W.
Stacy, William C.
Stansell, John G.
Stanley, Hobirt M.
Stanley, Thomas D. L.
Stanley, William Tasker
Stark, John B.
Sterns, Walter
Sterns, Perry (col.)
Stevenson, Edward K.
Stevenson, James Robert
Stinnet, Walter
Stinnett, Walter Obsbion
Stoker, Samuel
Stone, Dave*
Stone, Fletcher W.
Stone, James L.
Sumney, John B.

Sutherland, Elbert F.
Swanson, Ernest

Taliaferro, John W.
Tate, William B.
Taylor, John (col.)
Teasley, Edward Aaron
Terrell, Earl
Thogmartin, Will B.
Thrailkill, Roy P.
Thompson, Jeff E.
Tibb, John (col.)
Tipton, James E.
Towers, Ernest W.
Trevitt, Don C.
Trulove, Robert Don

Vick, James Bunion
Vick, Marvin
Vickery, Moses W.

Wade, Deedie M.
Wagnon, Vergil K.
Walders, John
Walston, Charles Henry
Walker, Paul G. (col.)
Wallace, Homer L.
Wallace, Joe E.
Wallace, Marvin G.
Walters, Louis G.
Walters, Walter G.
Warmack, Harry H.
Ward, Logan
Ward, William J.
Ware, John
Watkins, Clarence G.
Watkins, Ernest Leon
Westbrook, Joseph M.
Whaley, Benejah
White, Dallas Lxe
White, James Luther
Whitmire, Lee
Whittle, John T.
Wills, William F.
Williams, Edward
Williams, Flint H.
Williams, George W.
Williams, James H.
Williams, Joel S.
Williams, Russell Lee
Williams, William T.
Wilson, Clarence E.
Wilson, Louis (col.)
Wilson, Robert
Wilson, Sidney A.
Winstead, Paul L.
Winn, Brotho (col.)
Wood, Virgil H.
Wood, William Earl
Wood, William F.
Wright, George D.
Wyatt, William T.

Yaeger, Charles J.
Young, Amos L.
Young, Richard A.*

NAVY

Hamilton, Henry C., Ensign
McAfee, Phil, Ensign

Anderson, John Franklin

Judd, Morton Hubert, Ensign
Manly, William Judson, Ensign

Bankston, George Kitchens
Bohannan, Emmett William

---

*Deceased.

Burnette, Horace Clinton
Callaway, Harry Dunn
Carter, Fred
Cornelison, Linton
Counts, Willie Demer
Creswell, Truman Cyrus
Crow, Thomas Vinton
Cullen, John Lacewell

Dobson, William Alonzo

Earnest, Benjamin Watson
Elkins, Otis William

Frazier, Samuel*
Felker, Guy R.*
Finley, Lawrence Barrette
Gilbreath, James Columbus
Gregory, William Pharris

Hall, Henry Lee
Hassler, Faris Knoblaugh
Howell, Lenvel Jackson

Hudson, Jean Edwin

Kenemer, Henry Clay
Kenemer, Thomas Watson
Kimsey, Clint Cleborn
Kitchings, Doyle Bee
Kreischer, Charles Adams

Lockridge, Wheeler Franklin
Looper, Harry Stuart
Love, Overton Carter
Lynch, Willie Henry

McAuley, Hobart Babcock
McNabb, Dennis Manis
Maddox, Trammell S.
Mann, Joel Edmond
Maynard, Dennis Johnston
Mitchell, Clyde Washington
Mitchell, John Chester
Murphy, Carl John

Nelson, Philip
Newman, Minyard Lee

O'Hare, Hugh
Pitts, Mathews Otis
Puryear, Fred Bender

Richardson, Thomas Watso
Ritchey, Roy Sherman
Robertson, Vernon

Shields, John Luther
Smith, John Henry
Springer, Floyd Moody
Springfield, Wyatt Baker
Stewart, Henry W. Grady

Trammell, McAfee

Walters, Waco William
Walters, William Franklin
Wheeler, Clinton Warren
Wheeler, John Roy
White, Barrett David
Whitson, Joseph Lee
Wood, Samuel Cleveland
Wrinkle, Baxter Elbert
Wrinkle, Edward Earl

*Deceased.
*Officers.

Liberty League of Whitfield County, Georgia

WAR WORK CAMPAIGN COMMITTEES
DISTRICT COMMITTEES

J. G. McLellan, President   F. S. Pruden, Secretary

Cohutta

J. M. Wooten, District Chairman
T. J. Cooper, Cohutta

C. W. Woodward, Hopewell
Geo. Wilson, Keelers

Upper Tenth

V. B. Pullen, District Chairman
John Oliver, Mt. Pleasant

R. G. Shields, Tuckers
S. R. Shields, Prospect

Varnells

D. A. Speer, District Chairman
J. A. Speer, Varnells
J. T. Segars, Varnells

W. E. Bare, Mars Hills
T. J. Manis, Broad Acre

Lower Tenth

G. L. Broaddrick, District Chairman
W. R. Cline, Deep Springs

Joe Hays, Beaverdale
Judd Anderson, Good Hope

Tunnel Hill

J. E. Moore, District Chairman
G. W. Head, Tunnel Hill
W. H. Foster, Tunnel Hill

F. C. Black, Tunnel Hill
S. P. Reed, New Hope

Trickum

Matt Deck, District Chairman
A. M. Reed, Trickum
J. W. Fain, Nickajack
W. H. Westbrook, Gordon Springs
Green Carlock, Salem

Rocky Face

S. R. Hassler, District Chairman
J. C. Lynch, Rocky Face
J. A. Mosteller, Mt. Vernon

Mill Creek

James Nuckolls, District Chairman
S. W. England, Mill Creek
J. L. Morris, Mill Creek

Carbondale

H. L. Nations, District Chairman
H. S. Redwine, Carbondale
L. E. Cline, Redwines
A. H. Phipps, Center Point

Tilton

Jno. Gentle, District Chairman
J. M. Hogan, Tilton
C. R. Nance, Union
W. L. Roberts, River Bend

Finchers

S. A. Glass, District Chairman
H. J. Vernon, District Chairman
A. B. Hill, Pine Grove
T. A. Burgess, Liberty Hall

Ninth

P. G. Poteet, District Chairman
S. W. Bennett, Harmony
W. C. Bryant, Dawnville
F. L. Lane, Bunker Hill
F. J. Dantzler, Cedar rValley

Dalton

W. C. McGhee, District Chairman
T. M. Rollins, Waring
J. L. Randolph, Temperance Hill
Miss Mary Hamilton, Crown Point
J. H. Smith, Antioch
Eugene Evans, Antioch
R. A. Williams, Union Point
Mrs. G. V. Freylach, Dug Gap
Miss Clemmie Cavender, Five Springs
Mrs. W. J. Watt, Pleasant Grove

CENTRAL COMMITTEE

J. S. Hall, Chairman
J. G. McLellan, Chairman Liberty Bond
E. P. Davis, Chairman War Saving Stamp
W. C. Martin, Chairman Red Cross
J. J. Copeland, Chairman Junior Red Cross
W. C. McGhee, Chairman Y. M. C. A.
Frank Manly, Chairman Council of Defense
Mrs. W. C. Martin, Chairman Woman's Council of Defense
F. K. Sims, Chairman Four Minute Men
W. M. Jones, Food Administrator
J. S. Hall, Fuel Administrator
T. S. McCamy, Director Publicity
Mrs. R. M. Herron, Ch. Women's Work

COUNTY COMMITTEES

W. C. Martin, T. S. McCamy, G. J. Jernigan .... Deep Springs
J. G. McLellan, H. B. Farrar, J. G. McAfee .... Varnells
T. D. Ridley, F. A. Hamilton, R. L. Denton .... Dawnville
B. L. Heartsill, W. A. Broadrick, Walter Bowen .... Mt. Pleasant
G. P. Mills, H. L. Jarvis, C. M. Hollingsworth .... Mars Hill
M. C. Tarver, C. W. Moorre, J. B. Chitwood .... Trickum
W. M. Sapp, Chas. Connally, J. E. Whitson .... Tuckers
F. K. Sims, P. B. Fite, G. L. Westcott .... Tunnel Hill
S. P. Maddox, Robt. Loveman, R. H. Sapp .... Broad Acre
H. J. Smith, E. C. Coffey, Dennis Barrett .... Gordon Springs
H. L. Smith, J. J. Copeland, T. B. Wright .... Cohutta
A. L. Edwards, J. B. Brown, C. D. McCutchen .... Tilton
J. S. Hall, C. L. Hamilton, F. K. McCutchen .... Rocky Face

LIBERTY LEAGUE OF WHITFIELD COUNTY, GEORGIA   229

F. F. Farrar, J. A. Carter, H. J. Wood ....Mill Creek
J. H. Watson, J. M. Johnston, J. L. Buchanan ....Center Point
E. P. Davis, T. S. Shope, J. P. Neal ....Mt. Vernon
B. A. Tyler, P. B. Trammell, Sr., S. H. McKnight ... .Carbondale
Frank Manly, R. P. Gregory, G. W. Hamilton, Jr. ....Pine Grove
F. S. Pruden, G. M. Cannon, Jr., G. E. Horan ....Cedar Valley
W. E. Mann, D. A. McBrayer, H. L. Erwin ....Waring
Julian McCamy, L. J. Allyn, J. L. Palmer ....Pleasant Grove
W. K. Moore, J. A. Crawford, L. B. Lawton ....Union Point
J. T. Duncan, P. B. Trammell, Jr., Dr. J. C. Rollins ....Five Springs
Josiah Crudup, Buell Stark, John Williamson ....Antioch
Lee Routh, Carter Stacy, John Camp ....Temperance Hill
S. W. Looper, W. C. McGhee, J. T. Wills ....Keelers
W. C. Bowen, W. E. Nants, W. F. Summerour ....Hopewell
W. M. Denton, L. H. Crawford, W. M. Hardwick ....Union
C. C. Maples, A. G. Brown, Van Kettles ....Prospect
W. M. Jones, J. C. H. Wink, J. B. Denton ....Beaverdale
J. A. Dantzler, W. H. Prater, Dr. W. E. Wood ....Good Hope
J. S. Thomas, J. D. Hammond, R. M. Herron, Sr. ....New Hope
J. A. Looper, L. B. Hubbs, C. C. McCamy ....Nickajack
C. A. Deakins, T. A. Hopper, W. R. Cannon ....Dug Gap
J. P. Godwin, J. N. Caylor, Dr. W. C. Fincher ....Harmony
R. D. Bazemore, Joe Black, F. D. Percy ....Bunker Hill
J. H. Steed, W. S. McCarty, J. J. Duane ....Salem
W. M. Lynn, O. C. Alley, W. T. Kenner ....Liberty Hall
F. T. Hardwick, R. L. Harlan, G. W. Hamilton, Sr. ....River Bend
H. J. Ault, R. P. Neal, W. M. Mitchell, R. A. Shatzer ....Redwines

PLATFORM

"We are ready to do anything our Government asks, ready to make any sacrifice, putting up with any inconvenience in order to serve our country best."

Red Cross

The Red Cross was organized in Dalton during the World War. After the war the organization was continued and is functioning today. Mrs. M. E. Judd is the president.

Pioneer Citizens of Dalton and Whitfield County*

This list contains the names only of those known to have been residents of the county before 1860.

Captain Ed White	Major James Bard	Judge Ebert S. Bird
Franklin B. Morris	Mark Thornton	John Hamilton
Major James Morris	Col. I. E. Shumate	Judge Underwood
Dr. F. T. Black	Dr. John Allen	Wilson Green
Thomas Cook	Lewis Bender	Joseph Lynan
Dr. John Harris	Dr. M. R. Banner	J. N. B. Cobb
John Anderson	Dr. Foute	Jack Cobb
Garland Jefferson	Dr. Waugh	Thomas Henderson, Sr.
C. C. McCrary,	Frank Jackson	Captain A. P. Roberts
Wick Earnest	Robert O'Neill	Henry Davis
Charles Adams	John Hill	Warren R. Davis
Charles Barry	Bob Hill	Col. Charles E. Broyles
Dr. J. Bailey	Ralph Ellison	Amos Sutherland
Jabex Pitman	John Beaty	Rev. A. Fitzgerald
R. S. Rushton	Judge Dawson Walker	A. E. Blunt, (Blount)
James Buchanan	Wiley Farnsworth	Mr. Holt
Jack Oliver	Anderson Farnsworth	Nathaniel Harben

HISTORY OF WHITFIELD COUNTY

Prof. John Tyler
Judge John P. Chester
Col. J. A. R. Hanks
Col. J. A. W. Johnson
Judge Leander Crook
Dr. B. B. Brown
Rev. Levi Brotherton
Rev. George Selvidge
T. S. Swift
Col. Patrick McCowan
Col. J. T. Whitman
John Norris
Andrew Norris
Mr. Hawthorn
Mr. Spencer
Mr. Thompson
John Reynolds
Mr. Wright
Jacob Wrinkle
Benjamin Clark
D. W. Mitchell
Andrew Norris
William Hammond
Lawrence Barrett
Ed. Craigmiles
Mr. Sims
Duff Green

Robert Burner
John Henry King
Rev. H. C. Carter
C. B. Welborn
Dickson Taliaferro
James Longly
Captain Fred Cox
Judge Jesse Freeman
Col. W. K. Moore
J. F. Denton
Richard Tarver
Dr. Winston Gordon
Col. Jesse Glenn
Ben E. Green,
Thomas Jolly
Albert Senter
Mr. Lother
Mr. Fincher
George Williamson
Tim Ford
John Hackney
Mr. Emory
Mr. Franklin
Mr. Bishop
Frederick Pentz
Mr. Paxton
Mr. Sasseen

Dr. Groves
John Bitting
Nick Bitting
Major Harden
Jesse Trotter
J. M. Crute
J. W. Sitton
William Nichols
John P. Love
James Fields
Mr. Cuyler
Mr. Crawford
David Ware
Henry Wrench
Mr. Cate
J. B. Nichols
Silas Mote
B. E. Morse
William P. Hackney ✓
David A. Speer
Dr. Geo. R. Harris
John Wesley Fincher
Robert Hammond Baker
Geo. W. Stafford
Benj. Clark
W. M. Worley

*List compiled by the late Mrs. Warren R. Davis and published in "Georgia's Landmarks and Memorials" by Lucian Lamar Knight, pp. 1056-1057.

PIONEER CITIZENS AND OTHERS

List of names of pioneer citizens and others from Dalton and Whitfield county that have been placed on marble tablets in the Memory room of the Central club house.

The dates appearing on these tablets represent the time when the citizens came to Dalton; they represent the birth date of those who were born here.

This building was erected by the Lesche Woman's Club and the Bryan M. Thomas Chapter, United Daughters of the Confederacy.

Cicero Decatur McCutchen, Jr., 1874
Laura A. Kelly, 1866
John E. Satterfield, 1891
Carrie Bitting Dyer, 1869
Minnie Watt Westbrook, 1895
Frank Dana Percy, 1910
Louisa Staples Vance, 1890
Sarah Dobson Copeland 1855
William A. Black, 1874
John King, 1880
William T. McCarty, 1866
Laura Scott McCarty, 1864
Flo Herron Clark, 1874
Edith Walker Munroe, 1861
John Q. A. Lewis, 1877
Susan McKamy Lewis, 1877
Dollie Lewis Dettor, 1887
Mary McCamy Parker, 1876
Laura Whitney Mecklin, 1886
David Bukofzer, 1867
William F. Fischer, 1852
Nathaniel P. Harben, 1858
Will N. Harben, 1858
Ida L. Nichols Fincher, 1858
Dr. J. Cleveland Bivings, 1866
Blanche Flaghler Bivings, 1869
Barney C. Bivings, 1866
Samuel Allen Frazier, 1878
Rev. Archibald Fitzgerald, 1855

Anthony J. Showalter, 1880
Carolyn W. Showalter, 1884
Henri Schoeller, 1874
Josephine Johnston Coyle, 1872
Herman Fox, 1904
George W. Stafford, 1845
Charles H. Snow, 1873
Maj. W. C. Lester, 1865
Flora Lester Blevins, 1874
Mabelle Thompson, 1888
Maj. Henry A. Russell, 1873
Jesse A. Holtzclaw, 1876
Sarah C. Holtzclaw, 1876
Thomas M. Felker, 1892
Col. W. H. Pruden, 1869
W. B. Farrar, 1875
Robert Hill Deakins, 1897
Wm. Patterson Chester, 1836
Mary Chester Harris, 1836
George Reese Harris, M. D., 1840
Daniel Earnest Allen, 1867
General Bryan Morell Thomas, C. S. A., 1881
Mary Withers Thomas, 1881
Emily Adams McCrary, 1848
Alexander W. Lynn, 1860
Lizzie McCrary Lynn, 1848
William K. Moore, 1849
Jane Lucky Moore, 1856

PIONEER CITIZENS OF DALTON AND WHITFIELD COUNTY

Dr. Miles M. Puckett, 1895
Margaret Jefferson Puckett, 1850
G. H. Hightower, M. D., 1899
Mary Frances Hightower, 1899
Albert N. Senter, 1850
Elizabeth L. Senter, 1857
David A. Speer, 1857
Lida Amanda Field, 1875
Sara Frances McDaniel, 1902
Charles Nicholas Vance, 1890
Mary Morris O'Neill, 1899
John Horan, 1879
Dr. F. A. Rauschenberg, 1851
John Wesley Fincher, 1852
William G. Liddell, 1886
Capt. Pearce Horne, 1867
Tallulah Johnson Horne, 1867
Julia Martin Sapp, 1872
Judson C. Sapp, 1875
William L. Lampkin, 1875
Sarah Lampkin, 1875
Richard Grier Huston, 1878
Col. W. J. M. Thomas, 1860
James White Walker, 1870
Martha White Walker, 1870
John Freeman Harris, M. D., 1891
Mary E. Harris, 1891
John J. Duane, 1903
Sarah Perry Duane, 1903
Ainsworth Emery Blunt 1843
Robert Hammond Baker, 1842
Martha Foute Baker, 1878
Martha Brotherton Graves, 1845
Joseph W. Barrett, 1874
Anne Johnson Barrett, 1874
John Franklin Robertson, 1888
George W. Oglesby, 1876
Ann Elizabeth Oglesby, 1876
David Knox McKamy, 1875
Cicero D. Gilbert, 1905
Mary Martin Gilbert, 1905
Samuel P. Maddox, 1872
Sarah R. Maddox, 1861
James Herron, 1874
Dr. W. J. Manly, 1865
Martha Willard Manly, 1865
Thomas R. Jones, 1872
Gertrude Manly Jones, 1865
Charles Peyton Gordon, 1865
Maggie Manly Gordon, 1865
W. F. Summerour, 1887
Judge Dawson A. Walker, 1860
Robert Watson Weatherly, 1876
Lucretia Blair Weatherly, 1876
Guilford McG. Cannon, 1870

George W. Hamilton, Sr., 1847
Bettie Lucky Hamilton, 1875
Maj. T. H. Pitner, 1837
Malinda Pitner, 1856
James H. Huff, 1840
Margaret McG. Huff, 1840
William T. Emmons, 1860
Henry Clay Hamilton, 1847
James A. Maddox, 1840
Ignatius Elgin Shumate, 1861
Elizabeth G. Shumate, 1861
Cicero Decatur McCutchen, 1854
Frances Kelly McCutchen, 1854
Frank T. Hardwick, 1873
John H. Bitting, 1850
James I. Lowry, 1867
John Francis Reynolds, 1872
Warren R. Davis, 1850
Melissa Bird Davis, 1858
Edward Paschal Davis, 1871
Rosa Bird Freeman, 1861
John Black, 1872
Maj. Joseph Guthrie, 1848
Albert C. L. Setzepfand, 1852
Paul Barclay Trammell, 1869
Fannie McAfee Trammell, 1860
Zenobia B. Trammell, 1869
Dr. J. R. McAfee, 1853
May McAfee Shumate, 1874
Mary Starr Pinkerton, 1900
Harriet Towns Comer, 1872
Dr. Benjamin Hamilton, 1862
George P. Fraker, 1861
James F. Miller, 1856
Berry R. Bowen, 1873
Charles R. Evans, 1900
Fannie Swift Lester, 1857
Laura M. Buchholz, 1859
Eugenia Kelly Bitting, 1863
J. C. Riley, 1855
Jesse Trotter, 1859
Salina Jane Trotter, 1859
Sarah J. Huff, 1885
Nettie Florence Huff, 1885
George W. Horan, 1882
Henry A. Wrench, 1847
Robert Adams Rushton, 1851
Anna Towns Rushton, 1872
Charles A. Kreischer, 1888
Samuel E. Berry, 1853
Rev. Z. M. McGhee, 1870
John Baxter Brown, 1865
Annie E. Cannon, 1870
William Fincher, 1856
Fleta T. Cannon, 1882

THE OLDEST INSCRIPTIONS FROM THE OLD PRESBYTERIAN CEMETERY AND WEST HILL CEMETERY

John Hamilton .... b. 1803-d. 1853
Rachelle Hamilton .... b. 1811-d. 1876
Sarah Cook .... b. 1798-d. 1858
William Henderson .... b. 1811-d. 1880
W. J. Underwood .... b. 1813-d. 1898
Jane Underwood .... b. 1822-d. 1898
Lucy Carroll Hudson, wife of William Hammond .... b. 1803-d. 1855
  (Daughter of Nathaniel Hudson, of Virginia, kinsman of Henry Clay.)
William Hammond .... b. 1792-d. 1858
  (Ancestors Hammond of Virginia, Howard of Maryland.)
Mary Hudson .... b. 1772-d 1858
T. S. Swift .... b. 1813-d. 1858
Mary (Wife of W. P. Chester) .... b. 1808-d. 1877
John Divver .... b. 1808-d. 1884
Lawrence Harrison .... b. in Donegal Ireland, Dec. 24th, 1808-d. 1899

General Index

CHAPTER I

Cherokee Indians of North Georgia	1
Early Cherokee History	1
First Mission Established	4
Later Missions	9
Civilizing Influences	11
Ancient Mounds	13
Fort Mountain	14
Historic Places in Dalton and Vicinity	16
Prominent Cherokee Indians	18, 22, 24, 26, 31, 35
Events Leading to Removal	29
The Cherokees Appeal to the Supreme Court of the United States	32
New Echota Treaty	34
Compulsory Removal	36

CHAPTER II

Whitfield's Beginning	39
Georgia Extends Jurisdiction Over Cherokee Territory. Land Lottery Organization of Cherokee County Later a Part of Murray with County Seat at Spring Place	39
Whitfield County	40
Rev. George Whitfield	41
Early description of the land, by J. C. Head	42, 43, 44, 45
Dalton the County Seat	46, 47
Hotels	49, 50, 51
Tunnel Hill	53
Early Towns	53, 54

CHAPTER III

War Between the States	55
Military History	55, 56, 57, 58
Defense of Dalton	58, 59, 60, 61, 62
War Memoirs	62, 63, 64, 65
Battles	66, 67
Restoration	67
Joseph E. Johnston Monument	69

CHAPTER IV

The Reconstruction Era _____ 71
  The North Georgia Agricultural and Mechanical
    Association _____ 72, 73, 74
  Old Homes _____ 74, 75
  Social Life _____ 76
  Dalton Post Office _____ 77
  Growth of Dalton _____ 78, 79, 80, 81, 82, 83

CHAPTER V

Churches and Schools:
  Dalton Methodist Episcopal Church, South _____ 85, 86, 87, 88, 89
  First Presbyterian Church, Dalton _____ 89, 90, 91
  First Baptist Church, Dalton _____ 92, 93, 94
  Saint Mark's Episcopal Church, Dalton _____ 94, 95
  Hamilton Street Methodist, Dalton _____ 95
  South Dalton Baptist Church _____ 95, 96
  East Side Baptist Church _____ 96
  Mount Rachel Baptist Church, Dalton _____ 96
  Green Street Baptist Church, Dalton _____ 97
  Crown View Baptist Church _____ 97
  Morris Street Methodist Episcopal Church _____ 97
  Church of the Nazarene _____ 97
  Catholic Church _____ 98
  Church of Christ _____ 98
  The Holiness _____ 98
  Antioch Church _____ 98, 99
Bethel _____ 99
  Carbondale Churches _____ 99, 100
  Concord Baptist Church _____ 100
  Cohutta Presbyterian _____ 100, 101
  Tunnel Hill Presbyterian _____ 117
  Tunnel Hill Baptist _____ 117
  Varnell Baptist _____ 117, 118
  Colored Churches of Dalton _____ 118
Schools _____ 119
  Dalton Public Schools _____ 119, 120, 121, 122
  County Schools _____ 123
  Dawnville Consolidated School _____ 124
  Cohutta School Building _____ 125
  Cohutta Consolidated School _____ 125, 126
  Varnell Consolidated School _____ 126
  Valley Point Consolidated School _____ 127
  Pleasant Grove Consolidated School _____ 127
  West Side Consolidated School _____ 128

Tunnel Hill District ---129
Cohutta Cumberland Presbyterian and Presbyterian
    Church, U. S. A. ---102
Mount Olivet Methodist Church ----------------------------103
Cohutta Baptist Church --------------------------------------103
Dawnville Baptist Church --------------------------------103, 104
Dawnville Methodist Church ------------------------------104
Dawnville ---105
Deep Springs Baptist -----------------------------------105, 106
Dug Gap Baptist ---106, 107
Good Hope ---107
Harmony ---107
Hopewell Baptist ---------------------------------------107, 108
McGaughey's Methodist ---------------------------------------108
Little Prospect Baptist --------------------------------108, 109
Mount Pleasant Methodist -----------------------------------109
Mill Creek Baptist --109
Mt. Vernon Methodist --------------------------------------110
Mineral Springs Methodist ---------------------------------110
Pine Grove Baptist --110
Poplar Springs --110
Red Clay --111
River Bend Baptist ---111
Rocky Face Baptist --112
Shady Grove ---113
Grove Level ---113, 114
Pleasant Grove --114
Shiloh Methodist Church ------------------------------114, 115
Tilton Methodist Church ----------------------------------115
Varnell Methodist ------------------------------------115, 116
Tunnel Hill Methodist --------------------------------------116
Tunnel Presbyterian ------------------------------------116, 117

CHAPTER VI

Organization of Clubs and Societies ----------------------------131
Fraternal Organizations ------------------------------------131
    Dalton Lodge No. 72, I. O. O. F. -----------------------132, 133, 134
    Rebekahs Important Part of Odd Fellowship ----------------134
    Laurel Camp No. 24, W. O. W. -----------------------------134, 135
    Fort Hill Camp, Modern Woodmen of America --------------135
    Dalton Council No. 30, Junior O. U. A. M. -------------------135
    Dalton Council No. 15, D. of A. ---------------------------135
    Cohutta Lodge No. 64, F. and A. M. -------------------136, 137
    Tunnel Hill Lodge No. 202, F. and A. M. ----------------------137
    Tilton Lodge No. 291, F. and A. M. --------------------------137
    Gordon Springs Lodge No. 463, F. and A. M. ---------------137

Rocky Face Lodge No. 678, F. and A. M. ----137
Dalton Chapter No. 65, O. E. S. ----137, 138, 139
Dalton Post No. 112, American Legion ----141, 142
Civic Organizations
    Civitan Club ----143
    Junior Chamber of Commerce ----148, 149
    Lesche Woman's Club ----144, 145
    Dalton Woman's Club ----145, 146
    Junior Dalton Woman's Club ----146, 147
Patriotic Organizations:
    Bryan M. Thomas Chapter, U. D. C. ----147, 148
    Central Club House ----148
    Gov. John Milledge Chapter, D. A. R. ----148, 149
    Service Star Legion ----157
    American Legion Auxiliary ----181
    Cherokee Chapter, Georgia Society, D. A. C. ----152
    Parent-Teacher's Association ----151
    Dalton Garden Club ----153

CHAPTER VII

Modern Whitfield ----154
    Whitfield County Medical Association ----156
    Hamilton Memorial Hospital ----156, 157
    Dalton's Progress ----157, 158, 159
    Disastrous Fire of 1911 ----161
    Dalton's Reaction to the World War ----161, 162
    Red Cross in the World War ----163
    American League for Women's Service ----163
    The Dalton Public Library ----164
    Bank of Dalton ----165
    Hardwick Bank ----166
    First National Bank ----167
    Dalton Building & Loan Association ----168, 169
    Marking Historic Sites ----170
    Negro Population ----170

CHAPTER VIII

Greater Whitfield County ----171
    Road Building ----171
    Industrial Location ----172
    Educational Facilities ----173
    Dalton, the County Seat ----173
    Whitfield Citizenry ----178, 179

Census of 1850 of Murray County, Georgia, of which Whitfield County Was Then a Part _____175, 184
Whitfield County Officers _____184
Judges Superior Court Cherokee Circuit _____185
Judges Inferior Court Whitfield County _____186
Judges City Court of Dalton _____186
State Senators Representing County _____186
Representatives of Whitfield County _____187
Ordinaries _____187
Solicitors General Superior Court Cherokee Circuit _____187
Solicitors City Court of Dalton _____187
Sheriffs of Whitfield County _____187
Inferior Court Clerks _____188
Superior Court Clerks _____188
Clerk City Court Dalton _____188
Tax Receivers _____188
Tax Collectors _____188
County Treasurers _____188
Surveyors _____189
Coroners _____189
Superintendents County Schools _____189
Justices of the Peace and Notaries Public _____189
Carbondale, Cohutta Districts _____189
Dalton, Fincher and Lower Tenth _____190
Mill Creek, Ninth, Rocky Face, Tilton _____191
Fincher, Tunnel Hill _____192
Upper Tenth, Varnell _____192, 193
Commissioners of Roads and Revenues _____193
Early Deeds of Record Whitfield Co. _____193, 194, 195
Will Book 1, Beginning March 1, 1851 _____195
Officials Who Have Served City of Dalton _____195, 196, 197
Water, Light and Sinking Fund Commission _____199
Former Members, Board of Education _____199
Municipality of Dalton _____200
Revolutionary Soldiers _____200
Soldiers of the War of 1812 _____200
Soldiers of Indian Wars _____200
State Capitol Records, Confederate Soldiers _____200
The Dalton Guards _____201
Muster Roll Co. B Phillips Legion _____201, 202
List of Dalton Guards _____202
Muster Roll Co. T, First Reg. _____202, 203
        Co. H, Eighth _____203
        Co. H, 36th Reg. _____204
        Co. A, 34 Reg. _____204, 205
        Co. B, 36th Reg. _____205
        Co. C, 36th Reg. _____206

    Co. G, 36th Reg. ------------------------------206, 207
    Co. D, 39th Reg. -----------------------------------207
    Co. I, 36th Reg. ------------------------------------208
    Co. C, 39th Reg. -----------------------------------209
    39 Reg. ---------------------------------210, 211, 212
    Co. B, 60th Reg. ----------------------------212, 213
    Co. C, 60th Reg. ----------------------------213, 214
    Co. D, 60th Reg. ----------------------------------214
    Co. E, 60th Reg. ----------------------------------215
    Co. F, 60th Reg. ----------------------------------216
Fourth Ga. Cavalry --218
Muster Roll 36th Ga. Volunteers -------------------------219
Roster of the Joseph E. Johnston Camp, Confederate
 Veterans ---220
World War Soldiers of Whitfield County ---------------225
Liberty League of Whitfield County ---------------------228
Red Cross of Whitfield County -------------------------230
Pioneer Citizens of Whitfield County -------------------230
Pioneer Citizens and Others --------------------------------231
Oldest Inscriptions from Presbyterian Cemetery and West
 Hill Cemetery --232

Index of Illustrations

Map of Whitfield County	Frontispiece
Prehistoric Indian Articles	14
The Vann House	22
Rev. George Whitfield	41
Whitfield County Court House	48
Hotel Dalton	50
Map of Battlefields of Whitfield County	63
Joseph E. Johnston Monument	69
Dalton Post Office	77
First Methodist Church	86
First Presbyterian Church	90
First Baptist Church	93
City High School	120
City Park School	120
Fort Hill School Building	122
North Dalton School Building	122
Dawnville School Building	124
Cohutta School Building	125
Varnell School Building	126
Valley Point School	127
Pleasant Grove School Building	128
West Side School Building	129
Tunnel Hill School Building	129
Central Club House	149
Hamilton Memorial Hospital	157
The Dalton Public Library	164
Bank of Dalton	165
Hardwick Bank & Trust Co.	166
First National Bank	167
Thornton Avenue Looking North	169

OFFICIAL HISTORY OF WHITFIELD COUNTY, GEORGIA
NAME INDEX TO TEXT
PAGES V through 164
Compiled by Polly Boggess

A
Acree, _____ 99
Adair, J. 2
Adair, George W. 11-35
Adams, H. J. 86-89
Albertson, G. W. 133
Albertson, M. A. 133
Allen, _____ 108
Allen, B. P. 89
Allen, D. E. 73-76
Allen, E. W. 139
Allen, Mrs. Earnest 49
Allen, Ivan VI-15
Allen, Mrs. Penelope VI
Alley, O. C. (Ogburn) 74-157
Alley, Mrs. O. C. 152
Allman, J. I. 121
Allyn, L. J. 60
Allyn, Mrs. L. J. 153
Anderson, B. R. 101
Anderson, Barney 135
Anderson, E. L. 135
Anderson, Jane 89
Anderson, John 51-89
Anderson, Capt. J. W. 76
Anderson, R. L. 133
Andrew, colored boy of
  J. I. Hamilton 89
Anthony, J. D. 88
Arbogast, B. A. 86
Archer, Clarence 144
Armstrong, S. F. 132
Armstrong, Sarah 102
Ault, Dr. _____ 155
Ault, Clayton 142
Ault, James 116
Ault, John 135
Ault, R. W. 109
Ault, W. A. 132
Austin, Arch 110
Austin, Clisbe 116
Austin, James 99
Austin, R. L. 103
Autrey, Will 108
Avery, Col. _____ 56
Ayers, Mrs. Harold 146

B
Babb, E. W. 109-128
Babb, F. M. 109
Babb, Francis 131
Babb, L. C. 107
Babb, L. M. 124-126
Babb, Mrs. Ruth 151
Bagby, E. W. 137
Bagby, Sarah 108
Bagby, Fred 103
Bagby, T. J. 103
Bailey, Henry 133
Bailey, J. M. 114
Bailey, J. W. 105-116
Bailey, N. A. 93
Baker, F. F. 132-137-138
Baker, Frank F. 139-140
Baker, Mary Foute 109
Baker, Robert 78
Baker, Robert H. 109
Bales, S. A. 95-99
Ballew, John C. 78
Bandy, Mrs. B. J. 152-153
Bandy, Joseph 109
Baniel, Robert 116
Baniel, Mrs. _____ 115
Bankston, W. J. 135
Bard, James H. 140
Bard, James D. 82
Bare, D. 130
Bare, Mrs. Doss 147
Bare, Mrs. Susan 118
Bark, Chief 7
Barnes, Riley 108
Barnett, A. J. 131
Barnett, John C. 115-116
Barrett, _____ 158
Barrett, Dennis 168
Barrett, Mrs. Joseph 146-152
Barrett, L. W. 72
Barrett, Nell 121
Bartenfield, Mrs. Henry 99
Bates, _____ 58
Bates, Mrs. Jesse T. 142-151
Batey, S. W. 139
Baxter, J. H. 89
Bearden, _____ 116
Beckwith, Bishop 94
Beeman, J. 139
Beeson, Mrs. J. L. 20
Bell, Jack 109
Bell, John 12-35
Bell, T. R. 98
Bender, John Lewis 114
Bender, W. F. 95
Benge, John 28-38
Bennett, G. A. 133

Bennett, S. M.	102
Bennett, Walter	107
Bennett, U. J.	121
Benson, Bishop ____	40
Berner, W. R.	91
Berry, Martin	73-123
Berry, Martin P.	114
Berry, Samuel E.	140
Betterton, T. C.	89
Big Bear, Chief	19
Big Half Breed	7
Bigham, R. G.	86-89
Bird, Judge Elbert S.	51-140
Bishop, B. P.	132
Bishop, William	23-32
Bitting, Carrie	121
Bitting, John H.	72-79
Bitting, Mrs. M. E.	69
Bivings, Miss Blanche	145
Bivings, J. D.	72
Bivings, J. W.	73
Black Fox	19
Black, C. A.	132
Black, Ernest	97
Black, John	95-121
Black, Mrs. W. A.	148
Blair, Joseph	117
Blair, Miss Ruth	VI
Blalock, J. H.	109
Blanton, Jacob A.	92-140
Blevins, Mrs. Flora L.	145
Blevins, J. A.	133
Bloody Fellow, Chief	5
Blunt, Ainsworth E.	10-50-51
(Blount)	64-75-78
	89-91
Blunt, Elizabeth R.	10
Blunt, Harriet E.	10
Bodenhamer, J. E.	133
Bogle, Miss Grace	148
Bogle, M. H.	76
Bolander, A. (Anthony)	51-114
Bolden, B. E.	97
Bonds, Luther	124
Boudinot, Elias	11-25-26
	33-34-35
Boudinot, Harriet Gold	26-28
Bowdry, ____	106
Bowen, W. C.	133-159-169
Bowie, ____	16
Bowman, ____	117
Boyd, ____	108
Boyd, Rev. J. A.	95-96
Boyd, James	109
Boyd, William	109
Boyd, W. H.	106-109
Boyles, Homer	124
Brackett, M. Q.	125
Bradford, N. A.	54-131
Bradley, Dr. ____	155
Bradley, Mrs. C. L.	95-150-152
Bradley, Felix	99
Bradley, M. V.	133
Bradley, Perry	110
Bragg, Gen. ____	56-57-66
Bramblett, Mrs. Glennie	136
Bramlett, Arthur	133
Branch, Harlee	157
Breeden, A. R.	100
Breeden, Arnold	109
Bridges, A. J.	109
Bridges, Mrs. Harriet	112
Bridges, Jerry	109
Bridges, J. H.	103
Bridges, J. M.	112
Bridges, J. W.	112
Bridges, Sarah	109
Bridges, Rev. W. B.	96-107
Bridges, W. H.	103
Brinsmade, Gen. D. D.	26-29
Brinson, W. W.	101
Brittain, J. M.	113
Britton, J. A.	131
Britton, Mrs. William	142
Broadrick, Arthur	168
Broadrick, Dr. ____	155
Broadrick, John	54-130
Broadrick, Miss Phoebe	123-124
Brooker, ____	114-158
Brooker, Henry	113
Brooker, Jane	113
Brooker, John	72
Brooker, John Lake	144
Brooker, John W.	130
Brooker, W. H.	76-131
Brotherton, Levi	87-88-139
Brown, ____	54-58
Brown, Mrs. Alfred	162-163
Brown, B. B.	73
Brown, Bean	49
Brown, David	27
Brown, James	38
Brown, John	75
Brown, Gov. Joseph E.	65-119-121
Brown, Col. J. R.	76
Brown, J. W.	132-140
Brown, L. A.	75
Brown, Mrs. Mary	138
Brown, Susan A.	115
Brown, Rev. Thomas	101
Brown, William	115
Brown, Rev. William B.	101
Brown, W. L.	111
Browning, Columbus	78
Brumlow, J. W.	132
Bryan, J. L.	95-99
Bryan, Thomas L.	118
Bryant, Mrs. D. C.	148
Bryant, Miss Eloise	VI
Bryant, Guy	127
Bryant, John	72-82
Bryant, T. J.	131
Bryant, W. C.	124-126
Buchanan, J. L.	132
Buchanan, Joe L.	135
Buchanan, Joseph	138

Buchholz, Rev. O. E. 91
Bukofzer, D. 73-76
Bukofzer, Jacob H. 140
Burch, Lee 108
Burch, Mrs. Lillie 136
Burdette, V. E. 135
Burgess, T. A. 109
Burke, Hugh 46
Burns, Frank 102
Burns, M. 82
Bush, Mrs. R. G. 146
Bushyhead, Rev. Jesse 38
Butler, ... 38
Buttolph, D. L. 101
Byhan, Gottlieb 5-6-7-21

C
Cady, _____ 114
Cady, Stephen A. 113
Cae-te-hee 35
Cagle, Howard 107
Cain, Joseph M. 53
Caldwell, A. L. 111
Caldwell, C. G. 111
Caldwell, Margaret 104
Caldwell, M. F. 132
Caldwell, Thomas 104-105
Caldwell, Rev. William E. 101
Calhoun, Adam 54
Calhoun, Mrs. Andy 60
Calhoun, Elizabeth 109
Callahan, William 113
Calloway, T. M. 94
Calloway, W. W. 131
Camp, Maj. W. A. 49
Candler, Gov. _____ 80
Cannon, Mrs. Blair 152
Cannon, Mrs. G. M. 145-148
Cannon, Mrs. W. R. 150
Canter, P. T. 139
Carder, D. H. 137
Carder, William 130
Cargal, Rev. J. H. 96-107-109
Carlock, Rev. E. B. 97
Carr, Mrs. Sanford 151
Carr, T. S. 138
Carr, Mrs. T. S. 138
Carrington, Miss Beulah 155
Carroll, Fiddella 108
Carroll, Gov. William 35
Carter, A. S. 135
Carter, Ben F. 81
Carter, David 27-28
Carter, Farish 12
Carter, J. W. 135
Carter, Rev. H. C. 91
Carter, Mrs. Lillian W. 160
Carter, Sam 13
Cash, J. M. 107-111
Cash, S. A. 107
Cash, W. M. 107
Cates, J. N. 139
Catlett, Mrs. J. E. 151

Cator, Rev. William 115
Cavender, Washington 99
Chamberlin, Rev. _____ 28-29
Chambers, George 35
Chambers, William 130
Chapman, Ed E. 51
Chappell, George 87-88
Charles, Count Frederick 51
Chastain, _____ 100-108
Chastain, C. 109
Chastain, G. L. 95-99-105
.... 116
Cheatham, _____ 58-60
Cherry, _____ 116
Chester, Charles 76
Chester, Miss Charle 152
Chester, Elmer 162
Chester, Mrs. Lula J. 116-117
Chester, W. P. 49-60-75
.... 76-78-140
Chipley, Mrs. Lula F. 145
Chitwood, Rev. S. P. 96-107
Chowalooka 38
Christian, G. M. 109
Christian, Prof. George 115
Christian, J. T. 89
Chuleola, Chief 6
Church, Dr. _____ 84
Church, Myers M. 95
Clark, Benjamin 53
Clark, H. C. 98
Clark, Sarah 109
Clark, Z. T. 107
Clark, Zachariah 109
Clauder, Henry C. 21
Cleburne, Gen. Patrick 57-58-61
.... 66-69
Clegg, J. L. 94
Clement, P. P. 133-135
Clemons, Silas 72
Click, George 109
Clifford, Father _____ 98
Cline, D. L. 54
Cline, Daniel 130
Clonts-Clontz, Rev. M. A. 88-140
Clonts-Clontz, Rev. M. L. .. 112-114
Clonts, William 111
Clontz, M. S. 109
Clore, Miss Agnes 134
Cobb, Gen. T. R. R. 56
Cochran, Charlie 99
Cochran, Dr. E. C. 109-116-131
Cochran, Ferdy 108
Coffee, W. W. 133-135
Coffee, Mrs. W. W. 134
Coker, W. H. Jr. 115
Cole, John 107
Cole, W. H. 135
Cole, W. L. 135
Collins, John 133
Collins, Moses 110
Combee, Mrs. May 136
Combee, William 105

Compton, John	99
Conklin, Augustus	97
Conly, W. F.	88
Connally, Mrs. Molly	98
Connally, Mrs. Nola	138
Conrad, Hair	37
Coody, Joseph	29
Coody, William S.	29
Cook, _____	57
Cook, Charles A.	54
Cook, Frank	108
Cook, Frederick	51
Cook, James	109
Cook, R. L.	140
Cook, Rev. T. Frank	97
Cook, Capt. Tom	56-62
Cooksey, Mrs. _____	118
Cooksey, W. W.	72
Cooledge, _____	118
Coolidge, Judge John	165
Cooper, George F.	93
Cooper, Irene	109
Cooper, James	109
Cooper, T. J.	100
Cooper, W. H.	94
Copeland, J. J.	63-123-163
Copeland, J. C.	168
Cordell, Henry	109
Corn, John	87
Cornelison, W. C.	137
Cornelison, Mrs. W. C.	137-138
Cornelius, Elias	18
Cotter, Rev. W. J.	7-22-32-53
Couch, A. B.	94
Counts, B. E.	135
Cowart, C. L.	132
Cowart, Thomas	132
Cox, E. A.	109
Cox, Capt. Fred	51-78
Cox, Hiram	117
Cox, M. C.	134-135
Cox, Mrs. Sarah	118
Crawford, John A.	78
Crawford, Mrs. Josie	78
Crawley, W. G.	89
Creasman, Mary	107
Creekmore, Edmond	130
Crenshaw, Rev. David	87
Creswell, J. W.	101
Cronic, W. H.	97
Crouch, James	105
Crouch, Lavinia	105
Crow, J. C.	107
Crow, Jesse	117
Crow, Robert	126
Crow, Spartan	162
Crow, Thomas	110-111
Crudup, Josiah	94-163
Crutchfield, Margaret V.	21
Cummings, Rev. David	86
Cunningham, D. B.	106
Cunningham, _____	108
Cupp, George	162
Curtis, Mrs. May G.	145

D

Dale, _____	105
Dalton, Mary	47
Dalton, Tristam	47
Damel, Moses	38
Daniel, F. M.	93
Daniel, Frank	133
Daniel, T. B.	139
Dantzler, A. P.	113-130
Dantzler, F. J.	137
Dantzler, Jacob	113-130
Dantzler, Rev. J. O.	95-96-99-104-107-109-110-114
Dantzler, Lemuel	130
Dantzler, Rowan F.	130
Dantzler, Susan	113
Darnell, W. G.	107
Darnell, W. J.	100
Davenport, W. D.	107
Davenport, William	100
Davenport, W. H.	111
Daves, Mrs. Alice	139
Daves, J. P.	52
Daves, Miss Pearl	138
Davis, Edward	144
Davis, Rev. E. O.	96-97-107
Davis, E. P.	163-167
Davis, Henry	73-75-93
Davis, Jackson	105
Davis, Jane	105
Davis, Pres. Jefferson	57
Davis, M. B.	132-135
Davis, McAfee Bates	135
Davis, Mrs. Nell King	145
Davis, Mrs. Warren	VI-150
Davis, W. H.	76-80
Dawn, E. F.	104
Dawn, Mary	104
Dawn, W. E.	96-107
Dawn, Will	107
Dawtrey, Joseph B.	86
Deakins, Charles	51
Deakins, Mrs. C. A.	151
Dean, Alexander	105
Dean, A. S.	104
Dean, Elbert	109
Dean, Elizabeth	105
Deck, J. T.	131
Deck, Matt	135
Deer-in-the-Water	19
Deitch, H.	135
Dellinger, W. E.	140
Dendy, Dr. Wilkes	91
Denson, Mrs. Lena	139
Denson, W. L.	139-140
Denton, _____	158
Denton, Miss Elizabeth	145
Denton, J. F.	91
Denton, W. M.	91
Denton, William M.	78

DeSoto, _____ 1-13-15
Dettor, Mrs. Dollie Lewis 49
Dick, George A. 135
Dickey, J. M. 88
Dickson, Mrs. J. K. 146
Dill, Melvin 162
Disney, George W. 62
Dixon, R. M. 89
Dobson, Joe 110
Dobson, W. M. 128
Dooley, J. M. 110
Dooley, J. W. 107
Dooly, J. N. 104
Doublehead, Chief 5-11
Douglass, Rev. Hiram 102
Drew, John 38
Drowning Bear, Chief 16
Duane, _____ 158
Duck Rev. Thomas 94
Duckett, I. G. 97
Duckett, L. B. 107
Duncan, John P. 89
Duncan, J. T. 121
Dunlap, W. C. 89
Dunn, Billy 106
Dunn, Giles 100-106
Dunn, Levy 100-106
Dunn, Gen. S. 76
Durham, R. H. 95
Dyer, E. M. 94
Dycus, Mrs. Betty W. 104

E
Earnest, _____ 108
Earnest, Alonzo 109
Earnest, Col. L. W. 76
Earnest, Mahala 109
Earnest, Mary 109
Easley, Dr. _____ 155
Easley, C. L. 18
Easley, G. M. 110
Easley, Sam M. 140-143
Eason, John 164
Eason, T. J. 72
Edmondson, R. A. 89
Edwards, Edward H. 78
Elders, Mrs. Mattie 97
Ellington, Mrs. Marcia B. 145
Elliott, _____ 100
Ellis, H. J. 89
Elrod, F. W. 115
Elrod, Mrs. F. W. 148
Emerson, Dr. _____ 116
Emerson, Mrs. _____ 116
Emerson, Mrs. Will 117
Emory, H. C. 89
England, Otis M. 130
Ensley, _____ 100-109
Ervine, W. T. 89
Erwin, Dr. _____ 155
Erwin, H. L. 163-170
Erwin, Lieut. H. C. 170
Eslinger, Alma 118
Eslinger, D. 130
Eslinger, Roy 162
Evans, William 131
Ezzard, H. H. 127

F
Fagala, Abigail 117
Fagala, George 117
Fagala, John 118
Fagala, Sarah 118
Fain, W. M. 115
Faith, Mrs. Bessie 136
Fallis, J. R. 132
Fann, Dr. _____ 74
Farnsworth, J. L. 138
Farnsworth, Mrs. J. L. 138
Farrar, _____ 158
Farrar, Rev. B. F. 96
Farrar, F. F. 162-163
Farrar, H. B. (Henry) 138-140
Farrar, Mrs. H. B. 138
Farrar, W. B. 92-161
Faulkner, Miss Flora 98
Felker, C. H. 127
Felker, Guy 162
Felker, S. B. 131
Felker, T. M. 82
Field, Minnie 121
Field, Capt. Old 38
Fields, Dr. Carter Dempsey 28
Fields, J. D. 123
Fielder, Mrs. May 116
Fincher, _____ 165
Fincher, Jesse 110
Fincher, Joseph 110-131
Fincher, J. T. 111
Fincher, John Wesley 99
Fincher, Lucinda 110
Fincher, Rhoda 99
Finley, Mrs. Carl 134
Finley, Mrs. Mae 138
Fischer, Lou 52
Fischer, Otto 52
Fischer, Will 52
Fitch, H. P. 94
Fite, Paul B. 121-143-157
Fitzgerald, Rev. Archibald 75-92
Fleming, O. D. 94
Flemister, F. J. 131-135
Flemister, Miss Grace 145
Flemister, L. S. 117
Fletcher, George 96-107-111
Flowers, Charles 95
Folsom, Dr. _____ 72
Foote, W. R. 89
Foster, Absolem 53
Foster, B. F. 99-106-107
.... 108-109-110
Foster, Mrs. Florence 116
Foster, Gordon 124
Foster, James 35
Foster, John 116
Foster, Mrs. Rufus 117

Foster, W. H. 116-117
Foster, Mrs. W. H. 116
Foreman, Charles F. 35
Forsyth, Gov. _____ 30
Four, Joe 107
Fox, Haney 117-131
Fox, Herman 157
Fraker, Andrew 54-105
Fraker, C. H. 132-133
Fraker, Mrs. Clarence V-VI-150-169
Fraker, Evaline 105
Fraker, George P. 54-73-104-105
Fraker, Margaret 105
Fraker, Mrs. Nita Miller 145
Fraker, Sallie 105
Fraker, Wesley 105
Franklin, _____ 100
Fraser, B. F. 89
Frazier, S. G. 103
Frazier, Samuel 162
Frazier, T. M. 137
Freeman, Benjamin F. 54
Freeman, Judge Jesse P. 54-79-131
Freeman, Miss Kate 146
Freeman, W. H. C. 54
Fullilove, L. 82
Fulton, Rev. D. F. 85
Fulton, W. D. 139

G
Gambold, Anna Kleist 8-20-21
Gambold, John 7-8-11
.... 20-21
Gambrell, J. M. 93-104-113
Gambrell, James 106
Garrett, H. G. 116
Garrett, W. M. 133
Gaston, Dr. A. W. 91
Gatlin, Miss Lucille 138
Gatlin, P. A. 94
Gatlin, Rev. Pryce E. 138
Gatlin, Mrs. Pryce E. 138
Gavitt, Miss Irene 153
Gavitt, Miss Margaret 153
Gentle, J. H. 137
Gentleman Tom 7
Gibson, _____ 95
Gidden, W. W. 73
Gilbert, John J. 99-104-112
Gilbert, H. D. 99-106-108
.... 110-113
Gilbert, H. S. 96
Gilbreath, Col. _____ 27
Gillian, William 117
Gilliland, Miss Jessie 138
Gilliland, R. R. 132-137-138
Gilliland, Mrs. R. R. 138
Gist, George 24
Gist, Capt. Nathaniel 24-25
Gladden, Berry 107
Glass, Chief 5
Glass, Sam 131
Glaze, _____ 60

Glenn, Col. _____ 56
Glenn, George 131
Glenn, Jesse 131
Glenn, Jesse A. 78
Glenn, Jesse P. 75
Glenn, J. W. 86
Glenn, W. C. 131
Goad, F. S. 134
Gober, _____ 99
Goddard, J. E. 132-133
Godfrey, J. W. 127
Godwin, J. P. 137-138-140
Godwin, Mrs. J. P. 137-138
Goings, William 98
Gold, Benjamin 26
Gold, Harriet 26
Goodwin, S. A. 94
Goodwin, T. B. 132
Gordon, Dr. C. P. 121-140
Gordon, Col. _____ 64
Gordon, Dr. W. 76
Gordon, Col. William 51-76
Gordon, Winston 46
Granberry, _____ 59
Grant, Clarence 162
Grasshoff, Anse 131
Graves, R. L. 139
Gravitt, Oba 136
Gray, John D. 52
Gray, W. E. 108
Green, _____ 116
Green, Anthony 112
Green, Col. Ben E. 49-72-94-95
Green, Miss Carrie 94-95-145
.... 150-151
Green, Duff 49-92
Green, Rev. E. M. 91
Green, E. W. 91
Green, H. H. 115
Green, Dr. W. J. 155
Greene, S. Percy 76
Gregory, Mrs. Amos 148
Gregory, R. P. 91
Grey, W. E. 103
Griffin, Mrs. Carolyn 139
Griffin, J. A. 131
Griffin, Miss Laura 138
Griffin, Mrs. Lucinda 115
Griffin, Mrs. Mary 137
Griffin, Needham 115
Griffin, Rev. Reece 115
Griffin, Thomas 115
Griffin, Walton C. 135-137-139
.... 140
Grove, John R. 135
Groves, J. F. 91-101
Gudger, Ben 80
Gudger, L. P. (Lorenzo) 74-78-79
Guess, _____ 28
Gunter, _____ 37
Gunter, John 35
Gunter, Edward 28
Gunter, Samuel 28

Guntz, Augustus 51
Guthrie, Major Joseph 116-117

H
Hackney, W. M. 102
Hackney, William P. 51
Haddock, W. H. D. 103
Haddock, W. C. 100-103-108
Hailes, W. J. 140
Hair, Isaac 54-114
Hair, Sam 109
Halfbreed, Jesse 109
Hall, Cass 98
Hall, Thomas 115
Hambright, A. R. T. 53-102
Hambright, Martha I. 102
Hamby, W. T. 99-105-116
Hamby, W. F. 95
Hamilton, Mrs. C. L. 146-153
Hamilton, Miss Daisy 137-138
Hamilton, Miss Elizabeth 145
Hamilton, E. F. 95
Hamilton, F. A. 132-133-137-140
Hamilton, George W. 91-131-140-155
Hamilton, George W. Jr. 91-169
Hamilton, Mrs. G. W. 153
Hamilton, Henry C. 76-131
Hamilton, Mrs. H. C. 151-153
Hamilton, Miss Jennie 145
Hamilton, John 46-47-51-52-74
Hamilton, J. H. 76
Hamilton, Miss Kate 145-148-162
Hamilton, Miss Mary 153
Hamilton, Miss Maud 150
Hamilton, R. E. 82
Hamilton, Mrs. Robert 152
Hamilton, Mrs. Scylla 147-160
Hamilton, _____ 99-105-116
Hammond, _____ 54
Hammond, J. D. 89-163
Hammond, Capt. William 87-88
Hampton, _____ 108
Hampton, Rev. W. L. 97
Haney, D. J. 140
Hanks, H. T. 93
Hanks, J. A. R. 75-81-93-118
Hannah, C. P. 135-140-144
Hannah, Mrs. C. P. 139
Hannah, J. E. 133
Harben, Will N. 74-159
Hardaway, G. W. 89
Hardcastle, Mrs. _____ 105
Hardee, Gen. W. J. 57
Harden, Judge Edward 92
Hardin, Amos 162
Hardin, Eugene 140
Hardin, Mrs. H. H. 134
Hardin, Mrs. Mary 142-151
Hardin, Oliver R. 144
Hardin, Mrs. O. R. 145-146-147
Hardwick, C. L. 82
Hardwick, F. T. 80-82-140-167
Hardwick, John 82

Hardwick, W. M. 167
Hardy, Mrs. Judith 116
Hardy, Mrs. Pearl 139
Harlan, Mrs. Anna M. 12
Harlan, Charles 131
Harlan, Miss Eloise 146-147
Harlan, Ellis 12
Harlan, George 12
Harlan, George W. 53
Harlan, Dr. George 115
Harlan, I. H. 109-116
Harlan, Joshua 110
Harper, Fred 100
Harper, William 121
Harris, Dr. _____ 155
Harris, C. A. 109
Harris, C. P. 89
Harris, C. P. N. 116
Harris, E. C. 132
Harris, Isaac N. 26
Harris, Miss Laura 145
Harris, M. G. 110
Harris, M. L. 95-99
Harris, S. A. 87
Harris, William M. 82
Harrison, W. P. 86
Hartsfield, Miss Sarah 118
Haskins, J. D. 100
Haskins, John A. 100-101
Haskins, Martha J. 100
Haskins, Mary J. 100
Haskins, Rachel K. 100
Hassler, Michael 112
Hassler, S. R. 124-126
Hastings, Mrs. Donald 152
Hasty, John 127
Hawk, Madison C. 87
Hawkins, Frank 95
Hawkins, J. M. 95-99-105-116
Hawkins, _____ 106
Hayes, W. A. 126
Haygood, A. G. 86
Head, George W. 117-131
Head, H. J. 109
Head, Henry 100
Head, James A. 42-53
Head, Capt. J. C. 42
Head, J. C. VI-109
Head, John 99
Head, Miss Mabel 118-145
Head, Sam 143
Head, S. J. 168-169
Headden, Dr. Robert B. 117
Headrick, Mrs. James 117
Headrick, W. M. 117-131
Headrick, W. 108
Headrick Wheeler 97
Heartsell, Buford L. 78
Heggie, J. L. 116
Hendershot, Rev. H. H. 97-98
Henderson, Charles 101
Henderson, Miss Cora 164
Henderson, Ed 49

Henderson, N. G.	109
Henderson, P. S.	132
Henderson, William A.	140
Hendricks, L. G.	116
Henley, Mrs. Q. B.	31
Henesley, W. F.	103
Henry, Rev. S. R.	105
Henry, Rev. W. A.	105-106
Henton, Miss Belle	111
Henton, D. C. Sr.	111
Henton, J. L.	111
Herndon, B. Z.	73
Herndon, E. O.	131
Herron, R. M. Sr.	80-91
Herron, Mrs. R. M.	V-VI-148-150-162-163-169
Herron, R. M. Jr.	161
Hiberts, C.	139
Hickey, William	87
Hicks, _____	11
Hicks, Charles	5-7
Hicks, Charles R.	18-30
Hicks, Mrs. Clarice	98
Hicks, Elijah	37
Hicks, George	7-38
Hicks, Leonard	11
Hicks, Nathan	18
Hicks, William	30
Higdon, T. A.	111
Higgins, Mrs. R. B.	152
Higgins, Mrs. R. D.	150
Higgins, W. W.	73
High, William L.	139
Hightower, G. H.	132
Hightower, Miss Susie	138
Hildebrand, Peter	38
Hill, Gen. _____	64-65-69
Hill, Augustus	110
Hill, B. H.	132-133
Hill, Mrs. Clarence H.	151
Hill, Dick	52
Hill, Edward	110
Hill, G. C.	132
Hill, Hardee	135
Hill, J. B.	127-135
Hill, John Sr.	95
Hill, Morris	135
Hill, R. M.	134-135
Hill, Richard	110-139
Hill, Tom	132
Hillhouse, Rev. James S.	101
Hillhouse, J. B.	101
Hindman, _____	58
Hirschberg, _____	74
Hix, Fred W.	133
Hogan, Rev. _____	96
Hogan, John S.	115
Holiday, Miss Cornelia	94
Holland, E. B.	111
Holland, James	98
Holland, H. P.	108
Hollingsworth, Mrs. C. M.	146-148-150-151
Hollingsworth, C. M.	94
Hollingsworth, Latimer	94
Holt, A. B.	76
Holt, R. A. Jr.	76
Hood, Gen. _____	60-61-66
Hooker, Gen. Joseph	57-58
Hopkins, Lewis	162
Hopper, Thomas A.	78
Horan, George	75
Horan, Miss Mary Louise	145
Horne, Miss Annie	95-153
Horne, Capt. Pearce	57-95-130
Houston, C. B.	132
Houston, Martin	118
Houston, W. H.	132
Howard, Mrs. H. A.	151-152
Howden, Mrs. L. Q.	117
Howe, W. W.	78
Howell, _____	23
Hubbs, Devine	140
Hubbs, L. B.	135
Huckabee, John	95
Hudlow, Rev. J. M.	96
Hudson, E. C.	106
Hudson, J. E.	96-109
Huff, J. H.	53
Huff, James	130
Huff, James H.	19-103-111-115
Huff, Mrs. Margaret McG.	19
Huff, Miss Mattie Lee	19-145-150
Huff, Mrs. W. C.	19-57-75
Huffaker, Jesse T.	100-107-108
Huffaker, Landon	133-135
Huffaker, Nancy A.	102
Huffaker, W. F.	103-108
Huffaker, _____	111
Hughes, A. J.	99-105-116
Humphries, _____	105
Humphries, John	138
Hunsucker, Mrs. Mattie	139
Hunt, Rev. B. F.	94-96-109
Hunt, B. H.	103
Hunt, C. D.	131
Hunt, Miss Irene	137-138
Hurley, _____	108
Huss, Judge _____	28
Huston, H. S.	127
Hutchinson, John	138
Hutchinson, Mrs. John	138
Hutchinson, J. W.	138-139
Hyer, Miss Lizzie	139

I

Ingram, _____	49
Innis, Mrs. Frank	146-152
Irvine, W. T.	86
Isbill, Martin	106-108-113
Isbill, W. H.	113-130-137

J

Jackson, Andrew	12-33-150
Jackson, Major Frank	57

Jackson, Col. J. F. B. 76	Keith, G. W. 16
Jackson, J. M. 55	Keith, H. D. 104
James, Henry 106	Keith, R. J. 73-110
James, James S. 105-106	Keith, Samuel 110
James, John A. 106	Kelley, Rev. W. M. 96
Jarvis, Mrs. H. L. 72	Kelly, Laura 121
Jefferson, Walter 81	Kelly, Dr. T. L. 76
Jenkins, Charles J. 47	Kelly, W. M. 103-108-110
Jernigan, Mrs. J. G. 153	Kenan, Judge _____ 17-53
Jewell, _____ 54-114	Kenemer, David 109
Johnson, _____ 53-61	Kenemer, David Lowry 115
Johnson, Archibald 88	Kenemer, Needham 131
Johnson, Rev. A. G. 91	Kenemer, Mrs. Olivia 142
Johnson, James 102	Kenemer, Mrs. T. W. 151
Johnson, J. C. 107	Kennedy, Dr. _____ 155
Johnson, J. A. W. 76	Kennedy, W. E. 105-116
Johnson, Rev. Joseph 53	Kennedy, W. R. 99-105
Johnson, L. G. 89	Kenner, Mrs. Gayle 146
Johnson, Matthew 108	Kenner, J. H. 82
Johnson, W. A. 133	Kenner, Joe 121
Johnson, Waylan 94	Kenner, Mrs. Walter Jr. 146
Johnston, A. G. 101	Kenner, W. H. 73-123
Johnston, Col. J. A. W. 75	Kettles, Gordon 82
Johnston, Gen. Joseph E. 57-58-59	Kettles, Jerry 111
. . . . 61-62-66	Kettles, Van 82
. . . . 68-69-147	Keys, Dennis 98
. . . . 169	Kimball, Francis A. 89
Jolley, W. L. 95-99	King, _____ 50
Jones, Col. _____ 53	King, Prof. _____ 73
Jones, A. A. 118	King, C. N. 21
Jones, Clark 143	King, David 105
Jones, Mrs. Clark 152	King, H. A. 95-99
Jones, Claud 98	King, H. G. 133-134-135
Jones, Mrs. Ellen Worthy 145	King, Henry 112
Jones, Mrs. Gertrude M. 144-160	King, J. L. 101
Jones, H. M. 113	King, Silas 111
Jones, Rev. John 89-91	King, Susan 105
Jones, John A. 118	King, William D. 105
Jones, Lee 168	King, W. C. 133
Jones, Mrs. Lona 136	Kingsbury, Cyrus 9
Jones, Nathan 105	Kingsley, R. E. 72
Jones, R. W. 72-91	Kinsey, Newt 115
Jones, Robert F. 88	Kirby, Caroline 98
Jones, Thomas R. 76-82-91	Kirby, Elijah 98
Jones, Violet 105	Kirby, Mrs. Lillie 8-10-75
Jones, W. C. 121	Kirby, Miss Lucy 145
Jones, Walter 121-143-169	Kirby, T. M. 76-91
Jones, Walter Jr. 144-168-169	Kirby, W. C. 108
Jones, W. N. 93	Kirby, Walter 98
Jordan, J. G. 133	Kirk, _____ 114
Jordan, W. S. 116-131	Kirk, James 114
Jordan, W. W. 109-116	Kirk, Thomas 133
Judd, Mrs. Hubert 146-151	Kirk, Troy G. VI
Judd, Mrs. M. E. 15-145-146-152	Kirkpatrick Dr. _____ 131
. . . . 162-163	Kirkpatrick, Charles B. 117
	Kirkpatrick Elizabeth A. 117
K	Kirkpatrick, Mrs. J. T. 117
Kaneaster, Hannah 117	Kirkpatrick, Luvenia 118
Kaneaster, Sylvanus 117	Kirkpatrick, Mary 118
Keister, Guy W. 132-134-140	Kirkpatrick, Sarah 118
Keister, M. A. 132-133-134-140	Knorr, Charles 51
Keith, Bailey 110	Kramer, William P. 89
Keith, Dyer 110-130	Kreischer, Adam 51

Kreischer, C. A. 132-133
Kreischer, Mrs. Charles 153
Kreischer, Mrs. Janice 150
Kreischer, Peter 51

L

Lackey, W. R. 110
LaGrange, Col. _____ 59
Land, J. A. 137
Land, Mrs. J. A. 138
Lane, F. L. 104
Lane, James 101
Langston, J. W. 130
Lanham, Robert 162
Lankford, Miss Edith 97
Lankford, Miss Frankie 97
Lansdell, Henry 76
Larmon, A. J. 130
Lasseter, William H. 110
Lasley, _____ 27
Lassley, William 35
Latimer, Gower 94
Lawrence, T. 103-115
Lawton, L. B. 95
Laymance, Elijah 117
Laymance, Mrs. _____ 117
Leak, James 115
Lee, Gordon 77
Lee, J. W. 89
Lee, Gen. R. E. 56-60-66
Ledbetter, S. B. 87-89
Ledford, Alec 98
Legg, John M. 95-99
Leonard, _____ 111
Leonard, Benjamin D. 102
Leonard, Thirza 102
Lester, Mrs. Fannie C. 118
Lewis, _____ 80
Lewis, Charles K. 87
Lewis, Dan 100
Lewis, J. Q. A. 49
Liddell, W. G. 91
Lindsay, Florence J. 100
Lindsay, Robert 100
Lindsey, Mrs. Kirk 136
Lingle, Dr. Walter L. 91
Linton, Charles W. 139
Lipham, C. M. 89
Lippman, A. 51
Little Turkey, Chief 5
Lockwood, Belva 72
Loftin, G. A. 93
Loner, Miss _____ 60
Loner, Carl 128
Long, Mrs. Nora 97
Long, Roscoe 97
Longley, Mrs. C. E. 137
Longley, J. A. 140
Longley, Mrs. J. A. 138
Longley, James 106
Longley, Jasper 106
Longley, Mrs. J. C. 138
Longley, J. M. 137
Longley, Lewis 106
Longley, P. D. 103-109
Longstreet, Gen. _____ 56
Looper, Mrs. Glenn 146
Looper, John A. 157
Loughridge, B. F. C. 73-76
Love, J. P. 65
Love, R. R. 63
Love, W. E. 115
Lovejoy, W. P. 89
Loveman, Robert 145-146-160-164
Lowe, J. T. 89
Lowe, Mary 102
Lowe, William J. 102
Lowery, J. M. 89
Lowery, _____ 28
Lowry, J. M. 91
Lowry, Miss Lissie 115
Lowry, Thomas 115
Lowry, W. M. 100-109-130
Lucas, Major _____ 95
Lucas, T. S. 121
Lumpkin, Pete 144
Lumpkin, Mrs. Pete 152
Lumpkin, W. H. 142
Lumpkin, Mrs. W. H. 151
Lumpkin, Mrs. William 152
Luther, W. C. 93
Luttrell, B. T. 73-74
Lynan, James 140
Lynch, J. C. 137
Lynn, _____ 158
Lynn, A. W. 91

Mc

McAbee, _____ 104
McAbee, Edward 104
McAfee, Dr. _____ 155
McArthur, H. P. 128
McAuley, Sherry 121
McBrayer, D. A. 95-99
McCall, M. N. 94
McCall, W. C. 93-113
McCallie, Andrew J. 100-101
McCallie, H. J. A. 100
McCamy, Miss Anne 152
McCamy, Bob 144
McCamy, C. C. 138-140
McCamy, Mrs. Carlton 147
McCamy, Carlton 144
McCamy, Mrs. Grace G. 145-153
McCamy, Mrs. Julian 162-163
McCamy, Mrs. Robert G. 152
McCamy, R. J. 82
McCamy, Mrs. R. J. 21
McCamy, S. B. 95
McCamy, T. S. 143-157-162
McCarty, John B. 144-168-169
McCarty, Mrs. John B. 152
McCarty, Miss Olivia 145
McCarty, Samuel R. 47
McCarty, W. T. 92-121
McClure, Thomas 112

Name	Page
McCollum, C. E.	127
McComb, _____	53
McConnell, _____	56
McConnell, F. D.	107
McCord, M. O.	121
McCoy, J. H.	132
McCoy, R. A.	137
McCoy, W. W.	139
McCraw, Cornelia	108
McCraw, Matthew	108
McCurdy, Ann	99
McCurdy, F. W.	46-139-140
McCurdy, Mary Jane	99
McCutchen, _____	49-74
McCutchen, Miss Annie Laurie	152
McCutchen, C. D.	72-121-123
McCutchen, F. K.	51
McDonald, C. H.	17
McDonald, G. T.	142
McDonald, _____	11
McDonald, John	31
McDonald, M. L.	112
McDougal, James E.	162
McEntire, H. L.	95-134
McFarland, _____	99
McFarland, Mrs. C. W.	16
McFarland, Donald	144
McFarland, Mrs. Donald	152
McFarland, James A.	143-161
McFarland, Mrs. J. A.	151
McFarland, Mrs. Lou	139
McFarland, R. H.	137
McFarland, Mrs. R. H.	137
McGaughey, _____	53
McGaughey, Mary C.	102
McGaughey, R. B.	108
McGaughey, Sarah J.	102
McGaughey, William	102
McGill, _____	116
McGhee, Ambrose	78
McGhee, Mrs. Carolyn K.	145
McGhee, J. W.	88
McGhee, Miss Mary B.	152
McGhee, Miss Sarah	145
McGhee, Mrs. Walter	148
McGhee, W. C.	121-162
McGhee, Z. M.	105
McHan, B. M.	95-99
McHan, Harvey	110
McHan, Tolliver M.	78
McIntire, James L.	72
McKamy, D. K.	80-121
McLellan, Miss Fannie	145
McLellan, G. J.	118
McLellan, J. G.	163-167-168-169
McLellan, Mrs. John	152
McLemore, J. S.	94
McMillan, J. W.	23
McNabb, William	104-130
McNair, David	12
McNair, Jane	104
McNair, George	130
McNut, _____	106
McRee, Ford	89
McSpadden, James	89-91
McSpadden, Susan	89
McWilliams, Mrs. Lee	145
McWilliams, Miss Rebecca	150
McWilliams, Mrs. Shelley	150
McWilliams, S. N.	169

M

Name	Page
Maddox, J. A.	73
Maddox, J. M.	73
Maddox, Sam P.	131-140
Maddox, Mrs. Swift	95
Mallory, W. C.	89
Malone, Col.	51
Mangum, William C.	76
Manis, John C.	107
Manis, Martha	107
Manis, T. J.	126
Manis, W. A.	107
Manly, _____	158
Manly, Frank	74-121-169
Manly, Judson	142-144
Manly, Mrs. Judson	152
Manly, Miss Martha Lin	145-152
Manly, W. J.	75-91
Mann, Alfred T.	86
Mann, A. J.	105-116
Mann, Gordon	141
Mann, Mrs. Luther Thomas	146-152-153
Mann, Mrs. W. E.	150-151-153
Manning, W. F.	135-140
Maples, C. C.	132-133-157-163
Maples, Rev. Charles	96-99-103-104-107-110-111-114
Maples, Rev. Joe	96-107
Maples, J. A.	97-114
Marney, H. M.	133
Marshall, John	33
Martin, C. L.	95-99
Martin, Mrs. Ella Lewis	145
Martin, John	12-31-32
Martin, O. L.	94
Martin, W. C.	V-VI-123-124-126-162-163-167-168-169-171
Martin, _____	11
Maston, John B.	103
Mathis, Anderson	108
Matthews, Dr. Mark A.	91
May, William	12
Maynard, _____	54
Maynard, R. B.	131
Meadows, C. D.	121
Mealor, Rev. _____	96
Mecklin, Dr. John	91
Meigs, Return J.	6-7-8
Melton, Samuel	108
Messimer, Peter	109
Metcalf, W. W.	133
Milledge, Gov. John	12-21-148-161
Miller, A. J.	105

Miller, Andrew J. 47
Miller, Claud E. 142
Miller, Mrs. DeWitt 151
Miller, James F. 105
Miller, John 76
Miller, J. H. 102-105
Miller, H. O. 98
Miller, Rebecca 105
Mills, Mrs. George P. 162-163
Mills, J. G. W. 130
Mills, W. B. 116
Millsap, Charles 97
Millsap, D. M. 97
Millsap, Miss Estelle 97
Millsap, Samuel H. 97
Minnis, Elizabeth 100
Minnis, Mary 100
Minnis, Samuel 100
Minnis, Susan 100
Minnis, Thomas 100
Mitchell, ____ 49
Mitchell, A. H. 94
Mitchell, Frank 132-135
Mitchell, George 130
Mitchell, Henry 108
Mitchell, J. C. 142
Mitchell, Mrs. J. C. 151
Mitchell, Mary 100
Mitchell, W. L. 52
Mitchell, William 52
Mixon, J. F. 86-89
Monroe, James 12
Montgomery, J. J. 131
Montgomery, Jesse 109
Montgomery, Sarah 109
Moore, Miss Alice 145
Moore, Miss Allie 121
Moore, Charles 35
Moore, C. A. 88
Moore, Mrs. C. W. 152-153
Moore, D. D. 89
Moore, Eliza Ann 113
Moore, Joe 131
Moore, Will 75
Moore, William K. 76-79-91-121
123-131
Moore, W. K., Jr. 91
Moore, Mrs. W. K. 148
Moore, W. T. 107
Morehead, Dr. W. K. VI-13-15
Morelock, Dave 116
Morgan, J. E. 114
Morgan, J. H. 137
Morgan, John 113
Morgan, Matilda 113
Morgan, R. 113
Morgan, Rudd 113
Morrell, A. S. 93
Morris, Rev. ____ 96
Morris, Miss Agnes 121-145
Morris, Churchwell 99
Morris, Franklin B. 47
Morris, James 47-76-82

Morris, J. M. V. 95
Morris, J. L. 109
Morris, J. V. M. 99
Morris, W. G. 109
Morse, B. C. 10-51-52
78-89
Morse, John Emery 89
Morse, Miss Lois 145
Morse, Martha E. 89
Morse, W. N. 91
Mote, Silas 51
Motley, Mrs. Howard 152
Moyers, B. 73-91
Mulkey, ____ 28
Murphy, John 88
Murphy, Marvin 103
Murphy, S. R. 111
Murray, W. M. 89
Myrick, D. J. 86-89
Myrick, J. D. 89

N
Neal, Alfred J. 107
Neal, Bob 144
Neal, John P. 143
Neal, Mrs. Onie 139
Neal, Mrs. Varner 152
Neely, J. H. 135
Neely, W. T. 135
Nelson, Bishop C. K. 94
Nelson, J. A. 76
Nevin, Henry 144
Nevin, Mrs. Henry 146
Nevin, H. W. 95
Newell, Ann S. 89
Newman, Mrs. Jennie L. ..137-138-139
Newton, ____ 58
Newton, Mrs. John 146
Nichols, Rev. J. T. 96-99-104-106
107-109-110-114
Nichols, ____ 165
Nichols, H. L. 99
Nichols, William M. 56
Nix, ____ 21
Norris, ____ 75
Northrup, Sarah 26
Norton, ____ 53
Norton, Margaret 100
Norton, Wilson 54-102
Nucholls, A. B. 107-111

O
O'Barr, G. L. 91
O'Briant, H. H. 133
O'Cain, Mrs. Harry 142-151
O'Dell, John 88
O'Dell, William 99-110
O'Kelly, ____ 107
O'Neill, Col. ____ 64
O'Neill, R. P. 74-76
Orr, J. G. 118
Orr, W. H. 134
Otterlifter 19

Oxford, Jasper 107
Oxford, Joseph 107
Oxford, LaFayette 107

P
Pace, Henry D. 99-105-116
Padgett, Joe 111
Palmer, C. F. 135
Palmer, L. D. 72
Palmer, R. L. 134
Pangle, Aaron 162
Parker, _____ 111
Parker, A. N. 135
Parker, Emily 102
Parker, P. O. 125
Parker, S. H. 102
Parks, John 52
Parks, W. A. 86-89
Parrott, J. C. 104
Parrott, Mrs. V. D. 139
Parson, W. H. 109
Parsons, _____ 108
Parsons, N. A. 95-99-105
Pate, Miss Zeph 153
Pathkiller 30
Patterson, Mrs. Glen 97
Patterson, R. A. 91
Patty, Joshua W. 100-107
Payne, C. A. 95
Payne, Daniel B. 87
Payne, J. B. 86
Payne, John Howard 34
Payne, Louis B. 88
Peak, R. I. 82
Pedigo, C. D. 135
Peeples, T. N. 134
Pendleton, A. B. 95-99
Pendley, J. T. 95-99
Pentz, Frederick 47
Pettus, _____ 58
Petty, Mrs. Eliza 137-138
Petty, E. W. 137
Petty, W. 138
Peyton, O. C. 94
Pfancokuche (Pfannkuche) Adam ... 51
Phillips, _____ 56
Phillips, Anderson 133
Phillips, Stephen 72
Pickens, John A. 102
Pickett, Albert J. 2
Pierce, A. M. 87-89
Pierce, G. J. 89
Piner, Mrs. Malinda 103
Pitner, John 103
Pitner, Major T. H. 53-72-79-101
.... 103-115-123-130
Pitner, Sarah 100
Pitt, _____ 108
Pittman, Judge C. C. V
Pledger, Thomas 99-105-116
Poag, J. M. 104
Poge, Sallie 98
Polk, Gen. Leonidas 61

Poole, Mrs. Martha 106
Pope, Ross 95
Posey, _____ 108
Poteet, J. R. 132
Potter, _____ 27-28
Prater, Benjamin F. ... 53-72-103-115-130
Prather, J. F. 73
Pratt, C. T. 98
Prothro, Scott 162
Pruden, Col. W. H. 121
Pullen, V. B. 124-130
Pyle, Samuel 132

Q
Quillian, A. B. 89
Quillian, Clayton 88
Quillian, Frank 87-89
Quillian, James 88
Quillian, L. W. 114
Quillian, Lewis 54
Quillian, Milligan 54
Quillian, W. F. 86-89
Quinn, Dr. Moses 72-73

R
Rackley, Joseph 133
Rackley, Lawson 133
Ragsdale, J. O. 107
Raines, Mrs. Frank 146
Raines, Strander 108
Ramsey, W. A. 101
Randolph, Buford 99
Randolph, Elizabeth 99
Randolph, J. L. 99
Ratcliff, John 142
Ratcliffe, John 95
Rattling Gourd 17-19-53
Rauschenberg, Charles 115
Rauschenberg, Mrs. G. H. 146
Rauschenberg, Henry 51
Ray, Mrs. Elvira 104
Ray, F. H. 95-99
Ray, John W. 135
Read, Samuel 108
Reaves, Mrs. Della 98
Redbird, Chief 16
Redwine, Henry 131
Redwine, John M. 131
Reece, C. A. 95-99
Reed, John 137
Reed, Mrs. Mattie L. 98
Reeder, Mrs. Belle McC. 145
Reid, Jane 108
Reid, Samuel 108
Reneau, Russell (Rineau) 86-87
Renfro, Henderson 105
Renfro, Nancy 105
Renfro, W. A. 95
Reynolds, Frank T. 81-131
Reynolds, J. W. 133-134
Reynolds, Jackson 87
Reynolds, John 97
Rhymer, William 103

Richardson, Mrs. Alfred 99
Richardson, A. M. 98
Richardson, Ann 99
Richardson, C. O. 127
Richardson, Claude 162
Richardson, Duke 113
Richardson, Eliza 99
Richardson, Miss Ella 99
Richardson, Emily 113
Richardson, James S. 131
Richardson, Jane 99
Richardson, John M. 88-99
Richardson, Lee 99
Richardson, Lewis 99
Richardson, Martha 99
Richardson, Miss Nan 99
Richardson, Nancy 99
Richardson, Simon P. 89
Richardson, Victor C. 113
Richardson, W. C. 79-123
Richardson, W. S. 141
Richardson, William 99
Richardson, William C. 99
Ridge, Major 27-31-33-34-35
Ridge, John 11-26-27-31-33-34-36
Ridge, Sarah Northrup 26
Ridley, George 108
Ridley, T. D. V-132-133-134-136
.... 138-139-140-143-162-167
Riley, _____ 23
Riley, Finley 51
Riley, James G. 78
Ring, Rev. _____ 85
Risner, Mrs. J. R. 137
Rittenhouse, Floyd 135
Roach, Carl 137
Robbins, J. B. 89
Roberts, A. P. 73-131
Roberts, Col. G. W. 76
Roberts, Miss Johnnie 147
Roberts, P. A. 138
Roberts, T. E. 132
Roberts, Rev. W. E. .. 96-99-104-107-114
Roberts, W. L. Jr. 144
Robertson, Rev. G. F. 91
Robertson, Joseph 46
Robertson, Joseph G. 113-130
Rodgers, Luther 99
Roebuck, F. M. 109
Roebuck, I. M. 113
Rogers, _____ 11
Rogers, Miss Addie 117
Rogers, Emma 116
Rogers, Joe 117
Rogers, Joseph 116
Rogers, Tina 116
Rogers, Robert 35
Rogers, William 35
Rogers, Rev. W. A. 118
Rogers, W. M. 137
Rollins, Dr. _____ 155
Rollins, J. S. 130
Rooney, R. C. 107
Roosevelt, F. D. 118
Rose, Jane 108
Rose, John 108
Rosenbaugh, Mary 89
Ross, _____ 11-28
Ross, John Chief 9-10-11-27-29
.... 31-32-34-35-36-37-38
Ross, Andrew 33-35
Ross, Daniel 28
Ross, Jack 27
Ross, Mrs. Quatie B. H. 31
Routh, _____ 166
Routh, Rev. E. C. 106
Routh, J. E. 132-134
Routh, Lee 169
Routh, Rev. Robert 106
Routh, P. M. 106
Routh, S. H. 130
Roy, Henry Lee 134
Roy, L. W. 101
Rush, William 87
Rushton, R. A. 76-91
Russell, Cynthia Ann 113
Russell, Gordon 81
Russell, J. E. 95-99-116
Russell, H. H. 112
Russell, Mrs. W. N. 112
Russell, William 113
Ryburn, P. B. 89
Ryman, Mrs. Milton 142-146-151
Rymer, W. C. 108

S

Sams, Dr. _____ 52-115
Sandiford, J. E. 132
Sapp, Miss Ethel 145
Sapp, Miss Eugenia 145
Sapp, George W. 73-130
Sapp, G. W. 72
Sapp, J. C. 123
Sapp, R. H. 133-136
Sapp, Miss Sadie 138
Sapp, Sarah 113
Sapp, William 113
Sapp, W. M. V-VI-136-138-139-
.... 140-141-143-165
Sapp, Mrs. W. M. 145-148
Schermerhorn, J. F. 33-34-35
Schmidt, John R. 20
deSchweinitz, Charles 4-5
Scott, Sam B. 82
Scott, Gen. Winfield 37
Scott, W. J. 86
Searle, Thomas A. 89
Seaton, Hillard 154
Seaton, W. W. 125-126
Sebastian, _____ 110
Self, Erwin 135
Self, Joseph M. 94-95
Selvidge, George W. 88-92-93
Sequoyah 24-25
Setzfand, John 51
Seven Nose 19

Name	Page
Sevier, Col. ___	11
Shahan, L. N.	132
Shatzer, R. A.	138
Shaw, E. Burton	95
Shellhorse, Dr. ___	155
Sherman, Gen. W. T.	53-58-59-62-65
	66-91-92
Shields, S. G.	81
Shope, T. S.	81
Short, Frank	135
Showalter, A. J.	91-158-160
Shugart, Rev. C. S.	96
Shugart, Mrs. H. F.	100
Shugart, Henry	101-130
Shumate, I. E.	140
Sikwayi	24
Simmons, ___	88
Simmons, J.	115
Simmons, J. C.	86
Simmons, K. T.	101
Simmons, Rev. William A.	139
Sims, Frank Jr.	143-144
Sims, Mrs. Frank Jr.	160
Sims, Dr. F. K.	91-157-162-163
Sims, Mrs. F. K.	146
Sims, J. W.	127
Sims, N. W.	134
Sims, Newton	97
Sims, Warren	144
Sims, Mrs. Warren	146
Single, Walter L.	142
Sisk, J. E.	109
Situwakee	38
Slaton, John F.	161
Sleeping Rabbit	19
Smith, ___	158
Smith, Achilla	35
Smith, Berry	112
Smith, Miss Bertha	97
Smith, Mrs. Bessie	138-139
Smith, Mrs. Clara	134
Smith, Mrs. Elizabeth	97
Smith, George C.	89
Smith, H. L.	91-143
Smith, Mrs. H. L.	150-151
Smith, H. J.	159-163
Smith, Horace J.	140
Smith, Mrs. Horace J.	146-148
Smith, Miss Ina	97
Smith, J. A.	109
Smith, J. F.	97
Smith, J. P.	132
Smith, Miss Jessie Baxter	160
Smith, Mrs. L. P.	151
Smith, M. C.	88
Smith, M. D.	95-101-140
Smith, Nat	37
Smith, R. W.	135
Smith, Rufus W.	118
Smith, T. Jeff	116
Smith, W. F.	96
Soper, Rev. John H.	95
Sosby, J. W.	114
Sourmush, Chief	6
Spann, Hannah	117
Spann, Joseph	117
Span, Seaborn	103
Spear, W. H.	95-99-116
Speck, ___	16
Speck, J. R.	95-99-105-116
Speer, D.	130
Speer, Leonard	116
Spencer, Mrs. Dollie	138
Spriggs, Thomas	110
Springer, Mrs. C. F.	139-151
Springer, Miss Ione	142-151
Springfield, ___	59
Stacy, Judge O. M.	VI
Stafford, G. C.	VI
Stancell, W. T.	140
Stancill, Catherine	102
Stancill, Mrs. R. B.	97
Stancill, Polly	102
Stanford, Frank	72
Stanley, Hal M.	82
Stanley, Jason	98
Stansberry, Rev. J. M.	93-111-113
	117-118
Stansberry, J. C.	112
Stanton, ___	53
Stanton, E. M.	95-99-105-116
Stark, Buell	132-168
Starr, Emmet	18
Starr, James	35
Starr, T.	82
Starr, Dr. Trammell	155
Steed, Dr. J. H. Sr.	141-155
Steed, Mrs. J. Q. Sr.	21
Steed, W. L.	138
Steiner, Abraham	4-5-6
Steiner, David (Tauchee-chee)	11
Stephens, Alexander	165
Stephenson, Adlai	162
Stevenson, ___	54-58
Stewart, ___	58
Still, Elijah	87
Stockburger, Joseph E.	102
Stockburger, Sarah H.	102
Stocks, John W.	73
Stokes, ___	109
Stokes, H. P.	108
Stone, J. M.	107-114
Stradley, Cephus	114
Strain, Mrs. Ben	147
Strickland, Rev. John	88
Strickland, Mrs. M. C.	134
Stringfield, Thomas	86
Sullins, Rev. Timothy	86
Summit, ___	108
Sutherland, Amos	75
Swan, S. C.	114
Swinney, F. M.	108

T

Name	Page
Tah-gaheske	35
Tah-yeske	35

Taliaferro, Dickenson 55	Treadwell, _____ 54
Tallant, W. C. 108	Trimble, Rev. Elisha 139
Talley, Mrs. Georgia 138	Triplette, H. 108
Tankersley, W. G. 138	Triplett, Thomas H. 78
Tartar, J. C. 87	Tucker, W. M. 130
Tarver, E. J. 73	Tudor, J. R. 98
Tarver, Etheldred 54-105	Turner, B. B. 131
Tarver, Malcolm C. 54	Turner, Berry 131
Tarver, M. C. 36	Turner, J. T. 95
Tarver, R. M. 130	Turner, J. R. 87-89
Tate, A. W. 107	Turner, John W. 88
Tatum, J. T. 97	Twiggs, L. M. 89
Tatum, R. P. 95-99	Tye, Thomas A. 114
Taylor, _____ 11	Tyler, _____ 140
Taylor, Rev. _____ 96	Tyler, Mrs. B. A. V-VI-150
Taylor, Mrs. Elizabeth 78	Tyler, B. A. 162-163
Taylor, Mrs. Frank 152	Tyson, J. F. 105-116
Taylor, J. T. 132	
Taylor, J. Troup 81	**U**
Taylor, Lee 107-114	Underwood, Judge William I. .. 51-52-78
Taylor, R. F. 101	Underwood, W. J. 72-76
Taylor, Richard 29-38	
Teasley, I. B. 111	**V**
Terry, Joseph 99	Vandiver, A. E. 93
Tes-ta-esky 35	Vandiver, Lampkin 109
Thacker, J. A. 97	Vann, _____ 11
Thigpin, A. M. 86-89	Vann, Clement 10
Thomas, Mrs. B. M. 121	Vann, David 27
Thomas, Gen. Bryan M. 67-68-95	Vann, James 5-6-7-10-22
.............................121-147	Vann, John 11-33
Thomas, F. A. 55	Vann, Joseph 22-23
Thomas, John S. VI-169	Vann, Margaret 7
Thomas, Mrs. John S. 148-152	Vann, Polly 6
Thomas, Col. John 47-76	Vann, Sally 6
Thomas, Mrs. Kincaid 146-152	Vann, Wa-Wli 10
Thomas, Nathaniel 110	VanVleck, Jacob 8
Thomas, Mrs. Ruth Allen 145	Varnell, Albert 108
Thomas, W. J. M. 56-82	Varnell, Columbus 105
Thomason, E. G. 95-99	Varnell, M. P. 103-116-117-139
Thomason, J. A. VI	Varnell, Mitchell 116
Thomason, L. W. 115-131	Varner, J. L. 95-99
Thomaston, A. J. 98	Vaughn, Joe 98
Thompson, Rev. _____ 29	Veatch, J. W. 95-99
Thompson, Miss Dorothea 157	Venable, G. F. 89
Thompson, Mrs. Emma Love 62	
Thompson, H. D. 133	**W**
Thompson, T. B. 82	Waddell, J. M. 89
Thompson, Capt. T. C. 95	Wade, A. P. 139
Thompson, V. 91	Wade, J. T. 101
Thompson, W. S. 134	Wade, Jesse 53
Thornton, Col. Mark 47-51-139	Wade, P. L. 139
Thornton, Rev. _____ 96	Wade, Rev. Peyton 53
Tibbs, _____ 57-75	Walden, W. F. 116
Tibbs, W. H. 49-72	Walker, _____ 58
Tiffany, Rev. E. T. 96	Walker, George 115
Tillman, Mrs. Eliza H. 99	Walker, Capt. John 63
Tillotson, Emily 89	Walker, Dr. Mary 65
Timmerman, J. A. 89	Walker, Mrs. Porter G. 150
Toomey, Mrs. J. M. 151	Wallace, Alexander M. 47
Towns, Gov. George W. 47-52	Wallace, B. L. 137
Towns, John 76	Wallace, Bart 128
Trammell, Paul B. 83-121-167	Wallace, Rev. J. A. 91
Trammell, Mrs. Paul B. Sr. ..148-150-163	Wallace, J. B. 138

Wallace, J. D.	137
Wallace, J. L.	132-34
Walraven, M. M.	95
Walston, E. H.	135
Ward, A. M.	109
Ward, J. E.	95-99
Ward, Lofton C.	133
Ware, J. A.	81
Ware, _____	108
Warmack, A. J.	130
Warren, Dr. R.	76
Warwick, _____	118
Waugh, Dr. I. S.	51
Waugh, William A.	76
Waugh, D. S.	89
Watie, Buck	11
Watie, Stand	36
Waters, R. H.	88
Watkins, Isaac	108-114
Watson, J. H.	121-163
Watt, Andrew	54
Watterson, Col. Henry	81
Way, Rev. E. W.	91
Wear, William	162
Weatherford, J. G. S.	56
Weatherly, _____	111
Weaver, Dr. _____ (dent.)	74
Weaver, W. A.	98
Webb, Achilles	108
Webb, Margaret	108
Webb, Jordan	104
Weems, L. A.	142
Weir, David	140
Welch, M. H.	97
Wells, B. E.	52-87
Wells, J. E.	88
Wells, J. H.	97
Wesley, Charles & John	40-94
West, William	99
Westbrook, M.	140
Westcott, Mrs. Fred	146-152
Westcott, G. L.	157
Westmoreland, Mrs. Rachel	97
Wheat, Richard	108
Wheeler, John F.	26-33
Wheeler, Gen. Joseph	56-59-60-62-66-126
Wheeler, J. R.	126
White, _____	85
White, Alvin	123-126
White, Capt. Edward	47-48-51-87-88-89-92
White, Fred	135
White, George P.	94
White, John B.	82
White, Miss Willie S.	V-VI-145-163-169
Whitefield, George	40
Whitefield, Thomas	40
Whitener, Calvin	105
Whitener, John	105
Whitener, L. C.	98
Whitener, William	99
Whiteside, John	139
Whiteside, Mrs. W. M.	151
Whittier, John G.	20
Whitman, J. T.	78-81-91
Whitman, R. G.	76
Whitson, Joseph E.	140
Whitten, _____	117
Whitten, James P.	108
Whittle, Miss Mary	118
Whitton, Mrs. John	117
Wiggins, Cynthia	104
Wiggins, William	104
Wilcox, C. R.	137
Wilhoit, J. B.	102
Wilkes, W. C.	93
Williams, Adolphus	115
Williams, Albert	98
Williams, A. W.	89-98
Williams, Miss Annie	107
Williams, C. H.	95-99
Williams, C. T.	109
Williams, Coleman	107
Williams, David	104
Williams, Mrs. Elizabeth	104
Williams, Rev. Felton	115
Williams, J. S.	100
Williams, J. W.	121
Williams, John	107
Williams, Lillie	98
Williams, Richard	107
Williams, S. C.	25
Williams, T. L.	135
Williams, W. Thorne	84
Williamson, J. D.	82
Williamson, J. W.	73
Williamson, John D.	114
Williamson, John F.	140
Williamson, Thomas	103
Willis, D. D.	107
Wills, J. T.	133
Wilson, _____	116
Wilson, Catherine	108
Wilson, Elizabeth	108
Wilson, Frank	108
Wilson, Haseltine Ford	108
Wilson, Henderson	108
Wilson, J. F.	130
Wilson, James C.	108
Wilson, J. A.	130
Wilson, John A.	108
Wilson, J. Augustus	108
Wilson, Josiah Felix	108
Wilson, L. E.	91
Wilson, Martha	108
Wilson, Mary	108
Wilson, Minerva	108
Wilson, S. H.	VI
Wilson, Thomas	108
Wilson, W. H.	108
Wilson, W. O.	126
Wilson, W. M.	108
Wimpey, John	162
Winstead, H. A.	100-107-114
Wofford, E. H.	132
Wohlfart, J. J.	6-7

Wollenweber, Mrs. A.	152
Wood, Miss Arrie	151
Wood, C. E.	133
Wood, E. D.	73
Wood, Judge Harlan	VI-54
Wood, Mrs. H. J.	139
Wood, Isaac	104
Wood, Isham	54
Wood, James H.	131
Wood, Joe	104
Wood, Rev. John M.	104
Wood, Kimsey	104
Wood, Lazarus	104
Wood, Dr. Lloyd	155
Wood, Lorenza	104
Wood, Pierce	104
Wood, Rebecca	104
Woodpecker	8
Wooten, J. M.	103
Worcester, S. A.	26-29-33
Word, Dr. _____	117
Workman, Martin	113
Workman, Nancy Ann	113
Worley, A. G.	89
Worthy, _____	61
Wrench, H. A.	V-81
Wrench, Mrs. Joe	146-152
Wright, Charlie	108
Wright, Mrs. Dewey	152
Wright, Col. D. P.	76
Wright, G. D.	142
Wright, Mrs. G. D.	146
Wright, Miss Kate	155
Wright, William A.	113
Wyatt, _____	81
Wyatt, Mrs. Jennie	116
Wyble, Dr. _____	116
Wylie, Thomas	51

Y

Yarbrough, George W.	89
Yarbrough, J. F.	87-89
Yarbrough, J. W.	86
Yeager, Augustus	51
Yeager, Herman	51
Young Deer	8
Young, Bennie	112
Young, John S.	23
Young, Mrs. Hamp	112
Young, Hamilton	131

Z

Zimmerman, R. P.	139

www.ingramcontent.com/pod-product-compliance
Lightning Source LLC
Chambersburg PA
CBHW030227100526
44585CB00012BA/282